HARVARD HISTORICAL STUDIES • 191

Published under the auspices of the
Department of History

from the income of the
Paul Revere Frothingham Bequest
Robert Louis Stroock Fund
Henry Warren Torrey Fund

A Full-Value Ruble

The Promise of Prosperity in the Postwar Soviet Union

KRISTY IRONSIDE

Harvard University Press

Cambridge, Massachusetts & London, England

2021

Printed in the United States of America

First printing

Library of Congress Cataloging-in-Publication Data

Names: Ironside, Kristy, author.
Title: A full-value ruble : the promise of prosperity in the postwar Soviet Union / Kristy Ironside.
Other titles: Harvard historical studies ; v. 191.
Description: Cambridge, Massachusetts : Harvard University Press, 2021. | Series: Harvard historical studies; number 191 | Includes bibliographical references and index.
Identifiers: LCCN 2020047483 | ISBN 9780674251649 (hardcover)
Subjects: LCSH: Ruble, Russian—Political aspects—Soviet Union. | Soviet Union—Economic conditions. | Soviet Union—Politics and government—1945–1991.
Classification: LCC HG1075 .I76 2021 | DDC 332.494709045—dc23
LC record available at https://lccn.loc.gov/2020047483

Contents

Note on Currency and on Institutions

One (1) ruble contains 100 kopeks. Prices after the January 1, 1961, currency reform are expressed in new money, that is, 1/10 of the 1947 ruble, which was itself 1/10 of the 1924 ruble. To make this clear when necessary, post-1961 money amounts are marked in the text with "(new money)". It should also be noted that two parallel currencies existed in the Soviet Union: cost-accounting or "bank" rubles, which were used for accounting purposes and inter-enterprise transactions only and were not convertible into cash, and cash rubles in circulation, which were used for wages and all other payments. This book is concerned only with the value of the cash ruble in circulation, not the ruble that was used for accounting purposes.

In March 1946, the Soviet government's "Commissariats" (*komissariaty*) were renamed Ministries (*ministerstva*). Accordingly, the position of "Commissar of Finance," for example, became "Minister of Finance." I have used "Ministry" and "Minister" throughout this book to maintain consistency.

Note on Translation and Transliteration

All translations from the Russian are my own. Russian is transliterated using the Library of Congress style, except in the case of commonly used transliterations of surnames, that is, Mikoyan, not Mikoian.

Glossary of Key Terms

Planning and Economic Concepts

Balance of the population's money income and expenses (*balans denezhnykh dokhodov i raskhodov naseleniia*): A calculation used to decide how many consumer goods to be released for retail trade and to decide how much currency to print in a given year, viewed by economic experts as an important synthetic indicator of the purchasing power of the ruble and functioning of the Soviet money economy.

Financial discipline (*finansovaia distsiplina*): Strict budgetary control and the reduction of wasteful expenditures within the government and in state enterprises.

Economic or cost accounting (*khozraschet*): the principle of accounting for income and expenses within enterprises and the expectation to turn a profit (*pribyl'*), introduced with the shift to the New Economic Policy in the early 1920s.

Commodity circulation (*tovarooborot*): The exchange of goods for money and vice versa, in line with Marx's ideas about commodification, but within the parameters of a socialist economy.

Prices

Unified state retail prices (*edinnye gosudarstvennye roznichnye tseny*): The retail prices charged in state stores after the December 14, 1947, currency reform, generally reflecting the midpoint between prior ration and commercial price levels.

Commercial prices (*kommercheskie tseny*): Higher fixed retail prices charged in state stores for scarce and luxury goods prior to the 1947 currency reform. Goods sold at commercial prices could be purchased in unlimited amounts.

Ration prices (*paikovye tseny*): The artificially low fixed retail prices for rationed goods charged by state stores from 1941 until the 1947 currency reform. Goods sold at ration prices could be purchased only in restricted amounts.

Market prices (*rynochnye tseny*): Fluctuating prices reflecting supply and demand charged by peasants and speculators in the collective farm markets and on the black market.

Procurement prices (*zakupochnye/zagotovitel'nye tseny*): The fixed prices paid to collective farms for their compulsory deliveries to the state.

Social Welfare

Fund for social consumption (*fond obshchestvennogo potrebleniia*): The sum of money allocated in the state budget to raising living standards by providing free or subsidized educational, cultural, health, and housing-related services or goods, among others.

Benefits (*l'goty*): Free or discounted social welfare benefits, also sometimes referring to tax exemptions and other economic privileges granted to special recipients (e.g., personal pensioners) or recognized needy groups (e.g., families of deceased soldiers).

Bread allowance (*khlebnaia nadbavka*): A top-up on wages and pensions introduced in the fall of September 1946 to compensate for increased ration prices, eliminated with the 1956 pension reform.

Personal pension (*personal'naia pensiia*): A pension assigned to a notable individual and/or to his or her family members at the Union- or republic-level, in an amount that typically exceeded regular state pension amounts.

Elevated pensions (*povyshenye pensii*): Higher pensions offered to prized workers in heavy industry beginning in the 1930s.

Labor period (*stazh*): The number of years worked required to be eligible for a state pension, ideally an uninterrupted (*nepreryvnyi*) period of time.

Taxes and State Bonds

Agricultural tax (*sel'skokhoziaistvennyi nalog*): The tax that was paid by collective farmers and "independent farmers" (*edinolichniki*) on the profits from their sales of produce from their private plots at the collective farm markets.

Turnover tax (*nalog s oborota*): A commodity tax built into the price of nonessential consumer goods.

Income tax (*podokhodnyi nalog*): A progressive tax taken off of workers' wages.

Tax on bachelors, singles, and small families of the USSR (*nalog na kholiastiakov, odinokikh i malosemeinykh grazhdan SSSR*): A tax on childlessness introduced in 1941, whose rates were increased and its range of taxpayers expanded, under the July 8, 1944, Family Law. Prior to 1958, it was paid by all citizens with fewer than three children, with limited health-based exceptions.

Personal exemption (*neoblagaemyi minimum*): The amount of a worker's wages that was considered nontaxable.

Bonds (*obligatsii*): A generic term used for state bonds, often referring to the semi-compulsory mass subscription bonds Soviet citizens were compelled to purchase through wage deductions 1927–1957.

Free-circulating/market bonds (*svobodno-obrashchaemye zaimy/rynochnye zaimy*): State bonds that were not purchased through mass subscription campaigns and which could be freely cashed in, typically more expensive than the semi-compulsory bonds.

Wages

Wage fund (*fond zarabotnoi platy*): The amount of money allocated to pay wages across the Soviet Union, subdivided at the republic-, industry-, and enterprise-levels.

Salary (*oklad*): A fixed salary that was not tied to hourly or other measures of compensation.

Additional earnings (*prirabotka*): Workers' earnings over the base pay rate, including piece rates, bonuses, and premiums.

Progressive piece-rate payment (*progressivno-sdel'naia oplata*): Piece rates that multiplied in value above a certain number of units produced.

Piece-rate payment (*sdel'naia oplata*): Pay per unit produced, either on top of a base wage rate or as the only form of payment.

Tariff system (*tarifnaia sistema*): The system of scales governing Soviet industrial wages, determining the base pay amounts (*stavki*) within an industry and the wage differentials between categories of labor, expressed as coefficients of 1, the lowest base wage rate in an industry.

Base wage rate (*tarifnaia stavka*): The amount of a worker's wages that was guaranteed before payment for piece rates.

Leveling, "vulgar egalitarianism," or equalitarianism (*uravnilovka*): Equalizing compensation without consideration for the quantity or quality of, or demand for, labor contributed.

Temporary cash allowance (*vremennoe denezhnoe dovol'stvie*): Temporary cash allowances introduced during the Second World War to supplement the incomes and cost of living of elite government employees, eliminated in 1957.

Timeline of Important Events

May 9, 1945	The Soviet Union celebrates Victory Day, marking the end of the Second World War.
February 9, 1946	Stalin promises consecutive retail price reductions at a meeting of voters in Moscow.
March 18, 1946	The Fifth Five-Year Plan for the Reconstruction and Development of the National Economy is decreed.
May 3, 1946	The first Bond for the Reconstruction and Development of the National Economy is decreed. These are issued annually through 1950. In 1951, the word "reconstruction" is dropped from their title and they become Bond(s) for the Development of the National Economy, which are sold through 1956.
September 17, 1946	Higher ration and lower commercial prices are decreed and a "bread allowance" is extended to workers, pensioners, and students to offset the cost of living.
December 14, 1947	The currency reform simultaneously introduces a new ruble and new banknotes, worth one-tenth of the previous currency in circulation. This is accompanied by the abolition of rationing and introduction of new unified state retail prices effective December 16, 1947.
April 10, 1948	Selected price cuts for expensive and "luxury" goods are announced.

March 1, 1949	The first of six spring consecutive retail price cuts occurs.
March 1, 1950	The second spring consecutive retail price cut occurs and new international exchange rates for the ruble are announced. The Soviet government also ceases to peg the ruble to the US dollar and puts it on the gold standard.
March 1, 1951	The third consecutive retail price cut takes place.
March 1, 1952	The fourth consecutive retail price cut takes place.
October 5–14, 1952	The Nineteenth Party Congress takes place. The Party resolves to continue the policy of consecutive retail price cuts.
March 5, 1953	Stalin dies.
April 1, 1953	The fifth consecutive retail price cut takes place.
August 8, 1953	Agricultural reforms including changes to the agricultural tax and raised procurement prices aimed at improving conditions in the countryside and increasing peasants' deliveries to the state are decreed. These are announced by Georgii Malenkov.
April 1, 1954	The sixth and last consecutive retail price cut takes place.
February 14–25, 1956	The Twentieth Party Congress takes place. In his keynote speech, Khrushchev promises to "more fully satisfy the population's growing material needs" and on its last day denounces Stalin.
May 8, 1956	A draft version of a pension law unifying workers' and war invalids' pension policies and increasing pension amounts is signed. Collective farmers remain ineligible for state pensions. Career soldiers, artists, teachers, and notable persons who receive "personal pensions" are covered by separate policies. The law is published the next day and the government invites the public's feedback ahead of finalizing it.

September 8, 1956	A new minimum wage is decreed, going into effect on January 1, 1957, raising the base pay rate to 300–350 rubles per month.
July 14, 1956	The finalized pension law is promulgated.
October 1, 1956	The pension law goes into effect.
April 19, 1957	The abolition of mass subscription bonds and a 20–25-year freeze on payments for existing investments is decreed.
May 15, 1957	The last mass subscription bond, the Development of the National Economy bond (1957 issue), is decreed.
December 18, 1957	Single women and married couples with children are exempted from the bachelor tax, pursuant to a decree going into effect on January 1, 1958.
January 30, 1958	Ticket sales for the new cash-and-goods lottery in the RSFSR begin.
April 28, 1958	Wages are scheduled to be restructured in heavy industry and a new shorter workday is scheduled to be introduced. The reforms are to be rolled out in stages and completed by 1962.
January 27–February 5, 1959	The Twenty-First Party Congress takes place and the Seven-Year Plan is announced. Khrushchev promises another minimum wage raise and the abolition of income taxes, among other measures to improve living standards.
May 5, 1960	Khrushchev announces a new currency reform, to take place on January 1, 1961, and the abolition of income taxes (not including the agricultural tax), to be implemented in a gradual way over the next five years.
October 1, 1960	The first round of tax cuts occurs.
January 1, 1961	The currency reform introduces a new ruble and new banknotes, and scales down all prices, wages, and other payments by a ratio of 10:1, old money for new.

October 1, 1961	The second round of tax cuts occurs.
October 17–21, 1961	The Twenty-Second Party Congress takes place.
October 18, 1961	Khrushchev unveils the new Communist Party Program and promises that communism will be achieved “in the main” by 1980.
May 31, 1962	The Central Committee meets to revise control figures for the Seven-Year Plan. It approves retail price increases and postpones planned minimum wage raises and the abolition of taxes.
June 1, 1962	Retail prices for meat and butter are raised by up to a third. Letters of complaint pour in across the country and workers strike and riot in Novocherkassk.
September 22, 1962	The abolition of taxes is indefinitely postponed.
July 15, 1964	Khrushchev announces that state pensions will be extended for collective farmers and wages for service workers will be raised.
October 14, 1964	Khrushchev is removed from office.
January 1, 1965	The law on pensions for collective farmers goes into effect.

A Full-Value Ruble

Introduction

The Ruble and Soviet Prosperity

Thirty years after the Bolsheviks came to power trying to abolish money as a hated vestige of capitalism, they launched a currency reform affirming it as an essential economic instrument of Soviet socialism.[1] Excessive emission, severe shortages, and rationing had decimated the ruble's value during and after the Second World War. The December 14, 1947, currency reform, formally announced the next day, simultaneously abolished rationing and introduced a new ruble, converting cash at a rate of 10:1, old money for new, and savings and investments at a sliding scale of preferential rates. In the decree's preamble, the government assured Soviet citizens that it was not implementing this reform at their expense, and it would bear the largest share of its burden; however, by resorting to such confiscatory conversion rates, it was admittedly asking them to make a huge "sacrifice [*zhertva*] . . . especially so it can be the last sacrifice." The reform, they were promised, would "liquidate the consequences of the Second World War in the realm of currency circulation, resurrect the full-value Soviet ruble [*polnotsenyi sovetskii rubl'*], and ease the transition to trade at united prices without rationing," but also "strengthen the significance of money within the national economy, raise workers' real wages and increase the value of the rural population's money incomes." Finally, it would "create the conditions for workers' increased material prosperity, reconstruct and develop the national economy, and further strengthen the power of the Soviet government."[2]

The "full-value" ruble, this book argues, was essential to the state project of creating "prosperity" (*blagosostoianie*) in the postwar Soviet Union. Since the mid-1930s, the Stalinist government had explicitly promised to bring prosperity to the masses during the socialist transition via this ruble: a currency with real purchasing power, one that was "strong" (*tverdyi*) in relation to major world currencies, brought increasing material satisfaction to consumers, helped raise the population's "cultural level" (*kul'turnost'*), and served as a compelling incentive for the hard work that building communism required.[3] That goal had proved elusive then and was completely impossible to achieve during the war; however, it was believed to be more realizable than ever before after the war and into the early 1960s.[4] In the eyes of Stalin- and then Khrushchev-era authorities, the full-value ruble helped the Soviet Union to ascend toward the fated abundance of full communism, when money itself would become obsolete and could be tossed into the dustbin of history, as Karl Marx had always predicted.[5]

A Full-Value Ruble is roughly bookended by the two currency reforms of December 14, 1947, and January 1, 1961, both of which promised to put a new ruble into circulation that facilitated the Soviet Union's growing prosperity and economic advance. As in 1947, the 1961 currency reform scaled down the value of cash by a factor of 10. Unlike in 1947, it also scaled down wages and prices and it was not launched in response to an economic crisis, at least not overtly. Instead, it was connected to ongoing efforts to devise more accurate plans. When he announced the reform, Nikita Khrushchev emphasized that the country's skyrocketing economic growth in recent years had forced planners to operate in enormous figures and thus the ruble needed to be redenominated in order to preserve and even increase its value. He argued that "the full-value Soviet ruble is of the utmost necessity for realizing the Party's and government's plans for a ceaseless rise in the people's prosperity based upon the rapid growth of the socialist economy."[6]

In contrast to the weak, inflated, and virtually unspendable ruble that circulated before and especially during the war, Soviet citizens were promised a ruble with vastly increased purchasing power, allowing them to not only meet basic needs but gradually enjoy more of the good things in life. They were promised ever more of these rubles as the Soviet Union's supposedly unstoppable economic achievements allowed the government to fund a generous welfare agenda, including price subsidies that kept retail prices and the cost of living down, minimum wage and pension raises, and free benefits (*l'goty*) like holidays and socialized health care that workers had to pay for with their own money under capitalism—an expression of the socialist authorities' great "care" (*zabota*) for their citizens' well-being. Rising real wages, more take-home pay, and growing savings to put toward big-ticket consumer purchases were all portrayed as incontrovertible proof that the Soviet Union was not only putting the war behind it but becoming an increasingly wealthy socialist society triumphing over capitalism and making big strides toward communism.

The postwar promise of prosperity was not just an empty slogan, but an ambitious, if ultimately unsuccessful, project containing many moving parts. Planners and other economic authorities attempted to achieve a "balance of the population's money income and expenses" (*balans denezhnykh dokhodov i raskhodov naseleniia*), a concept devised in the early 1930s and used to determine the appropriate amount of cash to release into circulation, set wage and tax levels, and plan consumer production, "one of the most important synthetic balance sheets of the national economy," as its key theorist, N. S. Margolin, explained it.[7] Maintaining this balance depended upon the population's active and enthusiastic participation, which necessitated inculcating rational economic behaviors in them, including appropriate labor, spending, and saving patterns. This helps explain the careful attention Soviet economic authorities paid to fine-tuning price, wage, and pension levels, which affected the ruble's incentive value, and to honing propaganda techniques and messages inducing citizens to see their labor and other investments into the economy as materially beneficial.

A secondary argument threading through this book holds that the turn to the full-value ruble to deliver upon the promise of postwar prosperity is an important continuity between the late Stalin and Khrushchev eras. These periods are often seen by historians as sharply divided by the advent of liberalizing reforms and a more sincere desire to improve living standards under the latter.[8] A substantial literature has documented Khrushchev's attempts to improve material conditions after the Twentieth Party Congress, in particular through improved access to consumer goods and the construction of mass housing.[9] However, I am not the first scholar to point to continuities between them in the project of creating economic prosperity. Commenting on recent welfare developments under Khrushchev as a contemporary observer in 1960, Alec Nove called the promised abundance of communism "a meaningless, even nonsensical concept" but emphasized that "it was always the intention of all Soviet leaders, including even Stalin, to raise living standards at some future date, once the painful sacrifices of 'primitive accumulation' were no longer necessary."[10] Nove suggested that Khrushchev may have aspired "to go down in history as the man who brought prosperity to the Soviet people—on the foundations laid by his grim predecessor."[11]

As *A Full-Value Ruble* shows, despite his critique of Stalinist monetary "excesses" (*izlishchestva*), such as the egregiously high salaries and wide array of monetized perquisites enjoyed by Stalinist elites, and despite his desire to get back to "Leninist" norms when it came to the use of money as a labor incentive, Khrushchev did not disavow Stalin's ideas about the importance of the full-value ruble during the Soviet Union's socialist transition. Instead, he sought to gradually extend the benefits of Soviet prosperity to peasants, who had long been marginalized in the Stalinist money economy, and to low-income citizens, whose wages and pensions had been allowed to stagnate since the early 1930s. When it came to raising workers' real wages, Khrushchev sought to shift focus away from a Stalinist obsession with price cuts toward improving consumer output and expanding social welfare benefits as drivers of real wage growth. His government combined this with direct cash injections into household finances in the form of minimum wage and pension increases and higher take-home pay. The full-value ruble remained at the core of Khrushchev-era policies to increase living standards during the Soviet Union's acceleration toward communism.

Money in the Soviet System

Many readers might find this argument surprising for two main reasons. First, the word "prosperity" is rarely associated with the Soviet Union, certainly in the West and especially during the hungry Stalin years. The Soviet Union is usually left out of or assigned only a marginal place in the history of postwar prosperity in Europe.[12] After 1945, Western European countries experienced three decades of unprecedented affluence and consumer abundance facilitated by relative political stability, high growth and productivity rates, increasing economic integration, and American assistance. The Soviet Union achieved impressive economic growth rates given the extent of the damage inflicted upon its soil, returning to prewar levels by the start of the 1950s.[13] However, this did not necessarily translate into improved living standards for a majority of its citizens. As Donald A. Filtzer points out, postwar rises in real wages and other "paper calculations" Soviet officials boasted of did not correspond to a higher quality of life off the page, and many, if not most, Soviet workers were left hungry, sick, and struggling long after the war ended.[14] Even in the Khrushchev era, despite increased investment in consumer production and propaganda that loudly proclaimed the Soviet Union was on the verge of overtaking its Cold War competitors, average living standards in the Soviet Union undoubtedly lagged behind Western Europe and North America.

Second, and more importantly, this story seems to contradict a basic fact about the Soviet system: money held very little value within it. Within the Soviet planned economy, money was not (or at least not always) the most basic unit of value.[15] Within the state enterprise sector, money was rigidly earmarked: money allocated for wages could not be used to pay for equipment, for example. Money was not always the basic unit of Soviet international trade. Despite the Soviet government's grandiose claims, the ruble was not "strong" in relation to other currencies because the Soviet Union was excluded from the twentieth-century global financial system and the ruble was nonconvertible. Although the Soviet government set foreign exchange rates for the ruble for accounting purposes, these had no effect on its purchasing power at home, because domestic prices were deliberately shielded from world-market prices. Any transactions with the capitalist West had to be conducted in scarce "hard currency" (*valiuta*) or in kind. After 1945, the Soviet government's economic dealings with its satellite socialist states in Central and Eastern Europe and with the decolonizing world were nominally accounted for in rubles but, in reality, often took the form of barter and clearing operations.[16]

Because money did not integrate all economic transactions and was not a universal means of exchange, and was both internally and externally nonconvertible, the economist János Kornai famously concluded that the "classical socialist system"—essentially, the paradigmatic Stalinist command economy built in the 1930s in the Soviet Union and imposed upon "fraternal" socialist countries in Central and Eastern Europe after the war—may have maintained the outward features of a monetized economy but, behind the facade, the role played by money was only weak or secondary. It was, in his view, merely "semi-monetized."[17] Firms operated with "soft budget constraints," including subsidies, negotiable tax rates, low interest on credit, and administratively controlled prices.[18] On the other hand, households within this system faced "hard budget constraints": they were restricted by their cash resources, which made them highly sensitive to changes in prices and income.[19] In the meantime, chronic shortages caused "monetary overhang," a massive glut of cash resulting from repressed inflation and unspendable forced savings piling up in households' hands that could only be partially absorbed by informal and illegal trade.[20]

Historians have mostly concurred with economists that money possessed limited value in the Soviet system, especially under Stalin. They emphasize that it was frequently less useful in citizens' hands than having privileged access and pull (*blat*); by working personal connections, people could obtain coveted goods and products that were in chronically short supply. Elena Osokina suggests that *blat* became an important survival strategy, especially under Stalin's hierarchical and exclusionary rationing system, which privileged those perceived to be most valuable to the regime's political and economic goals.[21] As Sheila Fitzpatrick has shown in her seminal study of everyday life in the 1930s, Soviet citizens frequently expressed the opinion that, without *blat*, "Soviet life was impossible."[22] "One must not have 100 rubles, but 100 friends," went an oft-cited proverb.[23] If a person had money, he or she could sometimes circumvent the long lines in shortage-ridden state stores and buy things from more expensive but better-stocked outdoor markets and commercial shops, but consumption was largely tied to privilege, having less to do with money and more to do with the coveted access that came with elite positions in the Communist Party, academe, industry, and the arts.[24] Yegor Gaidar, one of the architects of post-Soviet capitalist "shock therapy" in the 1990s, described this phenomenon more bluntly: "If you had money but no connections, you would not have access to goods in short supply. You were a nobody. Your money just demonstrated your lack of position in society. This was the economic reality not just for a year or two but for decades."[25]

Yet, money was not supposed to be useless in the Soviet system. The early Bolsheviks certainly tried their best to make it so during the heady period immediately after the revolution, deliberately stoking hyperinflation during War Communism through profligate use of "the Commissariat of Finance's machine gun," as the economist Evgenii Preobrazhenskii famously dubbed the printing press.[26] Ideological hard-liners argued, per Marx, that money's existence was incompatible with socialism and proposed revolutionary alternatives, such as the "labor unit" (*trudovaia edinitsa*, or *tred*), a measure of the energy expended by the working human body. The Bolsheviks also turned to rationing to feed workers and the Red Army, partly out of necessity and partly because some saw it as an important step toward the material exchange of goods that they believed would occur under communism and as an example of the scientific management of resources which would soon be extended to the whole economy.[27] Beginning in late 1920, the Soviet government also issued an interim money surrogate, a special promissory note known as the "Soviet token" (*sovznak*).

Already by then, the realists were beginning to prevail over the utopians in the Communist Party, and its leadership grew increasingly committed to the goal of currency stabilization.[28] With the onset of the New Economic Policy (NEP), which allowed for a mixed-market economy and the limited use of capitalist instruments, Vladimir Lenin, who had initially been on the more radical 'left' of debates about money, came out strongly in favor of postponing its abolition and revitalizing the ruble, as did Grigorii Sokol'nikov, who became Commissar of Finance in 1922. They grasped that the socialist regime's very survival depended upon it: as Steven G. Marks observes, "Money is a tool and symbol of political power, and its weakness suggested to contemporaries that the Soviet government's hold on the country was still precarious."[29] Over the course of 1922–1924, *sovznaki* were phased out, a gold-backed chervonets banknote was phased in, currency emission was curbed, and a new Soviet ruble was put into circulation.[30]

Despite his extreme anticapitalist worldview, money was one of the few capitalist instruments that Iosif Stalin accepted and which he believed the Bolsheviks could make better use of, an argument he first advanced in the mid-1920s and one that he would hammer on for the remainder of his life and tenure as Soviet leader.[31] Amid the factional squabbles that emerged in the Communist Party during the NEP and especially around the time of Lenin's death in 1924, Stalin attacked Bolsheviks on both the left and the right for harboring utopian and fallacious ideas about the role of money during the socialist transition. Radical Bolsheviks viewed the continuing use of money as a concession to capital, while more moderate Bolsheviks, such as Nikolai Bukharin, viewed it as a strategic maneuver during a period in which money was supposedly losing its significance.[32] Stalin rejected the suggestion that money was inherently capitalist or declining in importance: at the Fourteenth Party Congress in 1925, he attacked Sokol'nikov for allegedly suggesting that the Soviet monetary system was "permeated with capitalist principles." Stalin argued that it was "irrelevant" that money was "capitalist" for, during the socialist transition, capitalist economic tools could be used against capitalism; moreover, they could even "change in favor of socialism to the detriment of capitalism."[33]

After securing his hold over the Party, Stalin dismantled the NEP in 1928 and replaced it with a planned centralized command economy. Like others in the Soviet leadership at the time, he initially presumed inflation could not affect this type of economy.[34] In 1930, Stalinist financial authorities began building a monetary system that was supposed to serve as the "passive handmaiden of planning," as Paul R. Gregory and Aleksei Tikhonov have observed.[35] Cash and bank money would be strictly segregated: inter-enterprise transactions would be cashless, while household transactions would be purely cash-based. Credit would follow output plans, cash would follow labor-staffing plans, and the most important decisions regarding the economy would be made by planners in accordance with general directives emanating from the

Communist Party. This system did not work as intended, and turned out to be incredibly inflationary.[36] The State Bank (*Gosudarstvennyi bank*, or Gosbank) quickly lost control of money and credit supplies as enterprises turned to illegal credit, over-demanded state credit, and overdrew upon their accounts—taking advantage of the soft budget constraints Kornai emphasizes. As wages were bid up to attract workers and reward productivity during the rapid industrialization drive, money in workers' hands far exceeded the availability of goods for purchase. Inflation was further exacerbated by shortages caused by the state's prioritization of heavy over light industry and by the fallout from its clashes with the peasantry during collectivization. The government responded to the excess cash in circulation by restricting wage funds, resulting in the growth of wage arrears and the use of money surrogates like lunch vouchers in Soviet workplaces.[37] Under these conditions, the purchasing power of the ruble was abysmally low. In order to ensure workers were fed and clothed, the government was forced to reintroduce rationing, which it had eliminated with the turn to the NEP.

Despite money's low real value within the system he helped create, during the 1930s Stalin repeatedly portrayed himself as someone who, contrary to his political opponents, grasped that money was a powerful tool of socialist construction. At the Seventeenth Party Congress in January 1934—dubbed the "Congress of Victors," for it supposedly marked the end of the economic crises associated with rapid industrialization and collectivization—Stalin attacked the "leftist" misconception that money was "mere tokens" and could be abolished in the near future.[38] Money was an "an instrument of the bourgeois economy which the Soviet government has seized into its own hands and adapted to the interests of socialism," he explained, and the Soviet Union would use it "for a long time to come, right up until the first stage of communism, that is, when the socialist stage of development has been completed."[39] To suggest otherwise was to be like "Don Quixote" tilting at windmills, "lacking the most elementary sense of reality."[40]

Stalin laid out yet another important Bolshevik economic principle in the same speech: socialism entailed bringing a more "prosperous life" (*zazhitochnaia zhizn'*) to workers. In his opinion, it was more leftist "stupidity" to think that socialism could be "built on the base of poverty and privation."[41] "Who needs this so-called socialism?" he sneered. "That's not socialism, but a caricature of socialism." Socialism, he argued, could only be built upon the growth of society's "productive forces," with an abundance of goods, the prosperity of the working people, and a rise in the population's cultural level. This goal had always been at the heart of the Bolsheviks' plans, according to Stalin. "There was no point in overthrowing capitalism in October 1917 and building socialism for all these years, if we were not going to ensure that our people lived in material comfort," he suggested, insisting that "socialism does not mean poverty and deprivation, but the elimination of poverty and deprivation, and the creation of a wealthy and cultured life for all members of society."[42]

Stalin expanded on these thoughts later that same year, drawing a more explicit link between the necessity of strengthening the Soviet money economy and improving living standards when he mused about the abolition of rationing. If the early Bolsheviks had seen rationing as an important step toward communism, Stalinist authorities saw it as a huge step backward, one they took only reluctantly.[43] Rationing proved useful as an instrument of social control, allowing the regime to reward workers in the most-prized industries with better rations, and punish so-called former peoples and class enemies by withholding central supplies from them, but it was inefficient, diverted personnel away from productive tasks, and demoralized the population.[44] Rationing caused price distortions in the collective farm markets (*kolkhoznye rynky*), the last semi-legal venues for private trade after the demise of the NEP, where peasants were allowed to sell their 'surplus' produce at unregulated and invariably higher prices.[45] Finally, rationing undermined the ruble's value as a labor incentive at a time when the Soviet government needed workers, especially in priority branches of the economy, to put in their best effort. After a good harvest in 1934, the Soviet government seized the chance to abolish it.

As Stalin explained to his colleagues in the Politburo that November, the primary goal behind the abolition of rationing was "the strengthening of the money economy."[46] It was "one of the few bourgeois instruments of the economy that we, as socialists, should use to the bitter end," he reiterated. "It's very flexible, we need it, and we can turn it around, such that it gives grist to our mill and not to that of capitalism."[47] The money economy was also needed to deliver upon the Bolsheviks' promise to bring abundance to the masses. The Soviet citizen should be treated no longer as an abstract entity to whom products simply needed to be doled out, but as a consumer with tastes and preferences, he maintained. Creating a "rich commodity distribution network" and learning how to respond to consumer desires were among the preconditions for the communist exchange of goods without the use of money, Stalin argued. Until these had been achieved, to speak of dismantling the money economy was, in his opinion, "stupidity, absolutely anti-Leninist, anti-Marxist, having nothing to do with Marxism whatsoever."[48] "As money comes to be widely used, we will have a vogue for money, which we have not had for some time, and the money economy will be strengthened," he concluded. "The exchange rate of the ruble will indisputably become more stable, [and] strengthening the ruble means strengthening all of our planning and all our economic accounting."[49]

Rationing was abolished to great fanfare over the course of 1935. Citizens were promised that "every Soviet ruble introduced into circulation will be counterbalanced by a significantly growing mass of consumer goods sold at fixed state prices. This means you will be able to buy more and spend less."[50] The Soviet worker was promised he would now be able to procure an unlimited amount of goods, and his individual prosperity would depend upon "what he earns, upon the level of productivity he achieves in his workplace." The abolition of rationing would "trigger a new wave of initiative and creativity in the masses. It will unleash new stimuli for the growth of productive labor and, at the same time, hasten the construction of a socialist society in our country."[51]

Any gains the ordinary worker received were short-lived, however. By the end of the 1930s, the ruble was under renewed inflationary pressure, and, with war looming on the horizon, Soviet authorities were forced to renege upon their promises about its rising purchasing power. They raised retail prices on basic necessities in 1940, and withdrew resources from consumer production and redirected them to militarization; shortages quickly worsened and informal rationing and barter soon reemerged.[52] Nazi Germany's surprise attack in the summer of 1941 and the four years of destructive warfare that followed completely derailed their tentative accomplishments improving the purchasing power of the ruble through fiscal discipline and nonrationed trade. In order to cover the costs of the war, the Soviet government printed billions of "uncovered" (*neobespechennye*) rubles, that is, rubles that were not counterbalanced by consumer supply. By January 1, 1946, there were around 69 billion rubles in circulation, up from 19.4 billion at the start of the war.[53]

Excessive currency in circulation, combined with even more severe shortages than the country was used to, decimated the ruble's already-low purchasing power. Rationing was reintroduced on the home front in July 1941. This revived the prewar Stalinist ration system of 1929–1934, in which eligible recipients were entitled to buy limited amounts of necessities at artificially low fixed prices, but, due to shortages, low prices did not guarantee there would be anything to buy with money in state stores. The ration system was also rife with theft and abuse, serving as a conduit for rationed goods to the private sector for resale at exorbitant prices.[54] At the collective farm markets, prices skyrocketed. By the war's end, the countryside was believed to hold twice as much cash as the cities.[55] Peasants often refused urban customers' money, especially toward the beginning of the war, and bartered food for the consumer durables that rarely appeared in rural shops.[56] City dwellers grudgingly handed over their coats, shoes, and household appliances in exchange for sacks of flour and potatoes.

As supply tentatively improved in the second half of the war, the government made several attempts to improve the ruble's purchasing power by repressing market price inflation; for example, it cut commercial prices several times, and launched highly coercive mass fundraising campaigns that helped remove excess cash from circulation.[57] These efforts failed, in part, due to how resilient the private sector had grown by then. As both Julie Hessler and James Heinzen have observed, in the second half of the war, the Soviet government grew increasingly anxious about illegal economic activities that had taken off in its first half, when authorities were distracted with the German onslaught and they looked the other way at "survivalist" economic initiatives; by the mid-1940s, these initiatives had become much more entrepreneurial, entrenched, and, in the eyes of Soviet officials, unacceptable.[58] By the war's end, billions of rubles had accumulated in the hands of sinister "speculative elements." State officials and ordinary citizens alike argued it was unfair that the purchasing power of these ill-gotten gains would only increase as prices continued to drop and as supply increased in the wake of a Soviet victory.[59]

The Soviet government's economic thinking also emerged from crisis mode in the second half of the war, and it started making plans to resurrect the full-value ruble. As Hessler emphasizes, Stalinist leaders developed strong preferences about the Soviet economy in the second half of the 1930s, when they believed it was no longer beset by the problems that had dogged it since the revolution.[60] In the case of consumer trade, they developed an affinity for non-rationed trade and "cultured" customer service—practices that were more ideals than reality at that time. They emerged from the war with their prewar conceptions intact and set about creating a "properly functioning" version of what had been in place in 1935–1939.[61] They held similarly firm convictions about how best to strengthen the money economy and improve the purchasing power of the ruble drawn from the lessons of the late 1930s.

The wartime economy, on the other hand, was viewed both as an aberration and as proof of the superiority of the Stalinist principles that underlay it, as the 1947 currency reform demonstrates. The working group on reforming the ruble, drawing together representatives from the State Bank and the Ministry of Finance (*Ministerstvo finansov*), among other institutions, first met in January 1943.[62] As Soviet economic authorities debated how best to address the problem of excessive cash in circulation in the years that followed, "the main criterion for choosing one approach or another . . . was that it, as quickly as possible, simultaneously liquidated the ration system, developed Soviet trade, increased money's purchasing power and full value [*polnotsennost'*], and strengthened the role of the ruble throughout the entire national economy," one expert involved in these efforts recalled.[63] The resulting reform entailed no reevaluation of the basic structure of the Stalinist money economy. As the December 14, 1947, currency reform decree explicitly emphasized, the Soviet money economy had "withstood the severe trials of the war," and, despite the ruble's low purchasing power, it was not in need of "fundamental restructuring."[64] With this reform accomplished, the Stalinist government believed it could resume its stalled plans to bring prosperity to the masses via a full-value ruble.

The Political Economy of Postwar Prosperity

Historians of late Stalinism tend to discredit the Soviet government's efforts to improve the purchasing power of the ruble under the banner of its postwar recovery plans. P. Charles Hachten presents its concern with money in the late 1940s as a paradox: he argues that, while money played almost no substantive role in shaping the allocation of resources in practice, "the country was preoccupied with money."[65] Hachten concludes that the government exploited the "money illusion," that is, individuals' tendency to think in nominal rather than real values, an argument borrowed from the economist Franklyn D. Holzman, who advanced it 50 years earlier.[66] In Holzman's opinion, the Soviet government frequently made use of the money illusion, especially when it came to tax policy, to cushion Soviet citizens' reactions to painful economic shifts.[67] In other words, the Soviet state's postwar use of the money illusion promoted the impression the ruble was accruing value, though its purchasing power remained low.

Scholars have also primarily focused on the material hardships caused by the December 14, 1947, reforms, which wiped out many citizens' savings and came in the midst of a severe food crisis. Elena Zubkova suggests that, by then, not only officials but even many ordinary citizens were pushing to abolish rationing, believing that "it sufficed to take one correct decision, simple and wise, to leave behind all the fevered problems of wartime"; however, their ideals clashed with reality, forming a "complex of deceived hopes."[68] By leaving people with less disposable income and by not addressing the gap between supply and demand, the currency reform led to great disillusionment among the Soviet people—not just with this reform but with reform, in general.[69] Filtzer similarly sees the reform as inadequate, emphasizing that the price cuts associated with the abolition of rationing give a misleading picture of the cost of living because they primarily affected expensive items like clothing and shoes, whose supply was limited and whose prices were still too high for ordinary consumers, as were the prices of many basic food products.[70] Shortages of virtually everything persisted, including shortages of cash itself, which led to wage arrears in many areas that only exacerbated workers' everyday hardships.[71] The "full-value" ruble ushered in by the currency reform did not have a transformational impact on the process of postwar recovery, which Filtzer describes as "attenuated."[72]

The December 1947 reforms fell far short of producing mass prosperity, as this book acknowledges, but this fact does not clarify why late Stalinist authorities clung to the view that the full-value ruble was an essential tool of postwar recovery, or why Khrushchev-era authorities continued to express this view beyond Stalin's death. To understand why, we need to look more closely at—and take more seriously—Soviet political leaders' and economic experts' beliefs and assumptions about the functioning of the Soviet economy.[73] Postwar efforts to reform the ruble flowed from their belief that a ruble with real purchasing power in a system of open trade boosted labor productivity and economic growth and, in the long run, produced abundance. Stalinist authorities articulated this belief before the war during the abolition of rationing in 1934–1935, as discussed above, and they retained this belief as they set about rebuilding and developing the economy after it. Their choice to focus on increasing the ruble's purchasing power by abolishing rationing and tinkering with price levels does not let them off the hook for the hunger and deprivation millions of Soviet citizens suffered in the absence of more immediate, direct, and material interventions to improve their quality of life after a devastating war.

Soviet political leaders were not the only ones devising and steering these economic initiatives. Over the course of the postwar period, experts played an increasingly important role in formulating the policies associated with the promise of prosperity delivered via the full-value ruble. Of course, Stalin continued to hold forth on this and related subjects into the last years of his life. Stalin considered himself to be a great authority on Marxist political economy: he famously intervened in the writing of a political economy textbook in 1952;

dissatisfied with what the writers had come up with, he wrote his last major treatise, *The Economic Problems of Socialism in the USSR,* in response.[74] In this text, he rehashed many of his old criticisms about the Bolsheviks' ideological prejudices toward money, attacking those who held onto "outdated" ideas derived from Marx's critique of capitalism, such as hostility toward commodity production and the money economy, ideas that scarcely applied to Soviet socialism, in his opinion.[75] He insisted that consecutive retail price cuts, which he initiated in the late 1940s, were the most important drivers of real wage growth, despite the fact that, as will be demonstrated in Chapter 1, they merely exacerbated chronic supply problems that undermined the ruble's purchasing power.[76] As the country's dictatorial leader, he was the arbiter of any economic strategy that was pursued. That said, there were more opportunities for economic experts to insert their input into the process of policy making even under his watch. Stalin increasingly focused on the international situation and delegated authority over domestic affairs after the war, as Yoram Gorlizki and Oleg V. Khlevniuk have observed. His colleagues recognized that certain areas of the Soviet economy were in crisis, and devised reforms around him that were implemented only after his death.[77]

A Full-Value Ruble thus joins a growing body of recent scholarship emphasizing the expanding influence of experts in formulating Soviet economic policies, especially with the renaissance of the social sciences in the Khrushchev era.[78] Beginning in the mid-1950s, the Soviet government took increased interest in their recommendations. These were not always "big name" economists, such as those later associated with the famous theoretical mathematical-economic innovations of the late 1960s: as Artemy Kalinovsky has pointed out, economic specialists, often working in "relative obscurity," became important voices in debates on all aspects of the economy after Stalin's death, helping to "gradually dismantle one set of assumptions and lay the foundations for another."[79] Many of these individuals were not standard economists in a sense that would be immediately recognizable to Western readers. As Chris Miller has recently implored historians to remember, "Economic ideas are not only the purview of economists . . . understanding the history of economic thought in the USSR requires intellectual histories not only of economists, but also of planners, enterprise managers, political leaders, and others who thought about economic problems but would not have described themselves as economists."[80] Cold War considerations heightened the stakes involved in solving the Soviet Union's economic problems. As Yakov Feygin argues, the competition between the Soviet Union and the West shaped these experts' priorities and their assigned tasks: beginning in the 1950s, economic experts attempted to reinvent the Stalinist planned economy in order to make the Soviet system more competitive against America's and Western Europe's high-productivity welfare states.[81]

Economic experts' advice, it needs to be emphasized, was not always welcome or taken. The practicing economists, planners, and bureaucrats featured in this book, working at various levels of government within the Ministry of Finance, the State Planning Committee (*Gosudarstvennyi komitet po planirovaniu*, or *Gosplan*), the Ministry of Social Security, the Central Trade Union, the Council of Ministers, and other institutions, fed their recommendations up the chain of command to Stalin and Khrushchev, who accepted and implemented some and rejected others as incompatible with their own ideas of the country's priorities or their own understandings of what was ideologically permissible in a socialist system. These interactions were often fraught, and, especially in the Stalin era, the personal and professional risks were extremely high.[82] Although there were no more violent purges during his tenure as Soviet leader, Khrushchev was no less confirmed in his convictions than his predecessor, prone to erratic decision-making, and frequently shuffled key personnel. Moreover, he plowed ahead with plans experts urged him to approach with caution or reconsider, as will be seen in several episodes in this book, in particular during the campaign to abolish income taxes, a policy officials and experts attached to the Ministry of Finance repeatedly rejected as "inadvisable." This campaign, and other economic initiatives spearheaded by Khrushchev, had disastrous consequences for the full-value ruble that were undeniable by 1962.

Indeed, by then, it had become abundantly clear to both Soviet political authorities and economic experts that, despite their efforts to put more full-value rubles into citizens' hands, money remained frequently, at times painfully, useless. As it had before the war, the Soviet government eschewed any hint of "leveling" (*uravnilovka*) in wages, pensions, and other payments to the urban population as undermining productivity, justifying glaring income inequality, especially in the late Stalin years, but even after Khrushchev's wage and pension reforms of the mid- to late 1950s. Despite the state's great purported "care" for citizens' welfare, many still lived in debilitating poverty. Khrushchev's efforts to broaden access to the fruits of Soviet prosperity after Stalin's death and the Twentieth Party Congress resulted in significant gains relative to the period that preceded it, but consumption levels still lagged behind Khrushchev's ambitious projections and the Western capitalist countries he promised the

Soviet Union would soon overtake. Despite the average citizen's supposedly steadily improving economic prospects in the postwar period, many still struggled to get by or simply to spend their hard-earned rubles, a reality that often shook their confidence in Soviet power and in communism itself.

Structure of the Book

This book reconstructs central political authorities and economic experts' bird's-eye perspective on the Soviet economy and society. When it comes to developments on the ground, it is mostly focused on the Russian Soviet Federative Socialist Republic (*Rossiiskaia Sovetskaia Federativnaia Sotsialisticheskaia Respublika,* RSFSR). This reflects the sources consulted during my research in Russian state archives, but also the Soviet government's conscious and unconscious efforts to deliver prosperity to workers and urban citizens in the industrial heartland first. Rural areas and less-industrialized republics were a lower priority, especially in the Stalin era. I have tried to show the impact of the policies under consideration upon a diverse group of cities and areas within the Soviet Union and across the RSFSR, but the regional dimensions and impact of the project of creating postwar prosperity would be the subject of an altogether different book, one I would strongly welcome to be written.

Each chapter focuses on a state promise about the gains citizens would enjoy, and the policies adopted to deliver them, as the Soviet Union purportedly experienced prosperity underwritten by a "full-value" ruble in circulation. Chapter 1 focuses on the promise of lower retail prices and a lower urban cost of living after the war and into the early 1960s. Chapter 2 examines Khrushchev's post-1956 efforts to raise minimum wages, tackle poverty, and reduce the massive income inequality that had emerged over the course of the Stalin era, while still retaining the incentive value of differentiated wages. Chapter 3 looks at the campaign to raise and reform state pensions and bring much-needed "care" to Soviet society's nonworking and most economically vulnerable members from the late 1940s onward. Chapter 4 focuses on Khrushchev's late-1950s promise to increase workers' take-home pay by eliminating burdensome wage deductions, including direct taxes and tax-like subscriptions to state bonds. Finally, Chapter 5 examines the tangible consumer gains Soviet citizens were promised in return for voluntarily investing in state bonds and lottery tickets and depositing their money in state bank accounts in the late 1950s and early 1960s, as wage deductions began to be phased out and as Soviet authorities coped with a growing savings glut. In the conclusion, I look at the legacy of these economic policies in the late Soviet period and beyond.

These promises were intertwined. Each had an impact upon the planned balance of the population's money income and expenses, productivity and economic growth rates, and, most importantly in authorities' eyes, the Soviet Union's revolutionary development toward the abundance of communism, when money would no longer be needed to motivate workers' and peasants' labor or determine their access to goods and could be finally discarded. Soviet citizens, in turn, measured their own progress beyond earlier hardships and toward the glorious future, as well as their losses and their disappointments, in rubles and kopeks.

1

Our Low-Price Guarantee

Supply and demand were not the most basic determinants of retail prices in the Stalinist economy. In theory, Soviet retail prices reflected Marx's "law of value" (in Russian, *zakon stoimosti*), the proportional relationship between the labor expended to produce a good and its exchange value. They also reflected the Soviet state's welfare priorities and its struggle against vestiges of capitalism, that is, against kolkhoz-market vendors, black marketers, and other manifestations of the persistent private sector.[1] During the NEP, with its mixed-market system, the Soviet economy had been plagued by rising retail prices; with the shift to a planned command economy, retail prices were no longer allowed to fluctuate and were organized into a tiered system of fixed levels. The shortages and inflationary pressures associated with the onset of the First Five-Year Plan and collectivization also forced the Soviet government to resort to rationing. Under rationing, workers were allowed to purchase basic necessities in restricted amounts at artificially low subsidized prices, typically in the "closed" shops accessible only to employees of a given enterprise. As Sheila Fitzpatrick astutely observes, "The harder it was to get access to a store, the lower the prices of its goods."[2] The state simultaneously charged higher "commercial" retail prices in its network of "open" delicatessens and department stores that featured a relatively better selection of goods and were targeted at foreigners and elites. The latter often received special discounts entitling them to pay less than the sticker price.

This tiered, class-informed retail price system, in principle, promoted ordinary workers' economic welfare by shielding it from the vagaries of the market, and by asking those with more financial resources—not to mention class enemies and "former peoples"—to pay extra.[3] However, it also frayed the connection between retail prices and the costs of production, especially of basic foodstuffs and consumer goods, and it exacerbated shortages that allowed the private sector to continue to flourish. Price controls encouraged "speculation" (*spekuliatsiia*), the state's catchall term for illegal economic activities, for example, embezzling ration-priced goods from central supplies and reselling them at a steep markup. Workers might have enjoyed access to the lowest prices in the Stalinist economy, but there was often nothing to buy in state shops at any price; as a result, even they had little choice but to turn to what was left of the market. If supply and demand ceased to meaningfully inform state retail prices under Stalin, this was not the case with market prices, which were invariably higher and a more accurate reflection of the dismal state of consumer supply under his leadership.

This approach to retail prices, in sum, merely promoted the illusion of a low cost of living—a fact that was not lost on Soviet leaders. As Stalin, himself, acknowledged in a speech to the Central Committee of the Communist Party in the fall of 1934, ration prices were not "real prices" but an expression of the government's "class policy" and a "gift to the working class at the expense of the peasantry."[4] Peasants were intimately aware of this: in fact, they typically ignored ration prices and oriented their market prices around higher commercial prices, he emphasized. By abolishing rationing, Stalin suggested the government could move toward a "real policy" on bread prices, which would ultimately help to bring down its price and the prices of other essential goods.[5] This move would exert a positive impact upon market prices: "The peasant [*muzhik*] will drop prices as a first order of business," he insisted.[6] Eliminating the tiered price system would, furthermore, prevent opportunities for speculation because "when there are two or three prices for bread, speculation is automatic, it is absolutely inevitable." Stalin scoffed that he could hardly blame speculators "because this system we have, the system of two to three prices, is such that even the most honest person ought to sell bread and turn it to his advantage. That's how rotten our ration system has become."[7]

The Soviet government abolished rationing and united ration and commercial price levels "irrevocably and forever" in 1935, promising workers lower retail prices, and vastly improved purchasing power in the near future.[8] It struggled to make good on this promise for the remainder of the decade and, during the Second World War, was forced to abandon the policy altogether.[9] Just weeks after Nazi Germany's invasion on June 22, 1941, rationing was reintroduced on the home front, splitting the retail price system back into lower ration and higher commercial levels. Ration prices were frozen until the fall of 1946; however, centralized consumer production all but ground to a halt in the first half of the war, leaving virtually nothing to buy at these prices. During the war, workers cashed in their ration cards in their workplace canteens, which had steadier access to food supplies, and provided them with most of what they ate.[10] Even in the state's supposedly better-stocked and more prestigious commercial outlets, supply often fell far short of demand and prices rose exponentially prior to 1944, putting their products out of reach.[11] Prices in the kolkhoz markets skyrocketed: by late 1943, they were 13.9 times higher than in 1940.[12] They declined only in the second half of the war as supplies to the ration system improved, often undercutting commercial levels but remaining above ration levels.[13]

In the wake of the Soviet Union's victory, Stalin vowed to reverse wartime price deviations and their impact on the ruble's purchasing power as soon as possible. At a meeting of voters on February 9, 1946, he promised to "wild applause" that "special attention will be paid to expanding production of consumer goods, and to increasing workers' living standards by means of consecutive price reductions for all goods."[14] The Five-Year Plan for the Reconstruction and Development of the National Economy, adopted in March 1946, set lower prices and the expansion of retail trade as priorities.[15] The government made plans to abolish rationing by the end of that year. However, these plans were waylaid as a drought in the country's grain-growing regions burgeoned into a deadly famine; the government, in the meantime, continued to export grain, exacerbating shortages.[16] The Soviet government postponed the abolition of rationing, focusing instead on narrowing the wide gap that had opened during the war between commercial and ration prices by increasing ration price levels in September 1946.[17] As it had done when it abolished rationing in 1935, it extended a cash supplement to the urban population, a so-called bread allowance (*khlebnaia nadbavka*), to soften the impact of raised prices, but this could only go so far to mitigate the high cost of living when there was little bread to buy in state stores.[18]

In the eyes of postwar political and economic authorities, abolishing rationing and bringing down prices was essential for reining in the hated private sector, but also to deliver upon their stalled mid-1930s plans to improve workers' purchasing power—the core promise of the full-value ruble. The punitive terms of the December 14, 1947, currency reform deliberately wiped out collective farmers' and speculators' illicit cash profits. The reform simultaneously abolished the ration system that had helped them to accumulate so much money, replacing it with the "open" retail trade and "united" price systems of the late 1930s. As it had in 1935, the Soviet government promised workers that even lower prices were in store. By the time of Stalin's death, not only had retail prices been reduced, but the consecutive price cuts heralded by Stalin in February 1946 had become a new annual ritual and an economic doctrine, the Communist Party's primary mechanism for raising workers' real wages, as Stalin insisted in his last major treatise before his death, *The Economic Problems of Socialism in the USSR*.[19] Each spring through 1954, the prices of dozens of categories of food and consumer goods were slashed to great fanfare. Consecutive retail price cuts were presented as clear evidence of Stalin's fatherly "care" for workers' bread-and-butter interests and of the Soviet Union's steadily increasing prosperity.

Although he publicly praised the policy of consecutive retail price cuts during the last years of Stalin's life and even promised to continue them after the dictator's death, Khrushchev changed course soon after securing his leadership in the mid-1950s.[20] He recognized that the spring price cuts did not reflect reduced costs of production or greater efficiency; rather, they were facilitated by costly subsidies and the ongoing exploitation of the Soviet peasantry, which was paid virtually nothing for the ever-cheaper food they put on workers' and other urban citizens' dinner plates. Collective farmers, in turn, "exacted their 'revenge' at the market," as the Soviet price expert A. N. Malafeev put it, charging prices that exceeded not only procurement prices but also the state's retail prices (emphasis his).[21] Workers, in turn, had little choice but to pay these steep prices because the Soviet government still could not fully provision them from central supplies.

At the Twentieth Party Congress in February 1956, Khrushchev publicly eschewed further consecutive price cuts, promising that real wages would rise, and the ruble's purchasing power would steadily improve, due to a larger and more stable supply of food and goods in state stores. The government would no longer squeeze the countryside to feed the cities but would give peasants a tangible interest in voluntarily increasing their deliveries to the state—in short, it would pay collective farmers more money. Light industry would be increasingly prioritized, at no loss to heavy industry, and the Soviet Union would "catch up and overtake" the capitalist West in consumer output. A more concrete correspondence between retail prices and the cost of production, and between supply and demand, would be established. "Economically sound" (*ekonomicheski obosnovannye*) price cuts would take place only on selected items whose prices remained severely inflated after the war.

Workers' purchasing power noticeably improved in the late 1950s, but shortages persisted that sent them to the private sector, where prices remained higher. In January 1961, Khrushchev revalued the ruble once again, a reform that applied to wages and prices this time. Unlike the confiscatory 1947 currency reform, Soviet citizens were promised the new currency reform would result in no financial losses for them whatsoever. In fact, it caused slight price rises in state stores and sharp rises in the collective farm markets; in the meantime, many citizens' wages, pensions, and other state payments were rounded down. These developments did not go unnoticed, especially by low-income members of Soviet society who were sensitive to even minor shifts in the cost of living. More problematically, Khrushchev underestimated the significance of Stalin's consecutive retail price cuts in the urban population's eyes. After years of being promised continually lower prices, many felt deeply betrayed when, in June 1962, Khrushchev announced that prices were going up.

The Return of "Open" Retail Trade

The December 14, 1947, decree announcing a new ruble and the end of rationing resurrected Soviet authorities' preferred "open" retail system of the late 1930s, in which (at least in principle) any good could be purchased in any quantity by anyone possessing enough money. As with the abolition of rationing in 1935, the tiered price system was eliminated and replaced with "unified state retail prices" (*edinnye gosudarstvennye roznichnye tseny*).[22] The new prices went into effect on December 16 in all urban retail stores and rural producers' cooperatives across the country. Three price zones were established, down from eight, as well as higher prices for consumer goods in rural areas.[23] Workers were promised that the new prices for food and consumer goods either were decreased from ration levels or now "tend[ed] toward the level of existing ration prices."[24]

The newspaper *Pravda* jubilantly assured its readers that, "instead of the currently circulating ruble with its low purchasing power, the population is receiving a full-value ruble."[25] In the days that followed, Soviet citizens flocked to state stores to see for themselves. Across 55 major cities in the Soviet Union, shops collectively exceeded their imposed limits for the day for purchases of bread, cereal, meat, milk, and butter, among other basic food items.[26] Demand for some items, such as white bread and shoes, far exceeded supply, though increased deliveries were scheduled to coincide with the introduction of the new prices.[27] Shops reported massive lines. By December 18, there were still around 5,000 people lined up outside the Central Department Store (*Tsentral'nyi universalnyi magazin,* TsUM) in Moscow first thing in the morning, waiting for its doors to open.[28]

Yet, demand for consumer goods in the days after the currency reform was considered disappointing. As trade reports noted, customers mostly bought basic clothing, like cotton socks and shoes, and food.[29] As one official in Sverdlovsk observed, "There is a huge amount and selection of manufactured goods on the shelves: prefabricated dresses, winter coats, and silk fabrics, but customers evidently do not have enough money to buy them, everyone just walks on by and considers the price. There are no lines whatsoever."[30]

While the December 14, 1947, reform did not apply to the unregulated prices charged in kolkhoz markets, the decree's preamble promised that "consumers will receive significant gains from the further lowering of prices, since unified prices in open state trade often entails lower prices in the kolkhoz market."[31] Reports from across the Soviet Union indicate that on December 16, peasants' prices did, in fact, plummet. Kolkhoz markets in most urban centers were virtually empty that day. In Kiev, the handful of peasants who showed up at the markets sold their products at prices that were half of what they had asked for only one day earlier.[32] Across the RSFSR, the average market price of potatoes dropped 2–3 times, milk 2 times, butter 2–2.5 times, and meat by 20%–25% in some cities.[33] By the end of the month, Soviet statisticians reported that market prices for most food products had dipped below state prices.[34]

Retail trade was anything but fully "open" after the abolition of rationing, placing a very practical constraint on the ruble's purchasing power. By the start of 1948, the Soviet Union was only beginning to recover from the famine, and severe grain shortages continued to leave many regions without bread for days.[35] In the city of Kaluga, for example, despite being allocated additional supplies of flour, shops reached their purchasing limits within three to four hours of opening, a situation that "elicits great criticism from the population and disrupts normal life," as one local Party secretary reported.[36]

Due to these shortages, "closed" distribution practices persisted. Many "departments for workers' provisioning" (*otdely rabochego snabzheniia,* ORSes), factory stores catering only to the workers of a given enterprise that remained in operation after the abolition of rationing, set internal limits on how much bread could be bought by one customer. Though it was prohibited, some stores sold bread only "according to the lists" (*po spiskam*) of shoppers who were granted access. Party and state officials, along with other elites, were often allowed to exceed purchasing norms for bread, while ordinary workers struggled to procure it.[37] Bread lines often started in the early hours of the morning and stretched out into the street.

Though the amount of money they spent on it declined after the December 1947 reforms, workers continued to spend far more money on food than on consumer goods with the advent of open retail trade. According to family budget studies, in the RSFSR in 1948, food constituted 46% of workers' reported expenditures, down from 55% the year before.[38] Food still occupied the lion's share of expenses because workers still purchased much of it at the kolkhoz markets, where prices still exceeded those in state stores—a situation that engendered enormous discontent among them. Many complained bitterly when new operating hours for retail stores were decreed in January 1948, giving retail shop employees the same workday as most day laborers and forcing the latter to have to shop in more expensive after-hours shops and in the kolkhoz markets. One group of Moscow office workers wrote that collective farmers, by inflating their prices, were exploiting the "desperate situation" faced by those who did not have "housekeepers or grannies and aunties" to go to the shops for them during the day, and demanded that the hours be changed "since it turns out the opposite is true: 'He who works, does not eat'" (underlined in original).[39]

The Soviet leadership was nevertheless convinced that the December 1947 reforms rapidly and substantially increased the purchasing power of the ruble. A group of leaders from Gosplan, the Ministry of Finance, Gosbank, and the Central Statistical Office confidently reported to Stalin in April 1948 that purchasing power had increased 41% since the reforms.[40] The sum of trade in state and cooperative shops in the first quarter of 1948 dropped by 13.4 billion rubles compared to the same period in 1947 due to decreasing prices for food and consumer goods; however, this was believed to have had less of an impact than decreased market prices.[41] Purchases in the kolkhoz markets totaled 8.1 billion rubles in the first quarter of 1948, 18.4 billion rubles less than purchases in the first quarter of 1947. Real wages had also increased overall, the report concluded, due to a 7% increase in workers' money incomes during the same period in 1947.[42] In the first quarter of 1948, the purchasing power of the ruble reportedly increased by 41.7%.[43]

There was still some cause for worry, however. In particular, shortages of bread and other basic necessities persisted into 1948 and large stockpiles of unsellable consumer durables and processed foods were beginning to accumulate in state warehouses because their prices were still too high. Soviet industries were required to maintain reserve supplies consisting of a certain number of days' worth of projected retail trade turnover, but these goods were accumulating well beyond desirable levels. By the spring of 1948, the state had a massive oversupply of alcohol on its hands. The price of a half-liter bottle of "Moskovskaia" vodka was, by then, seven times its prewar level.[44] Enterprising individuals had figured out that it was significantly cheaper to buy bread, sugar, and yeast at state retail prices and make their own homebrew or distill their own moonshine (*samogon*).[45] Goods with longer shelf lives, like vodka, could be relatively easily stored, but perishable foods like caviar and beer could only be held on to for so long before their quality was affected and the products were wasted. These industries pressured the central government to reduce retail prices in order to clear out their reserves.[46]

In response, on April 10, 1948, the prices of overstocked and luxury goods, including cars, vitamins, watches, and alcohol, were reduced by 10%–20%. This initiative was publicly depicted as the next step in the process of bringing down prices heralded by Stalin in 1946 and begun during the 1947 currency reform, "a new display of Stalin's care for workers" that would be gratefully and happily received by all Soviet people and would "inspire toilers in the cities and countryside alike to dedicate new deeds of valor to the glory of the Fatherland."[47] No mention of the trade system's desperate need to clear out stockpiles was made. Moreover, ordinary workers benefited little, since the reduced prices of many of these goods remained exorbitant. A Moskvich car cost 10,000 rubles—even with a 10% decrease, a 9,000-ruble expense was out of the question for most citizens, to say nothing of the enormous difficulties involved in purchasing one of the most deficit items of all in the Soviet consumer economy.[48]

Unsatisfactory trade turnover and swelling reserves thus persisted after the April price cuts. As of January 1, 1949, reserves of unsold consumer goods reached a total retail value of 48.4 billion rubles, up from 30.1 billion rubles on January 1, 1948.[49] As one report noted, these goods' prices had been set when they were being produced in much smaller amounts, and had not been adjusted since.[50] Nearly 3 billion rubles worth of shoes, 3.3 billion rubles of tobacco, 4.5 billion rubles of vodka, and 3.4 billion rubles of salt were held in reserve. The latter constituted more than 1.5 years' reserve supply. Trade officials explicitly blamed high retail prices for excessive stockpiles: in 1940, one kilogram of salt cost 11 kopeks and, as of January 1, 1949, it cost 1.50 rubles.[51]

Growing stockpiles were worrying to Soviet leaders not only because they required scarce storage space and because stored goods deteriorated in quality, but because of their impact on planned balances in the Soviet money economy. The retail prices of nonessential consumer goods contained the "turnover tax" (*nalog s oborota*). Though Soviet officials strenuously denied that it was a commodity tax, this is effectively what the turnover tax was (see Chapter 4). It could exceed half an item's retail price. The price of vodka had a particularly high share of turnover tax built into it. The turnover tax was the Soviet state's largest source of all tax receipts; sluggish retail trade turnover threatened its primary source of tax revenue.[52]

More importantly, massive stockpiles of unsold goods unsettled the precarious balance of the population's money income and expenses, tipping it toward the former and leaving excess cash in circulation that undermined the goal of a full-value ruble. In 1949, the Ministry of Finance emitted 3.3 billion rubles, a 14% increase over 1948, but retail trade rose by only about 8% and the wage fund by about 7.4%.[53] This increase in the cash supply did not exert a major influence on kolkhoz market prices, which continued their post–December 1947 decline, as one report noted: instead, it resulted in the accumulation of excessive sums of unspendable money in the population's hands.[54] Much of this money was deposited into Soviet savings banks while citizens waited to accumulate the necessary financial resources to purchase big-ticket consumer goods and for deficit items to become available (see Chapter 5), especially after rumors began to circulate at the end of the year that the government was planning to bring down prices once again.[55]

The rumor mill was on to something: already by then, the Council of Ministers was making plans to cut prices once again, this time, not only on overstocked goods and, this time, on a much larger scale. The cuts announced on March 1, 1949, brought the prices of over 40 categories of products down by 10%–30%.[56] The move was presented as yet another step in the process of raising the purchasing power of the ruble begun by the 1947 currency reform, a "pure gain" (*chistyi vyigrysh*) for workers and a "loss" (*ubytok*) to the state budget that was bestowed upon workers "regardless of the serious difficulties [the government] would have to bear."[57] High-demand food staples like bread and meat saw their prices cut, as well as a range of consumer luxuries, including household appliances, dishes, radios, and jewelry. "As a result of the new price cut, once again the purchasing power of the ruble soars and its exchange rate with other foreign currencies is improving, once again the real wages of workers and the intelligentsia seriously increases, and once again the cost of buying manufactured goods for peasants drops," read the front page of *Pravda*.[58]

"THIS IS POSSIBLE ONLY IN OUR COUNTRY!" another headline trumpeted (capitalization in text).[59]

The March 1949 price cuts were more successful at stimulating demand for processed foods and consumer goods than previous efforts. In 40 major cities across the Soviet Union, sales of meat products rose by 13.2%, oil by 27%, cheese by 57.9%, salt by 16.4%, vodka by 57.9%, and wine by 67.4% over the previous month.[60] Across 35 major cities, purchases of consumer goods multiplied: bicycles by over 4 times, gramophones by 4.5 times, watches by over 2 times, and radio sets by nearly 2 times. However, these increases appear to have dropped off toward the end of the month, for total retail trade turnover in March increased by only 6.6% over February 1949.[61] Sales of some products, such as bread and tobacco, even dropped compared to the previous month, but this was attributed by trade authorities to citizens diverting money to purchases of consumer durables. Shortages undoubtedly caused sales to taper off. As one anonymous letter writer reported, many of the musical instruments, watches, radios, and bicycles whose prices had been slashed were nowhere to be found or their selection in stores was abysmal. "You've decreased the prices of goods that are not for sale," he accused, adding that this had only heightened the importance of *blat* in procuring goods and had contributed to longer lines.[62]

Many Soviet citizens felt that the state's price cuts did not go far enough to reverse wartime price distortions. Ration prices were increased 2–3 times in the fall of 1946; the prices of necessities were then lowered on December 16, 1947, and on March 1, 1949, from these elevated levels. This meant that the prices of most foods and consumer goods continued to substantially exceed prewar levels. Wages and pensions, in the meantime, had not been adjusted for the cost of living since the bread allowance offered in the fall of 1946 to offset higher ration prices. "My wife asks me: when will we live well? Like we lived before the war?," the writer of an anonymous letter wrote in June 1949.[63] "The wages are the same as they were in 1935, and the prices for all goods and groceries are higher, for one thing, you need to spend 240 rubles a month on bread for the family, when you only had to spend 81 rubles before," he complained. "Don't forget about people like us," he urged Soviet leaders. "We are waiting for lower prices, we want to live normally, like we did before this war."[64]

Consecutive Retail Price Cuts

In the early 1950s, Stalin lived up to the promise he made in February 1946: each spring, the prices of dozens of categories of food and goods were consecutively slashed by up to 50%. It is unclear who proposed making retail price cuts a yearly ritual, but the available evidence points to him. According to the propagandist Dmitrii Shepilov, Stalin reasoned that in the absence of private manufacturing and with virtually no domestic competition among enterprises, a monopoly on foreign trade that shielded the country from the world market, strict control over prices, and even with a shortage of consumer goods, "systematically lowering prices is the most effective means of stimulating higher productivity and better quality. Lowering consumer prices prevents sloth and stagnation and is the best way to raise wages in real terms."[65]

The annual price reductions continued to be aimed at reducing stockpiles. Soviet authorities acknowledged this when they issued a round of price cuts in 1950. Gosplan reported in May 1949 that, already by April 1 of that year, stockpiles of many products, including vodka, textiles, perfume, and soap, were still 44% above normative reserve levels.[66] By January 1, 1950, an estimated 7 billion rubles more money than what was needed for "normal" consumption were in circulation.[67] As a result, March 1, 1950, saw the retail prices of 236 categories of goods reduced by 10%–50%, for a total of not less than 80 billion rubles in "savings" to Soviet consumers.[68] Although it was not admitted to consumers, this list included substantial discounts on many of the same goods that were in oversupply.

Publicly, the Soviet government also connected the 1950 price cuts to larger forces in the global economy. While the prosperity of the Soviet Union was ceaselessly increasing, its Cold War adversary, the United States, could merely boast of increases in the prices of basic necessities, unemployment, poverty, and hunger, *Pravda* claimed.[69] On the same day as the government unveiled that year's price cuts, it also announced new international exchange rates for the ruble. These supposedly reflected the effects of the currency reform, the abolition of rationing, and repeated price cuts on the ruble's purchasing power in 1947–1950, as well as the concurrent depreciation of the other major world currencies during the same period, especially the American dollar and the British pound.[70] With this move, the Soviet government ended its practice since 1937 of pegging the Soviet ruble to the American dollar; now, it would be pegged to "more stable" gold.[71] As Franklyn D. Holzman suggests, this shift likely had little to do with domestic economic developments, and everything to do with the Soviet government's foreign trade ambitions at the time. Stalin wanted to raise the international prestige of the ruble, which he wanted to become the dominant currency of an emerging socialist trading bloc in Eastern

Europe.[72] At the end of the day, raised exchange rates meant little to the Soviet consumer: he or she could not buy dollars or pounds with rubles and Soviet retail prices were deliberately shielded from world-market prices, as Shepilov indicated above.

Compared to the 1950 price cuts, the next two annual price decreases in 1951 and 1952 were much more modest, featuring reductions on only 46 and 48 categories of goods, for savings of 27.5 billion and 23 billion rubles, respectively.[73] Already by 1952, retail prices had already been cut in half, on average, from 1947 levels. Yet, at the Nineteenth Party Congress in October 1952, Soviet citizens were told they could expect even more retail price cuts, founded upon the country's massive successes in industry and agriculture. The Party resolved to "unswervingly conduct further retail price reductions on mass consumer goods, keeping in mind that, lowering prices is the primary means by which the real wages of workers and peasants are systematically increased."[74] That year, in *The Economic Problems of Socialism in the USSR,* Stalin argued that a major precondition for "real and not just declaratory communism" was the "cultural advancement" of society, which depended upon "a rise in real wages through direct wage increases and the systematic reduction of retail prices."[75] By the time of the last consecutive price cut in 1954, the prices of all goods had been reduced, on average, to 43% of retail price levels in the fourth quarter of 1947, before the currency reform (Figure 1.1). Altogether, the annual price decreases were argued to have resulted in 302 billion rubles in gains for Soviet citizens.[76]

Soviet citizens were encouraged to think of each spring price reduction as cause for celebration. "The prosperity of our country's workers is ceaselessly rising on the basis of the constant growth of the national economy. With each passing day, life becomes ever richer and more prosperous [*bolee bogatoi i zazhitochnoi*]," the front page of *Pravda* gushed on March 1, 1950. It attributed these achievements to the wise leadership of the Communist Party and to "our father and friend, great Stalin's unceasing care for the needs of workers."[77] Readers were reminded that rationing was ongoing and prices were steadily rising in England and other "Marshallized" countries of Europe that had accepted American financial aid to rebuild after the war, which the Soviet Union had rejected and had also forced its satellites in Central and Eastern Europe to reject.[78] The capitalist media, Soviet citizens were told, maliciously downplayed or concealed the Soviet government's enormous achievements in this realm—in April 1952, *Pravda* remarked scornfully that the *New York Times* had run only a tiny clip about that year's price cuts.[79]

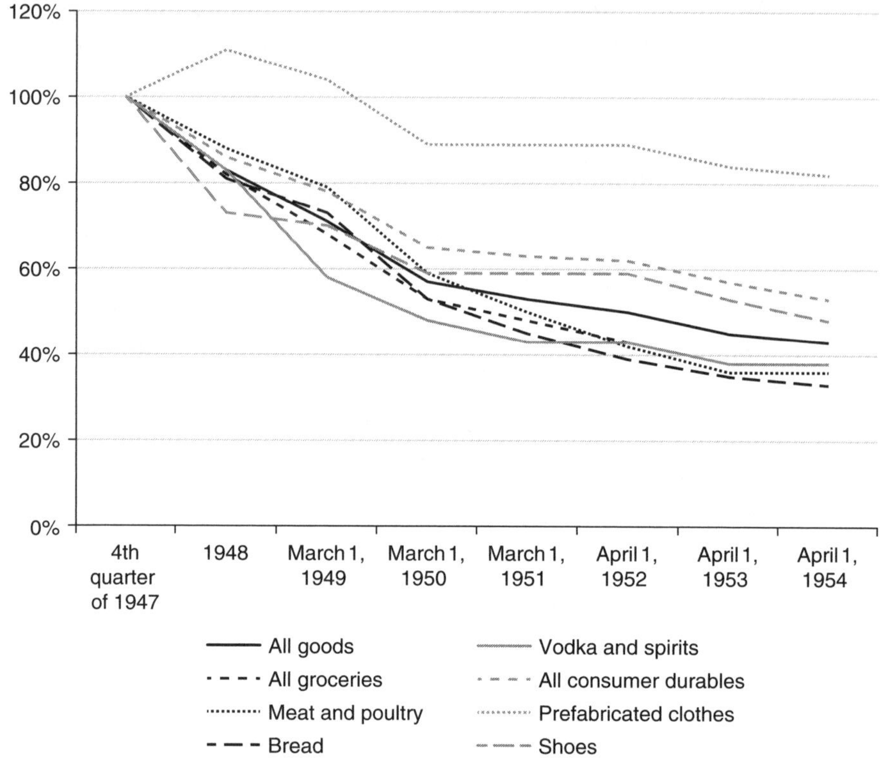

Figure 1.1 State Retail Price Reductions, 1947–1954
Data source: Tsentral'noe statisticheskoe upravlenie pri Sovete Ministrov SSSR, *Sovetskaia torgovlia: Statisticheskii sbornik* (Moskva: Gosstatizdat, 1956), 132.

The media coverage surrounding the price decreases employed the long-familiar trope of gifting on the part of the state and gratitude on the part of citizens, which Jeffrey Brooks has identified as a core Soviet value.[80] This ritualized thanking went beyond media reports; it was used as a tool for boosting productivity. In workplace meetings and rallies, activists responded to the new prices by pledging Stakhanovite labor as a token of gratitude for their increased purchasing power, and by issuing calls (*prizyvy*) to their peers to do the same. In response to the March 1949 price cuts, a forewoman in the Krasnyi Treiugol'nik rubber factory in Leningrad, a certain Nikiforova, urged her co-workers to "deploy socialist competition with renewed strength to improve our output of high-quality products and lower our costs of production. In this way, we can ensure the consecutive lowering of prices."[81] Although the supply of consumer goods in the countryside continued to be uneven if not wholly absent, rural activists made similar pledges. A milkmaid named Popok, of the "Soviet Belarus" farm in Minsk oblast, pledged to produce 3.5 thousand liters of milk from each of the 12 heads of cattle she had personally reared, while the head of the farm's gardening brigade promised to increase that year's harvest by 500 hundredweights per hectare out of gratitude for the 1951 price cuts.[82]

A recurring line in both media depictions and reports on the popular mood (*svodki*) was that trade in state shops in the days following the spring announcements proceeded "like a holiday." The Stalinist government had long released reserves of foods and luxury items like champagne and chocolates around the time of state holidays like International Women's Day or the anniversary of the October Revolution to popularize these events as new Soviet rituals.[83] The price decreases of the early 1950s were similarly accompanied with increased supplies, at least in department stores and in the major cities. Ahead of the last consecutive retail price cut of April 1954, the government drew upon its reserves to provide shops in Moscow with an additional 325 million rubles' worth of goods, including silk fabrics, garments, stockings, and shoes.[84] In the days following the announcements, newspapers, newsreels, and magazines depicted well-stocked stores, sumptuous displays of neatly organized food and goods, and customers, usually women, leaving with radiant smiles and saddled down with purchases.[85]

Alongside each price cut, workers were promised that they would receive additional savings from decreased prices in the kolkhoz markets due to the natural regulatory influence state retail prices were believed to hold over market prices. Prices in the markets did tend to dip immediately after the spring announcements: for example, in Moscow, Gorki, Sverdlovsk, and other major cities, the price of a kilogram of beef in the kolkhoz markets dropped by 1 or 2 rubles after the price decrease on March 1, 1949.[86] Butter prices dropped by around 5 rubles per kilogram, staying slightly below state prices by the end of the month. However, as soon as shortages inevitably emerged in state stores, market prices crept upward again. Workers dispatched angry complaints about the perpetually large discrepancy between the two sets of prices. "Products like potatoes are as needed as the air we breathe, but they are always a deficit in Rostov-on-Don," one worker wrote. "In the shops, they cost 1.10 rubles but at the bazaars, the speculators sell them for 3–4 rubles. The collective farmers sell them for 2–3 rubles and buy them in shops at state prices. We are now transitioning from socialism to communism . . . shouldn't they only be allowed to sell food and goods at prices that are lower than the government's prices?"[87]

By the early 1950s, the disastrous state of Soviet agriculture meant that ever-lower food prices were unsustainable. The countryside suffered a massive labor shortage due to heavy wartime casualties and postwar flight that left rural residents disproportionately aged and female. The fixed procurement prices (*zakupochnye tseny* or *zagotovitel'nye tseny*) paid to collective farms for their compulsory deliveries to the state had not been adjusted since the 1930s and, by the early 1950s, did not cover their costs of production. Peasants worked on the collective farm virtually for free. While state farms paid money wages, albeit ones that were lower than average industrial wages, collective farms paid using a peculiar measure of value: the 'labor day' (*trudoden'*).[88] All tasks on a farm were valued in labor days, with locally determined norms and higher labor days assigned to more skilled tasks. All members, even adolescents, were required to contribute mandatory labor days to the kolkhoz. After paying taxes, allocating cash to an "indivisible fund" (*nedelimyi fond*) for capital reinvestment, and covering any remaining costs, the kolkhoz divided up what was left at the end of the year among its members based upon the number of labor days they had individually contributed in a year. A peasant had no way of knowing what his or her labor days would amount to because the sum received depended upon the "dividend" available.[89] Many collective farms had no money left and thus paid their labor days in kind rather than in cash, and some paid out nothing at all.

The low and uncertain returns on labor invested in the kolkhoz caused many collective farmers to invest more effort into their private plots, though they were required to make mandatory deliveries to the state from what they produced there and any income they derived from selling their produce at the kolkhoz markets was subject to the punitive "agricultural tax" (*sel'skokhoziaistvennyi nalog*). Under the agricultural tax law in effect from 1939 to 1952, tax was paid on set income norms per tree, hectare of crop, head of cattle, and work animal employed. Progressively higher rates were then levied per tax bracket, with the highest amounts assigned to "independent farmers" (*edinolichniki*) who refused to join the kolkhoz. Because peasants were taxed amounts that could have only a tenuous correspondence to their actual income, they often found themselves in arrears. They were also squeezed hard for tax revenue during and after the war. The income norms were raised 3–4 times in 1943 to account for rising market prices, and the republics were given the right to adjust norms up or down by up to 30% in order to account for regional differences.[90] The average annual amount levied upon one peasant household rose from 142 rubles in 1941, to 679 rubles in 1943, to 716 rubles in

1945.[91] The 1947 currency reform deliberately drained the peasantry's wartime cash profits; moreover, as a consequence of the consecutive retail price reductions that had occurred since then, the market prices of vegetables and fruit, the mainstays of market trade, fell steadily and peasants' incomes followed suit. Despite peasants' declining money incomes, their tax burden was not eased. By 1952, the average agricultural tax paid by one household was 528 rubles, lower than wartime peaks, but still more than 2.6 times the average amount paid before the war.[92]

Stalinist authorities were reluctant to alleviate peasants' tax burden for two main reasons. Though market prices had declined since 1947, they were still noticeably higher than retail prices in state stores. For example, as of April 1, 1953, one liter of milk cost 2.90 rubles in state stores in Moscow and an average of 4.10 rubles at the market.[93] In Stalingrad, on the same date, the difference was even starker: a liter of milk in state stores cost 2.50 rubles and 6 rubles at the market.[94] By the spring of 1953, Soviet workers were still making an average of 28.8% of their food expenditures at the market, where they grudgingly paid these high prices.[95] More problematically, market prices' rate of decline vis-à-vis retail prices was beginning to slow by the early 1950s. After the March 1950 retail price cuts, the market price of one kilogram of beef had dipped 2–5 rubles below state prices in Moscow, Leningrad, Gorki, Stalingrad, and Chelyabinsk by the end of the month; however, by late March 1953, market prices were still 2–8 rubles higher than state prices for meat.[96] Consecutive retail price cuts were no longer having as significant a downward influence upon market prices as they had in the past, reflecting the increasingly worrying state of the food supply.

The Soviet government, for the moment, stayed the course. Stalin was aware of this emerging food crisis in the last years of his life, but he was only willing to contemplate solutions that would have increased meat to the cities and at the expense of another tax hike for collective farmers; although he staked out the possibility of agricultural reform, his views were, as Yoram Gorlizki and Oleg V. Khlevniuk argue, "unshakably conservative."[97] Similarly, though his heirs were aware of its knock-on effects for the food supply and its impact on market prices, Stalin's death on March 5, 1953, did not immediately inspire a reevaluation of the policy of consecutive retail price cuts. On April 1, the collective leadership that took over launched yet another round of cuts, promising 46 billion rubles in savings to workers. They claimed that this year's price cuts constituted "one of the biggest gains workers have received from lower prices in the entire postwar period" because they extended to all categories of mass consumer goods and because they were most substantial on basic foodstuffs like bread, flour, grains, fish, sugar, meat, and vegetables.[98]

These products' retail prices were cut despite the fact that, as the government was fully aware, peasants' deliveries were insufficient to meet demand at existing, let alone lower, prices. Anastas Mikoyan, the Soviet Union's long-serving Minister of Trade, acknowledged this one day before the cuts were announced to the public: although meat prices were scheduled to be reduced by 15%, "we are, for now, mainly satisfying demand for meat and meat products in the major industrial centers. In other cities, we are provisioning cafeterias, but the supply of meat in stores is insufficient."[99] The same shortages applied to animal fats and potatoes. Mikoyan insisted that food prices needed to be cut because they were still very high after the war, and potatoes and vegetables occupied a place of "vital importance" in the diets of low-earning workers who could not afford meat. He claimed that cost-cutting measures in their production and transportation had facilitated slashing their prices.[100]

The main contenders for Stalin's mantle repeatedly assured workers that they had no intention of abandoning consecutive price cuts, even as they launched desperately needed agricultural reforms aimed at boosting peasants' productivity later that same year, including cutting the agricultural tax and substantially raising peasants' procurement prices.[101] Georgii Malenkov, Stalin's successor as Chairman of the Council of Ministers and, at that time, the frontrunner in the leadership race, promised that the government would lower peasants' taxes and increase procurement prices "without raising retail prices in trade and ceaselessly realizing the principle of their further reduction."[102] In his speech on the Party's agricultural initiatives on September 3, Nikita Khrushchev, another main contender, reiterated that raising procurement prices was designed to give collective farmers a "material interest" in increasing their deliveries to the state.[103] Like Malenkov, he promised that procurement price increases would entail no losses for Soviet workers: "Retail prices for livestock products, potatoes and vegetables will not rise but, just the opposite, will fall every year. Henceforth, we will unswervingly adhere to the [Party] line of reducing retail prices for consumer items." Raising retail prices, he emphasized, "is not in the people's interest. It goes without saying that the Party and the Government can't and won't go there."[104]

As Anatolii Strelianyi puts it, "Simply recognizing the miserable condition of the countryside constituted a revolutionary step."[105] These basic reforms brought immediate rewards, including doubled production of milk in Ukraine and a 65% increase across the Soviet Union.[106] Increased procurement prices also injected much-needed cash into the countryside. By 1954, collective farms' money incomes had risen by 13.7 billion rubles, or by 27.6% since 1953, and by 46% since 1952.[107] This allowed collective farms to increase the monetary compensation they offered their members. The average money equivalent of the labor day rose by 41% across the Soviet Union, and a mere 0.9%, or 813, of all collective farms reportedly handed out no money when distributing labor days in 1954.[108] Yet, these increases were unevenly distributed across the country and across different types of farms. For example, although cattle farms' incomes rose by 60% over 1953 as a result of increased procurement prices for meat and milk, the average labor day paid to these farmers declined slightly and they earned less money than those involved in crop farming because of the higher costs of production associated with cattle rearing.[109] In sum, the agricultural reforms in the summer of 1953 were a salve, but they were far from a cure.

Soviet authorities then turned their attention to shortcomings in the "open" retail trade system. In October, they promised the "uninterrupted sale" of food and basic necessities in every city and rural milieu would be accomplished within two to three years, admitting that the Soviet retail trade system was beset by many problems, most importantly, unfulfilled consumer demand.[110] The Soviet government planned to dramatically increase production of basic food products, promising 2.3 times more meat by 1955. It also planned to increase the production of consumer durables like clothing and furniture, and construct thousands of new shops and eating establishments in the years to come.[111] Special attention would be paid to improving retail trade in the countryside, ensuring that deliveries were distributed evenly among the regions and republics, a tacit acknowledgment that Moscow and other major industrial cities had long received the vast majority of state-manufactured consumer products.

Despite "interrupted" sales that persisted into 1954, the government launched its last consecutive retail price cut on April 1, 1954, featuring reductions on 70 categories of goods, 5%–8% cuts to bread prices, and at least 20 billion rubles in savings to Soviet consumers.[112] These cuts merely exacerbated ongoing food shortages: as one anonymous letter writer complained, bread sales were "severely disrupted" in his town of Kamensk-Shakhtinskii, with lines exceeding 500 people, a situation that had only worsened since last year's price cuts.[113] By that summer, bread was reported to be critically scarce in many areas.[114] In their letters of complaint, many citizens remarked upon the discrepancy between the increased output they were promised and the empty shelves they encountered in state stores, as well as the high prices this led to in the kolkhoz markets. Some even reported instances of informal rationing.[115] The same kinds of complaints were sent to authorities the following year. "I can no longer remain silent about the difficult situation our Soviet people are living in," a worker in Novocherkassk named Fedosina wrote to Khrushchev in 1955: "There is nothing to eat. The stores are empty. We hand over all our wages to speculators and live on the verge of starvation."[116]

By late 1955, Khrushchev had concluded that consecutive retail price cuts merely contributed to the Soviet Union's chronic supply problems. In a report to the Central Committee ahead of the upcoming Twentieth Party Congress—where, on its last day, he would deliver his famous "Secret Speech" denouncing Stalin and tighten his grip on power—he recommended against further consecutive price cuts. Khrushchev argued that "until we can fully satisfy demand for manufactured goods, it does not make sense for us to reduce their prices."[117] In his opinion, it was a better idea to focus on producing enough meat, butter, vegetables, potatoes, and fruit to ensure that workers could purchase such staples entirely at state stores, as well as eat low-cost state-subsidized meals in socialized eating establishments, instead of being forced to shop in the expensive kolkhoz markets. Khrushchev suggested that price reductions should apply only to the small number of consumer goods whose prices remained significantly inflated after the war.[118]

In the summary report he delivered at the Congress on February 14, 1956, Khrushchev promised a host of measures to "more fully satisfy the population's growing material needs," acknowledging that "we still haven't resolved many serious issues connected to improving workers' material welfare."[119] He identified insufficient consumer production as the main culprit behind persistent shortages. By increasingly prioritizing light industry and boosting consumer output, in tandem with direct injections into household income including minimum wage and pension raises (see Chapters 2 and 3), he promised that the government would raise workers' real wages by 30% and peasants' real wages by no less than 40%. "All of these initiatives, of course, require massive funds. Where are we going to get them?" he asked.[120] "It will be necessary, first and foremost, to use some of the money accumulating in the national economy as a result of the growth of labor productivity, maintaining a strict regimen of economizing, liquidating various 'excesses,' and further reducing the administrative apparatus," he answered. Khrushchev then proposed a more controversial source of funding. He stopped short of saying that consecutive price reductions would cease entirely, but suggested: "It is possible it will be necessary to use some of the money that was set aside to cover the government's costs in connection with reducing retail prices. . . . As a result, in the coming years, price reductions will occur in smaller amounts than was previously the case, so that some of the money for planned price reductions can be put toward realizing the aforementioned initiatives."[121]

Rising Consumer Spending

In the wake of the Twentieth Party Congress, workers spent an increasing amount of money on food and consumer goods, and, for once, this reflected not just price inflation but the rising purchasing power of the ruble due to increased and more consistent supply. By 1957, workers participating in family budget studies reportedly purchased the vast majority of the meat, milk, and butter they consumed in state stores.[122] By 1958, the Central Statistical Administration calculated that industrial workers in the RSFSR handed over only 17% of the money they spent on food to peasants and private citizens instead of state stores, down from 20% in 1956 and 24% in 1953.[123] Prices in the kolkhoz markets remained more expensive, on average, than prices in state stores: by 1959, they were estimated to be around 54% higher than state retail prices for food, which, Soviet trade officials emphasized, accounted for the relatively large share of expenditures kolkhoz market purchases still occupied in household budgets.[124] In the case of potatoes, for example, market prices were 56% higher, while for vegetables, meat, and milk, they were 85%, 44%, and 35% higher, respectively.[125]

Workers' expenditures on consumer durables also rose significantly in the mid- to late 1950s (Figure 1.2). Much of this money was spent on clothing, which was in perpetually scarce supply during the Stalin years and remained in high demand under Khrushchev.[126] Already in the first half of 1956, workers across the Soviet Union were estimated to have purchased 94% more textiles than in 1940, 3 times more wool, 17 times more silk, and 43% more shoes.[127] By 1958, around 68%, 71%, and 67% of the money spent on nonfood manufactured goods by industrial workers, state farm workers, engineers and technical workers (*inzhenerno-tekhnicheskie rabotniki,* ITRs), and white-collar workers in the RSFSR, respectively, went to fabric, clothes, underwear, knitwear, and shoes.[128] Another 8%–10% went to furniture and household items, a category of purchases that rose by 22% among workers and 21% among ITRs and white-collar workers between 1957 and 1958.[129] Amid Khrushchev's concurrent mass housing construction program, millions of Soviet citizens moved into their

Советские люди, улучшая свое питание, все большую долю средств тратят на приобретение промышленных товаров, особенно товаров длительного пользования.

Figure 1.2 Increasing Purchases of Consumer Durables. Upper caption (in the television screen): "The portion of expenses on manufactured goods (1940) 36%, (1958) 45%, (1965) 47%." Lower caption: "As they improve their nutrition, the Soviet people are spending ever more money on the acquisition of manufactured goods, especially consumer durables."
Molodoi kommunist, No. 7 (1959): 107.

first private apartments and spent more money than ever before furnishing and decorating domestic spaces.

With their increasing money incomes resulting from repeated procurement price increases, tax cuts, and, after 1957, the introduction of cash advances that guaranteed money income for their work on the collective farms, peasants were also spending more money on consumer durables.[130] Their increasing disposable income was attributed by Soviet authorities to the rising average cash value of the labor day. By 1958, that was 8.17 rubles, up from 7.45 rubles in 1957, across the Soviet Union and across all types of collective farms.[131] In the first half of 1956, collective farmers across the Soviet Union purchased twice as many textiles as they did in 1940, including 3.5 times more wool and 15 times more silk, and 65% more shoes.[132] By 1958, collective farmers in the RSFSR were earning 3.6 times more money than they had in 1953, and 11% more since 1957.[133] Though they still spent less money than workers on nonfood manufactured goods, already by the end of 1956, the gap between them had begun to narrow: if in 1952, peasants spent 3 times less than workers and in 1954 2 times less, by 1956, they spent only 1.6 times less. By 1958, collective farmers in the RSFSR were spending an estimated 2.9 times more money on consumer goods since 1953, but still 1.7 times less than what workers and employees spent.[134]

Peasants' lower spending on consumer durables reflected not only their lower money incomes vis-à-vis workers, but also the fact that the rural stores continued to be more poorly stocked than urban stores and consumer trade remained only partially monetized in the countryside. Many rural stores insisted on payment partially or fully in kind—a phenomenon that reflected the government's traditionally extractive relationship to the countryside and its long-standing suspicion toward the peasant's presumed petit bourgeois mentality. By the late 1950s, eggs had virtually become a parallel currency in the countryside. Many peasants were furious that the purchasing power of their rubles, which were rare in rural milieus to begin with, was further weakened by the requirement of paying partly or fully in eggs.[135] N. I. Popov, a collective farmer and Communist Party member, wrote in a 1958 letter of complaint that, in addition to a money price, the rural cooperative in his area demanded 10 eggs for one meter of cotton fabric, 15 eggs for a pair of pants, 10 eggs for one kilogram of sugar, and 1,000 eggs for a sewing machine.[136] Most of the farmers in his region did not keep their own chickens; therefore, this policy effectively deprived them of the right to buy consumer goods. Members of the rural intelligentsia who did not have their own private plots, such as veterinarians, were often forced to purchase eggs and other commodities in the market to be able to shop in cooperatives. When the market price of eggs was factored into the price of a consumer good, it turned out they were far overpaying, as V. M. Kovrigin lamented in a similar complaint. "Why is it only in the cities that they sell everything for money?" he demanded.[137]

Despite placing a new emphasis on improving the population's consumption, the Soviet government stopped short of orienting the economy around consumerism; heavy industry was still seen as the most important or, in their words, "leading" sector. It also still did a poor job of anticipating and responding to consumer demand. As of 1957, sales of consumer goods in state stores and cooperatives had more than doubled since 1950, yet, as trade officials worriedly noted, the plan for retail trade was still unfulfilled by 9.9 billion rubles that year due to shortages of a wide variety of consumer goods.[138] That year, retail stores were not able to fully satisfy the population's growing demand for cotton fabric, stockings, wool suits, refrigerators, televisions, and furniture, in particular, and output projections for these items did not look especially promising, they warned.[139] They pleaded for another 8–10 billion rubles' worth of goods to sell, especially clothes, and floated the possibility of importing them.

In the absence of across-the-board price cuts, many foods and goods remained prohibitively expensive for low-income citizens even as they became more available. Khrushchev's March 1957 promise to catch up and overtake the United States in per capita production of meat, butter, and milk was supposed to put more meat on their plates, but meat remained one of the most expensive items on their shopping lists.[140] A 14%–15% decrease in the retail prices of pork products and a 12.5% decrease in the retail price of goose and duck meat was thus unveiled on November 1, 1957, supposedly facilitated by a 22% increase in their production since the 1953 agricultural reforms and 446 million rubles in state subsidies.[141] Goose meat was traditionally consumed on special occasions, and the announcement of its lower price came just before celebrations for the fortieth anniversary of the October Revolution.[142]

January 2, 1958, saw the launch of the most comprehensive retail price adjustment since the spring of 1954, this time to "establish a more correct price relationship between various manufactured goods that are not basic necessities and introduce new, higher retail prices . . . in order to further the struggle against speculation in those goods."[143] After repeatedly reducing alcohol prices, the prices of all alcohol products except beer were raised by 21%. Publicly, this was presented as discouraging alcohol's consumption; behind the scenes, this price hike helped cover the lost revenue from expanding personal exemptions from the Soviet state's unpopular "bachelor tax" (see Chapter 4) on citizens with small families or no children. Higher prices went into effect for rugs, cars, and motorcycles—the latter two highly coveted deficit goods that often fetched high prices on the black market—while certain makes of televisions and cameras had their prices reduced.[144] Bread prices, on the other hand, were rounded "primarily downward"—due to a perpetual shortage of coins, conflicts often arose at the cash register when customers tried to pay and cashiers could not make change, which "hindered the release of bread to the population."[145] The new bread prices were not only lower, citizens were promised, but they would be easier to pay.

By the turn of the decade, the old problem of growing reserves of too-expensive and low-demand luxury goods had reared its ugly head once more. Its price having been adjusted upward in January 1958, stockpiles of wine grew rapidly thereafter, doubling from 2.4 million decaliters to 5.2 million decaliters by March 1959.[146] Of the 14.5 million wristwatches produced in 1958, only 9 million were sold, while only 2.7 million of the 3.6 million bicycles produced the same year were purchased.[147] In spite of the January 1958 price reductions and initially promising sales projections, 460,000 cameras soon lay stockpiled for a retail value of 390 million rubles.[148] Stockpiles of rayon fabric grew by nearly 20% between January 1, 1958, and March 1, 1959, while 175 days' worth of rayon fabric trade was held in reserve compared to just 26 days' worth of cotton fabric.[149] The commission on prices within the Presidium of the Council of Ministers strongly urged the government to consider raising the retail price of cotton, which was disproportionately inexpensive compared to increasingly easier- and cheaper-to-produce synthetic fabrics.[150] In order to move these overstocked products, price decreases ranging from 16% to 21% were announced as of July 1, 1959, for an alleged total of 6 billion rubles in "savings" for Soviet customers.[151] No mention of stockpiles was made.

A New Ruble and New Prices

In a lengthy speech on May 5, 1960, in which he promised a host of ambitious measures to increase the Soviet people's prosperity including the abolition of income taxes (more on this in Chapter 4), Khrushchev abruptly announced the government would introduce a new ruble and a new price scale (*masshtab tsen*) effective January 1, 1961.[152] As in 1947, the new ruble would be exchanged for old rubles at a rate of 10:1. Unlike in 1947, all prices and payments would also be converted, not just cash in circulation. Coins were unaffected by the reform. Khrushchev argued that the revaluation of the ruble was necessary due to the Soviet Union's astronomical economic growth during the Seven-Year Plan and due to the fact that the existing price scale had been devised when the volume of Soviet industry and commodity circulation, as well as Soviet wages, were several times lower than they were at present. They now no longer corresponded to the Soviet economy's "attained level" (*dostignutyi uroven'*), he explained.[153]

The 1961 currency reform appears to have been more hastily conceived than its 1947 precursor. Unlike then, no working group of economic experts was struck to debate approaches to the reform.[154] After the Central Committee adopted Khrushchev's suggestion to redenominate the currency in October 1958, Arseny Zverev, the Minister of Finance and one of the main architects of the 1947 currency reform, was instructed to come up with suggestions on how to approach this task.[155] Evidence suggests he was less than enthusiastic about it: Zverev either quit his job or was sent off on a pension in May 1960 after reportedly arguing with Khrushchev about the necessity of another currency reform so soon after the last one.[156] Vasilii Garbuzov assumed the post of

Minister of Finance the same month, a job he would keep until 1985. Khrushchev's son Sergei claims that the driving force behind the currency reform was not his father, but Aleksei Kosygin, the newly appointed Deputy Chairman of the Council of Ministers, best known for launching "optimizing" economic reforms after Khrushchev's ouster in 1964. In 1961, he was a rising star in the central leadership. Kosygin advocated a currency reform for purely "technical reasons," the younger Khrushchev alleges: by then, Soviet planners were operating in billions of rubles, which, in a precomputerized era, led to mistakes and abuses.[157] Kosygin had also recently accompanied Khrushchev on a trip to France, where he consulted with French economic officials about their own currency reform, in which they had lopped a digit off the franc. The elder Khrushchev was convinced by the French example that a similar redenomination would result in no harm to the Soviet Union, for "capitalists never ventured into anything that might be harmful to themselves."[158]

The currency reform may also have been tied to the Soviet government's ongoing efforts to expand foreign trade with the capitalist world. In connection with the reform, the gold quantity of the ruble was raised to 0.987412 grams. Its exchange rate versus the US dollar was also changed from 4 rubles (old money) to 90 kopeks (new money) in November 1960, going into effect on January 1, 1961.[159] As when the Soviet government had announced new exchange rates in connection with lower retail prices and the increased value of the ruble back in the spring of 1950, the new foreign exchange rates supposedly reflected rising purchasing power at home. However, as Holzman suggests, these adjustments may, in fact, have been an effort to overcome the earlier overvaluation of the Stalinist ruble vis-à-vis foreign currencies and put its purchasing power into greater equilibrium with foreign currencies in planners' calculations.[160] As in 1950, the move was also likely aimed at increasing the prestige of the ruble, giving the illusion that it had significantly appreciated in value, when, in reality, the reform constituted a depreciation, as will become clear momentarily.[161]

The 1947 currency reform was announced out of the blue only one day before its implementation; the 1961 currency reform was announced over six months in advance. During this time, the Soviet government engaged in a "mass-explanatory" campaign to prepare Soviet citizens for the "painless" advent of a new ruble and new prices.[162] They were repeatedly and explicitly promised that, if the 1947 currency reform had asked them to make a "sacrifice," the redenomination of the ruble in 1961 would require no sacrifices whatsoever. Many nevertheless expressed anxieties, especially about how rounding up and down prices and wages would work. In a Q&A published in *Pravda* in October 1960, Garbuzov responded to the many queries the government had received about how the currency reform would affect prices. He explained that, if a decimal consisted of less than half a kopek, the price would be rounded down, while if it was more than half a kopek, the price would be rounded up to a whole kopek. In the case of essential food products, including bread, kefir, and milk, as well as certain children's goods, their retail prices would always be rounded down: for example, a 400-gram sliced loaf of bread made with first-class flour, currently priced at 1.35 rubles, would now cost 13 kopeks.[163] Garbuzov promised that the new price scale would result in a "gain" of 115 million rubles per year to Soviet consumers. Some citizens arrived at different conclusions. After waxing nostalgic about the consecutive price decreases of the late Stalin years, P. N. Maslov, a disabled pensioner from Moscow, asked: "If it needs to be done, then why not take the related expenses upon yourself, and just drop the five kopeks [paid when rounding up]?"[164]

As the date of the currency reform approached, Soviet trade officials, themselves, grew anxious about its effects, especially upon market prices, which they could exert much less control over. They—rightly, as it turned out—did not trust collective farmers to automatically scale down their prices in line with the new state prices, and they feared that many would even seize the opportunity to raise prices. Trade officials requested to draw upon additional reserves and imported supplies of potatoes, meat, and other food products to sell in state stores on January 1, in order to prevent shortages and panic buying that sent hordes of customers to the markets and caused prices there to spike.[165] They also instructed that measures be put in place to ensure that peasants did not deliberately restrict supply in order to drive up prices, but made full deliveries to the markets that day, and that Party representatives be dispatched to monitor market activity.[166]

The new currency and new prices were introduced as planned on January 1, 1961. Reports indicated that the new ruble went into circulation in a "normal" and "uneventful" manner.[167] The population reportedly greeted it with "great confidence." The RSFSR saw increased demand for certain big-ticket consumer goods, including clothes, wool fabric, silk fabric, shoes, cultural goods, and jewelry. By January 4, 1961, trade in state stores had increased by 22% over 1960 figures.[168] Some problems were reported, in particular, state stores failing to scale down prices on time.[169] Some shops also reported not having enough small change or bills to conduct trade at the new prices, while others refused to accept the old 1, 3, and 5 kopek coins, unaware that the coins' value was unaffected by the reform and they remained legal tender.[170] Unlike in the days following the 1947 currency reform, market prices did not dip dramatically in response to the 1961 currency reform but stayed relatively stable that day. During the first few days afterward, there was a slight increase in the market prices of meat and milk from December 1960 levels, and a slight decrease in the prices of apples, among other products.[171] By January 8, however, there were significant fluctuations in the market prices of many products in some cities, reflecting the emergence of shortages as the state's additional supplies ran out.[172]

Although Khrushchev's currency reform was not deliberately confiscatory in the same manner as the 1947 currency reform, workers took a hit due to retail prices in state stores that were rounded up and prices in the kolkhoz markets that were not scaled down or were even increased, not to mention wages and pensions that were also rounded down.[173] This led many to conclude that the 1961 currency reform was, despite the government's repeated assurances, a devaluation of the ruble. In his memoirs, Khrushchev wrote that, as a pensioner, he was frequently accosted by individuals who argued that raising prices had been the government's intention all along, an accusation he vehemently denied.[174] He argued that price increases in state stores had only taken place with goods produced after the currency reform, and he blamed incidences of price raising on "drunkards and swindlers and hooligans and people who break discipline." His interlocutors angrily informed him that many peasants continued to charge precisely the same prices as before, telling their customers: "I don't understand your monetary reform. Parsley used to cost ten kopeks, and if you want some, you can have it now for ten kopeks." Khrushchev insisted that this was a different problem altogether, having nothing whatsoever to do with the currency reform.[175]

Price Hikes for Meat and Butter

The losses associated with the redenomination of the ruble in 1961 contributed to a growing sense of anxiety at the turn of the decade about the rising cost of living in the Soviet Union. By then, Khrushchev's successes in increasing agricultural production had begun to falter, with dire consequences for urban citizens' purchasing power, especially when it came to the meat and milk products he promised would soon be in abundance. Through the abolition or amalgamation of several ministries and creation of regional economic councils (*sovety narodnogo khoziaistva, or sovnarkhozy*)—the so-called Sovnarkhoz reform—Khrushchev decentralized much of the state's economic decision-making, especially in the countryside. This was supposed to promote more accurate and efficient agricultural plans by devolving greater authority to the local levels, but resulted in reduced control over the rural workforce.[176] In a concession to collective farmers, in the summer of 1957, he abolished the long unpopular practice of compulsory deliveries to the state from peasants' private plots. By December, trade officials worriedly noted that this had resulted in an overall decline in pork deliveries.[177] In 1958, he liquidated the machine-and-tractor station (*mashino-traktornaia stantsia*, MTS) network that had performed mechanized work for the collective farms for payment in kind since the onset of collectivization, arguing that they had outlived their purpose and farms would use agricultural machinery more efficiently if it belonged to them. The machinery was sold to collective farms at high prices, and loans extended to them to buy it were expected to be repaid within short periods of time, leaving many farms in debt.[178] Khrushchev advocated planting corn on a massive scale to serve as fodder for a growing body of livestock, but it did not turn out to be the wonder crop he hoped for and the corn campaign brought him a great deal of public and private derision.[179] The early successes of the Virgin Lands campaign, which involved planting crops in "uncultivated" territories in Siberia and Kazakhstan to serve as fodder for a growing body of livestock, soon gave way to failing harvests. On top of this, many of the massive increases in meat and dairy output lauded by Khrushchev and in Soviet newspapers turned out to be the result of cheating and fraud.[180]

Khrushchev also limited the allowable size of private plots and the number of livestock permitted to be held privately in the late 1950s, restrictions that affected the market supply of meat. Beginning in March 1956, the kolkhoz was urged to base private landholding upon members' degree of individual participation in collective labor, and it was given the right to reduce the maximum amount of livestock its members were permitted to privately own.[181] When he announced the dismantling of the MTS in the summer of 1958, Khrushchev raised the question of whether or not state farm workers should be allowed to maintain private plots and hold private livestock at all.[182] He argued that they no longer needed these plots and livestock to feed themselves and they presented a "serious obstacle" to increasing these workers' productivity. He claimed that, as of January 1, 1958, around 700,000 cows, 1.1 million pigs, and 3.5 million sheep and goats were held privately by state farm workers, adding that "it's no secret this livestock is being fed state farm fodder and, as a result, this limits the development of socialized herds and the country's and the people's ability to procure meat and milk."[183] The following year, the government prohibited urban citizens and state farm workers from owning their own livestock.

These developments conspired to cause market prices for meat and milk to rise sharply in the early 1960s, turning workers' sentiment against speculators and state authorities alike. "Since May of this year, there has been absolutely no meat or meat delicacies for sale, which has led to high prices on the bazaar-kolkhoz markets, not less than 25–27 rubles per kilogram," wrote Oksana Maksimovna Piletskaia, of Tambov, in late September 1960, adding: "The poor provisioning of city residents has caused a terrible mood among the population and many have sent complaints to the government's address."[184] I. I. Zhukov wrote that rumors were going around town that the local authorities would prohibit private vendors from charging more than 20 rubles per kilogram for meat. He dismissed this solution outright: "No, we don't need these kinds of decisions. We need action instead of words, that is, we need to beat [high market prices] through the government [*sbit' po linii gosudarstva*]. We need to shock them."[185] Zhukov bemoaned the demoralizing effect of the high cost of living: "It's so difficult to get by, there is nothing to be happy about in life. You think, 'This year I scrimped and saved and next year, it'll get better.' But nothing changes. There is no use denying it: our whole wages go to food. If you want to buy clothes, you do so at the expense of your stomach."[186] He saw only two possible solutions: raise workers' wages or reduce retail prices.

Many expressed great nostalgia for the consecutive retail price cuts of the late 1940s and early 1950s.[187] They selectively remembered the increased supply in state stores around the time of the spring announcements, and not the shortages that appeared soon afterward. "People waited for those days, which relieved us from want," Gavriil Petrovich Miroliubov of Riazanskaia oblast reminisced, emphasizing that high prices placed a heavy burden upon elderly pensioners like him, who lived on fixed incomes.[188] "They've got everything in the shops now," wrote Nikolai Mikhailovich Siniutin, a worker in Volgograd, "but it's very expensive, and if you want to buy a coat, on average, it costs 90–100 rubles, the same amount as your monthly salary. You'll be in big debt for that coat and have nothing left to feed your family with." Siniutin reminded the government that "even after the war, when times were hard, amid the devastation and bad harvests, the Party and the Government managed to lower prices and now they put the prices of everything up."[189]

Those who harbored hope that the Soviet government might revive the Stalinist ritual of consecutive retail price cuts were roundly disappointed. By the early 1960s, economic reformers had successfully lobbied Khrushchev to introduce a new, more rational approach to price setting.[190] In the summer of 1960, Khrushchev gave the go-ahead to the State Economic Advisory Council (*Gosudarstvennyi nauchno-ekonomicheskii sovet*, or *Gosekonomsovet*), a new planning organ formed in the wake of the Sovnarkhoz reform that took over "perspective" or long-term planning functions from Gosplan, to initiate price-setting reforms.[191] That entailed introducing "prices of a unified level" (*tseny edinogo urovnia*) and allowing planners to use prices to allocate resources more efficiently. Under the proposed reform, the Soviet Union's convoluted system of multiple sector-specific price levels would be harmonized, creating a more consistent correspondence between the costs of production and price levels and reducing price discrepancies across industries. Supply and demand would play a larger role in setting retail prices than ever before. As one of the reform's architects, Viktor Belkin, put it, "socially necessary labor," the Marxist concept that was believed to regulate commodity-exchange values, would still be taken into consideration, but only simultaneously with supply and wage levels.[192] The Communist Party's Third Party Program, adopted at the Twenty-Second Party Congress in October 1961, confirmed that the Soviet Union had begun its final ascent toward communism and that there would be no "gifts" to the working class in the realm of retail prices during this time. "Prices should increasingly reflect socially necessary labor time, cover the expenses of production and circulation and provide some profit to each normally functioning enterprise," it instructed, clarifying that "the systematic, economically grounded lowering of prices upon the basis of a rise in productive labor and lowered costs of production, that is the main direction of price policy during the period of building communism."[193]

While the Soviet government contemplated a new approach to setting retail prices, the meat and milk supply both in state stores and in the kolkhoz markets dramatically declined. Soviet authorities were well aware of these problems, as evidenced by the many letters of complaint they received, cited above. In mid-May 1962, Khrushchev approved a draft decree raising retail prices for these products to offset the cost of raising procurement prices to stimulate peasants' livestock production and alleviate shortages. In doing so, the Soviet government employed essentially the same strategy it had used back in the summer of 1953 to quickly boost peasants' productivity and their deliveries to the state, but, this time, it was asking workers to pick up the tab: under the emerging doctrine of "economically sound" price cuts, an increase in the cost of production had to be balanced by a corresponding increase in prices.[194]

In a June 1 address to the Soviet people that covered the entire first page of *Pravda* and other newspapers, the government explained that it had decided to speak "plainly": agricultural output was insufficient to meet demand for livestock products.[195] This was attributed to the Soviet Union's rapid postwar population growth and to citizens' increasing money incomes, the most significant portion of which was still spent on food. Despite repeated increases, the state's procurement prices still did not cover collective farms' costs of production. Limiting peasants' income was rejected outright, since this would not stimulate their productivity, as was diverting funds to meat production from defense and heavy industry amid the hostile international climate of the Cold War. To cover the cost of raising procurement prices on livestock products by 35%, the government would raise the retail prices of meat and butter by an average of 30% and 25%, respectively. Meat prices, citizens were reminded, were already very low compared to other essential products like vegetable oil, sugar, and potatoes, since they had been reduced several times in the past "without sufficient economic grounds," that is, via Stalinist price subsidies. The price hikes were portrayed as a temporary measure that would soon be reversed with increased mechanization and rising productivity. As a concession, the retail price of sugar was reduced by 5%, while rayon fabric and its derived products were reduced by 20%.[196]

The Soviet government closely monitored market price behavior following the announcement. Predictably, market prices for meat and dairy rose sharply. In Tula, the price of one kilogram of beef rose from 2.80 rubles to 3.50 rubles, the price of one kilogram of lamb rose from 3 to 3.50, and the price of one kilogram of pork rose from 1.80 to 2.40 rubles.[197] Price increases were also recorded in Penza and Leningrad, while Arkhangel'sk saw a slight decrease in the market price of lamb meat alone.[198]

The government also paid close attention to the popular mood. Reports from the State Security Committee (*Komitet gosudarstvennoi bezopasnosti*, or KGB) emphasized that most Soviet citizens received the policy "correctly" and accepted the justifications offered by the government; however, they admitted that incidences of inappropriate reactions and "anti-Soviet provocations" had also occurred.[199] Flyers circulated around Moscow, saying, "Today they're raising prices, what will they do tomorrow?" and "Workers, fight for your rights and for lower prices!"[200] Some expressed "philistine assessments," suggesting that, if the money needed to be found to increase procurement prices, elites' salaries should be reduced or the Soviet Union should deny financial assistance to Third World socialist countries.[201] In some towns and factories, citizens called upon their coworkers and neighbors to strike.[202] One worker suggested that the entire Soviet government should be rounded up and mowed down with a machine gun.[203]

Letters to the authorities flooded in. They were not all critical: for example, M. S. Glazunova wrote that she had experienced hunger firsthand during the Leningrad blockade, but fully endorsed the new measure and thanked Khrushchev for his concern for pensioners.[204] Agapovich, a first-group invalid living in Gorki, wrote that "there could be no other decision" than the one taken by the government, before requesting better housing for himself.[205] The tone of most letters, however, was angry and reproachful. "In raising prices on meat and butter, you may think you're making a better life for the working class, but you are deceiving us, just like you deceived us before and I think that, after this, the working class will finally understand what's going on," one anonymous letter scathed.[206] Some were insulted by the reduced price of unwanted and perpetually overstocked rayon fabric. "You put down the price of rayon, and who needs it?" demanded T. A. Laletina. "You couldn't have put down the price of calico?"[207] "It's difficult to convince a person what is beneficial and what is not, when the words sink to the bottom of an empty stomach," she added. "If you have to raise prices, don't do it for the most essential products."[208]

Many condemned Khrushchev's leadership, suggesting that Malenkov, who had lost the post-Stalin power struggle and had been pushed out of the Soviet government by 1957, would have done a better job. Indeed, one of the reasons for Malenkov's downfall in the mid-1950s was his "woebegone-economist" heresy of arguing that light industrial output could rise faster than heavy industry.[209] "Stalin died and Malenkov took over, and people really started to live better," wrote A. O. Vershinin, of Novyi Altaisk, adding: "He cut [agricultural] taxes, he reduced prices 1953–1954 and in 1955, people started to feel like themselves again."[210] Vershinin attacked Khrushchev's leadership directly: "You took over the post of Chairman of the Council of Ministers and what did you do for workers? Nothing! We just heard that you are raising prices. . . . How much 'easier' it will be for the worker! There is no difference between you and Stalin, they licked Stalin's boots and now they lick yours."[211] A certain Savel'ev, a miner in Rostov, wrote that rumors were going around about strikes in Novocherkassk, and people were whispering that "Malenkov would have ruled the government differently than Khrushchev."[212]

The most dramatic backlash to the new prices did, in fact, occur in Novocherkassk, where several thousand workers took to the streets on June 1. The food crisis in Novocherkassk by the summer of 1962 had reached desperate levels, with citizens standing in line into the night for potatoes and frying up their peelings to eat.[213] The day before the new retail prices were announced, directors at the Novocherkassk Budenny Electric Locomotive Construction Works factory announced lower piece rates in connection with Khrushchev's wage reform (see Chapter 2). Higher retail prices coupled with the prospect of lower wages outraged workers, who walked off the job and protested outside the administration's office, where they quickly attracted the attention of other factory workers and townspeople. The protest spread throughout the city, barricades were erected, and rioters stormed local Party offices and the police station, looting and clashing with police. Eventually, either the KGB or the Red Army fired on the crowd, killing some and wounding even more. The events in Novocherkassk were kept secret until 1992, though, as evidenced by Savel'ev's letter above, rumors circulated at the time about what had taken place.

Against this wave of popular discontent, Khrushchev stuck to his guns. He claimed that the Soviet government had no choice but to raise retail prices in order to resolve the discrepancy between the artificially low retail prices at which meat was sold to the public, and the low procurement prices paid to collective farmers, which did not reflect the value of that meat or the value of the labor farmers put into producing it.[214] He acknowledged this was, in essence, asking workers to pay more. "Is the increase in prices beneficial to the consumer?" he asked at a meeting of administrators.[215] "Upon formulating the question thus, a person might respond: 'What exactly are they trying to prove to me? They raised the retail prices of meat and they're still saying it benefits me.' If we get to the heart of the matter, it is in fact beneficial, this measure was taken with the interests of the entire population in mind," he maintained. If the Soviet government had preserved the previous retail price levels for meat, this would not have allowed it to increase meat production; moreover, "the consumer's money would go straight into the pockets of speculators, and meat production would not rise." He claimed the Party had "opened the floodgates" to increasing livestock production on collective and state farms. Khrushchev railed against ingrained thinking about price setting to "thunderous applause," saying: "We know that even some communists sometimes say: 'We adopted a resolution at the Twenty-Second Party Congress to build communism, and right after that, we raised prices. So, where are we going: forward or backward?' That's what those who are looking backward argue, but those who are looking forward, they can see clearly the direction we're headed in."[216]

Khrushchev's confidence was not matched by reality. According to family budget studies, in the months that followed the price hikes, workers curtailed their meat and dairy consumption. Statisticians observed that they spent 16% more money on meat and 7% more on milk between June 1 and the end of the year, but their caloric intake dropped by 5% in the same period.[217] Workers spent 13% less on textile goods and their "cultural" expenses, such as theater tickets, declined by 8%.[218] In short, they were paying more money for less meat and milk, and were, once again, diverting money from nonessential consumer purchases to food. On the other hand, collective farmers' incomes went up, a development that was attributed to the government's increased procurement prices and to farmers' increased deliveries of animal products to the state. They reportedly consumed 7% more meat and 19% more sugar after the new retail prices went into effect and spent 14% more money on food and 8% more on consumer goods.[219]

Deficits of meat and milk persisted in state stores for the remainder of the year, as did shortages of bread and other essential foods, souring the popular mood. The fall of 1962 saw a disappointing harvest. By then, Soviet authorities noted that letters of complaint regarding food shortages addressed directly to Khrushchev were of a "sharp political character," and contained bold expressions of "distrust in the press and radio, [arguing that] when they report on the enormous achievements in the realm of agriculture and provisioning the population, they do not always coincide with the reality on the ground."[220] They called upon the government to clamp down on speculators and resellers, as well as high market prices. Some even called for the return of dreaded rationing.[221] Shortages continued to worsen into 1963, a year that saw another drought and an even more disastrous harvest. The sharp decline in agricultural production in 1962–1964 was, in historian Philip Hanson's words, "an unkind time for Khrushchev" and, although other political factors helped seal his fate, it contributed to his downfall.[222] As workers felt their grasp on economic stability slipping, they pointed their fingers at shortages and at high prices, but also at Khrushchev.

Conclusion

In the late 1940s and early 1950s, the Stalinist government resumed the stalled mid-1930s project of delivering prosperity to the population via a full-value ruble. Repeatedly reducing retail prices was presented as the most effective means of increasing the population's purchasing power toward that end; however, as V. F. Zima writes, "The legend of the postwar price decreases as a huge boon does not hold up to scrutiny."[223] Price cuts helped stimulate short-term demand for manufactured goods, which was necessary to clear stockpiles, balance the population's income and expenses (at least on paper), regulate the cash supply, and ensure a steady flow of state revenue in the form of the turnover tax, but they were not based upon a real reduction in the cost of production and, in the case of food products in particular, bore little relationship to existing supply. The price cuts were paired with temporary increases in supplies to the capital and the major cities, helping to produce the illusion of abundance, but were not accompanied by more consistent availability of manufactured goods across the country. Lower prices meant precious little when there was nothing to spend one's money on. "On the face of it, I can't complain about a thing: I have a job, an apartment, a family, and money," S. I. Shukin, an auto mechanic in the small town of Mednogorsk, lamented in an unpublished letter of complaint he sent to *Pravda*. ". . . But alas! There is not a single thing to buy with this money."[224]

Retail price cuts nevertheless held great symbolic value. They were a dramatic gesture to urban workers after the wartime hardships they had endured, reestablishing the Stalinist hierarchy of consumers in which, in principle, they sat at the very top. They tapped into lingering resentment toward peasants and wartime profiteers and reinforced the urban population's status as priority recipients of the socialist state's "care." They also served as a propaganda weapon in the Cold War, which saw living standards quickly emerge as a battleground in the economic competition between East and West. Decades later, responding to the question of why the Soviet government pursued this policy immediately after the war and why price cuts became a new ritual, the Foreign Minister at the time, Vyacheslav Molotov, answered matter-of-factly: "It was the correct policy to lower prices after the war. Everyone remembers it fondly and received it well . . . we reduced prices seven times after the war. By two to three times in seven years. That's good, that's outstanding! And they still had rationing in England."[225]

Bestowing artificial abundance upon workers was unsustainable. As Elena Zubkova notes, workers gradually became habituated to the state's "beneficence" and "little holidays" and began to develop a dependency complex and, as their basic needs began to be met, their demands began to grow.[226] Those needs were met using the prewar strategy of subsidizing the prices of basic necessities. Although they were presented as a zero-sum transfer of wealth—the state's loss at workers' gain—the price decreases also came at the expense of the country's food producers, a policy that grew ever more unfeasible as demand for cheaper food increased and agricultural output lagged further behind. The new lower prices were not the "real" lower prices that Stalin had desired when he championed their crucial role in strengthening the money economy and improving the purchasing power of the ruble in the mid-1930s.[227] They were simply another "gift" to the working class.

Khrushchev's decision to focus on solving the problem of output and reconciling the perpetual discrepancy between supply and demand rather than reducing prices was more economically rational by contrast, but it underestimated both the political significance and popularity of Stalinist price cuts. As his initiatives to boost output began to fail, the high cost of living became a touchstone for popular discontent with his leadership. Moreover, the large sums of money workers handed over in state stores and in the kolkhoz markets were widely viewed as clear evidence that, despite Khrushchev's claims to have opened the "floodgates" of production, state supply was still inconsistent and insufficient.

Yet, Khrushchev's pivot away from consecutive retail price cuts cannot be judged a complete failure. Living standards noticeably improved in the second half of the 1950s. Soviet consumers gradually spent more money in state stores, rather than at the market, and they spent less money on food and more on clothing, furniture, and other consumer durables. Although shortages persisted and new stockpiles accumulated, and the Soviet Union did not catch up to the West on the consumer front, thousands of new consumer goods entered the state retail market and trade turnover ballooned. The period saw the development of a consumer culture that was increasingly accessible not only to privileged elites, but to low-skilled workers and peasants.

Khrushchev's bold proclamations and promises about imminent prosperity fueled ordinary citizens' hopes and gave them a standard to measure their current economic circumstances against. The high cost of living, coupled with disruptive changes to their wages in the late 1950s and early 1960s, as will be discussed in Chapter 2, undermined his promises about the full-value ruble. Khrushchev struggled to convince low-income citizens, in particular, that real wages could be increased by means other than cutting prices. When they felt the pinch, many longed for the paternalistic price cuts and "savings" bestowed upon them in the late Stalin years rather than the selective price adjustments of the late 1950s and the more abstract "economically sound" price regime Khrushchev and a cabal of economic experts advocated. Like communism, the advent of lower prices seemed to be perpetually postponed.

2

Income Redistribution without "Leveling"

As Khrushchev prepared his summary report for the upcoming Twentieth Party Congress in the fall of 1955, he decided that minimum wage raises should be included under the banner of the Communist Party's measures to "more fully satisfy the population's growing material needs." Wage regulation (*uporiadochenie zarabotnoi platy*), he argued, was one of the most important issues affecting the Soviet Union's economic development at present. "We all know, and we've talked about it more than once, that, over the last couple of years, many abnormalities have emerged on this score," he wrote.[1] The Soviet wage system had grown extremely convoluted, encompassing great "variegation" (*pestrota*) in pay levels, often for the same jobs within enterprises and between industries. Khrushchev considered the main abnormality to be the fact that "we have a large number of low-paid workers, especially auxiliary workers, who cannot make ends meet on their wages. On the other hand, we have a small group of workers who receive very high wages."[2] This problem, he insisted, "cannot be solved only by increasing productivity, reducing retail prices and other measures. It's obvious the only solution is to directly increase the lowest paid workers' wages."[3] In order to pay for these raises, Khrushchev recommended reducing skilled workers' wages and the intelligentsia's salaries in a manner that ensured they continued to be well provided for, but no longer allowed for "excesses that give rise to a variety of unhealthy phenomena."[4]

In the speech he delivered at the Congress, Khrushchev promised raises to the Soviet Union's lowest-paid workers in tandem with sweeping reforms aimed at establishing more "correct" relationships between wages, qualifications, and jobs' difficulty levels. He chastised Soviet authorities for allowing wage-setting problems to go on for far too long. "A massive political and economic task falls to the Party," he claimed, "that is, to bring proper order to labor compensation [*nadlezashchii poriadok v oplate*]."[5] It was necessary to re-establish a more direct connection between the quantity and quality of each worker's labor and to make fuller use of the "powerful lever of material self-interest" (*moshchnyi rychag material'noi zainteresovannosti*). At the same time, skilled workers and managers' incomes should more strictly depend upon concrete measures of performance—a subtle allusion to the Stalin era's emphasis on quantity over quality. This system of determining compensation would better correspond to socialist principles of labor compensation, he maintained, and "the correct resolution of this problem will facilitate an increase in productivity and the prosperity of our people."[6] On the last day of the Congress, the Party resolved to raise low-paid workers' wages and to increase all workers' real wages by 30%.[7]

In the context of his broader campaign to raise living standards, Khrushchev's plan to redistribute more full-value rubles to struggling low-paid workers was a logical, yet extremely fraught, proposition. For decades, the increasingly unequal incomes of the urban population had been justified by a struggle against "leveling," otherwise known as "vulgar egalitarianism" (*uravnilovka*).[8] In the early years of its existence, the Soviet government had put its utopian principles into practice, equalizing payment for workers' labor regardless of skill level and type of job, but this had merely contributed to frequent, chaotic turnover (*tekuchka*) on the shop floor and did not incentivize the development of skills or disciplined work habits among a generation of workers recently transplanted from the countryside. By the early 1930s, Stalin had emerged as a fierce opponent of leveling. Under his leadership, industrial wages were aggressively differentiated on the basis of skill level and importance to the national economy and were raised dramatically in the so-called leading industries (*vedushchie otrasli*), such as metallurgy and machine building. In an effort to foster interest in increasing their individual output, a majority of workers' incomes thereafter depended upon "additional earnings" (*prirabotok*), including piece-rate pay (*sdel'naia oplata*), premiums, bonuses, and other payments above the "base pay rate" (*tarifnaia stavka*), the minimum payment that was guaranteed for simply performing one's job. Before long, a massive gap between high and low wages emerged, one that continued to widen during and after the Second World War.

In the meantime, salaries rose dramatically for Stalinist "cadres," the intelligentsia, and political elites.[9] White-collar workers' average wages rose from 1932–1933 onward, rapidly overtaking those of industrial workers.[10] In 1932, Stalin canceled the "Party maximum," a ceiling on the *nomenklatura*'s earnings set in 1921 that had limited the salaries of Party workers to amounts not exceeding the wages of skilled workers. Party workers' incomes climbed thereafter. In addition to these higher salaries, elites had privileged nonmonetized access to the good things in life, such as preferential housing, consumer luxuries, and cars. By the 1950s, the "Kremlin rations" (*Kremlevskii paek*) some members of the *nomenklatura* received, which had initially consisted of free food deliveries, had evolved into an array of money allowances, credit in special closed stores, and other perks that supplemented their incomes and lifestyles.[11]

By the time of Stalin's death in 1953, the struggle against leveling had resulted in a glaring gap between the wages of low- and high-skilled workers, between the wages of workers in light and heavy industry, and between the incomes of the working masses and Soviet elites. As discussed in Chapter 1, collective farmers were excluded from the state wage system altogether, contributing to their marginalization within the Soviet money economy. Millions of pensioners—including many injured war veterans who received pensions "the size of a sparrow's beak," as one postwar commentator put it—lived in extremely straitened circumstances, the subject of Chapter 3.[12] In the eyes of many communists, such a pronounced level of income inequality was patently unacceptable for a socialist society, let alone one that was supposedly edging ever closer to communism. It also presented a serious obstacle to the creation of mass prosperity in the postwar Soviet Union. As Chapter 1 demonstrated, Khrushchev's approach to increasing the ruble's purchasing power was premised upon boosting consumer output, rather than repeatedly cutting retail prices. That approach threatened to fall flat if most ordinary workers and other low-income groups continued to earn enough money to buy little more than bare necessities.

In tackling the problem of income inequality via wage policy, Khrushchev tried to have it both ways: raising too-low wages without reducing the incentive value of the ruble in the most important and productive workers' and cadres' hands. He restructured and "rationalized" high wages in an attempt to promote high-quality labor and eliminate opportunities for manipulating the wage system, and he scaled down some of the most visible and "excessive" monetized benefits enjoyed by industrial, cultural, and political elites. Leveling was still off the table, however, because it would not promote the high levels of productivity upon which Khrushchev's consumer promises were founded. The "struggle against leveling" (*bor'ba s uravnilovkoi*), a rallying cry of the 1930s, was recast as a Leninist, not Stalinist, imperative supporting the development of higher skills and more efficient work habits. The associated reforms were implemented in stages over the course of 1956–1962.

Khrushchev's efforts to reduce income inequality in Soviet society fell far short of radical redistribution. Minimum wage raises were not nearly as significant as the propaganda that surrounded them claimed they were, and they did not address the structural problems in the Soviet economy and in wage policy that left women the lowest-paid members of the Soviet industrial workforce. Because industrial wages remained oriented around individual output, especially in priority branches of the economy, opportunities for some workers to manipulate their norms and far outearn others remained. In the absence of significant retail price cuts, and as market prices began to rise again, low-income citizens still struggled to make ends meet. Real wage growth began to slow for both low- and high-income workers in the late 1950s and early 1960s; by 1962, a serious imbalance between the population's money income and expenses had emerged. In the meantime, elites maintained many of their traditional nonmonetized material privileges, fostering conflict and resentment between the Soviet social strata in a society supposedly composed of equals.

Curbing "Excesses"

Khrushchev's plan to pay for minimum wage raises by curbing "excesses" came in the immediate wake of a series of public scandals involving the Soviet Union's highest-earning citizens and their pernicious attitudes toward money. When he spoke of the "unhealthy phenomena" associated with excessively high income, it was undoubtedly these incidents to which Khrushchev was referring. This was not the first time Party members, managers, technocrats, and members of the cultural elite's higher salaries and monetized perks had come under public scrutiny. During the 1930s, ordinary workers frequently complained about the new "millionaires" the Soviet system produced, especially among the cultural elite.[13] Sheila Fitzpatrick suggests that the latter's privileges were even flaunted in the press as a means of deflecting attention from communists, who tended to "misrecognize" their own privilege.[14] Attacks on elite privileges in the mid-1950s were rooted in the power struggle that occurred in the wake of Stalin's death and the sea change of de-Stalinization. By then, Soviet ministers, managers, technical personnel, and the intelligentsia owed their elevated social standing and the financial benefits that came with it to the Stalinist system, making them obvious symbols of its moral and economic shortcomings.

After Stalin's death, criticisms of wealthy elites' excessively high incomes regularly appeared in feuilletons, newspaper articles that highlighted Soviet social problems. A recurring theme involved the children of well-off elites who, it was suggested, were not learning the right lessons about the inherent connection between honest labor and monetary gain from their parents.[15] A November 1953 feuilleton titled "Blight," one of the first to attack fashionable, Westernized youths (*stiliagi*) and the first in a series of articles criticizing the lifestyles of prominent citizens' offspring, described how three sons of high-ranking scientific, technical, and military personnel murdered a friend after he refused to participate in a robbery to fund nights of carousing in Moscow's cocktail halls.[16] The writers asked: "How could such a foul blight arise in the healthy environment of our Soviet youth, these people without honor or conscience, without a goal in life, people for whom money was the highest measure of happiness?" The answer: blinded by love, these gilded youths' parents had catered to their every whim and supplied them with large sums of pocket money. Their parents failed to instill in them a proper respect for labor, the true source of monetary reward.[17]

Not only young people had developed the wrong ideas about where money came from and how it should be spent. A March 1954 feuilleton attacked the socialist realist writer and four-time Stalin Prize winner Nikolai Virta, who had recently moved to the countryside, allegedly to be closer to the heroic subjects of his novels.[18] Upon arriving, Virta promised 10,000 rubles of his own money toward the construction of a cultural center, to be built with the local Komsomol's volunteer weekend labor (*subbotniki*). Virta reportedly never handed over the money and did little to help improve the struggling collective farm nearby. His complaints about the area's lack of electricity dissipated when he procured a private generator for his dacha. The article insinuated that the dacha, a two-story "mansion" shut off behind a high blue fence that overlooked the villagers' squat huts, was in fact the "cultural center" the Komsomol had built. Virta was accused of living a double life, "one in his books, another on his private estate." The local elderly peasant women had even taken to calling Virta "our master." In the ensuing scandal, Virta was expelled from the writers' union for "amoral and antisocial acts incompatible with the calling of Soviet writer."[19]

The sheer size of the sums of money mentioned in these feuilletons shocked and angered many readers, who compared them to their own meager wages and salaries. By the mid-1950s, the minimum wage had not been touched since the state extended a so-called bread allowance to compensate for increased ration prices in September 1946. That had de facto raised the minimum wage to 200–260 rubles; however, Soviet workplaces were explicitly forbidden from raising wages per se.[20] In response to a feuilleton mocking two singers at the Bol'shoi theater, in which it was mentioned in passing that one had earned 126,000 rubles for just 14 concerts and had canceled one in Kuibyshev after he did not receive his asking price, A. D. Gorbova wrote bitterly: "As a pediatrician, I earned 247 rubles in the first half of December. Can I go to the theater on such a miserable wage, subscribe to newspapers and journals, and satisfy my basic everyday needs?"[21] V. V. Gul'st, of Moscow, asked in exasperation: "How are those who earn [only a few hundred rubles per month] supposed to survive, especially if they have children? How can we assign such wages to them?"[22] He found the official explanation that low wage-earners lacked skills and qualifications unsatisfactory: "Maybe so, but they still need to eat and buy clothes."[23] V. I. Prokhorov called the subjects of these feuilletons "money grubbers" (*khapugi*) and asked how such large salaries could be permissible when many workers earned 300–400 rubles per month.[24] "It's far too big a contrast!" he exclaimed, emphasizing: "I am outraged, as is everyone else, but I am not, of course, thinking about leveling."[25] He proposed more modest reforms, including bringing down base pay rates higher than 2,000–3,000 rubles per month and cracking down on the common practice, especially among academics, of earning a second salary outside one's primary workplace.[26]

Some attacked the enormous pay gap that had now existed between manual and intellectual labor in a society whose propaganda constantly praised the essential contributions made by ordinary workers. An anonymous letter decried the fact that machinists and coal workers were having their piece rates revised, while "the rates of one category of workers' labor are not being revised, though they receive enormous sums, incomes not needed for a Soviet person."[27] In its ranks, he listed writers, playwrights, translators, composers, and artists. Indeed, members of the cultural intelligentsia could receive substantial royalties and prizes in addition to their salaries. Stalin Prize laureates like Nikolai Virta took home up to 100,000 rubles for their achievements, far more than even the most productive Stakhanovite.[28]

Much of the harshest criticism expressed in these letters was reserved for the Communist Party. Many attacked the enormous gulf that had emerged between the wages of Party officials and those of ordinary workers since Stalin's cancellation of the Party maximum. In an anonymous letter from "the deceived paupers and beggars" to Nikolai Bulganin, Kliment Voroshilov, and Khrushchev, the writer complained that ministers and high-ranking Party members received salaries of 3,000–30,000 rubles per month, which, "indeed, is creating a new class of rich people, of capitalists."[29] He criticized the fact that, in addition to their salaries, these individuals received thousands of rubles to cover their medical needs. On top of this, officials had privileged use of state-owned cars. "Why does a cleaning lady earning 200–400 rubles per month need to pay her own way to and from work, while others receive salaries of 30,000 rubles at the government's expense and they come and go in their own ZIMs [limousines]?" the writer demanded.[30] He advised Soviet leaders to think hard about what he had written.

Within the Communist Party, excessively high salaries and monetary perks came under fire after the "Aleksandrov affair" of early 1955. In February of that year, Khrushchev allegedly received an anonymous letter from a distraught mother who claimed that her daughter had been seduced and disgraced by the playwright Konstantin Krivoshein.[31] According to the letter, Krivoshein had lots of money, a lavish apartment in the capital, and a dacha in Moscow oblast, and he maintained a "house of ill repute" (*priton*) frequented by all the stars of Soviet culture, including the Minister of Culture, himself, Georgii Aleksandrov. Aleksandrov was accused of carrying on trysts with young aspiring actresses while in Krivoshein's company. The "affair" was most likely politically motivated: Aleksandrov owed his allegiance to Malenkov, who had appointed him to the post, with whom Khrushchev was in competition for the Soviet leadership.[32] By March, Aleksandrov, along with some of his fellow "degenerates," was disgraced and had been removed from his position.

Lapses of communist conscience such as Aleksandrov's greatly troubled the Soviet leadership. Amid the economic and social crises of the postwar period, there were fears that the Party was losing its enthusiasm and initiative; misconduct by communists, as Edward D. Cohn argues, both symbolized the regime's failure to transform society and threatened its ability to combat the country's problems.[33] In the meetings held to discuss Aleksandrov's fall from grace and in their letters to authorities, Party members fixated on the morally corrupting influence of the *nomenklatura*'s big salaries.[34] S. A. Figurin wrote: "It appears to me that such rot [*gnil'*] results from the fact that, for certain categories of managers, scientists, literary workers, artistic milieus and others, there are unlimited opportunities for personal enrichment. It's no secret that many of these people have become millionaires."[35] Figurin suggested that, perhaps in the past, it had been necessary to attract talented people to prestigious Party, cultural, and scientific positions through the prospect of higher salaries, but now that the Soviet Union had developed its own cadres, "there is not only no reason for it but, in my opinion, it is dangerous to use such incentives and to bring back old capitalist traditions."[36] E. Livshitz, a Party member since 1917, suggested that the Leninist principle of frugality (*skromnost'*) needed to be revived, adding that "as a rule, big money drags people down."[37]

Aside from the moral deficiencies excessive incomes facilitated, many criticized the fact that Party and managerial elites received extra income outside regular pay channels that was not subject to the full range of deductions ordinary workers paid from their wages, including taxes, bond subscriptions, and Party dues. Party members frequently concealed how much income they earned in order to reduce their dues, which constituted a percentage of their income, by omitting to include bonuses and other payments they received.[38] After the December 1947 currency reform, high-ranking government and Party workers received nontaxable "temporary cash allowances" (*vremennye denezhnye dovol'stvii,* VDD), which, by the mid-1950s, were obviously no longer temporary.[39] Although, as discussed in Chapter 1, the Soviet government publicly claimed that the ruble's purchasing power was fully restored after the 1947 currency reform and workers' real wages immediately improved, it offered a small group of political elites these allowances to tide them over while the cost of living, in reality, remained extremely high. VDD increased recipients' overall income 2–3 times, depending on the recipient's position.[40] As of December 1955, an estimated 6,136 Party employees received VDD for a sum of 169 million rubles.[41] These allowances were preserved after Stalin's death, though the amounts received were adjusted: amid his rivalry with Khrushchev, in May 1953, Malenkov secretly raised the amounts that some leaders could receive in an effort to maintain their loyalty and reduced the amounts received by others.[42]

Several letter writers argued that it was high time to abolish such additional cash payments. In a letter to Khrushchev and Bulganin in April 1955, one Party member, V. Kolotov, suggested that VDD payments had perhaps been necessary in the past, but had since become an unsupportable practice. They enabled "money hoarders" (*skopidomy*), created "artificial demand" (*isskustvennyi spros*) for deficit goods, and led to the moral degeneration (*razlozhenie*) of leaders' children, and even of some leaders themselves. As Aleksandrov and others like him demonstrated, "money spoils a person."[43] Comrades Potapenko, Astakhov, and Belkin of Leningrad argued that the practice of paying extra sums of cash in "envelopes" (*konverty*) should be abolished and the money should be integrated into regular pay if it was truly needed.[44] They harshly condemned those who willingly accepted these payments as exploiting those who did all the heavy lifting in the Soviet economy: "Indeed, this category of [elite] workers calls on [regular] workers to take on the entire burden of building communism themselves, while they live like it was before communism and get whatever they need, but don't always work according to their abilities."[45]

Additional cash payments also appeared to some communists to contradict the goals of an ongoing campaign for "financial discipline" (*finansovaia ditsiplina*) in the wake of the 1947 currency reform. As the Minister of Finance, Arseny Zverev, argued in 1948, the purchasing power of the ruble depended not only upon an increase in the production of goods and upon improvements to the trade system, but upon "observance of a strict regime of economizing—the most indispensable condition for strengthening the achievements of the currency reform."[46] In 1952, Zverev emphasized that "financial discipline and intensified control via the ruble" were needed to improve all branches of the national economy in qualitative and quantitative terms, and that financial discipline was "a major factor behind our advance toward communism."[47] Within enterprises, that entailed strict adherence to plans, meticulous accounting, and eliminating overspending and wasteful expenditures that undermined enterprises' productivity. To some, VDD payments appeared to be a particularly egregious example of the latter. "We talk a lot about economizing on state expenses, about being thrifty with every government kopek, we talk about people who display vestiges of capitalism, and at the same time we notice how we are inculcating capitalist habits in the Soviet people and creating new capitalists out of communists," a group of Party members from Rostov-on-Don observed.[48] Since the war, managers' workdays had been shortened, their responsibilities had been lightened, and retail prices had been reduced several times over; there was no good reason why managers and Party workers could not live on their salaries alone, they concluded.

Though leveling was still explicitly rejected, some communists implied that the government had gone too far in its struggle against it, using it to justify the existence of unacceptable levels of poverty and suffering among low-income citizens. As one anonymous letter writer from Moscow scathed, "The 'affair' of Aleksandrov, Virta and their ilk was possible only because the government unfairly compensated them for their labor at the expense of workers," he wrote.[49] In his view, the root of the problem was not the state's ignorance of the plight of the low-paid, but a lack of will to initiate serious reforms: "The difficult and sometimes simply dismal material situation of the enormous mass of pensioners, war invalids, the elderly, employees who were laid off from their enterprises and those who can't find work, among others, is also well known. It's long, long since time to start thinking about that. And not just think about it but do something about it."[50]

Khrushchev wanted to do something about it. In late 1955, as he prepared toward the Twentieth Party Congress, he and the Central Committee began devising reforms of the VDD system.[51] The payments were reduced in March 1956 before they were stopped altogether in 1957.[52] During the Khrushchev years, "Leninist" frugality and thriftiness (*berezhlivost'*) were held up as virtues to be praised and cultivated in Soviet citizens, especially among youth.[53] Amid increased investment in consumer production, Khrushchev promoted not acquisitiveness and consumerism per se but "rational consumption," as Susan E. Reid has argued. That entailed self-discipline and voluntary submission of the individual to the collective will and keeping "irrational" consumer desires, especially those believed to be held by women and youth, in check.[54] The government engaged in didactic efforts to cultivate austere, modern tastes that harked back to the utopian campaigns of the 1920s for the "new way of life" (*novyi byt*) and the stripped-down, modernist aesthetic that entailed.[55] This was contrasted to the decadence of Stalinism, which only the upper crust of Soviet society had had the means to enjoy firsthand, while the rest were left to make do with the sumptuous spreads depicted in propaganda posters.[56] "Excesses"—moral, aesthetic, and monetary—were incompatible with the more inclusive vision of prosperity Khrushchev laid out at the Twentieth Party Congress.

The New "Struggle against Leveling"

Khrushchev's efforts to rein in income excesses necessitated revisiting the question of the ruble's appropriate use as a labor incentive, and the question of the acceptable extent of wage differentials across and within the various branches of the Soviet economy. These were highly sensitive matters. Much like the Stalinist dictum that real wages could be increased most effectively by means of consecutive retail price reductions, the idea that any attempt to close the wage gap by raising low-paid and unskilled workers' wages undercut incentives and thus constituted dangerous leveling was deeply ingrained by the mid-1950s. Wage leveling was viewed as antithetical to the goal of rapidly increasing productivity, which was needed to live up to Khrushchev's consumer promises.

The experience of the radical postrevolutionary period, and Stalin's solutions to the problems he inherited from it, fundamentally informed Soviet leaders' thinking about this issue well into the Khrushchev era. Though Khrushchev sought to rekindle the enthusiasm of those early years, he could ill afford a repeat of that period's high labor turnover and low productivity. After October 1917, the principle of equal pay was introduced in Soviet workplaces and workers began to be paid in kind and in food rations, a policy that partly reflected the Bolsheviks' conscious attempts to abolish money and "naturalize" the economy after the revolution, but also a practical necessity due to the reigning economic instability and hyperinflation of those years. Unsurprisingly, meager rations proved to be a poor labor incentive: many workers grumbled at the new socialist authorities' policies and, even worse, walked off the job. Soviet leaders soon realized that communist slogans were not enough to motivate workers if they were struggling to survive; what they needed were tangible material incentives and wages that covered at least the minimum cost of living.[57] "We should not count on going straight ahead to communism," Lenin admonished in 1921: "We need to build every major branch of the economy on the basis of self-interest [*lichnaia zainteresovanost'*]."[58] From then on, workers were increasingly paid in money and Soviet workplaces abandoned the policy of equal compensation. Soviet workplaces increasingly turned to output-oriented piece-rate payment (*sdel'naia oplata*), despite the Bolsheviks having critiqued piece rates as mechanisms for extracting workers' surplus labor under capitalism.[59]

At the same time, and with the support of the trade unions, the early Soviet government set limits on the permissible extent of wage differentiation through the "tariff system" (*tarifnaia sistema*), a set of regulations that was rolled out across industries over the course of 1919–1921 and which stayed in place for the remainder of the Soviet Union's existence. The tariff system established correlations between wages and acquired skill levels, the difficulty and danger involved in performing jobs, and jobs' assigned importance to the Soviet economy. The first tariff system comprised three overarching categories of high-, mid-, and low-skilled workers and 35 tariff grades.[60] Within those grades, workers' base pay rates consisted of coefficients of 1, the lowest rate paid to the lowest skilled worker in a given industry. The difference between the lowest and highest coefficient was initially set at 1 to 5. The introduction of the tariff system was supposed to bring order to the chaotic and inconsistent wage system that the Bolsheviks' utopian experimentation and subsequent adjustments for inflation had produced, and provide more effective incentives for workers to enhance their skills.[61] However, as prices continued to rise during the Civil War, the lowest wages were raised to compensate and the difference in pay between unskilled and skilled labor was diminished. The tariff system was reformed in 1921–1922, when the number of grades was reduced to 17, and again in 1927–1928, when rates were revised on the basis of a "declining curve": the difference in coefficients between the base pay rates diminished as one went higher up the wage scale. Not all industries had the same number of skill grades; therefore, the wage difference between the lowest and highest coefficients was greater in industries with more categories of jobs, and smaller in industries with fewer. For example, in the textile industry, it was 1 to 3.5 and in metalwork it was 1 to 2.8.[62] This effectively narrowed the difference in base wages between high- and low-skilled labor.

For most of the 1920s, during the NEP, unemployment was rampant across the Soviet Union. Stalin's Great Break, with its shift to a command economy and the acceleration of industrialization, reversed this trend. It created a massive shortage of workers, especially skilled ones. Managers bid up wages in order to attract workers to their factories and meet ambitious quotas, which, in turn, caused discrepancies in tariff rates and overall pay for the same jobs between enterprises and across industries, and contributed to massive labor turnover.[63] Moshe Lewin famously dubbed this chaotic state of affairs a "quicksand society": workers, most of them low-skilled and of recent peasant origins, moved from factory to factory in search of real or fictitious differences in pay and provisioning, while administrators, specialists, and officials left before they could suffer retribution for shortcomings in their performance.[64] This caused bottlenecks and stoppages, and engendered discontent among high-skilled workers, who were often forced to do jobs below their skill level, while low-skilled workers were often asked to perform tasks they were unqualified to do, leading to shoddy work and frequent accidents.[65]

In an oft-quoted speech to Soviet managers in 1931, Stalin singled out leveling as the primary cause of labor turnover and of workers' low productivity. He criticized the fact that, in many Soviet enterprises, there was no significant difference between the wages paid to a sweeper and the wages paid to a machinist, and little to no difference between wages in light and heavy industry. As a result, this caused the average worker to have no real interest in developing his skills: "He feels like a 'summer visitor' [*dachnik*] of industry, working only temporarily, 'moonlighting' a little bit and then taking off 'to seek his fortune' somewhere else," Stalin claimed (emphases his).[66] Stalin argued that, to destroy this "evil," the practice of leveling wages needed to be abolished, the old tariff system needed to be "crushed," and a more substantial difference between wages for qualified and unqualified labor, as well as between jobs in heavy and light industry, needed to be established. "We can no longer tolerate that a machinist working in railroad transportation makes the same as a sweeper," he maintained. "We cannot tolerate that a machinist earns the same as a copyist."[67] Stalin emphasized that both Marx and Lenin had predicted that differential wage levels would persist under socialism, even after the destruction of classes, and that "whoever decides to build the tariff system on the 'principles' of leveling, without taking into consideration the difference between qualified and unqualified labor, is breaking with Marxism, is breaking with Leninism."[68]

The "struggle against leveling" became the banner under which Stalinist wage reforms proceeded in 1931–1933. Murray Yanowitch emphasizes that, although it was essentially a way of focusing attention on the need to effectively utilize monetary incentives to promote the development of scarce skills and disciplined work habits, like all the other campaigns of this period, it had "all the earmarks of a frenzied struggle against 'enemies.'"[69] As with Stalin's attack on those who claimed that money needed to be abolished or that it was inherently capitalist, leveling was portrayed as an ideological aberration espoused by Stalin's enemies in the radical left and by "petit bourgeois" right opportunists.[70] The trade unions, headed by Mikhail Tomskii, were accused of artificially narrowing pay levels between low- and high-skilled workers by limiting piece rates, and of ignoring the economic interests of workers in the leading industries.[71] Tomskii, who was forced out of his position in 1928 and later arrested during the Great Terror, was singled out as a promoter of leveling and as an obstacle to the goal of rapidly increasing productivity.[72]

During the wage reform campaign, the Stalinist government dramatically differentiated the wages paid to skilled versus unskilled workers and raised wages in the leading industries, such as metallurgy, mining, and machine building. Wages in heavy industry soon outpaced those in light industry. Over the course of the 1930s, workers' incomes increasingly depended upon piece rates and other earnings above the base pay rate, which was deliberately set low as an incentive to produce more than the bare minimum. By 1953, 77% of Soviet workers earned piece rates.[73] Soviet ideologists drew a dubious distinction between the use of piece rates under socialism and the use of piece rates under capitalism: in the case of the latter, they were exploitative because they were aimed at "intensifying production," whereas under socialism, they "encouraged workers to take the maximum amount of interest in the results of their labor."[74]

Because of this emphasis on results, income levels varied from worker to worker, and from month to month, depending upon their norms and their personal accomplishments. In 1935, Aleksei Stakhanov mined a record amount of coal in a single shift at a Donbass mine, far overfulfilling his norm, a "spontaneous" but, in fact, carefully planned act that began a mass movement to emulate his example. Stakhanovism produced an explosion in earnings for those who could keep up with faster and increased norms, but for regular workers, it often resulted in lower pay because they were expected to produce more to retain their original pay levels, as Donald A. Filtzer has observed.[75] Managers regularly overspent their allocated wage funds to compensate model employees who overfulfilled their norms. A massive discrepancy emerged between wages disbursed and the sum of money allocated to paying them in the state budget, that is, enterprises' shares of the centrally planned "wage fund" (*fond zarabotnoi platy*) to pay wages across all industries. This, as has already been discussed, contributed to the massive inflation that wracked the Stalinist command economy in the 1930s.

The Second World War exacerbated the income divide between low- and high-priority workers. Stalin's harsh wartime labor regime, which stepped up production pressures, instituted mandatory overtime, canceled holidays, and criminalized labor infractions, caused industrial wages to rise.[76] However, these increases were not evenly distributed: for obvious reasons, wages in the food production industry saw lower growth, having risen by only 2.5% by the middle of the war, compared to 25%–35% rises in the paper, textile, and other light-industry branches of the economy, and over 50% rises in the tank, weapons, and ammunitions industries.[77] In March 1943, coal workers' wages were significantly increased, making them the third-highest-paid industrial workers in the Soviet Union behind workers in the weapons and tank industries, up from tenth place in the first half of 1941.[78] Average wages across all branches of industry rose from 373 rubles in 1940 to 542 rubles per month by 1943. Over the course of the war, the annual wage fund increased, from 162 billion in 1940 to 195.6 billion in 1945.[79] Because of rising prices, increased taxation, and coercive wartime state fundraising campaigns, any extra money earned did not necessarily constitute real gains for workers. Any savings acquired during this period were then decimated by the December 1947 currency reform.

As Filtzer argues, Stalinist wage policy was essentially coercive; however, the system never quite worked as intended and it gave rise to many abuses that only worsened after the war.[80] Because they were ultimately responsible for their workers' performance, managers manipulated their norms so they could be more easily met and overfulfilled, and they gave workers "specious and sometimes totally illegal" bonuses to supplement their income.[81] Workers, in turn, often shied away from difficult jobs in favor of tasks that made it easier to overfulfill norms and thus were more profitable. Piece-rate workers' earnings more than doubled after the war because of the artificially low norms managers offered to newer workers entering the workplace then, including women and youth. In the meantime, those who were paid on a "time" basis (i.e., by the hour) saw their wages decline after the war, since they had no norms to overfulfill, and some managers responded by placing those workers on higher pay scales to compensate for their losses.[82]

Stalin's heirs thus inherited an extremely convoluted and inequitable wage system in desperate need of repair. In mid-1955, a new institution was created, the State Committee of the Council of Ministers of the USSR on Questions of Work and Wages (*Gosudarstvennyi komitet sovet ministrov SSSR po voprosam truda i zarabotnoi platy*) under the Council of Ministers, to study the existing wage system, propose changes in policy, and exercise oversight over the reform process. Among its tasks were devising new "technically sound" (*tekhnicheski obosnovannye*) base pay rates, reworking bonuses, and devising new, more rational, and harder to manipulate norms. Prior to its creation, there was no body below the Council of Ministers that addressed these issues.[83] This was a new way of thinking about economic problems, as Alastair McAuley has observed, reflecting a growing interest in labor economics at the time.[84] The reform was to be carried out in a gradual manner: high-earning workers did not have their wages slashed; rather, they were promised that restructured and "rationalized" wages would entail no loss to them if they put in quality effort.

The Khrushchev-era government wanted to reverse Stalinist "deviations" when it came to wage policy, but it did not want to do so at the expense of productivity. As a result, it did not repudiate the struggle against leveling, but changed the ideological justifications for continuing it. Before the Twentieth Party Congress, it was still possible to praise Stalin's shrewd approach to halting labor turnover and boosting productivity back in the early 1930s. A 1955 booklet on the subject identified the origins of "self-interest" in Marx's and Lenin's writings, and cited Stalin's famed 1931 speech to managers decrying the ills of misplaced egalitarianism during the socialist transition; however, it explained that, at the July 1955 Plenum of the Central Committee, the shortcomings of the Soviet wage system had finally been revealed, including the proliferation of tariff rates, too-low norms, and an emphasis on overfulfilling norms at the expense of quality.[85] The booklet explained that harnessing material interest was essential for building communism, which required large stores of consumer goods, as well as workers' elevated consciousness and cultural-technical level, before it could be realized. Though work was inherently social and did not have a "private character" (*chastnyi kharakter*) under socialism, it was nevertheless an "individual affair" (*lichnoe delo*): self-interested work proceeded alongside attempts to develop workers' collectivist ideological-moral qualities.[86] In other words, labor performed in exchange for money wages occurred during the socialist transition while the necessary economic and social foundations for self-motivated labor under communism were being laid.

After the Twentieth Party Congress and after Khrushchev consolidated his leadership, the struggle against leveling was disconnected from its Stalinist roots. In his speech at the Congress, Khrushchev emphasized the Leninist qualities of the wage reform, reiterating Lenin's 1921 argument in favor of wage differentiation, which held that "we need to build every major branch of the national economy upon self-interest."[87] During the wage reform process in 1956–1962, Stalin was no longer mentioned in connection with self-interest and monetary incentives, which were now deemed explicitly Leninist tools for building socialism, then communism. A 1959 booklet titled "Why We Are against Leveling" articulated this most clearly: "The principle of material stimulus was developed by Lenin. He based this on the general experience of socialist construction in the USSR, the experience of organizing labor compensation. V. I. Lenin observed that we need to build communist society not on the basis of immediate enthusiasm, but with the help of enthusiasm, on the basis of workers' self-interest."[88] The only way to get tens of millions of workers on the correct path to communism, it claimed, was the correct employment of the principle of "self-interest in the results of one's labor."[89] The booklet listed five main features of "Leninist" self-interest: (1) it encouraged workers to improve their education and skill levels by better compensating skilled over unskilled labor; (2) it encouraged workers to learn and implement improved methods and to root out obsolete ones; (3) it encouraged the creation of permanent cadres and discouraged turnover in the labor force; (4) it better compensated risky labor performed under difficult or dangerous conditions;

and (5) it helped modernize production techniques and encouraged labor discipline.[90]

None of these features of "Leninist" self-interest were especially distinct from the earlier "Stalinist" variant. The main difference between Stalin's and Khrushchev's struggles against leveling revolved around the intended beneficiaries of the associated reforms. As the 1959 booklet emphasized, the principle of material interest would apply no longer just to the individual but to smaller collectives within workplaces and to the Soviet collective, as a whole.[91] The premium system would now reward "rationalizers" (*ratsionalizatory*), that is, those who made efficient use of resources and produced higher-quality output instead of simply overfulfilling norms, which had merely encouraged overblown and often low-quality output in the past. "Material interest" would be used to narrow the difference in money incomes between low- and high-skilled workers and between the city and the countryside, a clear allusion to the recent procurement price increases offered to collective farmers in exchange for voluntarily increasing deliveries, as discussed in Chapter 1.[92] In the new struggle against leveling, the material welfare of low-skilled and low-priority workers, as well as peasants, would be raised while preserving the opportunity for workers to earn more money as an incentive for improving skills, working in a disciplined manner, implementing rationalizing methods in the workplace, and achieving high productivity levels. In theory, this approach supported a much more equitable distribution of income in the Soviet Union; however, it never managed to root out abuses of the wage system or dismantle the country's existing wage-earner hierarchy.

Narrowing the Wage Gap(s)

By the time of the Twentieth Party Congress in February 1956, as Soviet authorities were well aware, the lowest base pay rate in the Soviet Union was far from a living wage. The government thus kicked off the wage reform campaign with a minimum wage raise, decreeing in September that, as of January 1, 1957, the minimum base pay rate for all full-time workers and employees across all industries should be no less than 300–350 rubles per month, while all remaining workers and employees should be paid no less than 300 rubles in the cities and 270 rubles in rural areas.[93] The new minimum wage was exempt from income tax deductions. Eight billion rubles were allocated in the state budget to offsetting the cost of raising the minimum wage by about 33%. "This is a happy day for us," a cleaning lady at a Leningrad school reportedly declared in response to the announcement: "The extra pay will be very noticeable, and it's significant that we won't have to pay taxes on it. Our own government found the money for this. Eight billion rubles—that's no small sum."[94]

In fact, the impact of the minimum wage raise on low-income workers' living standards was limited. For one thing, many workers earning the minimum wage were only nominally "'low-income" because of the piece-rate payment system and due to norm manipulations. Some workers who earned the minimum wage took home substantially higher incomes than their coworkers who were assigned higher base pay rates, because the former were often given lower norms, which they then overfulfilled.[95] Others earned "progressive piece rates" (*progressivno-sdel'naia oplata*): unlike "straight" piece rates, which were proportionate to output, progressive piece rates increased per-unit compensation for whatever amount was produced over the norm. Progressive rates could double or treble payment and, in some industries, even kicked in below 100% of the regular norm.[96] Overfulfilling norms, in turn, could entitle one to a substantial premium on top of one's wages.

More importantly, the minimum wage raise did not address the massive gap that existed between the earning potential of male and female workers. The Soviet Union's lowest-paid workers were typically female, concentrated in low-priority industries, such as textile production and food processing, and in low-skilled and poorly paid jobs. By the mid-1950s, it was possible to acknowledge that inadequate childcare facilities were keeping an "army of women," an estimated 20 million of them, out of the workforce; however, the idea that gender, itself, impinged upon a worker's earning potential was explicitly rejected.[97] The Committee on Questions of Work and Wages explored the possibility of a wage discrepancy between male and female industrial workers in the Soviet Union and, in 1957, concluded confidently that it did not exist. It reported that there was absolutely no difference in earnings between men and women who received fixed salaries (*oklady*), while for piece-rate workers, the base pay rates and piece rates men and women earned were also identical.[98] Even on collective farms, payment for labor days, both in money and in kind, were the same for men and women. The number of state-organized day cares for working mothers' children was also on the rise, it emphasized.[99] "All workers, whether they are men or women, who have the same qualifications, receive equal pay for equal work," it concluded.[100]

Wages were highest in heavy industry, which was dominated by male workers, while wages were lowest in light industry, which was dominated by female workers. According to family budget studies, by 1956, a high-skilled coal miner in the RSFSR earned an average of 1,784 rubles per month, over three times more than a low-skilled seamstress, who earned an average of only 565 rubles.[101] If one takes skilled and low-skilled coal workers' wages together, the average was still over twice the amount of skilled and low-skilled textile workers' average wages. Statisticians downplayed the size of the gap between these categories of workers' wages, emphasizing that coal workers tended to have larger families to take care of, which diminished pay per family member, while the textile industry featured far more single persons.[102] Although not explicitly stated, this undoubtedly referred to unmarried childless women and single mothers. Two years into the wage reform process, the gap was still approximately the same: an average coal worker earned 1,617 rubles per month, while an average textile worker earned 707.[103]

The Committee on Questions of Work and Wages then began revising the tariff system, which had been subject to no comprehensive reforms since the early 1930s, merely piecemeal changes to base pay rates within individual industries and categories of jobs.[104] Years of decentralized adjustments had produced the great "variegation" in wage levels Khrushchev criticized in the report cited at the beginning of this chapter. More problematically, the lower weight of the base pay rate in workers' incomes vis-à-vis the money they earned from piece rates incentivized manipulating one's production norms. The tariff system, as even Soviet economists had to admit, had lost its "regulating power" over wages: by 1956, the base pay rate constituted an average of only 45%–55% of piece-rate workers' overall income.[105] By contrast, it represented 65%–75% of time-workers' pay, whose wages were typically supplemented by premiums and bonuses.[106]

One of the reformers' main goals was thus to make the base pay rate the most important component of wages once again and an amount of money that served as an effective incentive to be productive in and of itself, before additional earnings were factored into a worker's income. Although piece-rate payment was not abandoned, reformers planned to phase out progressive piece rates and curb opportunities to manipulate norms. Norm setting was to be devolved to the local level, ending the practice of central economic authorities announcing new, usually higher, norms each spring. Simultaneously, the wage reform sought to reduce and simplify the number of wage grades and rates and eliminate the patchwork of anomalies and discrepancies that had emerged after years of decentralized adjustments.[107]

The worst offenders when it came to norm manipulations were typically managers and workers in heavy industry. In these enterprises, workers' incomes were heavily dependent upon earnings above their base pay, in particular for overfulfilling norms (Figure 2.1). On April 22, 1958, the Soviet government

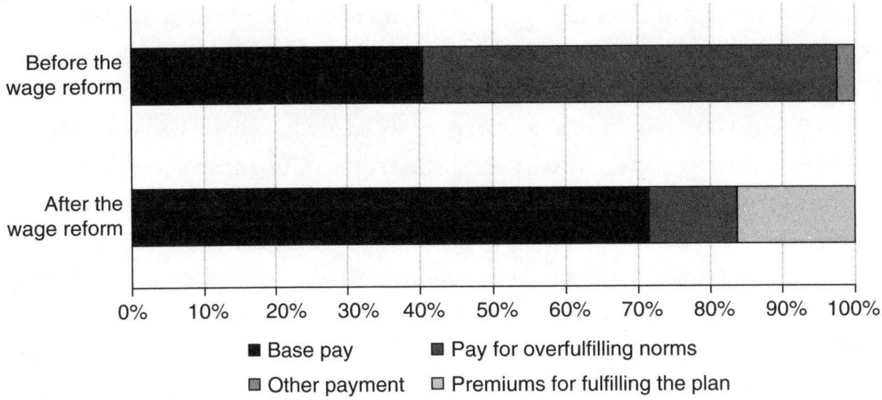

Figure 2.1 A Typical Wage Structure in Heavy Industry before and after the Wage Reforms, 1956–1962
Mariia Dynina, *Kak organizovana zarabotnaia plata rabochikh* (Moskva: Gosudarstvennoe izdatel'stvo politicheskoi literatury, 1961), 42.

unveiled its plan to make the base pay rate a more significant component of miners' and metalworkers' overall pay, and it introduced shorter workdays in these industries.[108] Workers in coal and other heavy industries would be gradually moved to a six-hour workday by the end of the year, while all other industrial workers would be moved to a seven-hour workday.[109] In November 1958, new base pay rates were announced for machine building, oil, and gas workers, putting them up to 70%–75% of overall compensation for piece-workers and 75%–85% for time-workers.[110]

Reformers also pushed to rethink the significance of premiums in workers' overall income. Premiums were supposed to be paid, at most, every six months or at the end of a season's work; however, over the course of the Stalin period, premiums steadily increased as a percentage of workers' income, and were paid out more often than initially intended.[111] By the mid-1950s, most recipients of these premiums had come to see them as guaranteed, integral components of their wages and salaries. As Filtzer emphasizes, they were frequently manipulated by managers: premiums were supposed to be rewards for economizing on materials, greater efficiency, increased output, and other achievements, but they were often paid out for a wider array of criteria than those specified by the regulations that governed them, often to smooth over labor disputes and to supplement time-based wages, which lagged behind piece-rate-based wages.[112]

Premiums helped to produce more content and loyal workers, but not necessarily more efficient ones. As Aleksandr Volkov and Viktor Grishin, of the Committee on Questions of Work and Wages and the Central Committee, respectively, complained in a 1956 report to Khrushchev, skilled and white-collar workers were paid premiums primarily for "quantitative indicators," namely, overfulfilling the plan, but not for "qualitative indicators," such as reducing the costs of production or increasing an enterprise's profitability. This often created a disconnect between an enterprise's finances and the amount of money it paid out in premiums.[113] They pushed to introduce premiums that depended upon "real results" and tight adherence to plans, and to bring an end to the policy of allowing regional premium norms and awards that reflected "narrow institutional interests" (*vedomstvennost'*)—the premiums paid to smooth over labor disputes and with other workplace concerns in mind that Filtzer has highlighted.[114] They also sought to reduce the weight of premiums in managers' and skilled workers' incomes by setting new caps on permissible amounts.

The bonuses and higher tariff coefficients offered to workers in some of the country's most remote regions, where heavy industry was often located, also came under fire as costly and inefficient at this time. Monetary incentives had long been offered to workers to attract them to undesirable and dangerous jobs in these areas, many of which were otherwise performed by prison laborers. These incentives were expanded after the Second World War. For example, following decrees in August and November 1945, workers in the Far North received a whopping 10% wage increase for every six months they remained employed there; in comparable areas outside the Far North, they received a raise of 10% per year.[115] In August 1946, workers and ITRs in the Urals region, Siberia, and the Far East were given a 20% wage increase as compensation for the harsh climate they worked in and for the difficulty of their jobs.[116]

These bonuses, when added to "regional coefficients" that raised base pay rates as a coefficient of comparable jobs in more central locales, helped to exponentially increase those workers' incomes. As Alan Barenberg notes in the case of Vorkuta, after 1945, miners' wages were indexed as 1.5 times the level paid to their peers in the Donbass, and, after 1955, as 1.8 times higher. The regional coefficient, plus Northern bonuses, could result in wages that were 3.6 times higher.[117] Only a tiny number of workers were eligible for these bonuses; however, by 1956, they cost the government an estimated 6 billion rubles per year.[118] Some categories of workers earned 3,000–4,000 rubles per month in Northern bonuses alone.[119] By the late 1950s, it was no longer believed that they were an effective incentive for workers to settle down and help develop the North, rather than work there long enough to earn big money and move on. Moreover, by then, and against the backdrop of the release of millions of prisoners from the gulag, the Soviet government was trying to shift toward less coercive recruitment practices in the North and the Far East. In 1959, Khrushchev announced that Northern wage bonuses would be scaled back, replaced with increased state investment in improving living conditions in these areas, which he acknowledged to be one of the main obstacles to labor retention in the North.[120]

At the Twenty-First Party Congress in late January 1959, the Communist Party abandoned the Sixth Five-Year Plan begun in 1956 and adopted an ambitious Seven-Year Plan for 1959–1965 that supposedly reflected the Soviet Union's enormous economic successes to date and planners' promising forecasts for the near future. In his speech on the "control figures" (*kontrol'nye tsifry*) associated with the plan, that is, the macroeconomic targets ministries and enterprises were required to hit to make the plan work, Khrushchev promised that one of its main goals was to "secure an uninterrupted increase in the population's living standards," predicated upon a 62%–65% rise in the national income by 1965.[121] This would facilitate unprecedented largesse on the part of the Soviet government, which could now offer workers such generous benefits as a shortened workday and workweek, tax-free earnings (see Chapter 4), and another minimum wage raise, among other investments in improving their living standards. Khrushchev promised that the minimum wage would be roughly doubled, from 270–300 rubles to 500–600 rubles. When combined with the effects of the 1956 pension reform (see Chapter 3) and new lower prices in socialized eating facilities, the new minimum wage would support a 40% increase in the population's real wages by the end of the plan.[122]

That fall, the Central Committee of the Communist Party, the Council of Ministers, and the Central Trade Unions vowed to implement the goals set at the Twenty-First Party Congress. All Soviet workers were promised that they would work only six hours per day by 1960.[123] "With no loss to productivity," the Soviet Union was slated to have the shortest workday in the world, "yet another clear demonstration of the Party's care for the further development of the socialist economy and increasing workers' material and cultural living standards."[124] Although this did not raise wages per se, it raised pay per hour and was therefore portrayed as conducive to the growth of real wages. A new, more modest minimum wage raise to 450–500 rubles, not 500–600 rubles as Khrushchev had initially promised, would be implemented by 1962. Finally, the

Committee on Questions of Work and Wages and the Central Trade Unions were instructed to work out new standard provisions for workers on piece-rate-premium (*sdel'no-premial'naia*) payment and time-premium (*vremenno-premial'naia*) payment scales. The wage reform process was scheduled to be completed for all categories of workers by 1962.[125]

According to the Soviet economists Rafik Batkaev and Vladimir Markov, Khrushchev's wage reform preserved the principle of wage differentiation while "resurrect[ing] the decisive role of the nationwide tariff system."[126] Filtzer, in his meticulous analysis of the reform and its implementation, grants that it reduced the number of workers on piece rates, which reduced the pressure on workers to overfulfill norms, and the government's wage spending dropped while overall productivity rose.[127] However, he emphasizes that these achievements were predicated on the gendered division of labor in the Soviet economy: they obscured how the reform disadvantaged women, whose wages were low to begin with and who tended to be employed in tasks that gave them less control over the labor process and less leverage to extract "looser" or more manipulatable norms.[128] This allowed local managements and the Soviet regime to tolerate violations of wage and norm regulations designed to protect the earnings of privileged male workers in favored industries and trades.[129] Valued, usually male, workers continued to exert influence to protect their high earnings, and managers continued to overspend on wages. Wage anomalies across industries persisted. Managers continued to pay out premiums and bonuses for dubious achievements. Although the wage reform sought to reestablish the relationship between the price paid for labor power and the amount of labor performed, a relationship that had broken down under the pressures of industrialization and in the last years of Stalinism, it did not, as Filtzer observes, "succeed in turning Soviet wages into a coherent, predictable, and centrally controllable system of incentives."[130] Nor did the wage reform, in his opinion, succeed in improving the plight of the low-paid, for its narrowing of wage differentials was modest at best.[131]

Slowing Real Wage Growth

Regulating the money supply and maintaining the real value of minimum and high wages alike during the reform process was challenging. Despite the new "technically sound" norms the reform introduced, the pressure to enthusiastically meet targets was not eased and managers continued to overspend from the wage fund to do so. As Filtzer notes above, valued workers and their bosses simply colluded to work around the new strictures. Soviet central authorities viewed this behavior as nothing short of sabotage. Wage overspending was cited as one of the main causes of excess money in circulation in the late 1950s, undermining real wages by creating "artificial demand" for consumer products.[132] "If we continue to overspend from the wage fund, there will not be enough goods and it could lead to financial difficulties for our country. This needs to be understood," Khrushchev explained to the May 1958 Plenum of the Communist Party. "Liberal" managers caused great damage to the government and should no longer be tolerated, he argued. "I don't know which whip we should chase them from the Party with," he went on, "but we need to give them the bum's rush, because they are our enemies and not our friends."[133] He pushed to prohibit extraordinary allocations of goods to areas where they were in deficit due to wage overspending, suggesting that local authorities would pay more attention to the problem and managers would be more disciplined about wage spending if their own workers suffered the consequences directly in the form of consumer shortages.[134] The Council of Ministers warned local authorities that the central government would no longer release extra goods from central supplies to help absorb the extra cash in circulation. As of a January 2, 1959, decree, Party, government, and managerial organs at the republic level were held more directly responsible for the state of the currency supply, for securing necessary supplies of consumer goods, and for strengthening control over the wage fund.[135]

The problem of wage overspending and the imbalance between money in circulation and consumer supply it exacerbated were especially serious in the parts of the country where heavy industry was concentrated. Miners, in particular, were paid some of the highest wages in the Soviet economy, leaving them with money to burn, but consumer goods typically did not reach their settlements in a timely manner or in sufficient amounts. The post-1947 unified retail prices of consumer goods in the country's most distant regions were the highest in the entire Soviet Union, but higher prices did little to sop up excess cash in circulation when factory shops' shelves were bare. Cheap alcohol was, perhaps, the one product that consistently made it to their way. Excess income was frequently cited as the cause of widespread alcoholism, as well as breaches of labor discipline and communist morality, among miners. Payday binge drinking was so common that miners' wives sometimes gathered at the factory to intercept their husbands' wages before they could be squandered on liquor, leaving nothing to feed their children with.[136] One mine manager offered a candid explanation for his employees' excessive drinking: "There's a lot of money around, and there isn't always something to spend it on. The demand for manufactured goods exceeds supply. People want worthwhile, costly items—pianos, for instance. It's absurd how few pianos we get for sale."[137]

These deficits persisted throughout Khrushchev's wage reform campaign, in spite of the central government's efforts to hold regional authorities and enterprise managers more directly responsible for achieving balances between wages and consumer supply. Thus, despite the fact that workers in heavy industry were promised their "regulated" wages would entail no loss to them if they put in quality effort, many of the Soviet regime's highest-earning and most valued workers perceived their living standards as stagnating or even declining, as one scathing April 1962 letter from a group of miners in Rostov oblast reveals. In it, they depicted living conditions as little improved from the Stalin years. They criticized the fact that "goods arrive at our trade base, but we never see them," suggesting they were snapped up by workplace elites who were granted privileged access to them, or they were stolen by trade employees and diverted to the black market. "Nikita Sergeevich, we would very much like to know how much longer the Party's leaders plan to live only for themselves and their near and dearest," they demanded, "for it is patently obvious that they live nothing like our workers. This is unacceptable."[138] They claimed that workplace authorities cared only about fulfilling the plan, regardless of any defects that went into the work, not so subtly hinting that the new emphasis on "technically sound norms" and rational use of resources went out the window to fulfill the plan, as per usual. Their superiors were seemingly unperturbed that the factory stores had nothing to sell, that workers were living in overcrowded barracks with some families resigned to the hallways or to rooms intended for single persons and pensioners, or that, due to plumbing problems, their water pressure had reduced to "teardrops."[139] The miners' claims were considered sufficiently serious to be investigated by the head of the local Party executive committee, who dismissed their complaints as unfounded, assuring Khrushchev that their factory store had a sufficient supply of meat, milk, and sausages for sale, and the settlement's plumbing and barracks were simply under renovation.[140]

The miners' collective letter pointed to another inconvenient truth: in spite of the push to eliminate excesses, cadres and political elites continued to have privileged access to goods and to make use of *blat,* which was still just as important as, often more important than, the full-value ruble in the process of consumption. Based on his interviews with Soviet émigrés in the 1970s, the British sociologist Mervyn Matthews observes that the elimination of Stalinist cash allowances by Khrushchev was simply replaced by the expansion of the Kremlin ration system and by not-so-secret closed distribution practices.[141] Instead of an envelope of cash, managers and other mid-level elites often received a "thirteenth month" of wages that was officially earmarked for medical treatment or "cure money" (*lechposobie*).[142] They also received special vouchers allowing them to shop in stores that, from the outside, appeared not to be stores at all, and that gave elite shoppers access to deficit Soviet goods and, in some cases, selected Western goods.[143]

Khrushchev scaled down many of the *nomenklatura*'s most obvious material privileges, limiting their free or discounted access to cars, dachas, furniture, and lavish holidays. However, this economizing did not apply to the entire government, as A. B. Konovalov has shown.[144] In 1959, for example, the *nomenklatura*'s access to personal cars was restricted in order to "liquidate excesses" and cut government expenditures on the cars' maintenance. Those who previously had the right to a car were to be compensated with a monthly cash bonus: 1,000 rubles for those with the personal right to a car, and 500 rubles for those who had as-needed access to it. This was supposed to offset the cost of providing their transportation and encourage them to be more economical about their use of cars. The reform was highly unpopular among officials and was almost immediately supplemented by a secret decree allowing top officials to continue to use cars, excluding regional secretaries. As Konovalov points out, a larger divide emerged between the living standards and material privileges of top Party members and those of lower-level functionaries, and between Party and governmental organs.[145]

In the meantime, low-income members of Soviet urban society were triply disadvantaged, having deficits of money, access, and personal connections to draw upon. They often struggled to afford basic necessities, let alone consumer luxuries. With the shift away from Stalin's consecutive retail price cuts toward Khrushchev's more abstract "economically sound" price policy, low-income workers were left wondering when they would enjoy the benefits of the new, celebrated consumer abundance on their wages. Khrushchev, himself, acknowledged that minimum wage raises were widely seen as less effective than Stalin's price reductions on this score. As he complained in May 1960, "Some comrades have stumbled into pushing us only toward lower prices, [for] they think this is the only way to improve workers' living standards." Khrushchev promised: "We have not lost sight of reducing prices, but you need to recognize the unequal conditions this creates for workers if you only go down this path, that is, the path of lowering prices, and if you don't achieve harmonization, pulling the lowest wages up to the highest. It's well known that the greatest advantages to be gained from lower-priced goods go to the categories of workers that receive the highest wages."[146] He insisted that narrowing the wage gap was a higher priority than reducing retail prices: "After the Second World War, too large of a gap appeared between the incomes of different categories of workers and that gap needs to be closed."[147]

Khrushchev sought to shift popular opinion on the sources of real wage growth and rising living standards, especially among low-income workers. If, in the Stalin era, real wage growth was argued to depend primarily upon consecutive retail price cuts, rising state spending on the population's social welfare was portrayed as one of its most important drivers in the Khrushchev era. Workers were repeatedly reminded that their free or discounted benefits (*l'goty*) like health care, education, and holidays, paid from the state's "fund for social consumption" (*fond obshchestvennogo potrebleniia*), as well as factory funds, needed to be kept in mind when assessing the state of their household finances.[148] These payments constituted an essential component of real wages and valuable source of supplementary income (Figures 2.2 and 2.3). As one steelworker and activist, Petr Ilich Ermolenko, wrote in a trade union journal in 1957, around payday, workplace chitchat often dwelled upon wage complaints, but he mused that "maybe we're adding it up all wrong."[149] In order to get a clear sense of one's family budget, he argued, "one needs to remember all the payments and privileges that don't make their way into the accounting books."[150] Ermolenko had recently been to the factory doctor several times for free, his family had regularly spent time in a house of rest (*dom otdykha*) either for free or at a steep discount, his children had been to Pioneer camps, and he lived in a new apartment building that had been built using government funds. "These are all the corrections you need to make when you're talking about family budgets, not only ours, but every worker's family in the Fatherland," Ermolenko concluded.[151]

Family budgets were frequently analyzed in newspaper and magazine articles in the late 1950s in an effort to demonstrate these shifts in concrete terms. A February 1957 *Komsomol'skaia pravda* feature, which was subsequently turned into a full-length book, invited readers to take a look at the Andrianovs' family budget and judge for themselves what the year 1956 had brought to this ordinary household of seven people: Semen Alekseevich, a skilled factory worker; his wife, Anastasia Grigor'evna, a coatroom attendant; and their five children.[152] As the figures showed, the family's living standards had noticeably improved: they had consumed more food and had bought more consumer goods that year

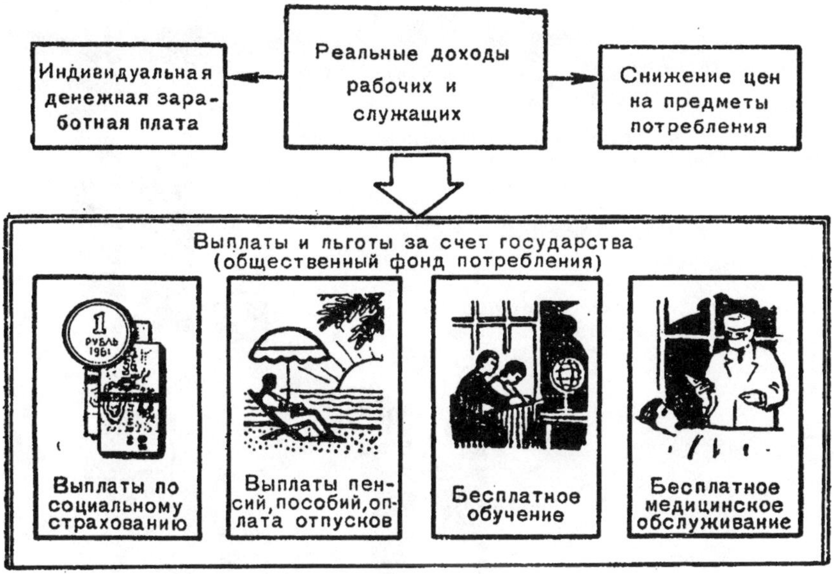

Figure 2.2 **The Structure of Workers' Real Wages. Caption: (from left to right) "Individual money wage payments←workers' and employees' real wages→ lower prices on consumer goods"; (bottom row) ↓"payments and privileges at the government's expense (the social fund for consumption)": (left to right) "payments for social insurance; payments for pensions, aid, holidays; free education; free medical services."**

Mariia Dynina, *Kak organizovana zarabotnaia plata rabochikh* (Moskva: Gosudarstvennoe izdatel'stvo politicheskoi literatury, 1961), 9.

and, just as importantly, they had spent less money on these purchases. Anastasiia Grigor'evna had transformed from a "bad housewife" into a thrifty and efficient one over the course of 1956 by spending less money on food—not by cutting down on her family's food intake, but by shopping less frequently in the kolkhoz markets, where prices were higher, and more often in state stores, where prices were lower.[153] More importantly, the Andrianovs had profited from substantial "invisible earnings" (*nezrimye dokhody*) in the form of increased state spending on their family's social welfare, readers were told. As a family of seven, the Andrianovs received around 3,100 rubles in subsidies from Semen's and Anastasia's trade unions to visit sanatoriums, Pioneer camps, and houses of leisure.[154] They, furthermore, had received 1,386 rubles' worth of cost-free medical care. Three of their children were currently studying at

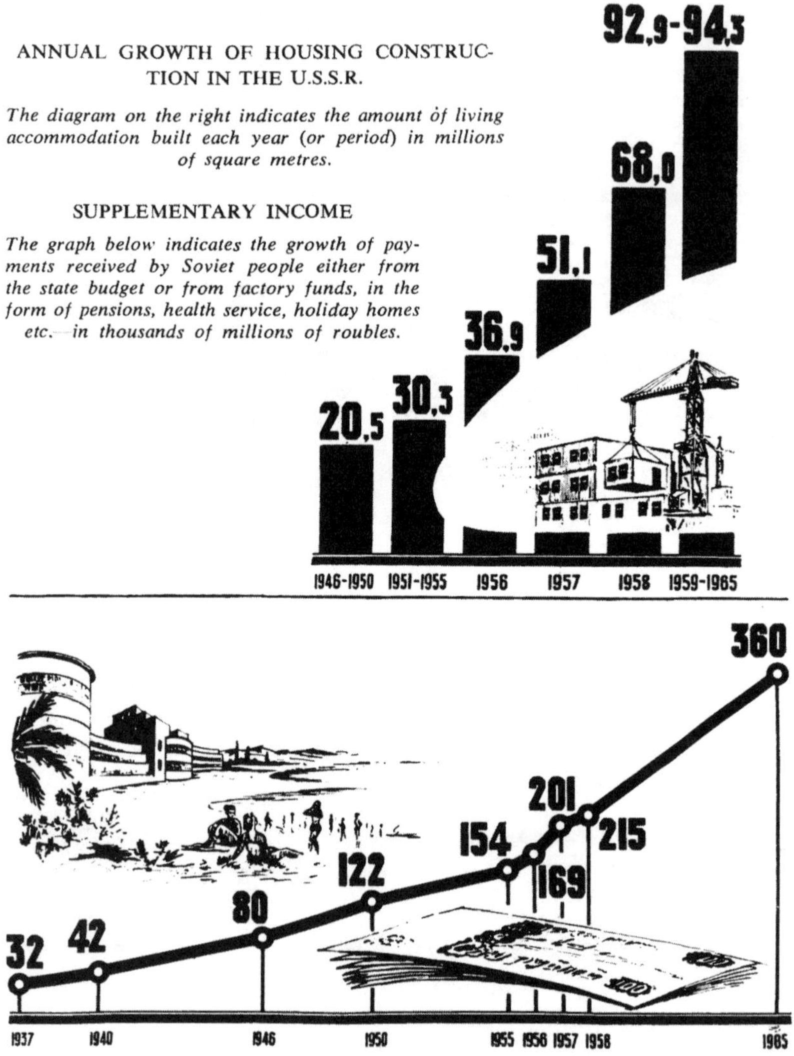

Figure 2.3 **Soviet Workers' Welfare Benefits Paid from the Fund for Social Consumption**

Arseny Zverev, *What Soviet Citizens Get besides Wages* (London: Soviet Booklets, 1957), 16.

no cost to them: including the stipends their two daughters received to attend university and a technical school, the state spent 11,670 rubles on their children's education. If one were to add up the Andrianovs' "invisible earnings," one arrived at a sum of 16,156 rubles, equivalent to one-third of the sum of money the family earned in a year.[155]

Khrushchev gestured to the new economic thinking the government sought to inculcate in Soviet citizens in his speech at the Twenty-First Party Congress, when he argued that "the material and cultural security of the Soviet people is determined not only by the sum of money they receive and by their individual distribution in the form of wages and price cuts."[156] He explained that, under socialism, the government strove to provide people not only with higher wages but with more and better housing, socialized eating establishments, communal services, day cares, educations, holidays, medical care, and cultural establishments. "Man is a social being," Khrushchev concluded, "his life is unthinkable, impossible outside the collective, with whom he has many diverse relationships. This social aspect of life is being ever more fully revealed on the path of communist construction. As a result, the satisfaction of each person's individual demands necessarily occurs alongside the growth of society's material and cultural well-being. It should occur not only via increased wages, but also through increased funds for social consumption, the role and meaning of which will only grow."[157]

In the meantime, however, the state's spending on nominal wages declined. This partially reflected its efforts to rein in wage overspending: in 1961, Gosbank officials reported that, of the 65.7 million rubles (new money) allocated to the wage fund that year, only around 65 million was spent, which was proof that wage expenditures were proceeding more "frugally" (*ekonomno*).[158] Yet, as the report noted, wages were primarily being constrained in light industry and low-priority branches of the economy. In other words, they were being constrained for jobs whose wages were lower to begin with, and not to the desired extent for high-income heavy-industry jobs. Many heavy-industry enterprises, meanwhile, were doing a poor job of implementing the January 2, 1959, decree on balancing wage payments with local supplies of consumer goods, and their managers continued to overspend on wages, they admitted.[159] In some industries, overspending actually went up after the wage reform began: the machine-building and metalworking industries overspent on average by 17.1% per month, up from 13.9% in 1959.[160] This was chalked up to poor implementation of new technology and procedures, as well as "excesses" in wage setting for some categories of workers.

Much of the decline in the state's wage spending was unintentional, however. Nominal wages rose by only 9.3% over the period 1959–1961, well below the 14% predicted in control figures, as Volkov and Grishin emphasized.[161] By 1962, the average wage was anticipated to be 42 rubles lower than control figures.[162] This was attributed to the measures put in place to constrain wage overspending and to reduce premiums and bonuses, as well as industries waiting until the last possible moment to put the mandated wage regulations and new output norms into place.

Real wage growth was also not hitting its targets. In a September 1961 report to Khrushchev on its progress during the Seven-Year Plan, Volkov and Grishin predicted that real wages would grow by only 13.6% in the first four years of the plan, well below the 21.1% predicted in control figures—substantial growth, but not at levels that would have a transformative impact on workers' living standards, as Khrushchev had promised.[163] Of those 13.6%, they calculated that 9% would be derived from nominal wage increases, 2% from lower prices, and 0.8% from lower taxes, and, despite its breathless propaganda about "invisible earnings," only 1.8% would stem from state spending on social welfare benefits.[164] In order to hit the government's promised target of a 40% increase in real wages, annual wage growth would need to be 7.2% per year, they informed him.

Under these conditions, the minimum wage raise Khrushchev had trumpeted at the Twenty-First Party Congress, which was slated for 1962, appeared increasingly unfeasible. Around 22 million people's wages were scheduled to be raised to 45–50 rubles (new money), mostly workers in education, health care, socialized amenities, and other branches of the economy providing services to the population such as childcare providers and cooks.[165] Within these industries, more than 25% of all workers, or more than 5 million people, received wages below 40 rubles (new money) per month.[166] Although Volkov and Grishin did not acknowledge this, these were among the most feminized industries and professions in the Soviet Union. The government had initially planned to spend around 800 million rubles on raising their wages; however, amid fears that this would throw off the balance of the population's money income and expenses due to shortages of goods to spend those wages on, Gosplan reduced that sum to 200 million. Even this lowered sum was now being "withdrawn" (*snimaetsia*) due the problem of inadequate consumer supply. Volkov and Grishin suggested that Khrushchev expand socialized amenities like laundries and repair centers to give citizens something else to spend their money on and thereby remove it from circulation. If these services could not be organized and sufficient consumer goods could not be found, they recommended excising the minimum wage raise from the wage reform process altogether and postponing it as late as possible.[167]

This increasingly worrying imbalance between wages and goods was addressed head-on during the May 31, 1962, meeting held to revise control figures for the remaining Seven-Year Plan. During this meeting, Khrushchev's planned minimum wage increases were postponed.[168] Aleksandr Zasiad'ko, the head of Gosekonomsovet, also asked to postpone the ongoing elimination of taxes, arguing that these measures were necessary to rebalance the population's money income and expenses (see Chapter 4).[169] Khrushchev consented, but not before launching into a tirade about the seemingly perpetual imbalance between goods and money in the Soviet economy. "It's killing us now," he exclaimed, "and that's why the ordinary person says: 'We want to buy meat.' And meat [production] has gone up, but only we know that, and the people don't live on stats, they live on kilograms and grams, and they can't buy meat. Why? Because we couldn't afford to increase payments to pensioners and other categories [of low-income citizens]." He complained that, on paper, a harmonious balance between the population's money income and expenses had been achieved, therefore, ". . . why do we have more money than we have goods?"[170]

The next day, June 1, the new higher retail prices for meat and butter were announced to the public. As discussed in Chapter 1, this led to a violent confrontation in Novocherkassk, where managers had announced lower piece rates under the banner of Khrushchev's wage reform just one day before. Like many other enterprises, they had postponed implementing the new and unpopular wage regulations until the very last opportunity. The prospect of lower wages and higher prices provoked outrage among those who walked off the job and who clashed with police. Another group that was particularly angry and distraught included those who earned inflexible incomes, a group whose number had increased substantially as the new wage regulations were implemented because they placed more workers on less lucrative time-based wages and restricted this group's ability to supplement their wages with premiums and bonuses.[171] It also encompassed millions of old-age pensioners who received fixed amounts based upon pre-pension earnings, and millions of mildly disabled citizens who were required to work to receive their benefits but were typically resigned to the simplest and lowest-paying jobs.

Able industrial workers earning piece rates had, to a greater or lesser degree, the ability to increase their output and earn more money through harder work or norm manipulations. Those who earned inflexible incomes had few legal strategies at their disposal to adapt to such abrupt economic shifts; improvements in their purchasing power thus depended more directly upon state interventions like reduced retail prices and minimum wage raises. "I am a second-group invalid since childhood, I work, I receive a salary plus a pension totaling 85 rubles," Nikolai Federovich Zlobin, a disabled 25-year-old worker from Krasnodar, wrote in June 1962.[172] "For each member of my family, that works out to be about 20 rubles. But can I, in fact, eat and buy clothes and shoes for 20 rubles?" he demanded. Zlobin elaborated that he was on his second day of skipping meals so his children could eat, and it had been three months since he had last been to the cinema. He appealed directly to Khrushchev: "I'm asking you: what can I do? I can't steal because I'm a legless cripple, and I can't earn more money . . ." Amid a confluence of dismal economic trends, the Soviet state asked for his patience and, in the meantime, told him to tighten his belt.

Conclusion

During the Soviet Union's ascent to communism, "distribution according to labor" (*raspredelenie po trudu*) supposedly governed access to the material benefits of membership in the socialist collective: since there was not yet a sufficient supply of goods to distribute solely on the basis of need, as would be the case under communism, and labor was not yet performed for its own sake but to secure the means of existence, the main factor determining distribution was the quality and quantity of workers' labor, expressed as money wages.[173] According to Khrushchev-era logic, this relationship—between labor performed, financial compensation for it, and money's function in determining one's share of food and consumer goods—grew distorted under Stalin. The lowest wages scarcely took need into consideration, while the highest wages became the product of status entitlements and skillful maneuvering, rather than the "results of one's labor." Excessively high wages, in turn, encouraged unhealthy acquisitiveness and the moral decay of socialist society.

During the wage reforms of 1956–1962, Khrushchev sought to establish a more concrete correspondence between labor quality and income level, promising that, if citizens worked more productively and efficiently, they would have more money to spend on the good things in life, of which, accordingly, there would exist naturally more. However, as we saw in both Chapter 1 and this chapter, the Soviet Union never managed to attain the high level of consumer output the fulfillment of this promise depended upon. In the absence of the necessary goods, the extra money in circulation caused by the persistence of elites' high salaries and extra perks and wage overspending in priority branches of the economy, as well as increasing payments to low-income workers, and, as will be discussed in Chapter 3, pensioners, tipped the balance of the population's income and expenses toward the former. This had ripple effects both for the full-value ruble's purchasing power and for Khrushchev's credibility as Soviet leader.

Khrushchev, for his part, appears to have believed the government did not hand over *enough* money to low-income citizens. Sergei Khrushchev similarly portrays his father's initiatives as stymied by bean counters in the Soviet government. He suggests the elder Khrushchev knew that minimum wage raises amounted to little more than "crumbs," but nothing more could be obtained because the Ministry of Finance "grumbled."[174] "Father understood their problems, financial officials' business is to offset expenses with income, to bring about an increase in the latter," Sergei wrote, "but you also can't forget about the people, about the fact that the budget is for the people and the people are not for the budget." Nevertheless, as he acknowledged, raising the people's real wages was trickier than raising nominal wages: "That's why you have to constantly balance, scrupulously monitor the relationship between expenses and income. God forbid money payments in 'empty' uncovered rubles should exceed the amount of consumer goods issued. . . . 'Spare' money simultaneously emptied the kiosks and necessitated bringing back rationing. . . . Father did all he could to make sure the past was not repeated."[175]

For obvious reasons, Khrushchev's efforts to reduce income excesses lost him the support of well-heeled cadres and elites whose privileges were reined in, as well as prized workers who benefited financially from the various opportunities to manipulate Stalinist wage policy. Khrushchev recalled that his elimination of VDD payments was never openly criticized by Party members, but he recounted feeling as if "he was being shot in the spine with their glares" as he walked the halls of the Central Committee and the Council of Ministers after the reform went into effect.[176] His broader efforts at income redistribution also failed in the eyes of many low-income citizens, who, in principle, stood only to gain. Minimum wage increases were too modest to bring about a dramatic improvement in their living standards. Furthermore, they were not accompanied by a serious reassessment of privilege in Soviet society. Visible material inequalities persisted despite Khrushchev's rhetoric of frugality and thrift, contradicting his image as a defender of the common folk's interests and his incessant invocation of Marxist-Leninist fundamentalism. "The average state farm worker earns 40–50 rubles [new money] per month. . . . And just how much does a member of the Central Committee earn? How much did Lenin earn?" one anonymous writer from Leningrad demanded after the price increases in June 1962.[177] As Sheila Fitzpatrick and Vladimir A. Kozlov note, praise for a golden age of "true Marxism-Leninism" and complaints about the current Soviet leadership's "distortions" became regular features of seditious sentiment after Stalin, a phenomenon they link to the Party's new approach to social policy and increased investment in consumer goods, which resulted in greater social stratification and growing privileges for Party bureaucrats.[178] As another seditious letter writer fumed: "We gave our labor and keep on giving it—but to whom? To false leaders. We received miserly pay for our work and we're still receiving the same pay. Who pays us this tiny amount of money? Those liars."[179]

Many felt that Khrushchev's wage reforms were less effective at widening access to the fruits of Soviet prosperity than Stalin's consecutive retail price cuts. Though they did nothing to solve the problem of insufficient consumer output and even exacerbated it, price cuts directly benefited those living on inflexible wages, because these individuals and their families were most acutely affected by high fixed retail prices, inflation, and market-price spikes. This is not to suggest that minimum wage raises played no role in improving living standards and were not felt at all. Earning even a handful of extra rubles was certainly helpful for those who earned the lowest amounts, for whom the cost of living could be a daily struggle. Some workers surely benefited financially from the monetary rewards associated with more rational and efficient performance of their jobs after the wage reforms went into effect. Yet, because Soviet consumption was a constantly shifting balance of access, availability, prices, and financial resources, more money to spend was not always all that was needed to improve one's living standards depending on where one lived, what one did for a living, and who one was within the Soviet socioeconomic hierarchy.

3

Socialist Security

While minimum- and low-wage workers struggled to get by in the late Stalin period, millions of elderly and disabled pensioners lived on even more miserable sums of money. This was due only in part to wartime inflation; it was also due to the convoluted and hierarchical pension system that had been in place in the Soviet Union since the 1920s. Prior to 1956, the Soviet pension system was governed by hundreds of contradictory rules and exceptions that resulted in a small number of elite and priority pensioners receiving relatively generous sums, while the overwhelming majority of pensioners received pitifully low amounts. By 1955, an estimated 70% of old-age pensioners received amounts that could dip below 150 rubles—the minimum entitlement of 50% of prior wages if one was lucky enough to be allowed to calculate the pension using the full wage cap of 300 rubles.[1] Many pension amounts were calculated using lower wage caps, or their recipients had simply earned less than 300 rubles per month during their working lives, and thus they were entitled to less than 150 rubles upon retirement. The remaining 30% of old-age pensioners received the so-called elevated pensions (*povyshenye pensii*) granted to priority workers in heavy industry, typically 400–500 rubles per month.[2] These pensions were calculated using higher wage caps or exceptions that allowed them to disregard the 300-ruble limit, but they still fell far short of the average industrial wage in 1955 of around 700 rubles per month. In the meantime, many urban citizens were denied an old-age pension due to an absent, inconsistent, or incomplete work record, while most peasants remained categorically ineligible to receive a pension.

Alongside retail prices and wages, Khrushchev targeted pensions as yet another area in which reforms were desperately needed in order to raise the population's living standards.[3] Pension reform went hand in hand with his efforts to create a more equitable distribution of income in Soviet society and reduce Stalinist excesses after the Twentieth Party Congress, as discussed in Chapter 2. In May 1956, the government heralded sweeping changes to the Soviet pension system. A more universal and generous pension system went into effect on October 1 of that year. Soviet propaganda portrayed the reform as a shining example of the great "care" (*zabota*) bestowed upon workers by the socialist state, a claim that reflected both its traditional paternalism toward workers and its idiosyncratic approach to pension financing. Soviet workers' pensions were fully funded, drawing upon payroll contributions from state enterprises toward a social insurance fund rather than individual contributions deducted from their own wages or a "pay-as-you-go" system.[4] State pensions were not an investment in one's future; rather, they were a reward for one's own or a family member's contributions and sacrifices in the service of the government's goals. Its ability to allocate billions of rubles to dramatically raising workers' pensions without requiring their own financial contributions was presented as clear evidence of the Soviet Union's growing prosperity.

Although historians typically date pension reform as beginning in the post-Stalin era and during Khrushchev's tenure as Soviet leader, the drive to reform the pension system, in fact, began well before his leadership, the Twentieth Party Congress, and even Stalin's death in 1953, as this chapter will show.[5] Pension reform kicked off during the last years of Stalin's life, though he evidently took no part in it.[6] As in other areas of postwar economic and social policy, his colleagues came to realize that the Soviet pension system was in crisis. The tangle of rules and exceptions that governed pensions was inefficient, and it was glaringly evident that the pension system—insofar as a coherent "system" could be argued to exist—did not widely distribute the care and financial security it claimed to. In their letters to the authorities during these years, many Soviet pensioners identified the pitiful sums of money they received as a major moral failing of the Soviet regime they had given so much to.

The Soviet government's various attempts to "unify" and reform pension policy were unsuccessful until 1956; nevertheless, the new pension law that went into effect on October 1 of that year capitalized upon existing momentum for pension reform within the central leadership. Furthermore, a close look at the resulting law shows that it remained grounded in Stalin-era ideas about pensions as labor incentives. As with wage policy, Khrushchev did not abandon the "struggle against leveling" when it came to pensions, but framed pension reform as furthering the state's economic goals without leaving low-priority members of the Soviet workforce and society behind. The new pension law eliminated the most egregious inequalities of the Stalin years by raising minimums and instituting new maximums, but it did not eliminate inequalities altogether. One's eligibility for a pension, the amount of money one received, and the extent of financial security one could enjoy in the absence of gainful employment still hinged upon maximized labor capacity and a demonstrable record of disciplined labor. The "uninterrupted labor period" (*nepreryvnyi stazh*), a concept that emerged in the Stalin years and referred to an unbroken stint of employment, typically in one industry but, even better, in a single workplace, remained the gold standard in pension policy after 1956, entitling a pensioner to a bonus.

The 1956 law thus recalibrated the state pension as paternalistic care for those who had lost their capacity for gainful labor but also as a monetary incentive for the actively employed. As a consequence, the new pension system continued to underserve those who struggled to find, maintain, or prove a history of stable employment, and it continued to prioritize the economic welfare of the city over the countryside and the factory over the farm. Collective farmers remained outside the pension system's purview until 1964, when they were finally brought in on an unequal footing compared to workers and in a manner that more explicitly linked the receipt of a pension to meeting the state's productivity expectations. The post-1956 pension system was nevertheless a significant improvement over the previous contradictory set of policies, providing more pensioners with more money and in amounts that correlated more directly to the cost of living. It gave an unprecedented number of Soviet citizens the financial means to stop working. At the same time, the expansion of pension coverage stoked officials' fears about declining productivity, and it bestowed more "uncovered" and unspendable rubles upon the Soviet population.

Pension Policy under Stalin

After the October Revolution, the Bolsheviks aspired to a modern comprehensive system of social insurance including pensions that provided assistance to the population's neediest members.[7] The system they put in place scarcely resembled their ideals; instead, it was a product of postrevolutionary turmoil, limited resources, and their economic priorities. Beginning in the early 1920s, Soviet welfare policy fragmented, drawing sharper distinctions between different categories of recipients of state assistance, as Maria Cristina

Galmarini-Kabala has shown. These distinctions increasingly revolved around a recipient's ability to engage in industrial labor and contribute directly toward the state's economic goals. After 1920, pensions for "invalids, peasants, and the indigent" fell under the jurisdiction of the Commissariat of Social Assistance, while pensions for workers fell under the purview of the Commissariat of Labor.[8] It was not until 1927 that the first old-age pensions for workers were paid out, however, starting in the textile industry in 1927 and extending to workers in other industries over the course of the First Five-Year Plan in 1927–1932.

Pension policy grew even more fragmented and hierarchical under Stalin's leadership. By 1935, there were already around 50 legislative acts governing pensions.[9] Pensions' prerequisites and terms varied by industry, type of job, and the grounds upon which a pension was assigned to its recipient. The first general guideline on pensions and recurring financial benefits, decreed in 1930, set the minimum retirement age for workers at 60 for men and 55 for women, having worked for no less than 25 and 20 years, respectively.[10] Old-age pensioners were entitled to no less than half their wages in pensions. As for so-called invalid pensions for disabled workers, preferential treatment was extended to those injured on the job over those who simply fell ill, and to workers in dangerous industries, such as mining. The same principle applied to the survivor pensions offered to dependent family members for the loss of a breadwinner (*kormilets*). Specialists including cultural workers, teachers, professors, doctors, and other medical personnel earned pensions upon achieving a certain "length of service" (*vysluga let*) rather than a labor period and regardless of age. In the countryside, state farm workers could receive pensions, but collective farmers were ineligible. The latter were encouraged to organize "peasant mutual aid societies" (*krest'ianskie obshchestva vzaimopomoshchi*) to help the elderly and those in need, drawing upon internal farm financial resources.

Pensions were also paid out on an ad hoc basis, regardless of recipients' ages and employment histories, as rewards for distinguished service or achievements on behalf of the revolution, the Soviet government, and socialist society. Old Bolsheviks, members of the political and cultural elites, and award winners like Stakhanovites, as well as other figures of significance along with their family members, were assigned "personal pensions" (*personal'nye pensii*) by decree at the local, republic, and Union levels. This category of pension was controversial: its critics pointed out that personal pensions lacked a clear legal basis and that they were a significant financial burden upon the government.[11] As a result, in 1928, a new law was passed limiting Union-level personal pensions to amounts not exceeding 1.5 times the highest base wage rate paid to a "'responsible" political worker, and, in 1930, they were capped at 500 rubles.[12] Personal pensions nevertheless typically exceeded the amounts received by regular pensioners and were a significant burden on the state budget for the remainder of the Soviet period.[13]

After the Great Break, the Stalinist government turned to pensions as a labor incentive, especially in priority branches of heavy industry. As Andrea Chandler notes, the right to an old-age pension, as well as the more general right to social welfare for groups unable to work, was replaced by the goals of improving conditions and benefits for active workers, and providing privileges to reward groups the regime considered worthy of special recognition.[14] In 1930, unemployment was officially "liquidated" and anyone without a job was now legally ineligible to receive the state's help.[15] In 1931, as the Stalinist wage reforms began and "struggle against leveling" in wages heated up, the Soviet government decreed that the "main aim" of Soviet social security was to benefit the most important proletarian cadres in industry, giving first priority to workers in the coal, metallurgy, chemicals, machine-building, and transportation branches of the economy.[16] In 1932, all workers' pensions were capped at a percentage of a 300-ruble maximum wage amount; priority workers in the leading industries, however, were often granted special waivers allowing them to exceed that amount. For example, if they had worked for no less than two years at the same mine, heavy machinery operators who worked underground were allowed to calculate their pensions using their actual wages, not to exceed a cap of 450 rubles.[17] They were also granted special privileges that allowed them to retire earlier than other workers.

Pensions were used as both a carrot and a stick in the struggle for labor discipline and against excessive turnover. The promise of financial security in old age or upon losing the ability to work was held out as an inducement to quickly settle into a job and work in a disciplined manner for as long as possible. Workers who alternated jobs frequently and who put in effort that was deemed shoddy or inadequate were considered unworthy of that sense of security. A December 28, 1938, decree on labor discipline railed against the "job-hoppers, slackers, shirkers and grabbers" (*letuny, lodyri, progul'shchiki i rvachi*) who "strive to give the government less work and snatch more money for themselves," who managed to "live off the government, off the people," and who received pensions on par with "conscientious" workers who worked in a stable and continuous capacity.[18] In addition to establishing stricter rules regarding sick leave, maternity leave, and the receipt of financial aid and holiday vouchers, the decree established a sliding scale of pension bonuses for labor invalids who achieved a continuous labor period beyond a set minimum, and new age-dependent labor periods for receiving an invalid's pension. Old-age pensioners who continued to work beyond the age of retirement were to receive their full pensions, regardless of the size of their wages.[19] The decree also cracked down on disabled pensioners who received a pension and continued to work, cutting their pensions by up to 50% if they earned amounts exceeding 100 rubles per month. Finally, it set new minimum pension amounts for all categories of pensioners.

The Second World War and mass conscription, more so than any deliberate effort on the part of the Stalinist government, provided more common terms for claiming a pension based on one's own or a family member's military service. Millions of Soviet families' breadwinners were conscripted into the Red Army and perished on the front. Millions of soldiers returned home with debilitating injuries that hindered their ability to engage in gainful labor. Wartime propaganda explicitly encouraged Red Army soldiers and their families to depend upon the state for the money they needed and portrayed them as priority recipients of its assistance. "The Soviet people have never grudged and do not grudge handing over all that is required to insure the Red Army," one pamphlet promised. "For patriots in our country, there is nothing higher and more honorable than care for the Red Army. . . . Care for soldiers and their families is the most important responsibility of all government organs."[20] State spending on social security benefits, including pensions and other forms of financial aid, more than tripled over the course of the war, from 7.9 billion rubles in 1940 to 26.2 billion rubles in 1945.[21]

Receiving the state's "care" after a soldier returned home injured or permanently disabled, or after a soldier died or went missing in action, was a different matter altogether. The Soviet government's generous wartime welfare commitments clashed with the reality of strained financial resources and its goal of rapidly putting the war behind it. Although it continued to promise "great care" for soldiers and their families, it applied stringent standards to the provision of survivor pensions for the families of deceased conscripts. It aggressively pushed disabled war veterans back to work and discouraged them from dwelling upon their misfortunes and relying upon state assistance.

Claiming a pension could be a byzantine process. For example, in order to receive a pension for the loss of a breadwinner, a widow required official certification from the military about the circumstances surrounding her husband's death or disappearance. Until a soldier was declared officially "missing in action" (*propal bez vesti*), his dependents received only the lower amount of recurring aid assigned to the families of mobilized soldiers, not the more substantial pension owed to families of the war dead; if it was later ascertained that the soldier had died on the front, the state would pay out the difference. The amount survivors received depended upon the breadwinner in question's employment history and wage level prior to mobilization: those designated urban workers prior to their military service were entitled to higher pensions than those who lived in rural areas or had any connection to agricultural production.[22] If a mobilized soldier died due to circumstances not directly connected to war service, for example, in an accident or due to illness while conscripted but not during combat, the family was entitled to a breadwinner pension through the social assistance system, but not through the military.[23]

It was common for families to go years without knowing what fate had befallen their conscripted husbands and sons, and, in the meantime, go without the pensions they were legally entitled to and struggle to make ends meet. By 1945, the government was still notifying family members about the deaths of their relatives during the chaos and disorganization of 1941–1942, which it acknowledged was delaying their receipt of survivor pensions.[24] As Zinaida Federovna Novikova wrote in late October 1946, in regard to her husband, Aleksei, whom she had not heard from since August 1941, she had received the same response from the military for the past five years: "There is no information about his location."[25] "All of this frays my last remaining nerves," she wrote. "I am not in a position to provide for my child on my salary alone. Do not deprive my child of what he is legally entitled to from his father! I cannot accept that, after five years, there can be no information about whether a person is alive or dead."[26] She demanded that her family be given the pension it should have received since his death or determined date of disappearance.

To receive their pensions, disabled war veterans had to prove that their injuries occurred on the front or while performing an official military task. They were required to visit medical expert commissions (*vrachebno-trudovye ekspertnye komissiia*), who assessed their injuries and assigned them to one of three disability categories, and to be routinely reexamined and their injuries reconfirmed, even if they were obviously permanent. The state's disability categories were established in 1932 and remained unchanged throughout the war and into the postwar period: first-group invalids were totally unable to work and required constant care; second-group invalids were unable to work but did not require constant care; and third-group invalids had diminished labor capacities but were deemed capable of some form of labor.[27] A war invalid's pension size depended upon his military rank and whether or not he was categorized as a worker or peasant prior to being conscripted. Length of employment and wages earned before the war also affected the amounts veterans received, a policy that disadvantaged collective farmers, who were not paid wages for their work on the kolkhoz, and younger war invalids, many of whom had left high school to go directly to the front and were never gainfully employed prior to their injuries. These individuals were eligible only for lower flat amounts.

If the prospect of a larger pension served as a labor incentive for the able-bodied, the dismal pensions offered to war invalids, especially to those in the largest, third group, served as a disincentive to avoid labor and expect to receive handouts. As Mark Edele argues, after the war, combat survivors became an "entitlement group," claiming a right to special treatment by the wider community, and making claims to scarce goods, services, and public esteem.[28] This was partially due to the wartime practice of making soldiers the Soviet Union's most valued citizens, as noted above. After the war, many veterans expected that their privileges would continue and, for a time, it even seemed as if veterans would become a "Soviet *soslovie* [estate]," as Edele puts it; however, this special treatment was curtailed by late 1947, as the state realized the steep cost these privileges entailed and that "no new Decembrist movement was in the making."[29] For example, initially, third-group war invalids were allowed to receive their pensions on top of their wages, but this policy was discontinued in August 1948, when the Council of Ministers decreed that the amount of a third-group invalid's pension plus salary was not to exceed pre-disability income, only 50% of the pension was guaranteed, and a refusal to work would be punished by cancellation of pension payments.[30]

Finding work could be an insurmountable task and the state provided little direct assistance, leaving many disabled veterans without the means to support themselves and their families. The steep quotas placed on factories during postwar reconstruction meant that managers were reluctant to hire them, especially as able-bodied soldiers were demobilized and returned to the factories in the late 1940s.[31] Work in *artels*, special workshops set up to employ the disabled, involved simplified tasks and correspondingly low pay. Many disabled veterans were forced to resort to illegal strategies to get by, including speculation, theft, and begging in the streets. A significant number of those deemed "anti-social parasitic elements" and rounded up during mass arrests of the homeless in the postwar period were disabled war veterans, many of whom were, in fact, receiving state pensions.[32] As Elena Zubkova emphasizes, receiving a state pension was by no means a guarantee against poverty.[33] The inadequacy of and wide variation in the pensions they received was a source of great discontent. Beate Fieseler notes that it eroded solidarity among them and precluded the development of a collective identity among "comrades in misfortune," for they "eyed each other warily, comparing, calculating, and suspecting others of receiving more."[34] They arrived at every level of the Soviet government virtually daily, complaining about the inadequacy of their pensions and petitioning to have them raised.[35]

Veterans were not the only pensioners to make such complaints. Inflation decimated the value of old-age pensions that had been assigned prior to the war when wages were much lower. Sofiia Briukhova, a schoolteacher in Yaroslavl' oblast who had retired in the early 1920s, wrote a desperate plea to Stalin in May 1946 petitioning to have her miserly pension of 51 rubles per month raised to the current minimum of 150 received by her colleagues who had retired more recently than she had.[36] Even personal pensions that had once been quite generous before the war were greatly depreciated. Sixty-seven-year-old Old Bolshevik M. L. Sosunov petitioned to have his personal pension raised in the summer of 1945.[37] His pension of 360 rubles per month had been assigned at the RSFSR level in 1937. Sosunov wrote that it was no longer sufficient, especially after the death of his two sons on the front, who had provided him with no less than 1,000 rubles per month in supplementary financial support. This was a common plea: in their requests for cost-of-living adjustments, pensioners frequently referred to the informal financial assistance lost when their children perished during the war. Sosunov's pension was ultimately raised to 500 rubles per month considering his history of "revolutionary struggle" and the tragic deaths of his sons.[38]

The government took a half step toward raising all pensions in September 1946, extending the bread allowance to offset increased ration prices to pensioners in the amount of 60 rubles per month. Amid severe shortages in state stores and the persistence of high market prices during the famine, this could only go so far in mitigating the inflated cost of living. Pension privileges for workers in the leading industries, on the other hand, continued to proliferate in the late 1940s, part of the state's ongoing efforts to attract workers to remote regions and dangerous jobs, as discussed in Chapter 2. In 1947, workers in extractive industries, including coal and oil, were given the right to early retirement with a shorter labor period and a pension calculated around a higher maximum wage amount, plus a percentage of what they earned above it, up to caps of 1,200–1,500 rubles.[39] As of April 1949, personal pensions were capped at new maximums of 600 rubles at the republic level and 300 rubles at the local level.[40] However, personal pensions were supplemented by additional noncash privileges: when they fell into financial straits, personal pensioners had the right to petition for "one-time financial aid" (*edinovremennoe posobie*) from social security organs at the levels of government that had assigned their pensions.[41] They were also granted a 50% discount on housing fees, the right to "suitable" accommodation and transportation, and priority access to specialized medical care and prostheses—benefits that surely won them the envy of those who received a "regular" pension, to say nothing of those who were ineligible to receive one.

Toward a "Unified" Pension Law

The Soviet government knew that the vast majority of its pensions were not enough to live on and that its lack of a coherent, standardized pension policy was the cause of a great deal of popular discontent. In a report to Stalin in October 1949, Boris Chernousov, Chairman of the Council of Ministers of the RSFSR, railed against the expanding mass of contradictory rules that governed pension policy: more than 200 decrees, instructions, and circulars had been added to pension legislation since 1938 alone, he noted.[42] He launched into a litany of examples: workers in the leading industries received pensions based on their full base pay rates or amounts that disregarded the 300-ruble cap, war invalids' and other categories of workers' pensions were capped at percentages of different maximum wage amounts, and some republics employed their own norms for calculating pensions. The widows of workers could continue to claim breadwinner pensions if they remarried, but not the widows of dead soldiers.[43] There were no consistent rules regarding the term within which one had to claim invalid status or how these pensioners' labor periods were calculated. Current law contained no provisions for labor invalid pensions in the absence of a complete labor period, and people with only one or two months lacking were often outright denied a pension. The "complexity and contradictions" of existing pension policy caused a great deal of confusion, as well as overpayment and underpayment, and an "excessive stream of complaints and petitions from workers," Chernousov concluded.[44] He urgently requested that the various relevant ministries work together to produce a single all-Union pension law.

By November, a special commission on pension reform was assembled, headed by Arseny Zverev and drawing together representatives from the central government, trade unions, and social assistance organs.[45] Its goal was to "unify" the Soviet pension system, in other words, to bring the various rules and exceptions that currently governed Soviet pensions together under a single law that applied to the vast majority of ordinary pensioners. More than 160 pension decrees and laws were scheduled to be annulled when the new pension law went into effect, plus many ad hoc memoranda, instructions, and circulars that had been sporadically issued over the years.[46]

The draft law they came up with preserved the basic principle of preferential pensions for high-priority workers, but also raised pensions for workers in industries deemed less strategically important. It did not cover all categories of pensioners: science workers, generals and officers of the Red Army, the Ministry of Internal Affairs, and the Ministry of State Security (*Ministerstvo gosudarstvennoe bezopasnost'*), as well as the regular police, were to be granted their own separate pension policies.[47] Its main innovation was to eliminate the 300-ruble wage cap for calculating pension size. It established three categories of pensions, regardless of which branch of the economy a worker was employed in, oriented around pension size: the first group earned up to 400 rubles per month, the second group up to 500 rubles, and the third group up to 600 rubles.[48] Each group's pension norm would now amount to 50%, 55%, and 60% of their wages, respectively, and could total no less than 210 rubles per month. Whatever amount a worker earned over 600 rubles would be calculated based upon a lower percentage of the remainder of his or her wages. Workers would receive a bonus of 5% for every five-year period they worked beyond the minimum labor period, not to exceed 75% of their prior wages. Men would be entitled to receive their full pensions starting at age 65 and women at age 60, while workers in dangerous and difficult lines of work could retire at 55 and 50.[49]

The proposed law reduced some elevated and privileged pensions from their current levels. Invalids' pensions would be set at the midpoint between the higher amounts currently received by labor invalids and the lower amounts received by "general" invalids: 70%, 54%, and 35% of wages would be offered to first-, second-, and third-group invalids, as well as minimum amounts of 250, 200, and 160 rubles, respectively, plus a percentage of wages earned over the norms.[50] The higher norms for survivor pensions that dependents of deceased workers in the most important industries currently enjoyed were to be extended to all families, and new minimums ranging from 130 to 200 rubles per month in the cities would be established. The draft law reiterated the already reduced norms for the assignment of personal pensions at the republic and local levels.[51] These cuts were necessary because the pension reform had to take place within the limits of the already allocated budget for paying pensions in 1950. No additional funds were forthcoming. To offset the remaining cost, the commission planned to eliminate the 1946 bread allowance, which would free up another 2.3 billion rubles.[52]

The new pension law was scheduled to go into effect on October 1, 1950.[53] However, the process of finalizing the law stalled, evidently due to disagreements within the commission about how the law would affect high-priority and privileged pensioners. Zverev asked the Council of Ministers to delay announcing the new law until June 26, 1950.[54] It was not announced then and, instead, went through another round of revisions. New provisions benefiting higher-earning and priority workers were added. The second draft proposed to give science workers and some government employees, as well as arts and culture workers, the option of choosing either their existing pensions under the old decrees that governed them or the new pensions.[55] Coal, metallurgy, chemical, and electrical station workers were to have their pensions calculated on the basis of their full base pay rates without any maximums imposed, or based on a percentage of their entire wages not to exceed 1,200–1,500 rubles.[56] The revised draft law was scheduled to go into effect on July 1, 1952. By then, the various parties involved were still dissatisfied with what they had come up with. The Central Trade Union aggressively lobbied to have the 1,500-ruble cap lifted or softened, pointing out that only around 3% of all workers earned wages above this level and it would not cost the government very much to raise this amount. Leaving the restriction in place would lead to "leveling" in pensions, it maintained.[57] If a cap needed to be imposed, the Central Trade Union wanted it doubled to 3,000 rubles. The pension commission rejected this suggestion. In the summer of 1952, the implementation of the draft law was postponed yet again, now to go into effect on January 1, 1953.[58] It missed this deadline, too.

In the meantime, many pensioners came to view the Soviet regime's lack of a coherent pension policy and the inadequacy of their pensions as major moral failings. As one labor invalid wrote, the state's pension policy divided pensioners into "beloved sons" and "stepchildren."[59] I. N. Egorov, an engineer and old-age pensioner in Sverdlovsk, dispatched an indignant statement (*zaiavlenie*) to the Council of Ministers and the Central Committee, which he titled with the proverb "A full stomach does not understand an empty one" (*Sytyi golodnogo ne razumeet*). In it, he charged Soviet leaders with "having forgotten and not thinking about those who bore the full weight of the struggle against Tsarism, the nobility, and the capitalists on their shoulders, who were the main force in the struggle for, establishment, defense, preservation, strengthening and development of Soviet power—the simple, rank-and-file people, the simple, rank-and-file workers."[60] This issue hit close to home for him: both his wife and his close friend did not receive the pensions they rightfully deserved, in his opinion, because in both cases they were deemed to lack the necessary labor period. Egorov argued that a unified law was needed, whereby every worker, upon reaching a determined age and labor period, should have the right to a pension in the amount of 50% of his or her prior salary, and this right should extend to every pensioner who had already stopped working.[61] In his opinion, a unified law would reduce the "deception and bureaucracy" that surrounded Soviet pensions at present.

After Stalin's death, pension-related complaints grew louder and more frequent. In April 1954, the Central Trade Union's newspaper *Trud* reported that it had received many complaints from pensioners over the years, but recently, around one-tenth of all letters coming in had to do with raising and reforming pensions.[62] "When we are young, we are all assured that, in our difficult moments and our old age, we will not be forgotten about, and we will be guaranteed a minimum standard of living. But this is not so," wrote S. Rushkevich of Sverdlovsk in one such letter, adding: "We are supposed to live on 210 rubles per month, and envy those who get 50% of their wages, even though many of us are of more use to the government than those who receive higher pensions."[63] Even the Soviet Union's most valued workers in heavy industry described complications when claiming their pensions. M. S. Piven', a miner who worked from 1936 to 1947 in the Lena goldfields, was diagnosed with chronic rheumatism and myocardia, whereupon he was transferred to light work.[64] It was common for third-group labor invalids to be transferred to less physically strenuous tasks, but such "light work" typically came with lower wages. Piven' returned to his hometown in Ukraine, where he took up work as a guard, earning a salary of 260 rubles per month before reaching the age of retirement. If he had retired as a miner, he would have been eligible for 50% of his wages and an "elevated" pension; however, his pension was calculated on the basis of his salary from his last, lower-paid job as a guard. His pension of 130 rubles plus the 60-ruble bread allowance rounded out to a measly 190 rubles. "I don't live, I just exist, which I find very shameful," Piven' wrote. "I lost my health in the mine, and I receive a pittance."[65]

In July 1953, a new pension commission was created. In March, May, and August of 1954, three new draft versions of a unified pension law were put forward removing the distinction between standard and elevated pensions but preserving higher urban norms.[66] None were approved. The government went back to the drawing table in the fall of 1954, efforts that resulted in yet another draft law which was sent to Khrushchev in March 1955.[67] Galina Mikhailovna Ivanova suggests that, although his name was not on the document, Georgii Malenkov's imprint was all over the proposal and, as Chairman of the Council of Ministers, it could not have been produced without his knowledge and input.[68] Like earlier reform efforts, it sought to unify the various pension policies under one law, raise the minimum pension amounts, and rein in "excesses." It explicitly linked the receipt of a pension to a worker's productive contributions to the socialist economy. As its preamble read: "The better a worker or employee works, the higher the quality of his work, the better he will be secured not only during his productive life, but also in old age and in the case of disability, and the better protected his family will be."[69] The proposal also envisioned a radically new way of financing Soviet pensions. In order to pay for the new pensions within the limits of the existing budget for 1955, the Soviet government would use some of the money derived from scaling down bonuses and premiums, which, as discussed in Chapter 2, had, by then, come under fire as problematic entitlements instead of incentives for efficiency and productivity.[70] After the new law went into effect, each month, 1% of workers' wages would be deducted toward a "personal savings fund" (*lichnyi fond sberezheniia*) separate from the state's social security fund, to which the state would add one-tenth of the amount workers contributed.[71] Ivanova suggests that Malenkov sought to pivot away from the state's traditional paternalistic approach to welfare benefits, amid his broader efforts to de-Stalinize the economy and reorient it away from its emphasis on heavy over light industry.[72]

The proposed pension law was supposed to go into effect on July 1, 1955. It did not. Instead, the Soviet government embarked upon yet another attempt to draft a new pension law that summer, this time under the supervision of the newly formed Committee on Questions of Work and Wages, the institution set up to devise rationalizing wage reforms and eliminate Stalinist "excesses." Initially, the Committee preserved the "Malenkov plan" to make workers pay into their own pensions through a personal savings fund, but it soon changed its mind; by late August, this measure was declared "impermissible."[73] The finalized law of October 1956 would explicitly guarantee Soviet workers that they would never be asked to pay for their own pensions through deductions from their wages. It was not until 1990, at which point pensions were helping to bankrupt the Soviet economy and the government was on the verge of collapsing, that Soviet authorities would revisit this approach to pension financing.[74]

The 1956 Pension Law

Like many of his colleagues, by the fall of 1955, Khrushchev had concluded that the Soviet pension system was broken. He connected its shortcomings to the same fundamental problems he believed had caused "'excesses" in Soviet wage-setting: if higher pensions had once served to attract workers to the most strategically important lines of work and reward their crucial economic contributions, they now resulted in abuses of the system and "such abnormal phenomena as relatively young and healthy people receiving great pensions, even though they don't work anywhere and live however they want. It provokes enormous criticism," he wrote in his report on the agenda of the upcoming Twentieth Party Congress.[75] "We need to change the legislation on pensions, to raise pensions for workers and employees receiving the lowest amounts and lower the pensions of those categories of workers whose pensions are too high." One source of funding he envisioned was simply reducing the amounts of money given to privileged categories of pensioners. Another was the savings gained by eliminating Stalinist consecutive retail price cuts.[76]

During his speech at the Twentieth Party Congress, Khrushchev lamented the pension system's "serious deficiencies" and disparities.[77] As with his wage reform, he proposed to similarly reduce the divergence in pension amounts by lowering high pensions and raising low pensions, and promised that a new unified pension law would go into effect by the end of the year. He scolded those who willingly accepted higher pensions than many workers earned in wages, as well as those who went on a pension when they still had productive contributions left to make on behalf of socialist society. He praised the example of Kirill Prokofevich Orlovskii, who, after fighting as a partisan in occupied Belarus during the war, losing a hand in battle, and being recognized as a Hero of the Soviet Union, could have fared "not badly" on the pension he received but, as a good communist, could not stand to be idle. Orlovskii demanded to be given work and became the Chairman of the "Dawn" collective farm, the first postwar "millionaire kolkhoz" in the Soviet Union. Khrushchev failed to mention, however, that moving to the countryside and taking up work on a collective farm entailed a financial hit for unremarkable war invalids, who then received only the lower rural pension norm.

Following the Twentieth Party Congress, a new pension commission was assembled, featuring some familiar faces such as Arseny Zverev, but also newer economic experts and rising stars, including Aleksei Kosygin.[78] By May 3, the pension commission had already come up with a plan, which it relayed to the

Central Committee of the Communist Party that day.[79] It proposed a new "unified" law that brought workers, rank-and-file soldiers, sergeants, and lieutenants, as well as members of these groups' families, together under a single set of regulations. It preserved some of the principles animating previous pension policy, in particular the privileges granted to workers in mining and in other dangerous professions, who would still be entitled to higher pensions and earlier retirement, and it continued to draw a division between urban and rural citizens. Anyone who permanently lived in a rural milieu would still only be entitled to a lower rural norm consisting of 85% of the urban norm.[80] Collective farmers remained categorically ineligible to receive a pension under the new law.

The draft law's most significant innovation was to increase pension amounts across all categories of recipients: pensions would rise by 2 times for old-age pensions; invalids' pensions by 41% and 49% for those injured on the job and off the job, respectively; breadwinner pensions by 54%; disabled war veterans' pensions by 48%; and veterans' families by 2 times.[81] Around 25.1 billion rubles were allocated in the state budget to paying pensions that year, which was admittedly not quite enough to cover the costs of implementing the new law; therefore, the government would have to draw upon reserve funds to cover a 12.6 billion ruble deficit.[82] By paying pensioners more money, the new law would dramatically raise living standards in the Soviet Union, the commission emphasized, especially those whose pensions previously had been capped at a percentage of 300 rubles. Just as importantly, it would eliminate the various discrepancies and excesses that currently existed, and it would finally allow most pensioners to stop working. On May 7, 1956, the Presidium of the Central Committee of the Communist Party voted to support the draft pension law, publish it in Soviet newspapers on May 9–10, and examine the law at an upcoming session of the Supreme Soviet, during which Nikolai Bulganin, the new Chairman of the Council of Ministers after Malenkov's ouster, would give the final report on it.[83]

In what was certainly a symbolic gesture to war veterans, the draft law of May 8, 1956, was published in all major Soviet newspapers the next day, on the eleventh anniversary of Victory Day.[84] As the preamble to the draft law boasted, "Pension security is guaranteed by the socialist structure of the USSR, in whose conditions the exploitation of man by man, unemployment, and insecurity is being constantly eradicated." It emphasized that pension financing came "fully at the state's expense," and would otherwise be covered by "socialized funds." The Soviet people's many economic achievements in recent years, under the wise leadership of the Communist Party, had allowed the government to "further improve its pension security."

The draft law echoed some of the proposed improvements included in earlier attempts at pension reform. Men and women retained the right to retire with old-age pensions at 60 and 55 years of age, respectively, with labor periods of not less than 25 and 20 years, while those who worked in dangerous, difficult, or hot conditions received the right to retire earlier with a lower labor period and higher pensions (see Appendix B).[85] The 300-ruble wage cap for calculating pensions was finally abolished. Instead, old-age pensions would be calculated as a percentage of average monthly wages on a sliding scale, from 100% of wages up to 350 rubles, to 50% of wages 1,000 rubles and above. Workers in mining and in dangerous jobs were entitled to 5% higher norms in all wage categories.[86] New minimum and maximum pension amounts were also established: although pensioners had the right to retain pre-1956 pensions if this entitled them to a higher amount, no amount could fall below the new minimum or exceed the new maximum. The law contained substantial bonuses for achieving a continuous labor period of 10–15 years for old-age pensioners, but also for the disabled and dependents of deceased workers.[87] Bonuses were also offered to pensioners upon whom labor-incapable family members were financially dependent, to offset the cost of their care.

The proposed provisions for labor and war invalids preserved the three existing disability groups oriented around a recipient's labor capacity. When it came to nonmilitary invalids, preferential treatment continued to go to those who were injured or became ill on the job, who were eligible for a pension regardless of the length of their labor period, while other invalids faced age and length restrictions and were entitled to lower amounts. The draft law offered better pensions to workers who became disabled as a result of work in the mining industry and other dangerous or difficult jobs, whose pensions would be calculated using higher norms. The same regulation for third-group invalids that required them to work to receive a pension and restricted the size of their pensions from exceeding wages remained in place; however, now, their pensions could not drop below 50% of that amount.[88] The most dramatic changes applied to the pensions of disabled veterans. The amounts they were eligible to receive still depended upon their wage levels prior to conscription, but the norms were increased to 65%, 90%, and 100% for third-, second-, and first-group invalids, respectively, plus 10% of what they earned over those amounts.[89] Those who had been employed in dangerous or difficult lines of work prior to the war were eligible to calculate their pensions using higher norms. Finally, new minimum and maximum amounts applied to all categories of pensioners.

The Soviet government invited suggestions for how to improve the draft law before it went into effect on October 1 of that year. By July, government organs and central newspapers had received more than 10,000 letters from workers, trade union representatives, and the heads of various ministries.[90] Responses published in the Soviet press were rather predictable: under banners like "For the Benefit of the Soviet People" and "A Display of Great Care," workers expressed their unanimous support for the law and their immense gratitude for their new pensions. In an article titled "The Country Is Growing Richer," Eduard Zhuravskii and Kuz'ma Popov, both workers at Leningrad's "Second Five-Year Plan" factory, asked rhetorically: "Could we have even dreamed about this before the Revolution at our factory, under the leadership of the capitalist San Galli [the factory's owner before the revolution]? All that was waiting for workers then was begging and hunger in old age."[91] A. Ignat'eva, a menial laborer in Leningrad, wrote that she began work at age 16 and worked continuously for the next four decades, 25 years in a single factory. Her husband and oldest son died during the war, and she depended upon state benefits as a widow to raise her younger son. "Of course, the years take their toll," Ignat'eva wrote, "but I don't worry about the future. And now that the whole country has learned about the draft law on state pensions, my spirits have lifted, my old age will be comfortable."[92] Everyone in Leningrad was discussing it in the factories and in the streetcars, she claimed, and all agreed that it was fair because the law reflected the principle "As you work, as you will be insured in old age."[93]

Published suggestions for improvement typically fell into two categories: reducing the required labor period, usually by another five years, and improving the pensions offered to the disabled. A group of railroad workers suggested that those who had achieved a longer labor period should be granted the right to retire early at age 55, since they had sacrificed more of their health in the service of their work.[94] Letters criticizing the provisions for invalids referred to the fact that the law made no allowances for those whose disabilities had robbed them of the chance to contribute their labor toward the socialist economy. Marta Timbovskaia, who had been paralyzed since childhood, wrote that she was totally dependent on her mother for care and had never been able to work, and was told she could receive a pension only when her mother died.[95] Timbovskaia argued it was unfair that the law contained no specific provisions for those who had been disabled their entire lives.

Citizens' and institutions' unpublished responses to the law expressed many of the same sentiments, but in a more critical manner. The labor period was a sticking point, both for those who had already completed a long one and for those who had not. Aleksandr Mikhailovich Barashkin complained that, under the old pension law applying to his industry, he was eligible to retire from his job at a train carriage repair factory at age 50, having worked for 34 years and completed the necessary labor period; however, under the new law, he would have to work another 10 years before he was eligible for an old-age pension. He suggested that the new law should allow those who had previously earned the right to retire to do so.[96] M. U. Gorlanov wrote that he had left high school to go to the front and had returned home a "cripple." "Why am I to blame because I was not able to achieve a labor period before the war and am now denied a pension on par with those who work?" Gorlanov demanded. He suggested that war invalids' age should be a relevant factor when determining their assigned pension amounts.[97] Numerous letters maintained that provisions for the disabled were inadequate. A letter from A. Tural'skii and B. Novikov, an economist and an engineer both living in Moscow, praised the new law but argued that pensions for those deemed invalids "for general reasons" needed to be much higher, possibly higher than old-age pensions: in general, they advised that "we need to be honest about the fact that for workers who have been given an evaluation of 'labor-incapable,' it is extremely difficult for them to find a job."[98]

Some Soviet bureaucrats found the new pension law out of touch with the specific needs of their industries. The current Minister of Culture, Nikolai Aleksandrovich Mikhailov, complained that the new guidelines applied awkwardly to many cultural workers—ballerinas typically stopped dancing professionally before the age of 55.[99] He requested to have culture workers' retirement ages reduced and to allow them to retire with 20 years of service, regardless of age. Another point of contention was the draft law's omission of preferential treatment for workers in the Far North and East, who had previously been granted early retirement privileges as one of the perks of an otherwise undesirable job. As the Secretary of the Magadan regional committee of the Communist Party explained, "Far from the industrial and cultural centers of the country, the difficult conditions of life and work in the Far North, the harsh climate of Kolyma and Chukotka . . . exert an intense exertion upon the organism, [and] therefore it is not by accident that the Decree of the People's Commissariat of Labor from 1930 on the regions of the Far North was applied to the most dangerous work in the harshest climates."[100] He requested that these workers have the privilege of retiring at age 50 continued.[101]

Soliciting suggestions was not merely a publicity stunt: their viability was assessed by Nikolai Bulganin and a special legal commission of the Supreme Soviet that was charged with examining the draft law and issuing final recommendations. In response to the most common suggestion, to lower the retirement age and reduce the labor period, Bulganin argued this was impossible because it would draw a huge number of labor-capable and relatively young people out of the workforce and, more importantly, cost another 900 million rubles per year.[102] However, he thought it was possible to do so for the blind and for "mothers of many children" who had to take more time off work for maternity leave. He suggested reducing these groups' retirement ages to 50 and their required labor period from 20 to 15 years. In response to the suggestion that workers in the Far North should be allowed to retain early retirement privileges, Bulganin argued this was unnecessary since they already received much higher wages than other workers, which automatically resulted in larger pensions, and they received several other benefits, like longer paid holidays.[103] He noted that the commission had received many letters about the fact that the law did not cover those who had been invalids since childhood; he thought it was possible to extend benefits to them on par with labor and health invalids. He also thought it possible to increase the bonus for pensioners' dependents up to 20%.[104]

Bulganin publicly evaluated the range of suggestions his commission had received during his concluding remarks at the Supreme Soviet's meeting on July 13.[105] In reference to his review of the many suggestions to lower the retirement age and labor period by five years, he explained that it could not be done because, if the government preserved a differential pension structure, this would reduce the lowest age of retirement to 45 and 40 for men and women in mining, which was far too young to retire. If they were to only reduce the age and labor period of the third group of retirees, the catchall category for all workers and employees who did not work in dangerous or difficult jobs, this would "take us down the path of leveling."[106] Bulganin explained that the government preferred to take a different route, to retain a higher retirement age and create more incentives for working into old age. The commission recommended raising the required labor period to 35 years for men and 30 years for women in order to receive the 10% bonus. The only changes to the labor period he proposed were for mothers of many children, who he argued should be allowed to retire earlier. The Chairman also recommended giving pensions to people who had been disabled since childhood if they worked for at least one year before claiming a pension. He agreed with the suggestion to scrap the clause tying disabled war veterans' pensions to pre-pension earnings, since this disadvantaged collective farmers and those who left school to go to the front, proposing to give these war invalids flat sums. Finally, he argued that the provision prohibiting pensions from exceeding previous earnings, which affected disabled war veterans most acutely, should also be discarded.[107]

In a jovial tone, Bulganin emphasized that his commission had not set out to determine if citizens' suggestions were right or wrong but had merely sought to balance them with financial considerations: "Living on one's means is an old and wise rule. We shouldn't get ahead of ourselves and live beyond our means."[108] Bulganin pointed to the already enormous expense of providing the new pensions, which, when amendments to the draft law were made, would total around 40 billion rubles. "This is a huge sum of money, even for our country," he emphasized. "This law, as you can see, is rich, not poor." Bulganin joked that some deputies of the Supreme Soviet had even suggested special pensions for those who lived in hot climates and for residents of cold climates. He concluded to laughter and wild applause: "Comrades, I believe there will come a day when we will have accumulated so much wealth, and that day is absolutely coming, that we will be able to offer [pension] privileges for the heat and privileges for the cold."[109]

The basic contours of the draft law remained in place, and amendments to the law largely corresponded to those proposed by Bulganin in his speech at the Supreme Soviet (see Appendix B).[110] Old-age pensioners were offered a 15% bonus on their pensions if they achieved a 15-year continuous labor period, with a total labor period of 35 years; women could claim a 10% bonus upon achieving 10 years of continuous labor and a total labor period of 30 years.[111] Blind workers were granted early retirement privileges, as were women who gave birth to five or more children who survived to the age of 18.[112] "General invalids" had to work for at least one year to claim a pension; workers who were injured or became ill as a result of their professional responsibilities could receive a pension regardless of the length of their labor periods. War invalids who had labor-incapable dependents now received a 10%–15% bonus and first-group war invalids received a 15% bonus to assist with the costs of their care.[113] Ten percent bonuses were extended to war invalids who had attained high military ranks, as well as the families of deceased high-ranking soldiers. Perhaps the most important amendment applied to war invalids who had not been workers before the war: they were guaranteed flat amounts that corresponded to the minimums assigned to war invalids as a whole.[114] Finally, the law preserved certain categories of specialists' pension terms based on "length of service," such as those offered to teachers and culture workers, indicating that the Council of Ministers would assign new norms for this category of pensioners at a later date.[115]

Increased Rewards, Diminished Incentives

Beginning on October 1, the day the new pension law went into effect, local executive committees' social security departments (*raionnye otdely sotsial'nogo obespecheniia,* or *raisobesy*), where pension affairs were handled, were inundated with visitors anxious to receive the higher amounts they were now entitled to.[116] One *raisobes* calculated that it saw around 29,000 pensioners in a matter of weeks, completely overwhelming its staff of 25 people, most of whom were young and new to the job.[117] Social security workers were ill prepared to deal with both the volume of visitors and the unforeseen complications engendered by the new law. They were frequently accused of displaying a heartless attitude toward pensioners and of being tactless and rude. In a summary of the many letters of complaint *Trud* received in October and November 1956, the editor wrote that many *raisobesy* had evidently "studied the law poorly, refused to admit to incorrect interpretations, and when in doubt, made decisions [about entitled pension amounts] at a loss to pensioners."[118]

These confrontations often boiled down to a contested understanding, or calculation, of the labor period. Demonstrating the necessary labor period for one's gender, line of work, and category of disability was the basic prerequisite for receiving a pension.[119] This required submitting employment records to the *raisobes,* including the workbooks (*trudovye knizhki*) that had been introduced in 1938 and distributed to all workers in state enterprises during the struggle for labor discipline and the battle against excessive turnover. The workbook recorded one's position and length of employment, any awards won, and the reasons for one's dismissal or transfer. It was supposed to be held for safekeeping by the workplace administration and given to a worker when he or she left the job; however, workers were frequently hired without presenting their workbooks, or they were not given their workbooks when they left. To make matters worse, not every workbook was filled out consistently or correctly.[120] Many workbooks, along with other employment records, were lost or destroyed during the war, especially in occupied territories. Former evacuees were frequently unable to prove their eligibility for a pension, as a result. In the absence of workbooks, many *raisobesy* requested other forms of documentation, such as affidavits and witness statements from managers and coworkers. The necessity of tracking down and submitting ever more documents amounted to bureaucratic red tape from many pensioners' perspectives. As A. S. Zhirkova, a pensioner in Moscow, wrote: "It seems Ariadne's thread, leading you out of the labyrinth, is usually but not always another slip of paper, confirming that you have submitted documents to the *raisobes*."[121]

Proving a "continuous labor period," was necessary to achieve the bonuses built into the new law; however, this was also difficult because the law, itself, did not specify what the word "continuous" meant. This caused, as V. A. Mandrik, an old-age pensioner from Tula oblast, put it, "Babylonian pandemonium [*stopotvorenie vavilonskoe*]."[122] "Everyone wants to know how to interpret article 25a of the law on state pensions requiring a 'continuous labor period,'" Mandrik went on, "that is, does it mean working in one place, or can it mean working at various workplaces without moving around too much?"[123] Virtually everyone's work life had gone through chaotic changes in recent years through no fault of their own. During the war, workers were conscripted into the Red Army or evacuated to distant parts of the Soviet Union. While some workers were evacuated along with their factories, many moved in a much more haphazard way or simply fled East, where they found it impossible to work in their regular professions and took up other jobs, sometimes even on collective farms.[124] Many returned from the war physically incapable of returning to their prior lines of work. Millions went to prison under Stalin's draconian labor laws. The October 1956 law contained no specific instructions on how to account for such disruptions.

Soviet social workers were also stumped by the conundrum of the continuous labor period, as evidenced by the repeated discussions of it in the magazine *Sotsial'noe obespechenie,* the profession's newly founded trade journal, in the winter of 1956–1957. Aside from calls to improve services to pensioners, hire more staff, and provide better training, social workers called for clearer information on how to determine a continuous labor period and more assistance in procuring the necessary evidence.[125] In March 1957, *Sotsial'noe obespechenie* published a legal definition of the continuous labor period in an effort to clear up the confusion.[126] "The continuous labor period," wrote V. Karavaev, a legal scholar, "constitutes lengthy, continuous work on the part of the worker or employee in one and the same enterprise or institute," which, in many cases, included moving from one job to another, breaks between jobs, and, in rare instances, a break in employment.[127] A worker was considered to have a continuous labor period, for example, if he was transferred to another job within an industry by its administration. If a workplace laid him off, or the workplace itself was dissolved, he maintained a continuous labor period if he found new employment within a month, but that month itself would not count toward the labor period. Workers with legitimate reasons to take time off work, for example, those who were declared a first- or second-group invalid whose health improved and who later returned to work, as well as those who received a doctor's note recommending sick leave, would preserve their continuous labor period, although the time off would not always be counted toward it. The article also clarified how wartime disruptions would affect the continuous labor period. Former evacuees were deemed to have a continuous labor period if they had found work within three months of arriving at a site of resettlement—the time it took to get there did not count toward it.[128] An exception was made for those who were residents of Leningrad between August 1, 1941, and February 1, 1944, for whom breaks in employment were forgiven due to the disruption caused by the blockade. If one had lived through Nazi occupation and there was no evidence tarnishing one's reputation, that is, if one was not accused of collaborating with the enemy, that period would also not negatively affect the continuous labor period. Time spent as a conscript in the Red Army and as a partisan counted toward it. Although Stalin's strict labor laws were formally annulled in April 1956, workers who were convicted under the laws and sent to prison were not automatically considered to have a continuous labor period.[129] Only those who were convicted prior to the July 1945 amnesty celebrating the Soviet victory were eligible to have their uninterrupted labor period reinstated.

Despite leaving many bewildered about its requirements, the new pension law had an immediate, positive effect upon most pensioners' living standards: it increased the amounts paid out overnight, and it narrowed the wide prior divergence between pension amounts. Before October 1, 1956, around 1.95 billion rubles in pensions were paid out across the Soviet Union, for an average pension of 149 rubles; as of October 1, that rose to over 3.5 billion and an average pension of 271 rubles.[130] Between October 1, 1956, and January 1, 1957, the number of pensioners in the Soviet Union jumped from 13.6 to 14.5 million people, with the largest growth seen in the number of old-age pensioners and "invalids for general reasons."[131] The average pension amount across all categories increased dramatically, from 155 rubles per month as of October 1, 1956, to 294 rubles per month on January 1, 1958, a whopping 90% increase (Table 3.1).[132] The amounts received by privileged pensioners like former miners also increased, rising to 1.5 times the amounts received by their peers.[133]

Table 3.1 Pension Increases as of October 1, 1956 (standard norms in rubles)

Type of pensioner	Average before October 1, 1956	New average pension amount	New pension as a percentage of the old pension
Old age	224	455	203%
Invalid due to workplace accident or work-related illness	247	357	145
Invalid for general health reasons	170	266	156
Breadwinner pension (for workers)	149	244	164
Breadwinner pension (in the case of a deceased soldier)	94	194	206
Invalids of the Great Patriotic War	151	254	168
Invalids of the Civil War and World War I	50	215	430

Source: GARF, f. 5446, op. 91, d. 577, l. 147–148.

These dramatic raises may have been gratefully welcomed by struggling pensioners, but they caused a headache for Soviet planners seeking to maintain the macroeconomic balances the full-value ruble depended upon. Increased pensions introduced more "uncovered" rubles into circulation, reducing the purchasing power of money in the hands of the actively employed population and non- or less-working pensioners alike. As Gosbank worriedly noted in a March 1957 secret report to the Central Committee and the Council of Ministers, over the period 1954–1956, the population's money income had increased by 22% over 1951–1953 levels.[134] During that period, the population took in 1,488 billion rubles in income, while only 1,403 billion rubles in goods were sold in state stores and an estimated 41 billion in the kolkhoz markets; only 29 billion rubles of the remaining money had been invested in state bonds and 15 billion remained in the hands of the population.[135] The main culprits for this unanticipated excess cash in circulation, it pointed out, were increased payments to collective farmers, whose incomes had more than doubled since the agricultural reforms, but, just as importantly, the new pension law.[136] By 1957, an average ruble now spent 34.7 days in circulation in 1956, up from 29.3 days in 1953. To prevent excess cash from entering circulation, which would have "a negative effect upon the population's prosperity," Gosbank requested that "further initiatives to increase the money income of the population should be conducted only under the conditions of simultaneously locating extra, real sources [of goods] for covering the government's expense."[137]

Table 3.2 Number of Pensioners and Average Pension Size across the USSR as of January 1, 1958

	Number of pensioners (in thousands)		Average monthly pension (in rubles)	
	October 1, 1956	January 1, 1958	October 1, 1956	January 1, 1958
USSR	13,610	15,686	155	294
RSFSR	8,835	10,044	160	299
Ukrainian SSR	2,525	2,989	152	284
Belarusian SSR	401	450	114	139
Uzbek SSR	269	321	140	272
Kazakh SSR	473	564	159	281
Georgian SSR	273	309	141	276
Azerbaijani SSR	172	203	150	301
Lithuanian SSR	57	79	155	276
Moldovan SSR	79	94	114	241
Latvian SSR	135	173	177	316
Kyrgyz SSR	89	99	137	269
Tadzhik SSR	58	67	144	273
Armenian SSR	113	130	154	274
Turkmen SSR	61	73	156	282
Estonian SSR	70	91	152	311

Source: GARF, f. 5446, op. 92, d. 622, l. 82.

The new pension policy also took more people out of the Soviet workforce, which, in turn, produced fewer goods and services for this money to be spent on. After October 1, 1956, millions of pensioners could now afford to stop working and get by on their pensions alone, an additional blow to productivity (Table 3.2). Around 59% of old-age pensioners still worked as of October 1, 1956, but, as of January 1, 1958, only 19% continued to do so.[138] Invalid pensioners saw a more modest decrease as a category, since the vast majority of these pensions were in the lowest, third category of disability, which required them to work to receive a pension. Among labor invalids and the "generally ill," 56% worked as of October 1, 1956; by January 1, 1958, this dropped to 47%. Among war invalids, if 84% worked in 1956, 70% did in 1958.[139] More dramatic decreases were visible at the level of individual categories, however: by January 1, 1958, the number of first-group invalids still working halved, while almost a quarter fewer second-group war invalids now worked—two groups who were not required to be working in the first place. Prior to the pension law, 93% of third-group war invalids worked; as of 1958, this dropped to 82%.[140]

The Soviet government soon began nudging pensioners back to work. In 1961, the Council of Ministers of the RSFSR asked for permission to allow pensioners, many of whom retired to the countryside, to work on collective farms and continue to receive their pensions.[141] Due to the ongoing depopulation of rural areas and the agricultural labor shortage this caused, workers were needed, especially on a seasonal basis, to help bring in the harvest. Under the post-1956 pension law, there was no incentive for pensioners to continue to work, though many were capable of doing so: if they worked, they risked losing their pension entirely or having it cut to 15 rubles per month (new money). In June, the central government sent out instructions permitting the Councils of Ministers of the various republics to allow pensioners to work on state farms and collective farms, with no bearing on their pension amounts.[142]

The number of working pensioners nevertheless continued to drop in the early 1960s. By 1962, it had reached a low of 9.2%.[143] This necessitated more proactive measures. As of a February 26, 1964, decree, old-age pensioners who continued to work were allowed to claim 50% of their pensions under the 1956 law, while those in the Urals, Siberia, and the Far East could claim 75% of their pensions if they continued to work.[144] The new law was touted as benefiting pensioners in moral and economic terms: as the Minister of Social Security of the RSFSR explained, the pensioner was not "severed from the work collective, he maintains his place in the ranks of the builders of communism. Continuing his work, he experiences moral satisfaction. At the same time, he improves his living standards."[145] The number of working pensioners crept steadily upward after the decree went into effect and, within 10 years, around one-quarter of old-age pensioners worked—a phenomenon that was certainly due less to the moral satisfaction of performing socially useful labor than to economic necessity, as inflation undercut the value of pensions assigned in the late 1950s and early 1960s.[146]

Against an "Egalitarian" Approach

One group remained almost completely outside the pension system after October 1956: collective farmers. Many collective farmers received state pensions because of a deceased spouse's or their own military service during the war, but, as a group, they were still ineligible to receive a pension for old age, labor disability, or the loss of a breadwinner. By the mid-1950s, pension provisions for collective farmers through the mutual assistance funds organized at the farm level were acknowledged to be inadequate and, in the case of many farms, nonexistent.[147] Many collective farms still struggled to pay out labor days in money, let alone pensions. Their exclusion from the pension system provoked great discontent among collective farmers, especially among older female peasants, who constituted the vast majority of rural residents by the mid- to late 1950s. As Liubov Denisova notes, many rural women felt that their hard work and sacrifices during the war were ignored, because the 1956 pension law denied them benefits on par with everyone else.[148]

As a result, in the late 1950s, many collective farm members supported transforming their kolkhozes into state farms, which made them eligible to receive workers' pensions at the rural norm, that is, at 85% of the urban norms. When this happened, it often deprived pensions to elderly peasants who could no longer work but lived on the same farm, since their previous agricultural labor did not always add to a complete labor period and their mutual aid pensions were discontinued when the collective farm was dissolved.[149] In late 1959, the Secretary and Undersecretary of the Party bureau of the Dubovo-Ovrazhskii rural soviet of the Krasnoarmeiskii raion of Stalingrad oblast wrote to Khrushchev asking for clarification on this issue.[150] When the "Leninist Path" collective farm in their region was converted to a state farm and renamed "Stalgres" in October of that year, around 98 elderly collective farmers lost the pensions they had been receiving from mutual aid funds, he explained. Per a 1954 decree, a former collective farmer could receive a pension only if he or she had a continuous labor period from 1939 onward and was employed by the sovkhoz at the moment of its reorganization. Many had already stopped working by the time of the conversion, which made them ineligible for a state pension. Though these elderly farmers had no other sources of income, the rural soviet was forced to deny them pensions due to this legal technicality. "If there is some decree that excludes this category of pensions, then we kindly request that you, Nikita Sergeevich, reconsider it," they beseeched him.[151]

The Soviet government approached the task of integrating collective farmers into the state pension system with great caution. Cost was undoubtedly a concern: extending pensions to collective farmers was considered in 1961 and rejected due to the massive additional expenditure the state would have to incur.[152] An equally important consideration was preserving labor incentives among an aging and thinning rural population. With economic growth slowing and acute food crises emerging in the early 1960s, the Soviet government wanted to impress upon the peasantry that they needed to enthusiastically produce the country's food supply. If Soviet pension policy for the urban population contained the implicit threat of economic insecurity as a negative incentive motivating the individual to work in a disciplined manner, Soviet pension policy for collective farmers was far more explicit in linking the receipt of a pension to meeting the state's productivity expectations.

At the February 1964 Plenum of the Central Committee, Khrushchev announced that economic conditions were nevertheless finally amenable to bringing collective farmers into the state pension system.[153] He proposed that all collective farms pay a set percentage deducted from their common income to an all-Union pension fund, just as state enterprises paid into the social insurance fund for workers' pensions. In 1964, that amount would be 2% and, starting in 1965, 4% of a collective farm's income.[154] However, pensions would necessarily be distributed to collective farmers on an unequal basis. Khrushchev claimed that the idea came from "the leaders of progressive farms," who had suggested that less productive farmers should not receive pensions on par with those who labored more intensively and generated more wealth for the country. He concurred: "He who labors more productively, who produces more, should receive more for his labor and should be better insured in old age. This will serve as a stimulus for the leading kolkhozes and for those kolkhozes that are economically weak at present."[155] "By the way," he went on, "workers engaged in industry, we also receive differential pensions. The size of [workers'] pensions depends upon their labor investments, on the character and conditions of their labor." "Therefore, in providing pension security to collective farmers, there should not be an egalitarian approach [*ne dolzhno byt' uravnitel'skogo podkhoda*]. We need to create a system that incentivizes and better insures those who work well, who make a big investment in production. It seems to me that this approach to pension insurance will be fairer and collective farmers will support the suggestion," he concluded, to applause from the audience.[156]

Later that year, at a session of the Supreme Soviet on July 15, Khrushchev announced sweeping measures to "fulfill the Communist Party Program in the realm of increasing the prosperity of the people," including extending state pensions to collective farmers and thus "uniting" the Soviet pension systems.[157] The government's concern with simultaneously preserving incentives while extending "care" to collective farmers was made clear. Khrushchev claimed that measures to improve the population's prosperity, including the new pensions, were possible due to the enormous successes of the Soviet economy, including 58% growth in industrial production instead of the planned 51%, but the government had no plans to stop there. "Economic growth and the increased prosperity of the people is, for us, the most important, the most interesting policy and ideology," Khrushchev declared. As *Pravda* elaborated: "The Soviet people know that the rapid realization of these and other measures to raise the people's prosperity depends upon a ceaseless rise in labor productivity. The more productive a worker is, the most opportunities society obtains to further improve the lives of all workers. From each to society, from society to each!"[158]

The discourse of productivity was even more explicit in the text of the pension law for collective farmers that was published on July 16. "The pension security of collective farmers should not take an egalitarian approach," its preamble read, reiterating Khrushchev's comments at the plenum earlier that year: "The higher the productive labor of collective farmers, the more a kolkhoz produces and sells to the government from a hectare of tillage, the higher its income and the level of contributions to the pension fund, the higher collective farmers' pensions should be. It is better to insure those collective farmers who work well and who make a big investment in socialized production."[159]

At the same time, the preamble echoed one of the main guarantees of the 1956 pension law, reaffirming that payments for pensions would come from the kolkhoz's collective income and from the state, but would not draw upon deductions from collective farmers' personal incomes. Male peasants would be allowed to retire at age 65 with no less than a 25-year labor period, while female peasants would be allowed to retire at age 60 with a 20-year labor period, and 5 years earlier with a 15-year labor period if they had five or more children. They were eligible to receive 50% of their monthly income up to 50 rubles per month and 25% of all earnings above that. The law established a sliding scale of invalid pensions depending on age and required labor period, from 1 to 20 years. The minimum pension amount was set at 12 rubles per month, while the maximum was 102 rubles—on par with the maximum amount allowed under the 1956 law for pensioners who permanently lived in the countryside. The 1964 law promised to gradually bring collective farmers' pensions up to the same level as workers. It went into effect on January 1, 1965, leading many to associate the reform with Leonid Brezhnev rather than Khrushchev, who had been, by then, kicked out of office and forced into retirement, himself.[160]

Conclusion

In his memoirs, Khrushchev wrote that "it could no longer be tolerated that widows of those killed during the war, as well as those who returned from the war unable to work, should be kept on short rations and paid a miserly pension."[161] He emphasized the immense popularity of the 1956 pension reform. "After we had increased pension payments, I remember I made a trip to

Rostov and was walking down the street, and the older people, the people of retirement age, literally shouted out their words of thanks," he reminisced, adding: "In our country some people liked to organize claques to shout out things that would be pleasing to the top leadership. There were actually people who signed up to shout such things. But in this case, the shouting was sincere. People were shouting: 'Comrade Khrushchev, thank you for the pension, thank you for the pension.'"[162]

Khrushchev acknowledged, in retrospect, that providing pensioners with more money meant more demand for food and consumer goods, which the state simply could not supply.[163] At the time of writing, he knew well the frustrations of living as a pensioner in the Soviet Union. This was not due to the terms of his own pension package, which were generous by contemporary standards: a personal pension of 500 rubles per month (new money), as well as guaranteed health care and use of a dacha.[164] Rather, he explained, ordinary people frequently approached him in his retirement regarding "everyday subjects," including the difficulty of making ends meet. Khrushchev, for his part, did not enjoy retired living. Unlike other pensioners who continued to work by choice or out of economic necessity, he was explicitly prevented from having a job for political reasons and was confined to his rural abode, which caused him no end of "moral suffering" and forced him to simply "live out my time," as he put it.[165]

Like wage reform, pension reform was politically fraught because it was fused to one of the Soviet Union's core economic problems: low productivity. The opportunity to earn a higher pension was seen as one of the most effective incentives to stay in one industry and work in a disciplined manner in pursuit of the state's economic goals. Like the Stalin era's wage policy, its pension policy had aimed to reward individual initiative and quality labor but had simultaneously contributed to widespread poverty by emphasizing economic over social welfare considerations. Total warfare had made more citizens than ever before eligible for state pensions, which were portrayed as an important reward for their sacrifices on behalf of the Fatherland, but which were far from enough to compensate for the income lost due to injuries and the deaths of family members. As Bernice Q. Madison writes, "What the 1956 act achieved was a degree of harmony, absent before that time, between the welfare needs of the population and the economic needs of the regime."[166] The 1956 law preserved pension inequalities that served as incentives to put in the best effort and eliminated pension inequalities that had become obvious instances of neglect. The struggle against leveling continued in the Khrushchev era in the realm of pensions but was no longer used as an excuse for extreme inequality.

The state's decision to focus on unifying its pension laws and reducing the disparity in pension amounts rather than reexamining the prerequisites for receiving its "care" nevertheless left cracks in Soviet pension policy that could easily be fallen into. Many citizens could not demonstrate the all-important labor period, let alone a continuous one. Post-1956 pension policy continued to differentiate and privilege those disabled on the job or during the war, putting them above individuals with lifelong health problems that prevented them from, or made it difficult for them to continue, holding down regular employment.[167] Collective farmers were not covered by Soviet pension policy until 1964, when they were given the right to receive pensions in lower amounts than those granted to workers and employees, and at a higher age of retirement. In 1968, collective farmers' retirement ages were reduced to urban levels, but their pension amounts continued to lag behind those of urban workers for the remainder of the Soviet period.

Despite the 1956 pension law's shortcomings, it was undoubtedly more equitable than the previous mass of confusing and contradictory pension regulations, and its positive impact upon the living standards of socioeconomically vulnerable citizens should not be ignored. It raised the amount of money most pensioners received and allowed more people to fully retire in old age or upon developing serious health problems, giving more people than ever before a sense of security about the future, as well as more tangible incentives to perform their jobs well in the meantime. It is no wonder why it was one of the Khrushchev era's most popular reforms. At the same time, as the government was all too aware, higher pensions had ripple effects for the full-value ruble. As with minimum wage increases, pension reform introduced more money into circulation that could not be covered by sufficient goods to spend it on. Putting more money into "unproductive" hands reduced the incentive value of money in "productive" hands, whose labor was crucially needed, in Soviet officials' view, to facilitate the economic growth and abundance that increasing the state's generous "care" for Soviet society's weaker and less productive members depended upon.

4

All Your Wages in Hand

In the Stalin and into the Khrushchev era, a host of deductions (*uderzhivaniia*) were taken off a Soviet worker's wages before he or she picked them up in cash from the factory cashier (*kassa*). These included penalties for any labor infractions he or she committed during a given pay period, such as wasting materials or breaking machinery, as well as deductions for direct taxes and tax-like, but technically voluntarily purchased, "mass subscription bonds"—a peculiar form of forced savings imposed upon the population in the period 1927–1957. Soviet authorities portrayed taxes and bond subscriptions as minimally burdensome and as economically beneficial to the worker who paid them: income lost to taxes returned to him or her in the form of free or subsidized social welfare benefits like health care and education, while income invested in the bonds, which also functioned like lottery tickets, returned in the form of cash prizes, interest, and, eventually, the principal.[1] Bond subscriptions were a "spontaneous" expression of the population's enormous enthusiasm for socialism, and their revenue was channeled to economic development plans such as completing the Five-Year Plan ahead of schedule or building hydroelectric dams.

When it came to taxation, as the economists Grigorii Mar'iakhin and Dmitrii Burmistrov emphasized in a textbook on the subject, taxes were not the foundation of the Soviet state budget, as they were for capitalist governments.[2] By contrast, the Soviet government financed itself with "the proceeds of state industry," much of which admittedly came in the form of the indirect turnover tax that was built into the wholesale prices of producers' goods and, as discussed in Chapter 1, into the retail prices of many consumer products. Though it strongly resembled it, Soviet financial authorities insisted that the turnover tax was not a commodity tax but a means of diverting enterprises' profits back to the state to put toward the people's needs.[3] Along with the tax on profits (*otchisleniia iz pribyli*), a payment state enterprises made to the government after covering their costs, the turnover tax was an essential component of socialist society's "pure income in money form," as the economist Aleksandr Bachurin wrote.[4] This money was, in turn, put aside for the purposes of "socialist accumulation" and the "fund for social consumption" that paid for workers' holidays, educations, and pensions, among other social welfare benefits not enjoyed by workers in the capitalist world.[5]

Writing as a contemporary observer in the mid-1950s, the American economist and expert on the Soviet economy Franklyn D. Holzman rejected these claims as obfuscation. Holzman suggested that Soviet taxation had a much less lofty goal: absorbing excess purchasing power.[6] In other words, taxes and semi-compulsory bonds helped to promote the full-value ruble by taking unspendable money out of citizens' hands or preventing it from ending up there in the first place. Taking together direct and indirect taxes, he calculated that, from 1931 onward, the Soviet taxpayer paid more than half his or her income back to the state and his or her tax burden was double that of an American, even when calculating using Soviet tax standards.[7] Because the Soviet Union had never experienced high living standards, the "psychological burden" of Soviet taxes was undoubtedly greater, in Holzman's opinion.[8] That was why the Soviet government cleverly disguised its taxes in the retail prices of state-produced consumer goods. Despite Marxists' criticism of commodity taxation as regressive—exerting a higher financial burden upon those with a lower capacity to pay—the Soviet government resorted to the turnover tax because it lacked an effective tax inspection and collection apparatus, especially in its early years, and because exclusive use of income taxes would have caused workers to moderate their efforts in the workplace based upon calculations of their after-tax earnings.[9] Commodity taxation thus preserved the value of money as a labor incentive. Elsewhere, Holzman suggested that mass subscription bonds, whose purchase was virtually compulsory, were better classified as a tax.[10] He therefore included them when calculating the Soviet worker's tax obligations, determining that the "tax element" of Soviet bonds was at best two-thirds of their price and, at worst, the entire price of the bonds.[11]

By the mid-1950s, Soviet financial authorities had also begun to quietly acknowledge that bond subscriptions and taxes exerted significant financial burdens upon workers, in stark contrast to their official claims. During the war, state bonds and taxes became more important sources of revenue as income from the turnover tax dried up due to severe deficits of the consumer goods whose retail prices contained it, the contraction of retail trade, and the proliferation of untaxable illicit transactions in the private sector. As a result of income and other tax hikes, direct taxes' contribution to state revenue rose from around 5% to 13% over the course of the war.[12] The sums workers and peasants were expected to pledge to state bonds also skyrocketed. Neither tax obligations nor expected bond subscriptions were significantly reduced from these elevated levels afterward. By the mid-1950s, the Soviet state's own financial obligations had also become cause for concern: after decades of borrowing billions of rubles from the population through aggressive bond subscription campaigns and encouraging "enthusiastic" overfulfillment of subscription norms, by the spring of 1957, the Soviet government owed nearly 260 billion rubles to its citizens, a debt that obliged it to make over 17 billion rubles in interest, prize, and early redemption payments that year alone.[13] Continuing to issue more bonds and accumulate more debt was unsustainable, while repaying what it owed threatened to introduce billions of "uncovered" rubles into circulation as the enormous issues of the war and postwar years matured.

Reducing collective farmers' tax burden was one of the most important ways the post-Stalinist government attempted to simultaneously improve the peasantry's living standards, boost their productivity, and put more food on workers' plates, as discussed in Chapter 1. In the late 1950s and early 1960s, the government turned its attention to the deductions it carved off workers' wages. Khrushchev promised they would soon take home virtually all of their wages at the end of the month: take-home pay—literally, "wages in hand" (*zarplata v rukakh*)—would rise as compulsory and semi-compulsory deductions for taxes and bonds were minimized and eventually eliminated, allowing workers to spend more of their own money on consumer purchases. The Soviet government reduced expected subscriptions to the bonds and then discontinued future bond issues as of January 1, 1958. It simultaneously froze existing bond issues for 20 years, paying out no interest and prizes in the meantime; however, Khrushchev promised that citizens' investments would be repaid in full when the country had become "rich."[14] He went even further when, at the turn of the decade, he unveiled an ambitious plan to fully eliminate income taxes over the period 1960–1965. The Soviet Union would realize workers' "long-held dream": a life free from taxes.

Postponing repaying the state's debt on the bonds kicked the can down the road, but exposed Khrushchev to enormous popular criticism in the meantime. The abolition of mass subscription bonds brought an end to the often dreaded public ritual of subscribing and freed up the equivalent of one month's wages for other expenses; however, the freeze was a big blow to the personal finances of older citizens who had thousands of rubles tied up in these investments and who had counted on getting back the principal within their lifetimes. Many bondholders would not live to see the money they had invested in socialist construction, victory in the Second World War, and postwar reconstruction returned to them. As a result, the freeze was widely seen as the theft of workers' "only savings," a repeated refrain in letters of complaint. The gradual abolition of taxes slightly alleviated low-income workers' tax burdens by raising the minimum nontaxable personal allowance (*neoblagaemyi minimum*), but, within just two years, further planned exemptions and discounts became unfeasible due to a fast-growing glut of unspendable money in the Soviet economy (see Chapter 5). In the fall of 1962, the government's planned tax cuts were indefinitely postponed. By eliminating taxes and bonds, Khrushchev scored points against Stalin's ideological compromises and excesses and, in the case of income taxes, against the capitalist West. These measures also deprived the government of two important levers it had long pulled on to regulate the currency supply.

Taxes in the First Socialist State

Well into the Khrushchev era, when discussing taxes, Soviet leaders made reference to Marx's 1847 essay "Moralizing Criticism and Critical Morality," in which he argued that "taxation is the existence of the state expressed in economic terms."[15] Bourgeois governments were a direct burden on workers in the form of taxes that paid for "civil servants and priests, soldiers and ballet-dancers, schoolmasters and police constables, Greek museums and Gothic steeples, civil list and services list—the common seed within which all these fabulous beings slumber in embryo is taxation."[16] Capitalists mediated this transaction, advancing workers the money they returned to the bourgeois state in taxes, thereby gaining influence over it.[17] If taxes were abolished, Marx concluded, wages would be reduced by the same amount that went into them.

Taxes levied on workers' wages were scorned as a primary source of revenue for the first socialist state; however, the use of taxes was not altogether prohibited, for even Marx and Engels had assigned them an important role in the socialist transition. In *The Communist Manifesto,* they suggested that a "heavy progressive or graduated income tax" could be established for the bourgeoisie, one of the "despotic inroads on the rights of property" the proletariat would take when seizing power from the capitalists.[18] This justified the use of punitive taxes as a weapon against those who lived on unearned income, a means of "expropriating the expropriators."[19] Shortly after the October Revolution, Lenin ordered those subject to Tsarist income taxes to pay them to the Bolshevik government, and, in 1918, the Bolsheviks demanded a one-time extraordinary tax of 10 billion rubles from Russia's propertied classes to fund the Reds' efforts in the Civil War.[20]

During the NEP, income taxes were used to contain the profits so-called capitalist elements could make within the limited private sector of the mixed economy.[21] A progressive income and property tax was introduced in November 1922, initially applying to individuals and enterprises together. After the process of nationalizing enterprise was deemed completed in 1924, the property tax provisions were removed, and income tax rates were established for four categories of citizens: employed workers; self-employed persons; those receiving income from enterprises, rent, securities, and other income classified as "unearned" or "nonlabor"; and juridical persons.[22] In 1926, new progressive rates were adopted for each group, with workers enjoying the most preferential rates. Stalin dismantled the NEP by the end of the decade but left the income tax system in place. Workers continued to enjoy the lowest income tax burdens under his leadership: although they constituted over half of all eligible taxpayers, under a 1926 law, they paid only an estimated 10% of all collected tax.[23]

Beginning in 1927, workers compensated for their low tax obligations through their contributions to mass subscription bonds. After repudiating the Tsar's foreign debt in the wake of the revolution, the Bolsheviks could not obtain foreign loans, forcing them to turn inward for the funds needed to complete the former Russian Empire's transformation into a modern industrial economy.[24] They briefly experimented with "natural" bonds (i.e., in-kind investments in grain or other commodities); however, by the end of 1922, the Soviet government had settled upon a more traditional instrument: lottery bonds paying out interest and offering the chance to win early redemption combined with cash prizes. Although, as will be discussed in Chapter 5, Soviet authorities initially harshly criticized lotteries and banned them during their attack on "bourgeois" gambling, they turned to lottery bonds for the same reason other governments have traditionally resorted to their use: lottery bonds tend to appeal to loss-averse and nontraditional savers, and are more effective than other types of investments when interest in saving is low.[25] With the rampant inflation and economic uncertainty of those years, Soviet citizens had more immediate uses for their money.

At the Fifteenth Party Conference in 1926, the success of rapid industrialization was argued to depend, in part, on better exploiting the Soviet Union's internal financial resources, including citizens' incomes and savings.[26] After a successful trial run in 1927, in which workers were pressured to subscribe to that year's 10% lottery bond within their workplaces, mass subscription bonds were issued to support each phase of the Five-Year Plans. These also took the form of lottery bonds: one could purchase interest-paying (*protsentnye*) bonds, combined interest-paying and prize-eligible (*protsentnye-vyigryshnye*) bonds, or noninterest-paying (*bezprotsentnye*) bonds that promised a better chance of winning a prize but offered no regular interest payments.

Revenue from the bonds supported flagship Soviet construction projects, such as the Dnieper hydroelectric dam in southeastern Ukraine. Because the money borrowed went directly into the national economy and toward "productive ends," socialist state bonds were portrayed as inherently superior to their capitalist counterparts, including the bonds sold by the former Tsarist government, which were used to finance oppressive imperial agendas (Figure 4.1).[27] Moreover, as one 1934 propaganda tract explained, capitalist countries typically resorted to increasing taxes to repay the money they borrowed, the burden of which necessarily fell upon the working class; by contrast, Soviet bonds would be repaid never by raising taxes but only with the "growing proceeds of the national economy."[28]

As with all other areas of the Soviet command economy, mass subscription bonds were subject to ambitious quotas at the level of the republics, oblasts, territories (*kraia*), and autonomous republics (ASSRs), as well for urban and rural subscribers. Workers' subscription quotas were determined by the sum of the average monthly wage fund. Ideally, workers subscribed for at least 100% of their own average monthly wage, taking into consideration their base wages, piece rates, and any premiums they earned. That sum was then deducted directly from their wages in 10 equal installments with a brief reprieve before the next year's campaign began. Peasants, by contrast, were expected to contribute minimum set amounts based on anticipated earnings from their individual plots of land. Because their subscriptions were demanded in cash and up front, rural residents were often more resistant to subscribing to the bonds than their urban counterparts and these areas often failed to meet their assigned quotas. According to one estimate, their prewar contributions to state bonds totaled only about 17% of all subscriptions.[29]

Figure 4.1 **Mass Subscription Bond Poster, 1929. "What the funds from state loans were spent on in Tsarist times and what they are spent on now."**
Ne Boltai: A Collection of 20th-Century Propaganda. Used with Permission.

Although the bonds' purchase was never publicly deemed anything but voluntary, an expression of workers' and peasants' enthusiastic support for Soviet power, the annual subscription campaigns were extremely coercive. Most of this pressure was applied by the Commissions for Contributions to State Credit and Savings (*Komissii sodeistviia goskreditu i sberegatel'nomu delu*, better known by the short form *komsody*). These groups of financial activists, who allegedly emerged "spontaneously" during the first mass subscription bond campaign in 1927, were embedded in every factory, office, and collective farm to oversee the subscription process. The *komsod* conducted "mass agitation-explanatory work" (*massovaia agitatsionnaia-ras"iasnitel'naia rabota*) during the subscription campaigns and provided services to bondholders afterward, such as routinely checking for their colleagues' unclaimed lottery winnings. This was, in fact, a somewhat valuable service, since the winning serial numbers were published in newspapers and personal subscriptions to newspapers were rare, meaning that many citizens' winnings went unnoticed for months and even years. Their unofficial task was to ensure that their coworkers met and ideally surpassed subscription norms. They organized competitions between factories and collective farms to achieve the highest subscription sums, pitting workers and brigades against one another in a manner that resembled socialist competition. This escalation of subscription sums was personally advantageous to *komsody* activists. Although these were technically volunteer positions, they were not unpaid: they were eligible for monetary bonuses consisting of a percentage of the total sum of subscriptions they individually collected.[30]

After it was announced on the evening radio, the bond subscription campaign typically kicked off with an assembly of all the workers in a given factory, office, or farm the next day. Activists and workplace authorities delivered rousing speeches about the bonds' vital importance to socialist construction. The sum a factory would collectively contribute was then put to a vote, and, as one Soviet citizen recalled, "There was never a vote cast against such a resolution."[31] After the speeches, the *komsody* distributed subscription sheets and kept a watchful eye on their colleagues' reactions. Workers could sign up individually or as members of a collective, settling upon a sum and divvying it up among its members. Those who refused to sign up or who gave less than everyone else could expect, at the very least, to be pulled aside for an "explanatory" chat with the members of their *komsod* or with workplace authorities, and, at the worst, to face political accusations. "You signed up just to have peace," another citizen recalled. "If you did not sign up you were regarded as counter-revolutionary and pro-capitalist and pro-fascist."[32]

The mass subscription bond campaign evoked the old concept of "collective responsibility" (*krugovaia poruka*) in which village elders used their local authority to compel their neighbors to meet their tax obligations to the imperial Russian state, a practice that resurfaced in many areas of Soviet life.[33] Party and Komsomol members, local authorities, Stakhanovites, and factory managers, among other upstanding citizens, were expected to serve as role models and enthusiastically subscribe to the bonds in amounts exceeding their peers. Eugenia Belova and Valery Lazarev observe that, within the Communist Party, candidate members were required to purchase state bonds as a token of their loyalty before they were admitted to full membership; in their view, such onerous expenses were part and parcel of a "promotion contract" in which activists, who typically held ordinary jobs, invested substantial time, money, and effort in order to be promoted to a position of privilege later.[34] Their enthusiastic contributions also helped to push up the baseline subscription amounts expected from their less enthusiastic peers.

Increased Obligations

As centralized consumer production ground to a near halt in the wake of the Nazi invasion in the summer of 1941, revenue from the turnover tax quickly dried up. Direct taxes and bond subscriptions took on vital importance as sources of state revenue and as means of preventing excess rubles from entering into circulation during the war, as well as retrieving some of the windfall that fell into peasants' hands due to skyrocketing market prices. By the end of the year, the number of eligible taxpayers in both the cities and the countryside had been increased significantly, as had the amount of money they were expected to pay in taxes. Within less than two weeks of the start of the war, a wartime premium was applied to existing agricultural and income taxes, increasing the former by 100% and the latter by 50% or 100% depending on income level.[35] In late November 1941, a "tax on bachelors, single persons and small families of the USSR" (*nalog na kholostiakov, odinokikh i malosemeinykh grazhdan SSSR*, hereafter the "bachelor tax") was introduced to help raise funds for orphanages and boost the birthrate, already seen as key to the Soviet Union's postwar economic recovery strategy in light of its massive casualties in the first months of the war.[36] With the introduction of the war tax in January 1942, the temporary premium on agricultural and income taxes was eliminated and a sliding scale of taxes, from 120 to 2,700 rubles, was now owed.[37] Both the bachelor tax and the war tax were poll taxes: no one who was eligible to pay on the basis of age and other criteria was exempt on the grounds of earning below a minimum threshold. However, recognized needy social categories, including the families of mobilized or deceased conscripts, as well as disabled war veterans, were offered "tax benefits" (*nalogovye l'goty*) reducing or eliminating their obligations entirely as demonstrations of the state's "care" for those most directly affected by the war.[38]

Workers' taxes were increased once again in the war's second half in response to rising income, excessive currency printing, and the state's desperate need for revenue and, in the case of the bachelor tax, to replace the war dead. With the introduction of a new income tax scale in 1943, workers began paying income tax on wages of over 150 rubles per month, the minimum base wage rate (Table 4.1).[39] Workers who had more than three dependent family members were now eligible for a 30% deduction on the amount of income tax they paid. With the introduction of a new Family Law on July 8, 1944, that provided recurring financial benefits to single mothers and mothers of many

Table 4.1 Income Tax Schedule for Workers as of May 1, 1943 (in rubles)

Monthly income	Sum of monthly taxes	
151–200	2.25 rubles	+ 5.5% of the amount of the monthly wage surpassing 150
201–300	5 rubles	+ 6% "___" 200
301–400	11 rubles	+ 7% "___" 300
401–500	18 rubles	+ 8% "___" 400
501–700	26 rubles	+ 10% "___" 500
701–1,000	46 rubles	+ 12% "___" 700
1,001 and higher	82 rubles	+ 13% "___" 1,000

Source: "Ukazy prezidiuma verkhovnogo soveta SSSR o podokhodnom naloge s naseleniia," *Vedomosti verkhovnogo soveta SSSR,* No. 17 (May 1, 1943): 4.

Table 4.2 Bachelor Tax Rates as of July 8, 1944

	Workers and employees	Collective farmers and independent farmers	All other citizens
No children	6% of income	150 rubles per year	90 rubles per year
1 child	1% of income	50 rubles per year	30 rubles per year
2 children	0.5% of income	25 rubles per year	15 rubles per year

Source: "Ukaz prezidiuma verkhovnogo soveta SSSR ob uvelichenii gosudarstvennoi pomoshchi beremennym zhenshchinam, mnogodetnym i odinokym materiam, usilenii okhrany materinstva i detstva, ob ustanovlenii pochetnogo zvaniia 'mat'-geroin' i uchrezhdenii ordena 'materinskaia slava' i medali 'medal' materinstva," *Pravda,* July 9, 1944, 1.

children, the bachelor tax rates were increased, and the range of taxpayers was dramatically expanded (Table 4.2).[40] All citizens with fewer than three children now had to pay the tax, and the childless rate was increased to 6% of workers' monthly income. Peasants and other citizens who did not earn standard wages continued to be levied lump sums, payable in cash to their local financial organs.

The Soviet government issued four war bonds over the course of 1942–1945. Subscriptions poured in in staggering amounts, far surpassing quotas and demonstrating the "fiery patriotism" of the Soviet people, but also stepped up coercive pressures.[41] Citizens bought so many bonds, their purchases frequently exceeded the bonds' physical availability; instead of the paper coupons, they simply received serial numbers. If before 1942, subscriptions among workers never reached the ideal sum of 100% of the average monthly wage fund, usually not surpassing two-thirds, by 1945, subscriptions reached 120%.[42] Budgeted expenses for paying prizes, interest, and redemption payments totaled 5.3 billion rubles by 1945, up from 0.9 billion rubles in 1940.[43] State debt to the population rose from 39 billion rubles on January 1, 1941, to 125 billion rubles by the start of 1947.[44]

Workers' increased tax and bond subscription obligations were not substantially reduced after Victory Day. The war tax remained in effect until the end of 1945, engendering much confusion and discontent in Soviet workplaces as workers returned to peacetime production norms and their wages correspondingly declined.[45] The last deductions for the war tax came off workers' December wages, and in January 1946, the government liquidated the 660 million rubles in arrears still owed by the rest of the population, mostly by peasants and individuals who paid their taxes not via wage deductions but in cash to local financial organs, money that financial authorities acknowledged was likely not retrievable.[46] Additional tax relief came later that year with the introduction of the "bread allowance" on September 21, 1946, when the tax-exempt personal income allowance was raised from 150 to 260 rubles.[47] Nontaxable stipend amounts for students were also raised from 210 to 260 rubles starting that September. After these provisions went into effect, there were no changes to the nontaxable income allowance for another 10 years.

Over the course of the early 1950s, the government repeatedly narrowed the range of bachelor taxpayers, but these cuts stemmed less from its desire to ease the population's tax burden than from its desire to reduce wasteful expenditure on hopelessly chasing arrears. In 1949, the taxation expert Mar'iakhin wrote a critical report on the bachelor tax in which he showed that, by 1948, around one-third of planned bachelor tax revenue simply failed to be collected and, in some republics, the sum of arrears exceeded 50% of what was owed.[48] Most of this money, he pointed out, was owed in cash by nonworkers, that is, primarily by peasants and others who did not work in industrial jobs, who could not have deductions taken directly off their wages. The bachelor tax, he emphasized, contradicted the Soviet principle of progressive taxation, especially in the countryside. Because they paid in lump sums, high-earning peasants paid less tax as a proportion of overall earnings compared to low-earning peasants: for example, a childless collective farmer who earned 1,500 rubles a year paid 150 rubles, or 10% of his or her income, in bachelor tax, while a childless collective farmer earning 9,000 rubles paid the same 150 rubles, which constituted only 1.6% of his or her income.[49] Moreover, the bachelor tax was more frequently paid in rural than urban areas because of the war's more severe demographic impact in the countryside, and a given peasant household often had more than one female bachelor taxpayer drawing upon the same household income.[50] After several attempts to reform the way peasants were levied the bachelor tax, including transforming it into a premium tacked on to the agricultural tax, peasants were finally mostly exempted from paying it altogether following the agricultural reforms of August 1953.[51]

The bachelor tax was also extremely regressive for some segments of the urban population. As discussed in Chapter 2, women typically earned among the lowest wages in the Soviet economy; the maximum 6% rate applied to the wages of millions of childless women was a very noticeable loss. It also put strain on the household finances of severely disabled first-group war veterans who were incapable of having children.[52] First- and second-group disabled war veterans' pensions were nontaxable, but many of their wives did not engage in paid labor because they took full-time care of their spouses (indeed, by definition, first-group invalids required constant care), meaning that their pensions were effectively taxed because they were the only source of household income. Their wives were still, in principle, capable of bearing children and thus still owed the bachelor tax.[53] The Ministry of Finance received many "quite justified" complains about this phenomenon, as Arseny Zverev acknowledged in the spring of 1951; that April, the wives of severely disabled war invalids were finally exempted.[54]

Alongside taxes, the Soviet state continued to lean heavily on mass subscription bonds as a source of state revenue and as a means of confiscating excess purchasing power after the war. Though the 1946 subscription quota was 7.3 billion rubles lower than that of 1945, it was still three times higher than it had been in 1940.[55] Subscriptions still poured in in enormous amounts. The first State Bond for the Reconstruction and Development of the National Economy of the USSR (*Gosudarstvennyi zaem vosstanovleniia i razvitiia narodnogo khoziaistva SSSR*) was issued May 4, 1946, for a sum of 20 billion rubles. That spring, the Chairman of the Soviet of Ministers of the RSFSR petitioned to bring down his republic's assigned subscription quota by 80 million rubles, arguing that it was unrealistic, especially for collective farmers, given the devastated state of farms that had survived occupation, as well as declining market prices.[56] By May 10, however, each republic, including the RSFSR, had overfulfilled its subscription quotas—in the case of the RSFSR, by 108.2%.[57] Total subscriptions across the Soviet Union equaled 100.1% of the monthly wage fund.[58] The second issue of the Reconstruction and Development of the National Economy bond, issued on May 4, 1947 also for a sum of 20 billion rubles, was similarly oversubscribed by more than 2.9 billion rubles.[59]

The December 14, 1947, currency reform revalued all mass subscription bonds held by the population prior to the Second Reconstruction and Development of the National Economy bond of 1947. All bonds subject to conversion had original terms of 20 years. The 2% lottery bond of 1948, into which all applicable mass subscription bonds were converted, extended the terms of citizens' investments by an additional 20 years beginning January 1, 1948. The conversion took place over the period May 3–August 1, 1948, and the bonds were converted at a ratio of 3:1, old for new. This significantly reduced the value of these bonds and freed the government of most of its wartime debt to the population. The government obtained an additional bonus in the form of bonds that were never presented for conversion, either because they were lost or destroyed or because the bondholder had perished. An estimated 18.1 billion rubles in bonds were not converted in 1948, rendering them worthless after the August 1 deadline, which was strictly enforced.[60]

These losses were not acknowledged by the Soviet government, which asked citizens to focus on public over private considerations when it came to the bonds' eventual payoff. Late Stalinist propaganda portrayed the rising revenue generated by the bonds as a collective "gain" to socialism, funding the Soviet Union's reconstruction efforts (Figure 4.2). Soviet activists thus pushed citizens to give to the bonds "enthusiastically" in the last years of Stalin's life, even as after savings were wiped out and as their household finances continued to be strained. During the war, it was common for wartime activists to pledge twice the amount of their monthly wages, sometimes more, while issuing a "call" (*prizyv*) to others to take up their challenge.[61] This practice persisted long after the war had ended. As B. S. Ivanov wrote in a 1950 letter to the Council of Ministers, he was happy to subscribe to the bonds, "knowing full well where those funds go," but social organizations promoting subscriptions were full of "zeal without knowledge" (*userdie ne po razumu*); in other words, they were fervently committed to a good cause but undermined it through their use of aggressive tactics.[62] These "leapers" (*pryguny*) tried to influence their peers to subscribe for ever more outlandish amounts with every passing year, he explained: this year, they were pushing citizens to subscribe to the current bond for 180% of their average monthly wage.[63] The Soviet government was clearly trying to create a prosperous life for its citizens, as evidenced by the recent repeated retail price decreases, he emphasized—it could not possibly want people to subscribe for more than they could afford, could it? Soviet citizens were

Figure 4.2 **Poster for the National Economy Bond, 1951. Bottom caption: "Our gain is their loss." In the background is a map of hydroelectric dams titled: "Great Construction Sites of Communism" and a 1951 bond. Off to the right side is a capitalist holding an atomic missile and a sign that says: "War plans."**
Ne Boltai: A Collection of 20th-Century Propaganda. Used with Permission.

free to subscribe for whatever amount they wanted, but mass attempts at influencing this decision were harmful and should be prohibited, in Ivanov's opinion.

Since each spring saw the announcement of a new bond like clockwork, it was not uncommon for local authorities to engage in extensive preparations, including informing citizens of the minimum subscriptions that would be expected of them and collecting "advance subscriptions" (*prezhdevremennye podpiski*) weeks beforehand. This provided extra time to convince reluctant citizens to cough up the money, especially among more intransigent rural citizens, and it allowed authorities to produce evidence of a rapidly fulfilled plan when the formal announcement was finally made. It also contradicted the spirit of "spontaneity" that supposedly animated the subscription process. Central authorities officially condemned the practice: on July 3, 1947, the Council of Ministers issued a decree, "On the Gross Distortion of the Practical Realization of the State Bond of 1947," in response to alarming reports it had received regarding the collection of advance subscriptions from peasants in Kirov oblast and an even more egregious case in the Azerbaijani SSR, in which peasants across the entire republic were levied 142.3 million rubles in subscriptions before the new bond had even been officially announced.[64] Advance subscription "discredits Soviet state bonds," the decree stated, adding that only "broad explanatory work among the population will ensure full receipt of funds for the Second State Bond for the Reconstruction and Development of the National Economy of the USSR."[65] Yet, reports suggest it continued to be tolerated at lower levels of government well beyond this point.[66]

Amid the high cost of living in the postwar period, steep bond subscriptions placed an onerous financial burden upon struggling low-income workers and pensioners, in particular. The bonds not only entailed withheld income, but it was extremely difficult to access the money invested in them before their redemption date, which was repeatedly postponed. Since 1930, when a so-called unification of Soviet state bonds took place and all previously issued bonds were converted into a new "Five-Year Plan in Four Years" Bond, extending the redemption date and lowering the interest rate, the *komsody* maintained "social control" (*obshchestvennyi kontrol'*) over the bonds. This granted them the right to decide if their peers were allowed to sell or mortgage their bonds under "exceptional circumstances," such as house fires, prolonged illnesses, or a death in the family.[67] The *komsody* were notoriously stingy in their decisions about Soviet bondholders' right to sell.

A Soviet citizen could, however, lend himself or herself a portion of the money that he or she had lent to the state. After 1936, when the bonds were converted a second time, a special decision from the workplace *komsod* was no longer required to mortgage one's bonds and workers could relatively freely obtain loans of up to 30% of the value of their bonds at a savings bank.[68] The loan garnered a low rate of interest: 0.5% for the first six months and 1% per month afterward. The one catch was that, during the loan period, mortgaged bonds were excluded from the draws for prizes and early redemption. Around 21.3 billion rubles were mortgaged in 1937–1941, before the practice was discontinued one day after Nazi Germany's invasion of the Soviet Union.[69]

Alternatively, Soviet citizens petitioned authorities at all levels of the Soviet government to be allowed to sell a portion or all of their bonds back to the state. In the late 1940s, especially at the height of the 1946–1947 famine, many petitioners arrived at the Reception of the Presidium of the Supreme Soviet desperately begging for the Chairman's help selling their bonds as (technically) the highest political authority in the country, something the Reception staff noted they had not seen even during the war itself.[70] N. M. Maralin, of Moscow oblast, a war invalid who had lost both his hands on the front, requested to sell 3,500 rubles of bonds in April 1947.[71] The Chairman, Nikolai Shvernik, agreed to help, and Maralin was allowed to sell back 1,000 rubles of his bonds. Others were not so lucky. In May 1949, Vasilii Nikolaevich Samoshkin, a disabled worker from Moscow, wrote a personal plea to Stalin asking for permission to cash in his bonds and put the money toward treatment at a sanatorium. Samoshkin admittedly bypassed the *komsod* in his workplace, "knowing that, only under exceptionally desperate circumstances, the State Credit commissions allow you to sell your bonds," and sent his letter to the Minister of Finance instead. He was denied, and so he turned to Stalin personally. "Iosif Vissarionovich! I have spent my entire working life on the job, working for the good of the Fatherland," he wrote. "All my savings accumulated during this time, for a sum of 8,000 rubles, are invested in Soviet state bonds, I have no other savings."[72] Samoshkin's request was denied a second time.[73] Samoshkin repeated his request a third time in a petition to the Council of Ministers, which, in September, asked that the Main Administration of State Savings Banks and State Credit (*Glavnoe upravlenie gosudarstvennykh trudovykh sberkass i goskredita*, or *Gostrudsberkass*), the branch of the Ministry of Finance that oversaw the bonds, reconsider his request due to Samoshkin's difficult circumstances and worsening health.[74] It is unclear if his request was finally granted.

A Growing Concern

The enormous sums of money produced by Soviet citizens' purported "enthusiasm" for state bonds made for excellent propaganda—the paper bonds, themselves, depicted the many economic accomplishments their revenue financed, including the construction of new factories, hydroelectric dams, and even Moscow's Seven Sisters skyscrapers (Figure 4.3). As a supposedly clear manifestation of that "enthusiasm," each "Reconstruction and Development of the National Economy" bond issued in 1946–1950 was substantially oversubscribed, in particular the 1950 issue (Figure 4.4). Yet, oversubscription to the bonds also caused the state's long-term debt to the population to grow to dangerously high levels and increased the government's burden of repayment. By 1951, when the word "reconstruction" was dropped from the bonds' title, the Soviet state's debt on these bonds already totaled 146 billion rubles, up from just 28.7 billion after the currency reform, which had lopped two-thirds off its total

Figure 4.3 **State Bond for the Development of the National Economy of the USSR, 1953. A 10-ruble issue of the 1953 bond. Depicted in the background are the accomplishments the bonds helped to fund, including factories, hydroelectric dams, and the Seven Sisters skyscrapers in Moscow.**
Reproduced from the author's collection.

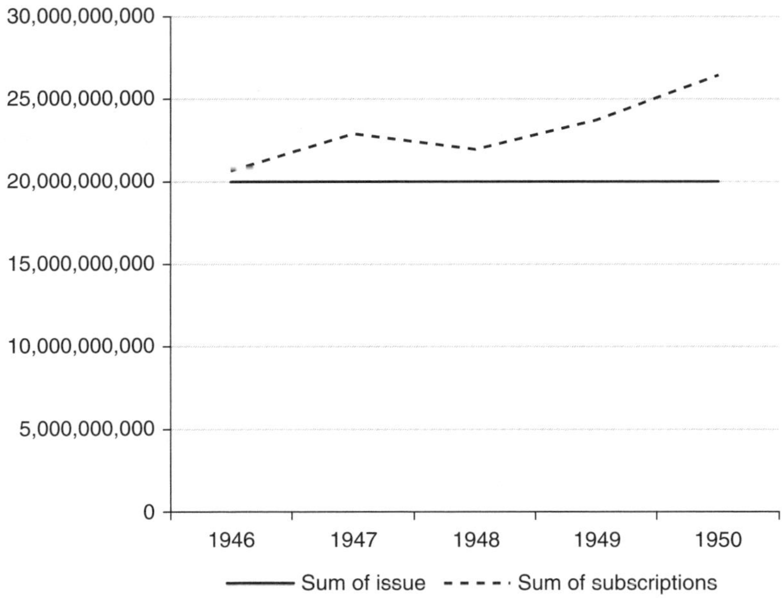

Figure 4.4 **All-Union Subscription Figures for the Reconstruction and Development of the National Economy Bonds, 1946–1950**
Data sources: GARF, f. 7523, op. 39, d. 968, l. 24; op. 40, d. 845, l. 21; op. 41, d. 888, l. 6; op. 42, d. 677, l. 19; op. 58, d. 3452, l. 49.

debt.[75] The state paid out 5 billion rubles to the population in interests and prizes that year alone.[76] The Ministry of Finance began to sound the alarm, not only about the size of the government's debt on the bonds, but about the serious consequences of releasing such an enormous amount of cash into circulation in the form of returns on those investments, money that could not be covered by sufficient consumer goods to balance the population's income and expenses.

In the early-to-mid 1950s, the Soviet government struggled to rein in the coercive social dynamics of the subscription campaigns that were the primary cause of oversubscription. After 1952's subscription campaign produced more than 6 billion rubles above the target of 30 billion rubles, bond issues in 1953 and 1954 were halved to 15 and 16 billion, respectively, and 1954's campaign was only slightly above target (Figure 4.5). However, the 1955 issue was back up to 30 billion. That year, Zverev instructed financial workers, republic authorities, and executive committees that "observance of the voluntary principle" (*nabliudenie printsipa dobrovol'nosti*) was now expected of them. Paradoxically, full participation by workers and peasants was still expected, and workplaces were instructed to collect subscriptions "in an amount exceeding that established by the Government."[77] Enterprises should not push workers earning less than 700 rubles a month to subscribe for any more than three weeks' pay, while workers earning more than that should not be allowed to subscribe for any more than one month's wages.[78] That year's subscriptions fell over 2 billion ruble lower than the target of 32 billion.

Bringing collected subscriptions closer to targets was not enough to avert a looming crisis, the Ministry of Finance argued. In a late January 1956 memorandum, Zverev warned that the state's payments on the bonds could not continue at current levels. By 1960, interest and prize payments would reach an estimated 37.7 billion rubles, up from 30.2 billion rubles in 1955, or a rise of 25%.[79] Although expected subscription amounts were scheduled to be reduced—in 1956, workers' contributions to the bonds were set at 71.5% of their average monthly pay, and this was planned to drop to 67.5% in 1960—the government now owed 228 billion rubles on the bonds.[80] By the end of the Sixth Five-Year Plan, that figure would rise to 350 billion and, in 1960, the Soviet government would pay out an estimated 21.5 billion. Zverev floated the possibility of having workers contribute only two weeks' pay toward them, and, by the end of the current Plan, the government should abolish the bonds altogether. He emphasized that this would have the added benefit of raising real wages and stimulating workers' productivity. Furthermore, it would let the

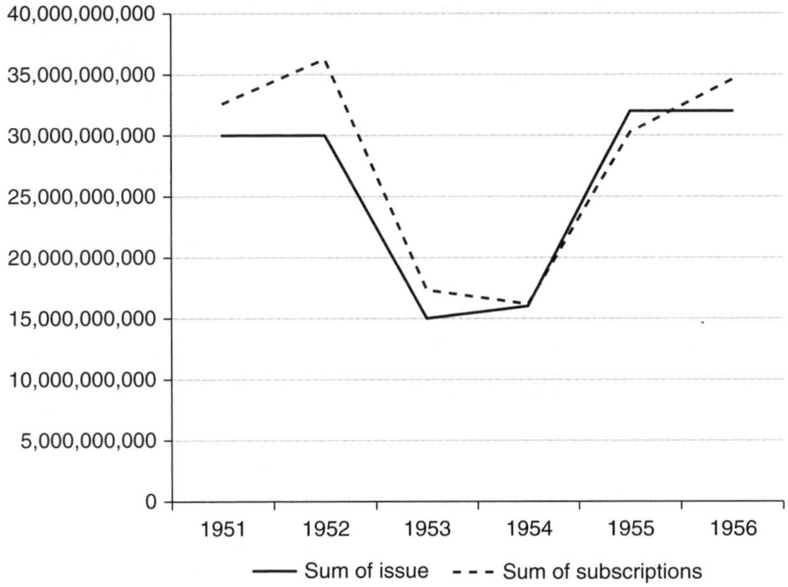

Figure 4.5 **All-Union Subscription Figures for the Development of the National Economy Bonds, 1951–1956**

Data sources: GARF, f. 7523, op. 58, d. 3471, l. 74; op. 85, d. 476, l. 2; op. 85, d. 489, l. 2; op. 75, d. 1663, l. 59; RGAE, f. 7599, op. 21, d. 106, l. 121.

government develop emergency financial reserves that the government desperately needed to pay for, among other social welfare commitments, its recent pension raises. Those funds were currently being wasted on paying prizes and servicing interest payments.[81] In the spring of 1956, as the new campaign approached, Zverev instructed financial activists not to allow their peers to subscribe for any more than three to four weeks' pay, and workers earning less than 400 rubles a month should only be allowed to subscribe for two weeks' pay.[82]

The Soviet government continued to encounter ingrained habits in the bond subscription process, however. In many workplaces, managers simply ignored the new subscription norms for low-income workers and activists continued to zealously hand over more than was expected as a public display of gratitude to the government—though, ironically, this was exactly the opposite of what it now wanted them to do. As a May 15, 1956, report on the campaign's progress explained, "fatherly care for the prosperity of the Soviet people," including the reduced workday, care for mothers and children, health care and holidays for workers, and the new law on pensions, all figured prominently in workers' declarations regarding how much they planned to contribute.[83] One Order of Lenin bearer and widow, a certain Comrade Miakushina, declared: "I pay nothing for my children's education and clothing. I recently received a good room, and every day I feel the government's fatherly care for me. My children are not orphans. I am subscribing to the bond because I want to thank the Party and the Government for their enormous care and I request that they accept my subscription in the sum of 1,250 rubles, that is, both my monthly wage *and* my pension" (emphasis mine).[84]

Workers who dared to pledge a lower amount, even one that complied with the new directives, were often pressured to give more than they could afford and suffered repercussions when they refused. A. T. Suslova detailed her experience of being pressured to commit a whole month's wages in a bitter letter of complaint to Aleksei Kosygin.[85] After pledging an unsatisfactory amount, she was called into the office of her foreman, who suggested that she subscribe in the amount of 640 rubles, the entire sum of her March wages. "Without saying a word," she took the pen from him and signed up for only 600 rubles. Shortly thereafter, the machine belt from her workstation was removed. She was informed that she was punishing her coworkers who had subscribed for "all that they could," and she would not be given any more work to do.[86]

By the spring of 1957, the government owed nearly 260 billion rubles on the bonds, having more than doubled its debt to the population in just 10 years (Table 4.3). Central authorities finally addressed the problem head-on at a meeting of the Presidium of the Central Committee on March 19, 1957. During this meeting, they decided that, after conversing with workers in flagship factories in Moscow, the government would discontinue future issues of mass subscription bonds and would default (*sdavat'*) on existing bonds, which would "stay in the hands of the bondholders (as a symbol of their investment in the common project of building socialism)."[87] The Presidium of the Central Committee returned to the matter again on April 4, meeting to discuss a draft version of a decree on the bonds and to decide whether or not it should issue a new bond before, simultaneously, or after the end of mass subscription bonds was announced, since one had already been budgeted for that year and the government could not do without its revenue.[88] It was decided to announce both simultaneously.[89]

Table 4.3 Government Debt on Mass Subscription Bonds as of April 1, 1957 (in billions of rubles)

Year of issue	Name of bond	Sum remaining in bonds	Sum of redeemed bonds	Amount of debt
—	State 2% Bond of 1948	29.8	5.4	24.4
1947	Second State Bond for the Reconstruction and Development of the National Economy of the USSR	22.1	6.1	16.0
1948	Third State Bond for the Reconstruction and Development of the National Economy of the USSR	22.2	5.2	17.0
1949	Fourth State Bond for the Reconstruction and Development of the National Economy of the USSR	24.1	4.6	19.5
1950	Fifth State Bond for the Reconstruction and Development of the National Economy of the USSR	27.1	4.2	22.9
1951	State Bond for the Development of the National Economy of the USSR	33.7	4.0	29.7
1952	State Bond for the Development of the National Economy of the USSR	36.8	2.6	34.2
1953	State Bond for the Development of the National Economy of the USSR	15.0	0.8	14.2
1954	State Bond for the Development of the National Economy of the USSR	16.5	0.6	15.9
1955	State Bond for the Development of the National Economy of the USSR	32.9	0.4	32.5
1956	State Bond for the Development of the National Economy of the USSR	33.0	–	33.0
TOTAL		**293.2**	**33.9**	**259.3**

Source: RGANI, f. 5, op. 30, d. 222, l. 19 (report to the Central Committee from Zverev on the state's debt on mass subscription bonds, circa late March 1957).

In early April 1957, Khrushchev publicly broached the topic during meetings with workers and peasants, not in Moscow as initially planned, but during a trip to Gorki. In a speech to agricultural workers on April 8, he praised the Soviet people's willingness to lend such enormous sums of money to their government over the years, which, he argued, demonstrated their enormous faith in Soviet power and in the Communist Party, and had helped to raise the Soviet Union from a backward, illiterate country to an industrial superpower within only a few decades.[90] The bonds had been integral to stabilizing the postrevolutionary economy and had funded rapid industrialization during the Soviet Union's years of capitalist encirclement and economic isolation, he went on. "The capitalists didn't lend us a farthing," he noted proudly.[91] The bonds had also helped to ensure a Soviet victory in the Second World War and to rapidly rebuild the economy afterward. Over time, however, they had become a drain on the state's finances. The government was now stuck in a "vicious cycle": in 1957, around 16–17 billion rubles would be spent on prizes and redemption payments, while in 1958, the government would pay 18 billion rubles, and by 1967, 25 billion rubles, almost the entire sum that would be obtained from planned proceeds of the bonds in 1957.[92] "It turns out that the government puts money from the bonds into one pocket and pulls out the same amount of money from the other to pay prizes," Khrushchev lamented.

Khrushchev proposed a compromise: the government would issue no bonds as of 1958, but it would issue a halved bond of 12 billion rubles, instead of the 26 billion-ruble bond originally planned for 1957. Doing without even those 12 billion rubles was impossible, he told the crowd, because the government had budgeted for this revenue and it did not have 12 billion rubles' worth of goods to release into the retail trade system to absorb the excess cash that would be left in Soviet citizens' hands. After this last bond was issued, the government would abolish mass subscription bonds altogether and freeze citizens' existing investments for 20–25 years, he went on. This was not what the Presidium of the Central Committee had agreed upon at its March 19 meeting, and it is unclear if Khrushchev proposed this measure spontaneously or deliberately against its wishes.[93] Khrushchev emphasized the great benefits of the proposed approach: the freeze admittedly asked workers to make a 20–25-year sacrifice of their savings, but it left them with more of their wages in hand right now. He compared it to the prizes won by the lucky bondholder: in the future, "each month he will win on his wages, in the amount of one month's wages per year. This is a more tangible prize, whether or not he wins."[94] He promised that payments on the bonds would resume within 20–25 years or the bonds would be cashed out, a decision that could be made later. "It won't make much of a difference," Khrushchev claimed, "because in twenty years' time, our country will have become rich."[95]

Khrushchev's statements in Gorki set into motion a series of meetings in workplaces across the Soviet Union to "discuss" the government's proposed resolution concerning the bonds. Agitators went into these meetings armed with evidence of the plan's many benefits. By postponing payment on the bonds, 62 billion rubles would be freed up before the end of the current Five-Year Plan, and 106 billion rubles over the course of 1961–1965, to devote to capital construction, including the construction of private apartments.[96] Agitators were to encourage Soviet citizens to focus on the many free social welfare benefits they had received from the government and would increasingly receive in the future, such as better housing, schools, hospitals, and cultural establishments, rather than on the damage to their personal finances.[97]

During these meetings, some called upon their coworkers not only to express their unanimous support for the government's plan, but to voluntarily cancel the state's debt and request that their bonds be counted as sources of state revenue. These donations recalled earlier cancellations of the state's debt during the war, when millions of rubles in bonds were contributed to the Red Army fund as citizens' personal donations to the war effort.[98] Auto garage workers in Tul'skaia oblast, for example, offered to hand over all their bonds to the government, calling upon their fellow workers to do the same in order to "strengthen the power of the Fatherland."[99] Just as they had earlier "sacrificed" toward the bonds, elites, activists, and Party members now eagerly forfeited decades worth of savings. Fifty-five-year-old A. S. Bakaliaev, a Party candidate member and instructor at a machine-building institute in Zaporozh'e, donated 40,435 rubles in bonds he had accumulated over the years.[100] Bakaliaev emphasized that he did not need the money: he had earned a good salary of 1,600 rubles per month before claiming his pension of 600 rubles, he had a good apartment in a new building, he received quality health care, and he was otherwise "materially secure."[101] Others made more humble donations: P. T. Samorukov, of Molotov oblast, declared: "I am a Party member and an invalid of the Patriotic War. I ask that you accept my modest savings toward the construction of communism."[102]

Negative opinions appear to have been far more widespread, if not voiced openly, judging by the higher volume of critical letters the Council of Ministers received in the lead-up to the freeze's formal announcement on April 19. Many letter writers called into question the legality of Khrushchev's proposal, and highlighted the manipulative character of the meetings held to discuss it. One group of workers decried the freeze as "a violation of socialist legality, such as existed under Stalin, Ezhov, and Beria."[103] An anonymous letter writer from Leningrad, who called the meetings "so much hypocrisy," pointed to a duality in the behavior of those who attended: "True, at the meetings you see only 'smiles' and you hear only shouts of approval—that's all for show. Indeed, under Stalin we also applauded and approved such decrees 'unanimously.'"[104] Many flatly rejected the state's argument that the freeze was in the interests of both the government and workers, calling it what it was: a default. "Extending the term of the redemption of government bonds by 25–45 [*sic*] years is equivalent to totally liquidating these bonds," a group of workers wrote, adding: "The remarks of Comrade Khrushchev, regarding the ongoing campaign to discuss the question of the bonds at the local level, appear to have been cunningly arranged in advance and are a psychological attack on the people, directed at the well-being of working families and their only form of savings."[105] Some emphasized that older citizens would be disproportionately affected by the policy, for they would reap none of the financial rewards that had long been promised to them. "Please bear in mind that freezing state bonds for twenty years will deprive [low-paid employees and pensioners] of the possibility to improve their material conditions with funds that actually belong to them," A. Ogureeva of Moscow pleaded.[106] "Older people who worked honestly on behalf of the Fatherland and pensioners will be hurt terribly," R. Ivanov of Michurinsk complained, adding that the "clamor" surrounding the bonds could be exploited by foreign enemies to win support for a counter-revolution such as had recently occurred in Hungary in 1956.[107]

The official decree issued on April 19 made no reference to any of these objections, claiming that an "overwhelming majority" of citizens across the Soviet republics supported the government's plan, a "unanimity" that demonstrated the measures were timely and necessary, and met the needs of both the Soviet state and the people.[108] The Central Committee of the Communist Party and the Soviet government expressed their "deep gratitude to all workers for their unanimous support and their vast satisfaction, a fact that, time and again, testifies to the superior political consciousness of the Soviet people and the indissoluble unity of the Communist Party, the government, and the people of our country."[109] The decree explained that, because revenues from state bonds had already been budgeted for 1957, a new, smaller bond had to be issued for a sum of 12 billion rubles and a term of five years. Subscription amounts were not to exceed two weeks' wages, and individuals receiving less than 500 rubles per month in wages, pensions, or stipends were to be exempt from subscriptions. As of January 1, 1958, no future mass subscription bonds would be issued.

The last Soviet mass subscription bond was announced on the radio on the evening of May 14, 1957. The lead article in *Pravda* the next day, titled "In the Interests of Government, in the Interests of the People," declared that the new bond would help to accomplish the historic goals laid out at the Twentieth Party Congress, especially the goal of raising living standards. The collection of subscriptions was to "strictly adhere to the voluntary principle," however; "there is no doubt that workers, collective farmers and intelligentsia will happily subscribe."[110] The issued sum of 12 billion rubles was almost three times lower than the previous year's bond, and less than half of the 26.6 billion rubles originally scheduled to be collected in the 1957 budget.[111] That December, Gostrudsberkass calculated that the bond was oversubscribed by over 6 billion rubles, for a sum of 18.43 billion.[112] "Enthusiasm" was expected of the Soviet people one last time.

Reducing the Worker's Tax Burden

In the wake of the abolition of mass subscription bonds, several workers suggested the government should go one step further and eliminate another unpopular, unnecessary, and burdensome deduction from their wages: income taxes. "You openly and directly announced that it is not economically feasible to continue to issue state bonds," wrote Ivan Mironovich Tokarev, a self-described "non-Party Bolshevik" and bearer of the Order of Lenin, in a letter he dispatched to Khrushchev the same day the abolition of the bonds was announced. "Now they have become obsolete. The whole country agrees with you," he went on, suggesting that "perhaps workers' income taxes have also outlived their usefulness."[113]

A popular complaint centered on the fact that the Soviet tax system had become extremely convoluted and the government should simply reduce workers' wages by the amount they paid in tax. "In response to the question 'How much do you make?' you frequently hear 'In net terms, I earn . . .' How strange is it that the term 'net income' has entered our workers' lexicon!" G. N. Chukaev exclaimed.[114] Would it not be easier, he asked, if the government simply reduced the wage fund by the amount it subtracted for income taxes and the bachelor tax? "The socialist system of accounting should be simple," he argued. Many bookkeepers, whose job it was to keep track of these deductions, agreed. In their letters of complaint, they pointed out that the state's system of multiple separate taxes on income was the source of frequent disputes between workers and bookkeepers when wages were paid out, not to mention an enormous amount of paperwork to contend with. "It's no secret that our current manner of calculating taxes is cumbersome, requiring much labor input and time to determine how much to withhold in taxes," one Leningrad bookkeeper, Fedor Vasil'evich Popov, complained.[115] The Ministry of Finance, whose raison d'être depended upon the administration of these taxes, consistently rejected the suggestion to abolish them outright. It pointed out that it was impossible to reduce wages by flat amounts because most workers' income still revolved around piece rates, which meant that their wages fluctuated, sometimes quite significantly, from month to month.

Yet, by the late 1950s, even financial officials were forced to admit that the Soviet income tax system had its share of shortcomings and, as some suggested, undermined the Party's stated goal of raising living standards. For one thing, it did little to improve the economic circumstances of those who responded to the state's postwar imperative to increase family size. In a late 1956 report, tax experts compared Soviet working parents' income tax burdens to their peers in the United States, England, France, and the People's Democracies of Eastern Europe. Capitalist countries, they concluded damningly, offered workers with children higher nontaxable income allowances than the Soviet Union: for example, in the United States, the nontaxable income for a family with three dependents, consisting of a wife and two children, was calculated to be 65% of the average industrial wage in 1956, while it was only 51% of the average industrial wage in the Soviet Union that year, 724 rubles.[116]

The bachelor tax had long been criticized as an unfair burden for the infertile and especially for single women. Due to the deaths of millions of men on the front, finding a partner with whom to have a child in or out of marriage was a virtually impossible task for many women into the mid-1950s, and single motherhood still carried a social stigma in some citizens' eyes. As a December 1956 report to Nikolai Bulganin noted, many letters of complaint singled out the bachelor tax as a "contrived and unwarranted, unnecessary measure" that was "not in accordance with moral norms," for it encouraged young men and women to have children regardless of if they were married and penalized those who did not. Moreover, they argued that the state should not be encouraging workers to have as many children as possible until those children could be adequately provided for.[117] "Is it fair to demand a tax on childlessness from a person who does not have the means to start a family and at the same time diminish the material conditions that would make it possible in the first place? No, it's not fair," one letter writer fumed, suggesting that a tax on childlessness would only be appropriate for citizens who earned enough to provide for a family and simply did not want one (underlined in the original).[118]

It is difficult to say if popular discontent eventually swayed the Soviet government's opinion on the bachelor tax. Within the Ministry of Finance, critics like the outspoken tax expert Grigorii Mar'iakhin had been emphasizing its regressive nature and pushing for reform, with limited success, since the late 1940s.[119] Khrushchev, however, remained a staunch proponent of it: in 1955, he publicly boasted that it was he who had originally suggested the tax during the war and claimed that, despite the many complaints the government received about it, the law was sound and the bachelor tax yielded "great benefits."[120] Nevertheless, in late 1957, he ordered the Ministry of Finance to study the question of whether it was now financially possible to do away with or significantly alter it.[121] Zverev responded that eliminating the tax altogether would necessarily involve "certain financial hardships" due to the ongoing discrepancy between the population's money income and expenses. Regardless, the Ministry of Finance agreed that the bachelor tax needed to be abolished. Given that year's financial constraints, it proposed doing so only for people who had one or two children, which would free 18 million citizens from paying the tax and would require finding only around 2 billion rubles to replace the lost revenue in the state budget. Zverev advocated postponing its complete abolition until the following year. To cover the government's additional expenses for the Family Law's provisions in the absence of bachelor tax revenue, the government planned to raise the price of vodka, "taking into consideration that it is not a necessity and that this will help to restrict its consumption."[122] In other words, it planned to plug the resulting hole in the budget with increased turnover tax revenue.

On December 18, 1957, the Supreme Soviet issued a short notice announcing that the new exemptions would go into effect as of January 1, 1958.[123] Increased alcohol prices went into effect the same day. The country's massive economic success purportedly allowed it to "strengthen the Soviet family and increase care for children and mothers," especially for low-income large families.[124] At the same time, the fundamental "fairness" of the tax was reaffirmed, especially for men who "do not have children and do not have the expense of raising them," for "preserving this tax for this category of persons is aimed at making them participate in the state's expense for providing material help to workers and employees with large families."[125] The decree freed 26 million people or 85% of all previous taxpayers from the tax, while around 4.3 million people would continue to pay it. Following the new exemptions, the tax now applied only to single men and married childless couples, but, to many citizens' chagrin, still made no accommodations for those who were physically incapable of having children.[126]

Soviet citizens were not the only ones who harbored objections to the way their income was taxed. In a 1958 report produced under the auspices of the Ministry of Finance's internal think tank, the Scientific-Research Financial Institute (*Nauchnyi-issledovatel'skii finansovyi institut,* NIFI), Mar'iakhin recommended completely overhauling the Soviet tax system, which, he pointed out, was a product of the Second World War and had not been significantly changed since.[127] Mar'iakhin stressed that his proposed changes would by no means entail increasing the Soviet citizen's tax burden, which, he emphasized, was "fully adequate."[128] Under conditions of commodity-money relationships and the ever-growing incomes of the population, taxes, especially the income tax, were an important means of redistributing income to the population, he went on. "Without supporting leveling," progressive income taxes helped to "diminish wage discrepancies and realize the principle of socialist payment for labor," he continued. Income tax reform could undoubtedly assist in raising the population's living standards, he concluded, but the current income tax system featured many flaws that prevented it from becoming a more effective tool in this "struggle."

Among its many deficits was the fact that it did not differentiate taxpayers on the basis of family size, which necessitated additional measures to rectify this "abnormality," including the bachelor tax; however, in Mar'iakhin's view, the bachelor tax "not only does not rectify this abnormality but exacerbates it," for it had absolutely no impact upon the finances of citizens with dependent family members.[129] The current nontaxable personal allowance, he went on, was pitifully low: after 1957's minimum wage raise, it was still only 450 rubles. With the "growing material-cultural needs of the population," the minimum living wage needed to be increased, as well as the nontaxable personal allowance.[130] More problematically, the lowest tax rate (5.5%) had not been changed since 1943, nor had the highest tax rate (13%), though wages had increased considerably since. The first two rungs of the income tax scale now fell below the lowest tax-exempt wages and the third and fourth did also when additional tax privileges were taken into consideration. This meant that, in effect, the tax scale was not 5.5%–13% but 7.5%–13% upon wages of 500–1,000 rubles and above.[131] Citizens whose incomes fell between 451 and 1,500 rubles per month contributed only about 18.6% of all taxes paid.[132] The rest came from citizens who earned over 1,500 per month, for whom the income tax was, in effect, a flat tax. In sum, the current income tax system led to much over- and under-taxing and resulted in billions of rubles in lost revenue for the Soviet government.[133] As possible solutions, Mar'iakhin proposed changing the tax schedule to more accurately reflect the current distribution of income levels, starting with incomes of 500 rubles and progressively taxing incomes up to 2,001 rubles and above.[134]

In a letter to Zverev, Bachurin, then the Ministry of Finance's head of taxes and collections and a representative of NIFI, endorsed Mar'iakhin's suggestions, especially his proposal to use taxes to better redistribute income to low-paid workers and to large families and to scrap the bachelor tax as a standalone tax.[135] The institute had also discussed the suggestion to abolish taxes altogether and reduce salaries by the same amount levied, Bachurin went on. This suggests that, already by the fall of 1958, the idea to completely abolish income taxes had begun to gain traction within the central government. However, NIFI concluded that the abolition of income taxes was inadvisable because it would complicate the piece-rate and premium payment system for workers. Instead, it recommended gradually raising the nontaxable personal allowance, freeing an increasing number of workers from paying taxes.[136]

Mar'iakhin's and Bachurin's recommendations fell on deaf ears. In early January 1959, the Ministry of Finance was ordered to figure out if the complete abolition of taxes was financially feasible.[137] After years of hostility to the mere suggestion, Arseny Zverev surprisingly responded in the affirmative. He reported that, as of then, 90% of all state revenue came from socialist enterprises, from the turnover tax and profits tax, and taxes from the people constituted only 7.8% of budgeted revenue.[138] Because taxes from the people constituted such a small amount of revenue, Zverev concluded it was indeed possible to abolish them. He recommended implementing the policy in a gradual way, through one-time salary decreases in the amounts that were previously paid in tax for time-workers, and by revising piece rates and base pay for those whose income depended upon fulfilling norms.[139] This, he argued, would ensure that the abolition of taxes did not represent a significant loss of revenue. Finally, Zverev recommended scrapping the long unpopular bachelor tax.[140]

Workers' "Long-Held Dream"

During his speech to the Twenty-First Party Congress on January 27, 1959, Khrushchev boasted that Soviet economic growth would rise to levels "unheard of in capitalist economies."[141] As discussed in Chapter 2, he identified this extraordinary growth as the main reason the government could now afford to raise minimum wages and pensions, and launch other measures to improve the population's living standards during the Seven-Year Plan. By its end, Khrushchev argued that the "socialist accumulation" of enterprises would become the single source of funds securing the Soviet Union's ongoing development and the continuing growth of living standards. "Under these conditions, the existence of taxes from the people is unnecessary, not from the point of view of their class meaning, as was the case in the past, to limit the earnings of capitalist elements, nor from the point of view of securing revenue for the state budget of the Soviet Union," he argued.[142] It was now possible for the Soviet Union to discontinue the practice of collecting taxes altogether.

Khrushchev wasted no opportunity to exploit the abolition of income taxes in the Cold War rivalry between communism and capitalism and between East and West. In his farewell speech during his September 1959 visit to the United States, he proudly announced: "In the near future we're going to abolish—and I repeat, abolish—all taxation of the people—and I think you will appreciate the significance of this step."[143] The statement was a provocative one given the context, taxes being one of the causes of Americans' own revolution. No American was less impressed than Franklyn D. Holzman. In an open letter to the *New York Times,* he dismissed the move as a sleight of hand on Khrushchev's part, explaining that income taxes were a less important source of Soviet state revenue than sales taxes, that is, the turnover tax. "The Soviets may prefer not to call their sales taxes 'taxes on the population' but in their most essential sense this is what they are," Holzman wrote. "And even if Khrushchev abolishes what he calls 'taxes on the population'—the income tax—this will not abolish the heavy burden on the population for Soviet government expenditures."[144]

Upon returning to the Soviet Union in the fall of 1959, Khrushchev met with an ad hoc commission on the abolition of taxes, and with the chairmen of the republics' Councils of Ministers. Representatives from the Councils of Ministers recommended doing away with both the agricultural tax and the bachelor tax in addition to the income tax; however, the commission concluded it was impossible to consider abolishing the agricultural tax without first revising procurement prices.[145] The agricultural tax was therefore left out of the proposal they submitted to the Presidium of the Central Committee in late February 1960. In their proposal, they recommended eliminating taxes beginning with the income tax paid by workers and employees, since it was the most substantial portion of all taxes paid—of the 59.2 billion rubles in taxes included as revenue in the state budget, 46.3 billion were income taxes from workers and employees, the bachelor tax comprised 5.5 billion, and the agricultural tax, 4.1 billion.[146]

The commission recommended that the abolition of income taxes should accomplish the following goals: echoing the language of the abolition of mass subscription bonds, it should "observe the interests of the government and the people"; help to reduce the income gap between the highest- and lowest-paid workers and employees; apply to tariff rates so as to ensure that the lowest-paid workers received more take-home pay and to avoid a multiplicity of rates; and, finally, low-income workers in the first tax bracket should be exempted first. While the taxes paid by workers in the lowest tax bracket were abolished, those in the next bracket would receive a 40% tax cut each October 1, from 1960–1962; in 1963–1964, workers earning 700–1,000 rubles would receive 40% tax cuts each October 1 before everyone's taxes were abolished on October 1, 1965.[147] Under this plan, the first tax cut, scheduled for October 1, 1960, would free 15.7 million, or 26% of the industrial workforce, from paying income taxes, and would see 7 million people, 12% of all workers, paying lower taxes. Simultaneously, the commission recommended freeing citizens from paying the bachelor tax in the same graduated manner. The abolition of the income tax and the bachelor tax would result in a predicted loss of 77 billion rubles in state revenue by 1965, which would be compensated for by reshuffling funds to make use of money that had been budgeted for further minimum wage raises, as well as savings from Khrushchev's wage reforms, and money set aside for retail price subsidies.[148] The plan nevertheless predicted a deficit in 1960–1962, which necessitated releasing no less than 5 billion rubles in consumer goods for purchase each year, to help bring in revenue via the turnover tax.[149] The end of income taxes would raise the real wages of workers and employees by 40% by the end of the Seven-Year Plan and workers would receive an average of 33% more take-home wages.[150] Afterward, the sum of taxes from the people (excluding the agricultural tax) would amount to around 3 billion per year and would consist primarily of taxes paid on irregular income, such as rent paid by boarders or compensation for repairs. The plan was approved by the Presidium of the Central Committee of the Communist Party, the Council of Ministers, and the Central Trade Union in late February.[151]

During his speech before the Supreme Soviet on May 5, 1960, the same speech in which he announced the 1961 currency reform, Khrushchev argued: "The end of income taxes is workers' long-held dream. But can it occur under capitalism? Of course not!"[152] He referred to Marx's argument that income taxes supported bourgeois governments and pointed out that a continuous increase in taxes was inherent to capitalist economic systems. The Soviet government, he admitted, had been forced to resort to income taxes in the past, not as a means of exploiting workers but in order to build socialism. However, since the Great Patriotic War, their role in the budget had continuously diminished. Furthermore, since Stalin's death, out of "care" for workers, the government had followed a consistent course of lowering taxes and had put more money into workers' hands by eliminating their onerous contributions to mass subscription bonds. Khrushchev linked the abolition of taxes to the government's commitment to raising workers' real wages and reducing income inequality as stated at both the Twentieth- and Twenty-First Party Congresses. The abolition of taxes would proceed "not upon the principle of leveling, but in a differentiated way," he explained, "from the premise that the wages that should rise most of all should be those of low-paid workers and employees. In this manner, the discrepancy between workers with low and high rates will be reduced."[153]

These tax cuts did not extend to collective farmers and the agricultural tax, Khrushchev admitted. The agricultural tax needed to be "temporarily preserved" because of its "well-known role in strengthening labor discipline in the collective farms and regulating collective farmers' incomes from their private agricultural activities."[154] Khrushchev emphasized that peasants' money income from collective farm labor was already nontaxable. At the same time, with collective farms' growing productivity, their incomes would increase; this, he promised, would make it possible for collective farms to increase their members' payment in kind and peasants' money incomes. The role of private plots would correspondingly decrease: "They will lose their meaning for collective farmers and, as a result, create the conditions for the abolition of the agricultural tax on personal agricultural economic activity."[155] In other words, as collective farms became more prosperous from their joint efforts, so too would their individual members.

The text of the official decree on the abolition of taxes was published in Soviet newspapers on May 7, outlining the elimination schedule and specifying how the tax cuts would apply to the highest wage-earners whose taxes would be cut last, on October 1, 1965 (Figure 4.6).[156] Its convoluted wording obscured the fact that these workers' base pay rates would be cut by a portion of what they had previously paid in tax.[157] No doubt the Soviet government wished to minimize this fact, since high-earning workers' wages were already being restructured and in some cases reduced under the banner of Khrushchev's wage reforms. As of 1965, the bachelor tax would be abolished altogether, with no corresponding wage reduction.

The abolition of taxes was accompanied by a massive propaganda campaign reminiscent of the fanfare surrounding Stalin's consecutive retail price cuts. The ritualized displays of gratitude workers performed were virtually identical. As they had during the retail price reductions, workers pledged to improve the quality and quantity of their labor as tokens of gratitude for their reduced tax burden, especially the most immediate beneficiaries of the initiative: low-skilled and low-paid workers. As E. Lukashenko, a cleaning woman in Magnitogorsk, declared in a published testimonial: "When a family doesn't rake in big wages, every ruble counts. If you buy something, you need to take

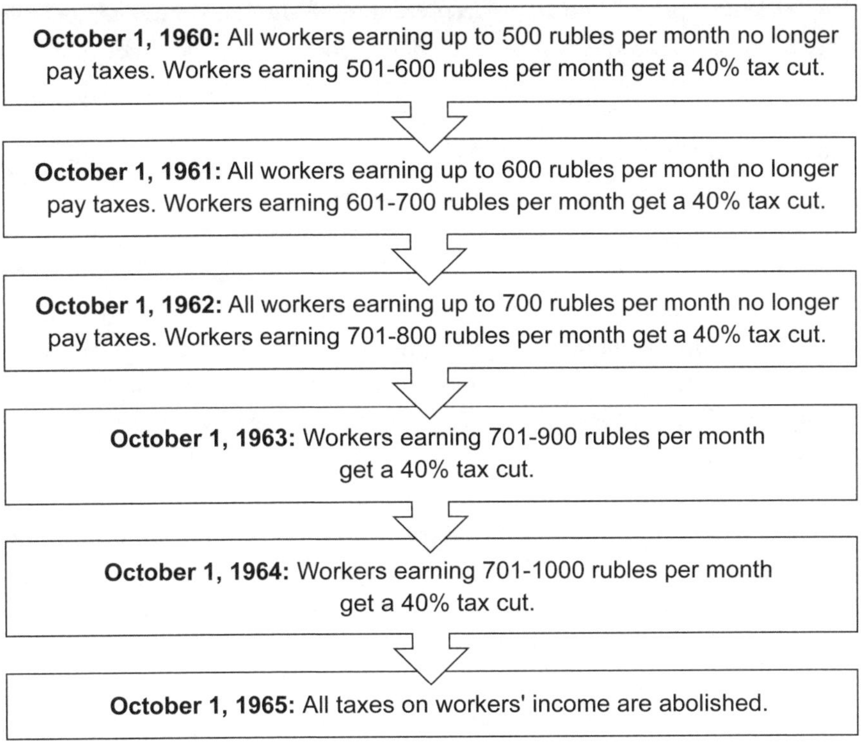

Figure 4.6 **Tax Abolition Schedule, 1960–1965**
Data source: "Zakon soiuza sovetskikh sotsialisticheskikh respublik ob otmene nalogov s zarabotnoi platy rabochikh i sluzhashchikh," *Pravda,* May 8, 1960, 1.

money away from something else. . . . So, imagine how carefully I listened to Nikita Sergeevich Khrushchev. It seems to me, he is speaking exactly about our family, he is glad that life will be easier for us simple, humble people."[158]

As it had during the price reductions, the Soviet government paid close attention to the foreign press's reactions and accused it of willfully diminishing the historic significance of its accomplishment. Indeed, a *New York Times* editorial on May 7 outright dismissed Khrushchev's initiative, calling it an insult to workers' intelligence, since he had eliminated only the income tax and not the more lucrative turnover tax.[159] Soviet tax experts, in turn, attacked this line of criticism as uninformed. "These statements are absurd, since the authors do not understand the nature of the turnover tax in the USSR," Burmistrov scoffed.[160] He downplayed the fact that the state budget relied far more heavily upon the turnover tax, explaining that it was only paid by industries that made excessive profits and that it represented an internal source of socialist accumulation, which the government then used to satisfy the needs of Soviet citizens.[161] Burmistrov argued that the turnover tax incentivized factories to cut their costs of production and improve efficiency in order to raise their profits. Soviet price policy, Burmistrov argued, precluded the possibility of using the turnover tax as a tax on consumption because retail prices were fixed and, in the case of many basic necessities, were set lower than the costs of production.[162]

Much of this propaganda fixated upon workers' tax burdens under capitalism, especially the plight of Americans, who were argued to be "the most taxed citizens in the world." The announcement of the abolition of income taxes in *Izvestiia* was accompanied by the Soviet political cartoonist Boris Efimov's 1952 drawing of an American being attacked and tied up by tax collectors who are shaking him down for money (Figure 4.7).[163] The American government was supposedly 99% reliant upon taxes as a source of revenue, *Izvestiia* readers were told.[164] Taxes were argued to hurt ordinary consumers most of all: on a single kilogram of bread, which was not subject to the turnover tax in the Soviet Union, ordinary Americans allegedly paid no less than 151 indirect taxes.[165] No mention was made of how much Soviet citizens indirectly paid when they purchased other goods subject to the turnover tax, such as vodka. American capitalists were the beneficiaries of "tax favoritism" that allowed them to shirk the taxes paid by the ordinary workers they exploited and maintain oppressive monopolies.[166] Khrushchev's abolition of taxes was also portrayed as a peace-promoting gesture in the Cold War, which, in the West, necessitated raising taxes to fund these governments' militarization and imperialism.[167] Finally, the Soviet Union was purportedly the first country in history to abolish taxes. Before long, "the word 'taxpayer' will disappear from our Soviet lexicon," one booklet claimed, adding: "We anticipate that, in time, this word will become a thing of the past."[168]

The Soviet Union's abolition of taxes scored points in the Cold War, but, as with pensions, it posed a major challenge for planners seeking to balance the money income and expenses of the population because it introduced additional cash into circulation that was not matched by consumer supply. Furthermore, its impact on low-income workers' living standards was negligible, since the minimum wage was already nontaxable. As Volkov and Grishin of the Committee on Questions of Work and Wages pointed out, if the government did not continue to raise minimum wages, this would create a "logical inconsistency" between the ongoing wage reform and the abolition of taxes.[169] On Oc-

Figure 4.7 **The American and Taxes. The signs at top read: "Pay your taxes!" The belt, coffer, and saw all read simply: "Taxes." The vacuum's label says "taxacuum," a play on "taxes" and "vacuum."** Ne Boltai: A Collection of 20th-Century Propaganda. Used with Permission.

tober 1, 1962, those earning 60–70 rubles per month were supposed to have their taxes abolished, while those earning 70–80 rubles would get a 40% discount. If the minimum wage was not raised, the 5 million workers who earned less than 40 rubles per month "will receive no benefit from this tax cut whatsoever."[170] In other words, this tax cut would benefit the wealthy and not, as had been explicitly promised, low-income citizens. Volkov and Grishin pushed to postpone the tax cut scheduled for October 1, 1961, to November 7, 1962—to the forty-fifth anniversary of the October Revolution, no less—a move that would provide the government with extra time to accumulate the revenue needed to raise the minimum wage.[171]

The second round of tax cuts took place on October 1, 1961, as planned, but there was noticeably less fanfare surrounding it. It was relegated to page-six news.[172] In the meantime, Soviet leaders were quietly beginning to wonder if putting millions of rubles into the population's hands instead of into state coffers was advisable after all. Due to the second round of tax reductions, the Supreme Soviet's subcommission on sources of state revenue reported a decrease of 451.1 million rubles (new money) in revenue from the income tax and a reduction of 65.5 million in revenue from the bachelor tax.[173] That money was left in circulation at a time when, as described in Chapter 1, consumer supply problems were steadily worsening and market prices were rising.

During the same May 31, 1962, meeting to revise control figures for the Seven-Year Plan, when the Presidium decided to raise retail prices for meat and butter and postpone minimum wage increases, it also decided to indefinitely postpone the remaining stages of the abolition of taxes.[174] The official announcement did not come for another four months, however, most likely because the government wanted to wait until the controversy surrounding higher retail prices had died down. On September 22, 1962, a decree from the Supreme Soviet stated briefly that, due to ongoing attempts to develop agriculture and industry, to increase the output of consumer goods and the construction of housing, as well as the need to strengthen the defense of the Soviet Union against "increased imperial aggression," the government was forced to increase budget allocations and temporarily suspend the income tax cut planned for October 1, 1962.[175] In a longer article in *Izvestiia,* the initiative was portrayed as anything but a complete failure: due to the previous two rounds of tax cuts in 1960 and 1961, a substantial number of low-paid workers no longer paid income taxes.[176] Moreover, not a single capitalist country decreased taxes that year, it emphasized, and the United States, in particular, was taking "energetic measures" to increase tax revenues—American citizens allegedly now lost 25%–30% of their wages to taxes. It enumerated the Soviet Union's many other achievements in the realm of raising living standards, especially in the construction of housing, which the government had no intention of defunding, it promised. Soviet citizens "know well these accomplishments," the article concluded, therefore "it cannot be doubted that the Supreme Soviet's decree, published today, will be understood correctly and will be unanimously supported by the people as a necessary measure dictated by the interests of all workers and the interests of the security of our country."[177]

Conclusion

When it eliminated mass subscription bonds and began the process of eliminating taxes, the Soviet government deprived itself of two of its traditional strategies for regulating the currency supply. One of the mass subscription bonds' major advantages—from the state's perspective, if not necessarily from that of bondholders—is that the screws in the coercive mass subscription machine could be tightened when the money was critically needed and when there was too much of it in circulation, as the government did during the war and again during postwar reconstruction. They could later be loosened to bring in fewer subscriptions and less revenue, as the government did in the mid-1950s when it tried to gradually reduce its acquisition of new debts and ease the burden of the bonds' purchase on low-income workers. Taxes performed a similar function in preventing excess cash from entering circulation in the first place, but, as obligatory and more clearly defined contributions, they were less flexible in this regard. Over time, payments on the bonds for prizes and interest not only became a drain on the budget, but the government's rising debt to the population became a liability, a tidal wave of cash that would hit the Soviet economy as the huge issues of the postwar period matured and destroy the equilibrium between money and goods the full-value ruble depended on. Reneging on repayment undermined the government's promises about the Soviet Union's growing prosperity, but the political cost of doing so proved preferable to the economic damage that would result from allowing that money to enter circulation.

Here, Holzman proved fundamentally correct. Writing at the time of the 1957 freeze, he suggested that mass subscription bonds eventually lost their appeal for the government due to the rising standard of living in the Soviet Union.[178] Unlike other governments that reneged on their debts because their bonds had become worthless due to wars and crises, the Soviet Union reneged on its debt because its bonds had become *too* valuable. Before 1947, a winning bondholder was unlikely to recoup the interest or principal on his investment; however, as Holzman argued, by 1956, "even if he didn't win a lottery, in twenty years he stood to recapture a real nest egg, possibly worth two or three times what he had paid for it," due to the steady reduction in consumer prices since 1947 and the rising purchasing power of the ruble.[179] Put slightly differently, the bonds ceased to function as taxes after the 1947 currency reform, and this was the main reason why they were discontinued according to Holzman. They turned out to be something akin to a Ponzi scheme or, in his words, a "hoax," and the decision not to pay back what the government owed was "one which could only be made under a totalitarian system."[180]

Although the prospect of bringing home a larger paycheck was appealing, many Soviet citizens felt deeply betrayed that the Soviet government backed out of its promise to repay the hard-earned rubles they had invested, often against their will, during years of great privation. In a seditious poem found in the bathroom of an apartment building in Rostov-on-Don in 1965, Khrushchev was called a new "Tsar" and was criticized for borrowing from the people to fund his pet projects in the Third World at the expense of those who had sacrificed their savings to build socialism at home. "Of course the people grumbled," the poem concludes, "but they didn't dare object . . ."[181] Indeed, despite the purportedly "open" discussions surrounding the freeze, the government had already decided its course of action before the plan was announced to the public; the discussions held were for show, and the public's input was not taken into consideration.

Holzman also turned out to be right about income taxes' anti-inflationary role within the beleaguered consumer market: when there were not enough goods to spend wages on, excessive currency in circulation not only led to grumbling workers, but threatened turnover tax revenue, the far more important source of state revenue than direct taxes. The socialist government was, furthermore, hamstrung by its Marxist commitment to low to no income taxes for workers and, as outspoken economists like Grigorii Mar'iakhin pointed out, the Soviet tax scale was in dire need of fine-tuning to reflect more accurate income levels by the late 1950s. Rather than reform the taxation system as Mar'iakhin recommended, using it to more efficiently redistribute income to needy social groups and progressively constrain higher earnings, Khrushchev chose to blow it up. This may have seemed like a triumphant victory in the context of the Cold War, but it was a fiscally disastrous move given the serious imbalances that had emerged in the Soviet money economy by the start of the new decade.

5

Real Returns

Despite the Soviet regime's repeated attempts to improve its citizens' purchasing power, they earned far more rubles than they spent for virtually the entirety of its existence. According to State Bank calculations of the balance of the population's money income and expenses, over the course of 1924–1990, it spent more money than it earned in just five years: 1933, 1940, 1946, 1947, and 1960—the first three years likely reflecting price increases and the last two years undoubtedly reflecting the panic buying associated with the December 1947 and January 1961 currency reforms.[1] Excessive income combined with chronic shortages depressed real wages, as discussed in Chapter 2. It also resulted in massive "savings" (*sberezheniia*)—the monetary overhang János Kornai argued was endemic to planned command economies.[2] Apart from the "deviant" war years, the amount of money deposited into Soviet state savings banks (*sberagatel'nye kassy*, or *sberkassy*) steadily rose: from 1.2 million rubles in October 1923 to 24.4 billion on January 1, 1953, to 63.7 billion as of January 1, 1957.[3] Over the course of the Seven-Year Plan, the number of deposits (*vklady*) exceeding 1,000 rubles rose by 2.9 times.[4] By 1964, deposits into Soviet savings bank accounts equaled about 17.9% of the population's average monthly income.[5] By the end of the Khrushchev era, in sum, most Soviet citizens were not effortlessly spending their full-value rubles and enjoying the fruits of the Soviet Union's postwar prosperity, but were accumulating substantial amounts of unspendable money.

Postwar Soviet officials publicly interpreted the phenomenon of rising savings as evidence not of the limited purchasing power of the ruble, but of a concurrent increase in citizens' living standards. The banking expert L. V. Valler linked the phenomenon of saving money to the socialist principle "From each according to his ability, to each according to his labor," which, he explained, "allowed for the harmonization of the worker's personal material interests with those of society."[6] "Payment according to labor" allowed workers to develop savings that helped them "more fully satisfy their material needs." They saved up to buy expensive items that they could not immediately afford, such as consumer durables and holidays.[7] In the Soviet Union, there was no need to put aside one's spare money for a "rainy day," he went on: unlike under capitalism, there was no such thing as unemployment, medical care and children's education were free, and citizens were protected against poverty. While their savings were not being spent "for one reason or another," these funds were directed toward the financial needs of socialist construction.[8]

Financial authorities remained mute about the fact that those savings were repeatedly confiscated during the Second World War and into the 1950s to prevent the emergence of more serious problems than frustrated consumer desire. Immediately after Nazi Germany's invasion in the summer of 1941, the government limited withdrawals from savings accounts to prevent a run on the banks, a restriction that remained in force until a Soviet victory was all but assured. It discontinued the practice of allowing citizens to mortgage their semi-compulsorily purchased mass subscription bonds. Money voluntarily saved in so-called market or free-circulating bonds (*rynochnye* or *svobodno-obrashchaemye zaimy*), the noncompulsory and liquid counterparts to mass subscription bonds, was frozen until 1946. The December 1947 currency reform converted money saved in bank accounts and invested in state bonds at preferential rates compared to cash, but the reform still entailed a significant loss to account holders and bondholders, especially those with large savings. Ten years later, the abolition of mass subscription bonds was accompanied by a 20-year freeze of existing investments to prevent an enormous influx of cash from entering Soviet citizens' hands as the massive issues of the war and postwar years matured, as related in Chapter 4.

After the 1947 currency reform, however, and especially in the wake of the abolition of mass subscription bonds, the Soviet government took an increasingly lighter touch in its handling of citizens' savings. It sought to foster increased confidence both in state banks and in the purchasing power of money deposited into them. Its "mobilization of the population's money" (*privlechenie sredstva naseleniia*), as its efforts to encourage savings deposits, playing the lottery, and investments in state bonds were known, began to revolve around positive incentives.[9] Soviet citizens were promised that their savings and investments would bring real returns after the losses and sacrifices they were repeatedly expected to make during earlier, more perilous stages in the Soviet Union's economic development. Market bonds were promoted as securing a tacitly middle-class lifestyle, and for the massive, exciting jackpots that could be won. Lottery tickets offered ordinary workers the chance to win large cash prizes or the coveted big-ticket consumer items that would soon be widely available under communism. Savings deposits, which came to be the state's preferred method for mobilizing the population's excess money, allowed industrial workers, urban citizens, and an increasing number of peasants to gradually acquire the resources necessary to purchase the trappings of a comfortable "cultured" lifestyle.

These efforts were led by the Main Administration of State Savings Banks and State Credit (*Gostrudsberkass*), a branch of the Ministry of Finance whose aim consisted of "provid[ing] the population with the opportunity to safely store their spare money and maintain bank accounts, and to promote the accumulation of money savings and their use in the interests of developing the national economy of the USSR."[10] Gosbank, by contrast, was responsible for the emission of money, housed enterprises' accounts, oversaw the cashless clearing operations between enterprises, controlled salary funds, and extended credit to the various branches of industry, among other higher-level economic functions. In the wake of the abolition of mass subscription bonds, there were proposals to make Gostrudsberkass subordinate to Gosbank, as had been the case before 1931; however, until 1963, it remained under the auspices of the Ministry of Finance due to the important role it played in state fundraising.[11] Citizens' savings, in bank accounts and in both voluntary and semi-coerced bonds, as well as money from the sales of lottery tickets, were counted as sources of state revenue.

After 1957 and the demise of mass subscription bonds, there were no more coercive efforts to mobilize citizens' excess money or abrupt confiscations of their savings despite worrying imbalances in the population's money income and expenses and the growth of massive cash surpluses in their hands; rather, this money and the pent-up consumer demand it represented was warehoused. This was not an effective strategy in the long term, as scholars have pointed out. Yakov Feygin argues that the Soviet state effectively went into debt to its own population: their savings became a constant liability on its balance sheet, one it could never discharge.[12] Serguei Alex Oushakine has linked the exponential growth of personal savings in the late Soviet period to the phenomenon of excessive unwanted inventory in the trade system. He observes that massive overstocking of goods, both unwanted and desired "deficit" goods, was accompanied by hoarding sizable sums of money. "In a sense, these incapacitated assets could be seen as perfect symbols for the period that would be characterized later as stagnation," he suggests. "Immense financial and material resources were frozen in time and space; their circulation was arrested—intentionally or inadvertently, potentialities were turned into a burden."[13]

In the late 1950s and early 1960s, however, the Soviet government was still confident it could correct imbalances in the money economy, and give these savings real value, once its investments in consumer industry and its efforts to boost workers' productivity paid off. Gostrudsberkass persuaded citizens to put their money into bank accounts, bonds, and, after January 1958, lottery tickets, thereby keeping it out of circulation, while shortcomings in the consumer economy were corrected. To accomplish this, the government invested heavily in propaganda that encouraged trust in the security and convenience of Soviet banks, that stoked citizens' consumer desire and channeled it toward appropriate ends, and that cultivated responsible saving habits. The diligence involved in the steady accumulation of the resources necessary to participate in rational consumption was portrayed as a virtuous quality befitting a builder of communism.[14] Even the frivolous expense of a lottery ticket was justified by its trivial cost, the "cultured" goods that could be won, and the laudable goals its revenue supported.

During this period, the ever-increasing amount of money put into market bonds, lottery tickets, and savings accounts was repeatedly portrayed as evidence of the population's rising prosperity; however, these investments' impact upon living standards was uneven, at best. Market bonds were expensive and primarily held by wealthier elites, whose status and privileges determined their access to consumer goods as much as their financial resources. Cash-and-goods lotteries benefited directly only the small fraction of ticket holders who won, and even of these, many struggled to claim their prizes. The money spent on losing tickets was, of course, irretrievably lost. The steadily rising amount of money held by Soviet citizens in state savings banks, as financial authorities were all too aware behind the scenes, was a stark indicator of the growing portion of the population's income that simply could not be spent.

Rubles for Reconstruction

After the Second World War, the Soviet government continued to rely heavily upon the virtually compulsory mass subscription bonds to fund reconstruction and channeled citizens' savings into them, as discussed in Chapter 4. It also increasingly encouraged citizens to make additional voluntary investments and savings deposits as a strategy for removing excess cash from circulation. The public's response to these initiatives was harder to predict and much more difficult to control. Though the government drew up plans for anticipated revenue from market bonds and savings deposits, unlike mass subscription bonds, it did not rigidly enforce quotas for their sale, nor were market bond purchases and savings deposits directly subject to collective input and the *komsody*'s hectoring. To convince citizens to invest their excess money in the state, the government had to foster confidence in the economic benefit of these investments to the individuals who made them. This was no small feat after their savings were virtually seized during the war and after the December 1947 currency reform decimated what remained.

On June 23, 1941, one day after the German invasion, the Soviet government limited account holders' withdrawals to 200 rubles per month, discontinued the practice of mortgaging mass subscription bonds, and prohibited holders of market bonds from selling back issues of the most recent internal lottery bond, the 1938 3% bond.[15] They eased up on the withdrawal restriction in August, permitting account holders to freely withdraw any sum from funds deposited after the June 23 decree; however, it had frightened off account holders. New deposits came to a near standstill in the second half of 1941, while withdrawals steadily increased. Financial officials worried that Soviet savings banks would be forced to give out all their remaining cash in 1942.[16] Despite proposals to remove the restriction on withdrawals and on cashing in bonds as incentives for the population to save and help correct the volume of cash in circulation, the restrictions remained in place until January 1944 in the case of savings and 1946 in the case of market bonds.[17]

During this time, the *komsody* implored their peers to save as a patriotic strike against the enemy, but, since such deposits were fully voluntary and made outside the workplace, and the contents of accounts were strictly confidential, they struggled to influence decisions to save in the same way that they exerted influence over mass subscription bond subscription pledges.[18] The government also turned to the prospect of material gain, offering increased interest and the chance to win prizes as incentives to leave money in the bank as long as possible: "time accounts" offered the account holder a relatively high 5% interest rate for every month he or she left money in the bank beyond an initial six-month term and "lottery accounts" gave the account holder the chance to win a percentage of the amount that remained by a certain date.[19]

Amid the economic uncertainty of the first half of the war, these incentives were largely ineffective; the slump in deposits continued until the second half of the war and the Soviet Union's victory at Stalingrad, after which citizens deposited money more consistently into the bank. This newfound interest in saving was due more to declining prices that left citizens with more money in hand and to their changing expectations about the war's outcome than to the state's propaganda efforts.[20] This bump in deposits also reflected increased saving on the part of frontline soldiers, who increasingly transferred money to their families at home or brought back money with them as they reentered the Soviet Union in the last stages of the war. Around 4 billion rubles were transformed into financial reserves in this manner by January 1, 1945, which Gosbank credited for allowing it to finally reduce currency emission that year.[21]

By 1947, there was more money in Soviet state savings banks than there had been before the war, and the number of accounts being opened, as well as the amount of money deposited into those accounts, was steadily rising. As of December 1, there were 16.5 billion rubles in Soviet savings banks, up from 7.3 billion on January 1, 1941.[22] The currency reform temporarily reversed this trend. Although it was formulated in strict secrecy, information leaked to the public in the weeks leading up to it. Savings banks across the Soviet Union recorded large withdrawals as panicked rumors circulated among citizens about what was going to happen to their savings, especially those that were not the product of honest labor. In Moscow and Leningrad alone, over the course of just three days, November 28–30, 113 million rubles were withdrawn.[23] Panic buying (*azhiotazh*) took place in Soviet stores and kolkhoz markets as citizens rushed to invest their money in clothes, furniture, paintings, and other consumer goods before their old rubles became useless.[24]

As it became clear that the reform would privilege money left in the bank, citizens rushed to do exactly the opposite. The first few days of December saw massive increases in deposits across the major cities of the Soviet Union.[25] The Ministry of Finance estimated that between the beginning of December and the formal announcement of the currency reform on December 15, no less than 2–2.5 billion rubles were hastily deposited.[26] In a letter of complaint, one Party member reported long lines outside the banks in his town before December 13. To his disgust, he observed individuals carting large sums of money "from their piggy banks" to the state saving bank, money they had "evidently held on to for quite some time . . . [for] the notes had lost their color and had turned into powder, or had been eaten by mice."[27] Many of his colleagues were much less scrupulous: Party members received advance warning of the currency reform's terms and many did not hesitate to take advantage of this knowledge. While cash was converted at the rate of 10:1, sums held in accounts up to 3,000 rubles were to be exchanged at a 1:1 ratio, while sums up to 10,000 were exchanged as follows: the first 3,000 rubles was exchanged at a rate of 1:1, and the remaining balance was exchanged at a rate of 3:2.[28] Accounts containing more than 10,000 rubles had the first 3,000 rubles exchanged at a 1:1 rate, while the remainder was exchanged at a ratio of 2:1.[29] Those who knew this in advance split their savings up into 3,000-ruble or smaller sums, spreading accounts between different banks, and putting them in their children's, relatives', and friends' names.

The central government was aware of these attempts to circumvent the confiscatory dimensions of the reform.[30] In fact, it had anticipated them: initially, it was proposed to convert all money deposited after December 1, 1947, at the harsher cash rate to penalize individuals trying to protect their savings, but this suggestion was jettisoned in favor of "securing a rise in the population's trust in savings banks in the post-reform period."[31] Many citizens complained this was unfair to those who played by the rules, who stood to lose a significant amount of money. "I was frugal my entire life, frugal to the point of being able to do nothing in order to save up for my retirement, because I have no children," an anonymous letter writer complained on December 9. "I put all my savings into the state savings bank. In my own name. What am I going to do now?" he demanded angrily.[32] V. Molchanov, an electrical engineer from Stalingrad, argued that "it would be very unfair if the savings of a Stalin Prize laureate . . . or those of a distinguished industrial worker or collective farmer, whose savings were accumulated over the years as a result of conscientious labor, were put on par with the sudden savings of some speculator, brought to the bank only so that he can preserve his capital, only to have the government give those savings right back to the same speculators, individuals without determined occupations, at the same or even at a better rate."[33] Molchanov suggested that all those who made such deposits should simply be arrested.

Following the reform's public announcement on December 15, it was risky but not impossible to split up one's savings and have deposits of old rubles backdated, especially if one worked for the government or was well connected. For example, S. V. Vladimirov, the head of the secretariat of the Ministry of State Security in Molotov, managed to convince the manager of a savings bank to allow him to withdraw 34,000 rubles on December 15 and have 14 bank accounts opened in the names of his coworkers and relatives.[34] Vladimirov was but one of several of the Ministry of State Security's workers in Molotov who violated the currency reform decree by manipulating their savings.[35]

Deposits in the fourth quarter of 1947 were higher than those of the same period in 1946, reflecting savvy and unscrupulous efforts to preserve the value of personal savings and mitigate the effects of the December 14 currency reform; however, the influx of money into Soviet savings banks in the first three quarters of the year was still two times lower than in 1946.[36] Lower than anticipated deposits continued into 1948, when large deposits all but ceased. Although the number of account holders rose by over 1.7 million, or 23%, over the course of that year, the average amount held in a savings account dropped from 1,546 rubles to 1,290 rubles, or by 17%.[37] This slump undoubtedly reflected the financial losses stemming from the currency reform, but also the high cost of living after the concurrent abolition of rationing and reintroduction of open retail trade, which left citizens with less money to put aside.

Savings held in market bonds were also hit hard by the currency reform. Issues of 1938 3% bonds could be purchased through 1947, since a new 4% lottery bond planned for 1946 never materialized.[38] By the end of that year, around 2 billion rubles in 1938 lottery bonds were held by the population, up from around 1 billion before the war.[39] These were revalued at the ratio of 5:1, old rubles for new, converting them into the new State 3% Internal Lottery Bond of December 13, 1947.[40] As Gostrudsberkass noted, these losses had a discernable impact upon investors' interest in the new 1947 issue: although higher than normal purchases occurred in January 1948, the bond failed to meet its projected target of 400 million rubles.[41]

In response to declining interest in saving after the currency reform, Gostrudsberkass ramped up its efforts to mobilize the population's spare money; however, it did not turn to the coercive methods that it still employed when it came to mass subscription bonds. Instead, a new strategy took shape, revolving around improving customer service and devising more compelling propaganda messages. In January 1948, the head of Gostrudsberkass, Nikolai Obolenskii, called for a "fundamental reform" of savings banks to actively encourage deposits, including expanding their regional coverage, improving customer service, and educating cadres.[42] Customer service in Soviet savings banks was widely viewed as abysmal and as a deterrent to saving by officials and ordinary citizens alike. Since the 1930s, there had been a push to create more "cultured savings banks," echoing initiatives to improve service and conditions in retail shops.[43] By the late 1940s, customer service in many savings banks still left much to be desired. Patrons reported long waits for money transfers, banks often did not have enough cash on hand for withdrawals and sent account holders home empty-handed, and cashiers were accused of being unprofessional and rude.[44] Following the reforms of 1948–1949, savings bank employees were required to attend training sessions and they were encouraged to take a more proactive approach to their role in state fundraising.[45]

Gostrudsberkass also stepped up its advertising efforts. In 1948, around 500 new advertising materials were created for use in banks and in workplaces, as well as by the *komsody* and other activists, including materials specifically targeted at collective farmers.[46] Although savings were still portrayed as crucial to the success of postwar reconstruction, the new propaganda materials were more subtle than those that called upon citizens to sacrifice toward mass subscription bonds, and explicitly linked market bonds and bankbooks to the tentative improvements that were beginning to appear in the postwar consumer economy. In 1950, perhaps the most well-known product of Gostrudsberkass's efforts appeared, a poster of a man seated in a new car purchased with his savings, grinning at spectators while he holds up his bankbook (Figure 5.1).

This propaganda emphasized that it was now possible for an increasing number of ordinary workers to afford the good things in life if they simply diligently saved up for them. A 1952 testimonial on the front page of *Literaturnaia gazeta* by P. Martynov, the manager of Savings Bank No. 171 in Rostov, exemplified this message. Walking along the main street in town, Martynov described his great pleasure in seeing the "widow's mite" (*skromnaia dolia*) of savings bank employees' work reflected in the new factories, stadium, and workers' quarters in town.[47] These public accomplishments were not the only evidence of the importance of savings. The hundreds of people who showed up at the bank each day to make deposits came there, he wrote, "because of their firm faith in the purchasing power of the Soviet ruble, because they know that today our ruble is worth more than it was yesterday, and tomorrow it will be worth more than it is today." The savings bank, Martynov concluded, was a "barometer of the people's prosperity." As soon as there was a price cut or premiums were paid out for Stakhanovite labor, the banks were packed with steelworkers from the nearby Azovstal'stroi factory collectively depositing hundreds of thousands of rubles. Walking down the street, Martynov often encountered these workers out shopping, on their way with their families to holiday resorts, and driving their own cars: more than 50 cars had been purchased with money saved at Savings Bank No. 171 alone, he claimed. While workers under capitalism had to save for a rainy day—for a doctor's visit when

Figure 5.1 **Savings Propaganda Poster, 1950. "I saved up and bought a car!"**
Ne Boltai: A Collection of 20th-Century Propaganda. Used with Permission.

they were sick and for bread when they were laid off—Soviet account holders did not have to fear hard times and "thus our people don't save money for rainy days, but for sunny days."[48]

Martynov's "observations" were hyperbolic to say the least; however, Soviet citizens did show a more enthusiastic interest in putting their money in the bank as the campaign to improve Soviet banking services and propaganda campaigns unfolded. The number of banks with accounts containing less than 5,000 rubles declined over the course of 1949: from 9,327 banks on January 1 to 4,994 by the end of the year.[49] By January 1, 1950, around 14.5 billion rubles were held in Soviet savings banks, approximately twice the sum held by account holders prior to the war.[50] This trend continued into the early 1950s: between January 1, 1951, and January 1, 1956, the sum of deposits in Soviet savings banks tripled and average savings deposit amounts rose (Table 5.1).

Although peasants were gradually saving more money, it was still the case that far more urban residents than rural residents held money in the bank. By 1954, an estimated 6.913 billion rubles were held in cash by the population, only around 3.8 billion rubles of which were believed to be in the countryside.[51] The money incomes of the entire population in 1955 had increased by around 3 billion

Table 5.1 Savings Deposits as of January 1, 1951, and January 1, 1956 (all-union figures)

	As of January 1, 1951		As of January 1, 1956	
Balance of the population's deposits				
	Sum	Percentage	Sum	Percentage
In cities	16,471,400,000	88.9	44,586,300,000	83.1
In the countryside	2,059,100,000	11.1	9,077,900,000	16.9
TOTAL	18,530,500,000	100.0	53,664,200,000	100.0
Number of account holders				
	Number	Percentage	Number	Percentage
In cities	10,467,000	73.0	24,195,000	73.8
In the countryside	3,877,000	27.0	8,604,000	26.2
TOTAL	14,344,000	100.0	32,799,000	100.0
Average size of savings (in rubles)				
In cities	1,516		1,834	
In the countryside	531		1,055	

Source: GARF, f. 7523, op. 75, d. 1641, l. 17.

rubles over the previous year, while peasants' money incomes rose by over 10 billion rubles due to the increased procurement and purchasing prices for agricultural goods after Stalin's death. Yet, the amount saved by peasants only rose by around 1.46 billion rubles.[52] Financial officials laid the blame on shortcomings in savings banks' work in rural areas, particularly the lack of mass-explanatory work among peasants and the lower quality of service in these areas.

Indeed, not all banks in the countryside offered the full range of services enjoyed by account holders in the major cities. Not all types of banks could be found there. There were three different types of savings banks in the Soviet Union—first rank, second rank, and agents—distinguished by the size of their staff, limits on monetary transactions, and the range of services they offered. First-rank banks employed complete staffs of controllers and cashiers and offered the full range of banking services including deposits, investments, storing of bonds, and processing of "letters of credit" (*akkreditivy*); second-rank banks employed only a controller, could process transfers of only up to 1,000 rubles, and could store state bonds for citizens; and agents were employees of other institutions or organizations authorized to perform limited banking functions, such as deposits.[53] First-rank savings banks tended to be located in the major cities, while second-rank banks and agents were more common in the countryside, where they were often attached to a post office, collective farm headquarters, or other state institution. Not all first-rank banks offered the full range of saving opportunities, either: for example, although there were 18,149 savings banks across the RSFSR by 1956, only 605 of them offered 3% lottery bonds for sale.[54]

The Soviet savings bank network was still recovering from the war's physical damage in the early to mid-1950s, exerting a very basic infrastructural constraint on Gostrudsberkass's ability to mobilize the population's excess money. By mid-1950, around 38,000 savings banks were counted across the country, only 89% of prewar numbers.[55] It was not until the middle of the decade that the number of savings banks in the Soviet Union finally exceeded prewar levels.[56] Many savings banks, along with their records, had been destroyed or displaced during the war. Many now shared facilities awkwardly with other enterprises, and operated with insufficient staff and cadres, as well as suboptimal security standards. This left banks vulnerable to armed robberies, theft, and embezzlement, often by savings bank employees, themselves.[57]

Fewer banks, poor facilities, and inadequate staff put pressure on the banking system's human resources; moreover, despite the push to improve the quality of customer service in banks since 1949, there was still much work left to be done in this department. Among Khrushchev's promised measures to "fully satisfy the growing material needs of the population" announced at the Twentieth Party Congress, one involved expanding the range of public amenities (*bytovoe obsluzhivanie*) and everyday conveniences available to Soviet citizens, such as laundries, cafés, hairdressers, and savings banks. As discussed in Chapter 2, these time- and labor-saving services were not only viewed as a means of improving citizens' everyday quality of life, but were also seen as a means of channeling more of the population's spare money back to the state, giving them something else to spend their money on besides consumer goods, thereby removing it from circulation. A November 1956 article in *Izvestiia* pointed out that propaganda posters informing customers that "you can reliably, profitably, and conveniently save your money in a savings bank" were hung up across the country; "there is no doubt about the benefits and the reliability," but, it asked, "is it really always 'convenient'?"[58] Even in urban milieus, patrons often had to wait in long lines to perform simple operations like depositing money. Financial authorities needed to "think more about account holders," the author concluded.

Gambling on Prosperity

Better propaganda, customer service, and regional coverage, both of banking infrastructure and of access to financial services and savings programs, were not the only strategies employed by Gostrudsberkass to encourage more citizens to hand over their spare money to the state. Since the early 1920s, and across several different financial instruments, the Soviet government had turned to the lottery mechanism as an incentive for participating in its fundraising campaigns, enticing citizens to risk a relatively small and inconsequential sum of money toward a potentially enormous payoff. It continued to rely upon the prospect of hitting the jackpot after the war and especially in the Khrushchev era.

This turn to the lottery is somewhat surprising at first glance: risk was supposedly anathema to the planned command economy. Gambling was, especially in the early Soviet period, viewed as a regressive and unhealthy "'bourgeois'" pastime. In 1903, Lenin expressed an iteration of the common argument that lotteries are a "tax on the poor and stupid" when he compared proponents of small-scale farming to lottery organizers, claiming that "those who say that lotteries are advantageous to the people are simply practicing deceit" because only the organizer of the lottery and the winner benefited, while the rest lost everything.[59] At the turn of the twentieth century, communists had looked upon the lotteries played by imperial Russia's aristocracy, for both gambling and charitable purposes, as a bourgeois indulgence.[60] They banned lotteries alongside other games of chance in 1918.[61]

As in other areas of the economy, their pragmatism soon outweighed their ideological reservations. Amid the Soviet regime's desperate need for revenue at the start of the NEP, the ban on lotteries was overturned. In 1922, Lenin signed off on a state lottery to the sum of 2 million gold rubles with 60,000 tickets to be sold, the same day the Soviet Union's first lottery bond, the 6% Gold Lottery Bond, was decreed.[62] After postponing the draw until May 1923 due to logistical problems, and once more to November 1923, the government issued a new decree on July 24, 1923, banning central and local authorities from holding their own state lotteries. This did not put an end to lotteries altogether: they could be held by social and voluntary organizations if they applied for and received special permission. Associational lotteries fundraised for a variety of social causes, such as paramilitary training, improving literacy, and building roads. In the meantime, Soviet citizens could play the lottery and potentially win big through the wide range of state lottery bonds issued after

1922, including the mass subscription bonds they were virtually forced to buy beginning in 1927. As James R. Millar observes, by the mid-1930s, lottery winnings had become the principal vehicle for returns to the Soviet bondholder, if he or she received any.[63] Beginning in 1931, the government even sold "guaranteed-to-win" (*besproigryshnye*) issues assuring the bondholder a prize within their term.

During the Second World War, the Ministry of Finance finally exercised its prerogative to organize a state lottery. The first of four cash-and-goods lotteries to fundraise for the war effort was launched in November 1941. The wartime lottery ticket sales campaigns were virtually identical to those of the mass subscription bonds.[64] Trade unions, workplace management, and, of course, the *komsody* ensured that ticket sales quotas were met and pressured their coworkers to pledge more than suggested minimum amounts. Money for the tickets' purchase was deducted directly from workers' wages in the same manner as bond subscriptions. Model lottery players soon emerged, contributing sums well over the minimum set percentages of their wages they were expected to spend on tickets.[65] The lotteries offered big cash prizes, but also scarce and coveted consumer goods like fur coats, silverware, and household appliances. Cash-and-goods lotteries were held annually each fall through 1944. A fifth lottery was planned for 1945, but it was canceled after the Soviet victory in May; cash-and-goods lotteries were thereafter abandoned as a state fundraising strategy for more than a decade.

Before the war, market lottery bonds were primarily held by skilled workers, craftspeople, and wealthier members of Soviet society residing in the major cities.[66] They continued to be held by the wealthy, urban, and privileged after 1945. At 200 rubles per bond, the 1947 3% bonds were twice as expensive as mass-subscription "Reconstruction and/or Development of the National Economy Bonds."[67] That these were targeted first and foremost at the beneficiaries of the postwar "Big Deal" was made obvious by the imagery of their promotional materials, which depicted smiling, well-dressed citizens noticeably marked as white-collar workers and urban elites. For example, a 1951 propaganda poster depicted a respectable middle-aged couple seated in the dining room of their well-appointed apartment overlooking a hydroelectric dam, holding up a 200-ruble issue above the caption "We won!" (Figure 5.2). At the same time, Gostrudsberkass sought to diversify ownership of the bonds and increase their penetration into the countryside and other more distant locales. For example, in the late 1940s and early 1950s, high-income workers in the Far East were pressured to buy the bonds during one-on-one conversations with

Figure 5.2 Poster for the State 3% Internal Lottery Loan, 1951. (top) "Buy 3% Internal State Lottery Bonds! State bonds make possible the further development of the national economy of the USSR"; (bottom) "We won!"
Ne Boltai: A Collection of 20th-Century Propaganda. Used with permission.

members of the *komsody* and they were forced to repeatedly watch a short propaganda film about them.[68]

The challenge for Gostrudsberkass was how to encourage citizens to buy as many 3% market bonds as possible, but also how to persuade them to refrain from cashing in their bonds for as long as possible. Unlike mass subscription bonds, market bonds could be cashed in at any time. To solve this problem, it once again turned to the jackpot: the longer money was left invested in a market bond, the higher one's chances were of winning a large prize. Beginning in the fall of 1948, in addition to the regular six draws per year that were held for 3% bonds, a bonus draw was held each September 30 into which only the serial numbers of bonds that had been held for a minimum of nine months could be entered.[69] Only bonus draws featured the grand prize of 100,000 rubles, and each bonus draw featured more prizes to be won than a regular draw.

The government also promoted the lottery draws as public spectacles. This was, in some ways, a throwback to the early days of their existence: in the 1920s, the draws were held in prestigious cultural establishments in the major cities of the Soviet Union and were promoted as cost-free outings, featuring musical acts and films in addition to agitational speeches.[70] A prize committee of notable persons and local authorities presided over the events, and the winning serial numbers were drawn out of the lottery machines by schoolchildren. This format became the norm for the mass subscription bond draws, as well as for other kinds of lotteries, for decades afterward. However, the compulsory and routine nature of subscribing to mass subscription bonds undoubtedly put a damper on citizens' enthusiasm for attending these events. Most citizens found out if their bonds had won simply by checking the official tables of winning serial numbers published in the newspapers. In the late 1950s, Gostrudsberkass sought to move beyond these admittedly "standard, dry announcements."[71] It promoted the draws as dramatic spectacles once again, dispatching radio and television reporters to the events for that purpose.[72]

Most ordinary workers, it should be emphasized, did not have the necessary financial means to buy expensive market bonds; however, they had other ways to engage in state-sanctioned gambling with their spare rubles. They could put their money into lottery accounts and win cash prizes that grew depending on the amount of money they left in the bank. Of every 1,000 bankbooks, 25 winning numbers were drawn twice per year: 1 for 200% of the sum left in the bank, 2 for 100%, and 22 for 50% of the average amount kept in the bank over the course of a minimum of six months.[73] These accounts never proved especially popular: by 1956, an estimated 63.9% of all accounts were basic accounts used for day-to-day transactions, while 34.9% were time accounts paying out higher interest rates, and only 1.2% were lottery accounts.[74]

During the April 1957 meeting of the Presidium of the Communist Party when it was decided to abolish mass subscription bonds, the Minister of Trade, Anastas Mikoyan, proposed a new state lottery as a viable alternative.[75] The government had reason to believe it would be successful. Though mass subscription bonds had effectively forced Soviet citizens to play the lottery, and the prize was a by-product of their forced savings rather than an incentive to buy bonds in the first place, the chance to win a prize was not always unwelcome. When Khrushchev announced the government's plan to freeze existing bonds in April 1957, several angry letter writers complained that this deprived them of the chance to win: "The worker waits for the draw as if it is a holiday," one unsigned letter explained. "Even 100 rubles is a huge amount to him if he wins. Those who make lots of money can easily do without this, but it's difficult for workers. Think about that, and come up with a better solution for common folk."[76] Cash-and-goods lotteries were that solution from the perspective of central authorities: unlike mass subscription bonds, whose interest, prize, and redemption payments were a constant drain on the budget, after paying out prizes to a tiny fraction of ticketholders, the remainder of their investments in lottery tickets were pure revenue.

A New Lottery with Old Problems

The new cash-and-goods lottery was not portrayed as the revival of a wartime fundraising instrument or a quick, low-cost solution to the Soviet government's economic woes. Rather, it was presented as a concession to popular demand stirred up by the Soviet Union's first postwar associational lottery organized by the Committee of Youth Organizations to fundraise for the World Festival of Youth and Students, which Moscow hosted in the summer of 1957.[77] Thousands of Soviet citizens won prizes ranging from cars to musical instruments, bicycles, and cash prizes in the festival lottery. In line with Khrushchev's decentralizing economic reforms, the new lotteries were implemented independently in each republic, which was allowed to keep a portion of the revenue. The first cash-and-goods lottery in the RSFSR, whose draw took place in May 1958, offered 14 million rubles in cash prizes and 100,000 goods prizes for a retail value of over 101 million rubles (Figure 5.3).[78] Cars, cameras, washing machines, comforters, fur coats, vacations, and even single-family homes featured among the coveted consumer items that could be won.

Figure 5.3 Lottery Ticket, 1958. A 5-ruble lottery ticket for the first postwar cash-and-goods lottery in the RSFSR, 1958.
Reproduced from the author's collection.

Echoing changes the Ministry of Finance had been attempting to implement since the mid-1950s when it came to mass subscription bonds, the republics' lotteries were instructed to be implemented according to "strict observance of the voluntary principle" (*pri strogom sobliudenii printsipa dobrovol'nosti*).[79] Lottery tickets would now be paid for in cash at the time of sale rather than through wage deductions, as they had been during the war. They would be available for purchase from the *komsody* in Soviet factories, offices, and collective farms, but they would also be sold at post offices, stores, theaters, cinemas, and newspaper kiosks.

Continuing to sell tickets primarily within the workplace and assigning responsibility for this task to the *komsody* gave the wrong impression of the sincerity behind these instructions. Those responsible for meeting ticket sales quotas turned to the same strategies they had been using for decades to ensure that quotas were swiftly fulfilled, to the state's chagrin. On February 1, 1958, in a joint decree of the Council of Ministers and the Communist Party, the Soviet government reiterated its expectation of adherence to the voluntary principle and highlighted several violations of that principle that had come to their attention.[80] For example, in some areas of Moscow, workers had been forced to attend meetings where they were informed of set percentages of the monthly wage fund that had to be contributed to the lottery. Enterprises compelled workers to subscribe for wage deductions, ignoring the new standard of paying in cash, and, in some cases, outright forced workers and employees to buy tickets against their will, "undermining the very idea of the lottery."[81] In fact, the violations were much more widespread than in Moscow, as an investigation instigated by the Collegium of the Ministry of Finance revealed. In the city of Riazan, for example, activists at a local hospital began hitting up employees for money for lottery tickets even before the paper tickets had been printed.[82] At a workshop in Ul'ianovsk, individuals who refused to contribute to the lottery in the amounts suggested to them had their names posted on a bulletin board in shame.[83]

The old methods for mobilizing the population's spare money were no longer tolerated. Following the February 2 announcement, the matter was discussed among Party, Soviet, and republic organs, and a flurry of instructions were sent to lower-level functionaries.[84] A large-scale verification (*proverka*) of the extent to which they were abiding by the voluntary principle was quickly launched across the Soviet Union.[85] Those who continued to violate it were warned that they would be held personally responsible for their transgressions. Pavel Dmitrichev, the head of Gostrudsberkass, was reprimanded for being aware of violations and not bringing the matter to the Collegium's attention immediately.[86]

Two changes were implemented in the wake of the February 2 decree. First, ticket sales were displaced from the workplace into more neutral locales like state stores, savings banks, theaters, and public parks. Citizens would now buy tickets in the same places where they voluntarily handed over money for other purchases, instead of from the *komsody*. This weakened Gostrudsberkass's ability to quickly meet sales targets, as it was the first to admit: officials noted that in the first half of February, around 12 million rubles were collected across the country, while in the second, after the February 2 decree was implemented, only 6 million were collected.[87] In the first five days of March, only 2.1 million rubles were collected and in the second five days, 2.7 million.[88] Financial activists and workplace authorities struggled to make sense of the new instructions. "Mass-agitation explanatory" work among collectives had all but ceased, one report noted, because comrades who were responsible for the distribution of tickets in the workplace were "afraid of violating the voluntary principle" and, as a result, simply avoided interpersonal methods altogether.[89]

Second, Gostrudsberkass produced advertising that evoked material desire in Soviet citizens. Advertising efforts for the first cash-and-goods lotteries were "weak," as Gostrudsberkass acknowledged: although lottery advertisements were placed in the Main Department Store (*Gosudarstvennyi universal'nyi magazine*, or GUM) and TsUM's shop windows and in some other streets in the capital, a more comprehensive and wider-reaching—and admittedly more expensive—advertising campaign involving television, radios, and newspapers was needed, it argued. Promotional efforts needed to be expanded in more high-traffic areas in the capital and elsewhere. In existing high-traffic zones where tickets were already being sold, such as the Arbatskaia metro station in central Moscow, more signs informing citizens that they could buy lottery tickets there needed to be put up.[90]

In the months that preceded the draw in May, as well as in subsequent lotteries, Gostrudsberkass expanded and intensified its promotional efforts across a variety of media. Despite the statistically higher probability of winning a cash prize, the resulting propaganda was almost exclusively focused on the goods. Where money was referred to, it was typically to emphasize the trifling cost of the lottery ticket compared to the expensive, desirable items that could be won. Occurring against the backdrop of Khrushchev's mass housing campaign, the lotteries offered as prizes many big-ticket items intended for the new domestic private spaces: refrigerators, sewing machines, vacuum cleaners, washing machines, furniture, and even single-family apartments themselves. The most fetishized prize, and the one that was most frequently targeted at men, was the car. A *Krokodil* cartoon from the first lottery of 1958 poked fun at this, depicting a middle-aged man drawing a car around his lottery ticket and affixing a license plate over the ticket's serial number.[91] Newspaper articles hyped up the draws by repeatedly reminding readers that a Volga car could be won, and wondering who the new car owner could be when a lucky ticket was drawn but the prize was not immediately claimed.[92] Shortly after the draws, follow-up "human interest" pieces on winners examined how these lucky citizens were enjoying their prizes. In January 1959, *Ogonek* gushed that thousands of lottery winners were flooding into Moscow department stores to cash in their tickets and depicted the Sopygin couple receiving a demonstration of their newly won sewing machine.[93]

The Soviet government also promoted the lotteries through the consumer goods, themselves. Except for big prizes like cars, motorcycles, and pianos, winners were supposed to pick up smaller prizes like sewing machines and alarm clocks at local trade outlets, which were sent larger than normal deliveries of these products around the time of the lottery draws. This promotional strategy often backfired because the goods were sold immediately, leaving nothing for prizewinners to claim after the draws.[94] Sewing machines, in particular, were repeatedly the subject of such complaints. S. V. Apollonova, of Voronezh, received hers not immediately after the draw but 71 days later, and only after complaining to the newspaper *Sovetskaia Rossiia* that she had all but given up hope of holding the prize in her own hands.[95] This should not have been the case for, as the Collegium of the Ministry of Finance noted in November, trade outlets had been sent three times the necessary number of sewing machines to hand out as prizes in the second quarter of 1958; only a small portion of these evidently made their way to the winners and the rest were immediately sold.[96]

The new cash-and-goods lottery was viewed as a great success, despite these hiccups. Moreover, although lottery tickets did not completely sell out, they came very close to targets (Figure 5.4). This experience prompted Gostrudsberkass to explore the possibility of expanding the scope and types of state lotteries across the Soviet Union. Gostrudsberkass conducted a study of state lotteries existing in the People's Democracies and capitalist countries in Western Europe (at the time, no state lotteries existed in the United States).[97] Among the options they considered were "permanent" state lotteries with monthly drawings, as were held in Bulgaria, Poland, and France. Other alternatives included "number lotteries," in which participants were asked to choose a series of numbers from 1 to 90, and "sport lotteries," in which they chose the winning teams in sporting contests across the Soviet Union—a precursor to the Sportloto lotteries that would be organized during the Brezhnev years. Gostrudsberkass recommended that, starting in 1959, the Soviet Union should institute a permanent lottery with monthly drawings, and set ticket prices at 3 rubles instead of the current 5 rubles.[98] It also recommended the establishment of a 2-ruble "instant-win" lottery (*lotteri-allegri*) in the major cities of the Soviet Union. The main difference between the proposed lotteries and the existing cash-and-goods model was that prizes would be paid out in cash only, although in the case of the permanent lottery, one could opt to take the money in the form of credit toward the purchase of certain goods. Dmitrichev argued that the lowered price of tickets across all three types of lotteries would encourage the broadest possible participation.[99] The enhanced frequency of these lotteries, as well as the entertainment afforded by choosing one's own numbers, would also promote interest in the lottery, as would the instant gratification provided by break-open tickets.

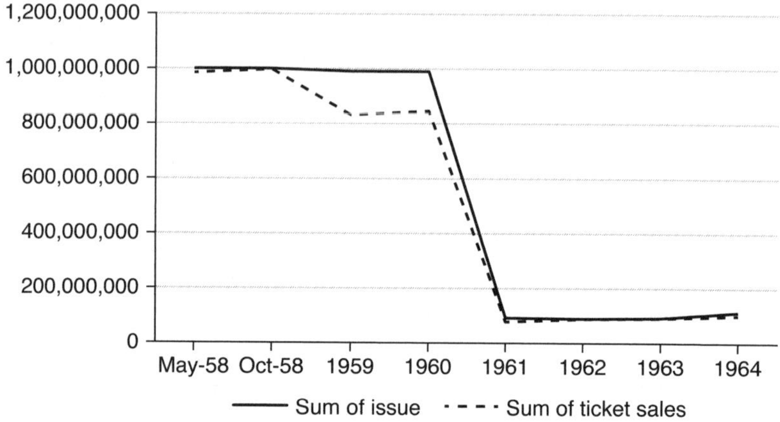

Figure 5.4 Cash-and-Goods Lotteries' Ticket Sales in the RSFSR, 1958–1964. Figures from 1961–1964 are in new money following the 1961 currency reform, scaled down by 10.

Data sources: GARF, f. 259a, op. 45, d. 1360, l. 11; d. 4452, l. 69; GARF, f. 472a, op. 1, d. 1670, l. 83; d. 1755, l. 22; d. 1756, l. 2; d. 1842, l. 2; d. 1928, l. 17; d. 2095, l. 92 (reports from Gostrudsberkass RSFSR on lottery sales tickets, 1958–1964).

Zverev and Dmitrichev submitted their proposal to the Council of Ministers in August 1958.[100] Their proposal was evidently rejected for, that October, another cash-and-goods lottery based on the existing model was held, though ticket prices were reduced to 3 rubles, as had been recommended in their proposal. In 1963, the number of draws held in the RSFSR was increased to six per year.[101] Cash-and-goods lotteries would continue annually up until the collapse of the Soviet Union with few changes to the original model.

There are two reasons why the Soviet government was likely reluctant to run strictly cash-based lotteries. First, goods prizes were more appealing incentives to play the lottery than cash because of the great difficulty involved in procuring the same items in the retail system, and Soviet citizens already had the chance to win big cash prizes through the purchase of 3% market bonds, if they were so inclined. Second, and more importantly, Soviet authorities were by then wary of putting more money into the population's hands for reasons that will become clear momentarily. Shortages boosted the popularity of the goods-oriented lottery, which helped to siphon the excess cash in circulation caused by shortages.[102]

Socialist Accumulation for the Account Holder

Already by the mid-1950s, savings deposits had begun to eclipse lotteries as the Soviet government's preferred means of mobilizing the population's excess money. As Khrushchev's wage reforms, pension raises, reduced wage deductions, and even lottery winnings put more money in citizens' wallets and as more consumer goods entered the retail market, the government told Soviet citizens that the surefire way to satisfy their material desires was through the gradual accumulation of the money needed to buy big-ticket items in a savings account. The steadily increasing sum of money held collectively by Soviet account holders was portrayed in savings propaganda as indisputable evidence of the population's rising prosperity.

Gostrudsberkass was assigned the key role in getting this message across, as was made clear at a convention for savings bank employees in late February 1957. Speaking before the crowd, Dmitrichev praised the great potential of savings as a source of state revenue and chastised his colleagues for not doing enough to secure it.[103] By then, Soviet savings accounts held over 10 times more money than they did before the war and, as of 1957, 26.8% of account holders lived in the countryside, up from 16.9% in 1956, a growth rate that surpassed that of new urban account holders.[104] These trends reflected the government's successful efforts to improve pay and living standards for collective farmers in the wake of the Twentieth Party Congress, he went on. Yet, the plan for 1956 was not fulfilled in every republic and oblast. Dmitrichev dismissed the suggestion that it was simply "too much for them."[105] Rather, the root cause was shortcomings in financial workers' hands-on work with the population, he insisted. "There is no reason to deny several international factors that took place in the fourth quarter—the [1956] events in Hungary—which had a negative impact upon deposits and the receipt of funds," he elaborated, "but the task of savings banks workers and the administration consists in organizing mass-explanatory work to counter against shortfalls in funds, to ensure the fulfillment of the plan."[106]

Dmitrichev acknowledged that the savings banking network was still suffering from many infrastructural deficits after the war and that more work needed to be done to ensure the delivery of "cultured" service in Soviet banks. As of January 1, 1957, there were 51,000 saving banks across the Soviet Union, including 33,000 agents; this constituted 22% more banks than had existed before the war, and in 1956 alone, 3,000 new banks were opened.[107] But regional coverage continued to be uneven: in many formerly occupied areas of

Belarus, Ukraine, and southwestern Russia, the number of banks had not yet returned to prewar levels. There was still a noticeable divide between urban and rural banking services across the Soviet Union. Many collective farms in the RSFSR did not have a bank nearby, while in Ukraine, there were only 128 banks near collective farms and only 64 in all of Tajikistan.[108] Without making it easier for them to get to a bank, it was difficult to encourage collective farmers to save their money, Dmitrichev acknowledged. At the same time, even when a suitable building was found or was built, "without adequate explanatory work, we'll just end up with a bank with very low amounts of money sitting in its accounts."[109] Simply correcting the deficit of banking infrastructure across the country would not compensate for the ongoing, more serious deficit of the population's trust in Soviet savings banks.

On the last day of the conference, Arseny Zverev took the podium and echoed many of Dmitrichev's sentiments, especially the need for savings bank workers to engage in better explanatory work. This included explaining the economic logic of related policy shifts, especially the move away from retail price cuts, he told the crowd. The government had already spent more than 35 billion rubles on increasing pensions, improving maternity leave, and other welfare initiatives, but, as Zverev claimed, "some people still say [to us], 'Alongside everything else you've done, you need to reduce prices.' They even say: 'We used to reduce prices and now we've given up reducing prices.' Some even say: 'We need to reduce taxes or get rid of them all together.'"[110] These opinions were "fully understandable," he said, but "we need to understand that all of this is being done in accordance with the planned development of our economy and with other considerations in mind, stemming from the national income." Price and tax cuts would resume in the future, but, in the meantime, workers needed to realize that the 35 billion rubles in benefits they had received constituted more than two times the sum of savings they had received from price cuts during the Fifth Five-Year Plan. "All of this points to the importance of the work you are doing, Comrades, the work on behalf of state credit," Zverev concluded.[111] This work was inherently different than levying taxes, which revolved around clear deadlines, places of payment, and determined sums; by contrast, Gostrudsberkass's success depended upon "well-organized and correctly targeted organizational labor, on the mass-explanatory and agitational work of savings banks," he elaborated.[112] Savings bank workers needed to encourage the population to become "more interested in the services of savings banks, to fully and completely trust them, to believe in their authority and believe in good and honest service to the population."[113]

This helps explain why, while Gostrudsberkass's promotional efforts when it came to lotteries increasingly moved away from interpersonal efforts and toward advertising that appealed to risk, pleasure, and gain, its efforts to promote savings still assumed more pedagogical forms. After the abolition of mass subscription bonds in 1957, the *komsody*'s efforts were refocused to promoting diligent savings habits among their peers. No longer required to hound their coworkers for subscriptions, their task now consisted of posting financial propaganda in public places, conversing with workers, and "widely promot[ing] the idea among workers, employees and collective farmers that it is necessary to regularly deposit money in savings banks or buy free-circulating bonds in order to save money to satisfy their growing material and cultural needs."[114] In participating workplaces, they raised awareness of and popularized new banking conveniences, such as "savings bank agents" who were directly embedded in factories, allowing workers to conduct their financial affairs without ever having to leave work, or programs that allowed workers to opt to have a certain portion of their wages automatically credited to their bank accounts.[115] Across the country, *komsody* activists were instructed to remind their colleagues that they could pay their telephone, gas, and electricity bills at savings banks directly from their bank accounts without having to withdraw cash—an autopay system *avant la lettre*.[116]

They did not wholly abandon mass and interpersonal methods for ensuring their peers' cooperation with the state's plans for savings deposits. They continued to shine a spotlight on model employees who invested their money in market bonds and who won prizes by posting their names and photographs in public places. In participating workplaces, they organized savings drives in which fellow workers signed up to have a certain portion of their monthly wages automatically transferred to their savings accounts. For example, in October 1958, at a machine-building factory in Smolensk oblast, 60 workers and employees signed up for this service, and over 20,000 rubles were transferred to their savings; by January 1, 1959, they had allegedly saved over 42,000 rubles.[117] The *komsody* could not, however, control when and how much these workers withdrew from the bank after the savings drives had ended.

The *komsody* were also supposed to take the lead in teaching young people that money in the bank was the cornerstone of rationally organized personal finances. In a 1958 article in *Izvestiia*, Dmitrichev wrote that more work needed to be done "in order to instill thrift in workers who have only recently entered industry, as well as in young collective farmers, to help them organize their personal budgets correctly."[118] The *komsody*'s official handbook informed them

Figure 5.5 **Saving for Socialism. "Money for buying expensive things can be accumulated in a bankbook."**
Ne Boltai: A Collection of 20th-Century Propaganda. Used with Permission.

that youth were particularly prone to poor decision-making regarding their spare money: "Getting their hands on their first earned money, [youth] sometimes do not know how to use it rationally or at an even pace."[119] They spent their money on alcohol and other frivolities, rather than newspapers and cultural products.[120] Furthermore, as the number and quality of clothes, motorcycles, cosmetics, and other goods entered the Soviet consumer market, some developed unhealthy acquisitive attitudes. Although savings propaganda reminded Soviet youth that it was acceptable, even encouraged, to save up toward expensive consumer items like motorbikes, they were never to lose sight of what they were really saving up toward (Figure 5.5). As one advertisement in the journal *Molodoi kommunist* read, "The more workers use savings banks to store their money, the more money our socialist Fatherland receives for fulfilling its grandiose plans for economic and cultural construction."[121]

In 1958, Gostrudsberkass began cooperating with a Moscow film studio to produce a "scientific-popular" film about saving money explicitly targeted at the country's youth. The resulting product, *A Strong Character* (Tverdyi kharakter), released the following year, "populariz[ed] the significance of monetary savings for the correct organization of workers' personal budgets."[122] The short film, running about 20 minutes in length, is a comedy consisting of a series of vignettes in the lives of newlyweds Kostya and Valya narrated by Kostya's mother.[123] In the opening scene, she praises her son as "a good son, a good turner [*tokar'*], and a good friend," but "Kostya has one big shortcoming: he doesn't value his hard-earned ruble." Kostya constantly borrows money from friends, spends money liberally on dining out and on entertainment, and lavishes expensive presents on his bride that clutter their brand-new private apartment. Valya, the film's eponymous "strong character," is frugal, diligently keeps track of the couple's expenditures, and is saving money toward major household acquisitions including a furniture set and much-needed bookcases for their growing library.

The couple repeatedly argues about the necessity of saving money, with Kostya insisting that only those who earn big salaries can afford to put money aside and Valya insisting it is possible to save even small amounts. On each payday, Valya diligently deposits money into the bank. On one occasion, she is tempted to give less than usual: as her mother-in-law explains, "Others were depositing thousands, and this time, Valya was lacking in character," for she planned to deposit only 25 rubles that day. Valya encounters another bank patron making a large withdrawal. The woman explains that she is heading out shopping and plans to make a long-awaited purchase: a fur coat that costs 2,100 rubles. When Valya marvels at her discipline and asks her how she has managed to save so much money, the woman tells her that she put aside sometimes only 25 or 50 rubles at a time because "it develops character." Valya changes her mind and deposits 250 rubles. As she leaves the bank, another patron comments on the striking resemblance between Valya and a woman depicted in a savings propaganda poster that hangs on the wall.

Valya and Kostya continue to fight over his frivolous spending habits and over her penny-pinching. After a particularly heated argument, spurred by Valya deliberately buying obstructed theater tickets to teach Kostya a lesson about what miserliness really looks like, Kostya accidentally reveals that he has forgotten their wedding anniversary is tomorrow. They sleep apart that night. The next morning, Kostya sneaks out and asks his friend Fedya, from whom he has borrowed money in the past, to meet him at the bank, to borrow more money for a gift for his wife. Fedya arrives and tells Kostya that his economic circumstances have changed and Kostya must return the money he borrowed immediately. Valya arrives right behind Fedya; Kostya is furious that she is checking up on him. Valya retorts that, since today is their anniversary, she will give Fedya the money Kostya owes him as her gift to her husband. Feeling guilty, Kostya asks about the furniture she planned to buy, and Valya replies that she bought it yesterday—with her savings.

The film ends with the mother's warning: "I hope this affair was a good lesson for Kostya. You can give presents, it's good to do so, you can go out and have fun at restaurants . . . sometimes . . . but you need to buy the most essential things first." As she speaks, the giant disorganized pile of books that Valya has been complaining about throughout the film transforms into an orderly bookcase. The camera pans around their now tastefully furnished and tidy apartment. Against the backdrop of factories and fields being worked, the film ends with the explanation that, from all those savings, the government obtains large sums of money that are put toward the development of the national economy and "all deposits, big and small, help industry and agriculture, and raise the people's cultural level and the well-being of the Soviet people." *A Strong Character* thus encapsulated the key message of savings propaganda in the postwar years, and particularly in the Khrushchev era: Soviet citizens should take pleasure in the new material goods the full-value ruble allowed them to enjoy, but, rather than expecting immediate rewards, these should be acquired responsibly and gradually through prudence and patience.

"Pent-Up Demand"

Savings deposits exhibited steady growth across the Soviet Union after the Twentieth Party Congress. Planned revenue from the population's savings in 1957 was far surpassed that year, over 3 billion more than the expected 9.6 billion.[124] This was due in part to rumors of another currency reform around the time of the mass subscription bond freeze: citizens across the Soviet Union hurried to deposit cash into the bank in order to obtain a preferential conversion rate, just as they had in 1947.[125] The next year also saw a big rise in the amount of money Soviet citizens saved: white-collar employees' savings increased 2.6 times, workers' 3.5 times, and peasants' by a whopping 7.2 times, for a total of a threefold increase over 1956.[126] By January 1, 1959, there were 42.9 million account holders holding about 80.6 billion rubles in their accounts.[127] That year, the plan was overfulfilled for a sum of around 11 billion rubles, well over the 7.2 billion planned.[128]

As in the Stalin years, the Khrushchev government continued to portray the population's increasing savings as unequivocal evidence of the country's growing prosperity; however, as Gostrudsberkass and other financial officials were well aware, these sums also reflected imbalances in the population's money income and expenses caused by inadequate consumer supply. Despite what its propaganda claimed, savings went up not only when there were more consumer goods to save toward, but also when there were not enough goods to spend money on. In 1958, for example, retail trade turnover went up by 6.9% on the whole, with dramatic increases when it came to the sale of expensive consumer goods: sales of televisions and radios went up by 27.6%, sewing machines by 24.3%, furniture by 18.8%, building materials by 16.6%, and appliances including refrigerators, washing machines, and electric goods by 14.6%.[129] Yet, as Gostrudsberkass lamented, "Demand for all manner of goods was not fully satisfied, meaning that a great sum of cash still remains in the hands of the population to purchase these goods."[130] This exerted a "serious influence" on the growth of savings the following year, accounting for the wild "success" of the plan in 1959: in the first three quarters of the year, it was already overfulfilled by around 6 billion rubles.[131]

The 1961 currency reform also had a significant impact upon the balance of the population's income and expenditures. In the wake of Khrushchev's May 1960 announcement of the reform, and despite the state's "systematic efforts to persuade the population that the value of their savings would be fully preserved," many citizens refused to believe the government's assurances and rushed to invest their savings in material goods once again.[132] The sum of goods for both retail and wholesale was estimated to be around 3.7 times higher than the total amount of money held by the population, and around 1.4 times higher than the amount held in savings accounts, by the start of 1960.[133] Panic buying, hoarding, and speculation rendered planned consumer supply wholly inadequate. The plan for retail trade was overfulfilled by 7 billion rubles in the second and third quarters of 1960 alone.[134] The currency reform had a noticeable impact on savings deposits: because of the introduction of new prices and smaller bills—and, although it was not mentioned, the loss of confidence in state banks after the population's savings were revalued for the second time in just 14 years—"certain groups of the population" thereafter now preferred to hold their savings in cash.[135] Increased savings held in cash, rather than in bank accounts, were extremely worrying to central officials because it made it harder for them to know how many goods to release for purchase and how much more cash to release into circulation.

Some Soviet economists began to eye the population's growing savings warily. In a report titled "The People's Savings and Their Accumulation via the Financial System in the Process of Communist Construction," Grigorii

Mar'iakhin pointed to an inconvenient truth. The state's propaganda emphasized that savings increased in tandem with rising living standards and the country's movement toward communism, but, in fact, "the growth of savings during the socialist period is a process that is inversely proportionate to the movement toward communism. The more society moves forward, the fewer reasons there will be to develop personal savings, the weaker the economic stimuli for accumulating money will become, and the less need there will be for making use of voluntary methods for mobilizing money via the various parts of the financial system."[136]

Although he stopped short of calling for the return of mass subscription bonds, Mar'iakhin pushed for a return to more heavy-handed methods for managing the population's out-of-control savings. He criticized Soviet economists who argued that the population's savings should no longer be counted as a source of revenue in the state budget. He argued this practice was, in fact, beneficial because "savings banks play a dual role: as well as accumulating additional resources for the national economy, they absorb the excess currency in the population's hands that does not make its way into the channels of circulation." Money surpluses, he conceded, "disrupt the proper balance between the mass of goods [in the economy] and the purchasing power of money, and thereby weaken the regulation of the monetary system." By absorbing the monetary surpluses caused and creating a means for this money to return to state coffers, savings banks played a critical role in regulating the country's currency supply. The welfare initiatives associated with the Seven-Year Plan would result in rising income and would put ever more money into savings accounts, he warned. Through the abolition of taxes alone (which, as discussed in Chapter 4, Mar'iakhin had vehemently opposed), workers' incomes would rise by another 74 billion rubles. The only way this would not be "financially disastrous," Mar'iakhin argued, was if workers saved money in "predetermined amounts," in other words, through something akin to the now-discontinued mass subscription bonds.[137] "Only under these conditions will it be possible to avoid the appreciation of the mobilized ruble [*udorozhanie privlechenogo rublia*]," he argued. Furthermore, the Soviet government was only adding to the glut, Mar'iakhin pointed out, by paying interest on those savings. This had been necessary in the past when the government needed to incentivize savings, but now it simply increased the value of already-large savings: in 1959 alone, banks across the USSR paid around 2 billion rubles in interest on accounts.[138]

Publicly, the state continued to laud the Soviet people's ever-increasing deposits and the amount collectively held by account holders in Soviet savings banks. In 1961, Petr Chetverikov, who replaced Dmitrichev as the new head of Gostrudsberkass, noted proudly that, in just the first six months of the year, over 560 million rubles were deposited, "evidence of the growing prosperity of the wide mass of workers in our country," and he praised the fact that the average length of time a single ruble spent in a bank account was now 420 days, significantly more than in previous years.[139] Rising savings were linked to increases in the population's real wages and purchasing power during the Seven-Year Plan, he claimed. As the Minister of Finance, Vasilii Garbuzov, explained in his announcement of the 1962 state budget, "The growth of savings proceeds based on the steady growth of Soviet citizens' income. This increase in saving facilitates the strength of the Soviet ruble and the increased trust of the Soviet people in savings banks."[140]

By 1963, at which point the government's control figures for the Seven-Year Plan had not been met and the government had been forced to implement austerity measures, it was abundantly clear to planners that the massive sum of money held by the population, in cash and in savings, was a liability more so than evidence of economic success. Since the start of the Seven-Year Plan in 1959, worrisome cash surpluses had developed because of shortcomings in the consumer economy, ending up in citizens' bank accounts and becoming a source of "pent-up demand" (*otlozennyi spros*) for consumer goods.[141] This exacerbated speculation in and resale of deficit goods and led to the accumulation of massive stores of money in some individuals' hands. Furthermore, in the wake of the currency reform, the growth of savings in cash had begun to outpace the population's savings in banks.[142] It made it extremely difficult for Gosbank to correctly plan how much money to print; excessive currency emission, in turn, simply fed the cycle that created more unspendable money, swelling savings, and grumbling citizens.

Because of this, and against the wishes of economists like Mar'iakhin, Gostrudsberkass and the savings bank network was removed from the Ministry of Finance and placed under the auspices of Gosbank in 1963. The move purportedly recognized the key significance of citizens' spare money and savings in planning the country's currency in circulation, insofar as they increased the cash supply and were needed by the government to cover important payments that led to the further "economic and cultural growth of the country."[143] It also brought an end to the long-standing approach to mobilizing the population's spare money as a form of fundraising—one producing results that, per the Soviet logic of "enthusiasm" and die-hard habits inherited from the mass subscription bond years, could only go up from year to year. It reflected growing recognition on the part of Soviet economic authorities that structural imbalances not only threw off their carefully constructed plans but undermined the real value of money in citizens' hands and the incentive to save it in the first place.

Conclusion

After the "last sacrifice" associated with the 1947 currency reform and especially after the 20-year freeze of citizens' savings held in mass subscription bonds in 1957, the Soviet government promised that money invested in the state would produce real returns: more immediate and tangible benefits for the bondholder, ticket holder, and account holder. Over the course of the postwar period, an increasingly explicit rhetoric of permissible monetary gain and the pleasures of consumption emerged alongside appeals to public considerations in the state's propaganda and in its official proclamations regarding the importance of savings accounts, state bonds, and lotteries to postwar reconstruction efforts and overall economic growth. Personal wealth and collective wealth were depicted as intertwined in the process of building a prosperous socialist society striding toward communism.

For this message to resonate and for workers to respond to the state's appeals, Soviet citizens needed to be able to consistently convert their supposedly "full-value" rubles into what they desired and were saving toward. Perpetual shortages of coveted consumer durables persisted throughout the Khrushchev years, and, as ever, access continued to play a crucial role in consumption. Shortages boosted savings deposits toward the consumer durables citizens were promised would eventually appear. This channeled increased revenue to the state budget and allowed Gostrudsberkass to fete its fundraising successes, but, by increasing the state's financial burden in the form of payments for interest, prizes, and redemption, it also created more unspendable money and undermined the government's claim that steadily rising savings necessarily corresponded to improved living standards.

This increased the popularity of the lottery mechanism in the eyes of at least some citizens and certainly in the eyes of financial officials. Unlike the thousands of rubles that citizens had tied up in semi-forced investments into mass subscription bonds, the 3-ruble expense of a lottery ticket could be quickly forgotten about when it lost, and it represented an enormous return on one's investment when it won. Unlike the billions invested in bonds, the money citizens invested in losing tickets did not need to be paid back. Furthermore, appeals to risk, pleasure, and material gain were far easier to devise than the slow and steady work of building confidence in banks and in the Soviet economy. Shortages in the state consumer economy fueled interest in the cash-and-goods lotteries; however, this strategy could, and often did, backfire. When Margarita Abramova won a "Saratov-2" refrigerator in the 1962 cash-and-goods lottery, for example, she was congratulated by her coworkers and cracked open a bottle of champagne but spent the next two months engaged in a wild goose chase around Moscow trying to find the deficit item. The delays and headaches she experienced were publicly criticized in a June 1962 feuilleton as "discrediting something that is valuable for everyone."[144]

By the early 1960s, it was clear that the Soviet population's savings were a massive liability; however, the government's options for addressing this burgeoning economic crisis were politically disastrous. The government's audacious decision to confiscate decades' worth of supposedly "spare money" invested in mass subscription bonds in 1957 was coupled with the promise to eventually pay it back, and it had eliminated the onerous burden of annual subscriptions, but the move had nevertheless been deeply unpopular, and it was widely seen as robbery in broad daylight, as Chapter 4 revealed. The violent backlash to Khrushchev's June 1962 announcement of higher retail prices showed the risks of asking the Soviet people to accept yet another economic sacrifice after years of promising abundance. As a result, when it came to the population's growing savings, the government took the path of least resistance: they were warehoused while the country's economic problems were tackled and, hopefully, solved. As with the mass subscription bonds, Khrushchev likely hoped that the problem of unspendable savings would solve itself organically with the advent of communism—the ultimate return on money invested in the socialist state. Following this logic, in 20 or so years' time, it would not matter what happened to citizens' savings because the country would be sufficiently wealthy to finally do away with money altogether. By then, communist abundance had still not been achieved, and the Soviet Union's money troubles were far from over.

Conclusion

Prosperity Postponed

At the midpoint of Nikita Khrushchev's tenure as leader of the Soviet Union, the Bolsheviks prided themselves on their many achievements in delivering prosperity to the Soviet people via the full-value ruble. After the 1947 currency reform, prices had been reduced, and after the Twentieth Party Congress in 1956, state spending on the population had been steadily increased, boosting real wages. Workers received higher minimum wages and pensions beginning in 1956, and more free or discounted social welfare benefits. The living standards of the neediest segments of the urban population had increased. Even collective farmers' personal finances had improved since Stalin's death and the agricultural reforms of August 1953 onward. The urban and rural populations alike were putting more money into big-ticket consumer purchases. The abolition of mass subscription bonds in 1957 and end of semi-compulsory, sacrificial contributions to the socialist economy left the population with more money to put into satisfying their "growing material needs." By 1959, the economy was growing so rapidly, and the country was sufficiently wealthy, that it could afford to abolish income taxes and fund the Soviet Union's generous social welfare agenda with the proceeds of state enterprises alone. The government's "grandiose program," unveiled at the Twenty-First Party Congress in 1959, predicted "steadily rising national income and internal accumulation based on growing labor productivity, reduced costs of production and maximally effective use of material, labor, and financial resources," necessitating a new, stronger ruble that reflected "the growing significance of money within the socialist economy."[1] That ruble was introduced on January 1, 1961.

Planners' calculations pointed to even more accomplishments along these lines over the next two decades. In a late February 1960 report to Khrushchev, Aleksandr Volkov of the Committee on Questions of Work and Wages expressed great optimism about the country's economic prospects.[2] By 1980, productivity was scheduled to rise by 4.5 times and the national wealth by 5 times, for a total of 7.2 trillion rubles (old money). The fund for social consumption would simultaneously grow to 2.25 trillion rubles by 1970 and 5 trillion rubles by 1980, or 1,500 rubles per person, up from 410 rubles in 1960—an increase of 3.6 times. Citizens' meat and milk consumption would rise by 1.8 times and 1.7 times, respectively, while their expenditures on consumer goods would also rise.[3] By 1980, the average Soviet citizen would earn 1,500 rubles per month and spend almost all this money on food and consumer goods because housing dues, medication, and transportation, among other everyday expenses, would be made totally free. This planned balance of the population's money income and expenses would "allow us to come ever closer to fully satisfying the needs of the population for the main food and consumer products, which is an important precondition for the transition to communist production," Volkov argued.[4]

The Soviet Union's social welfare system would increasingly integrate those who, at present, were inadequately or wholly unprotected by the socialist safety net, he went on. Low-income members of Soviet society would see tangible improvements to their living standards through further minimum wage increases, higher guaranteed minimum incomes for collective farmers, and, most importantly, increased social welfare benefits covered by the rising fund for social consumption. These would constitute 55% of the real wage by 1980, up from one-quarter in 1960. This represented a major step forward toward communism, Volkov claimed, for satisfying workers' needs via the fund for social consumption constituted "a transitional form of the communist distributional principle."[5] Other real gains would include a shorter workday and workweek, and holiday leave would increase to one month per year.[6] Price cuts would also resume and would help drive real wage growth: between 1960 and 1970, 25% growth would stem from lower prices, while, over the course of 1970–1980, this would rise to 42%.[7] Many of these price reductions would occur in socialized eating facilities, where workers would eat more low-priced and high-quality meals rather than cooking at home, saving them time and money. Over the next 10–20 years, the Soviet Union would be able to offer pensions to collective farmers and to those who had not managed to achieve a complete labor period. By 1980, an estimated 50 million people across the country would receive pensions, which would rise on average to 800 rubles in 1970 and 1,200 rubles in 1980, up from an average of 475 rubles in 1960.[8] In sum, Volkov argued, within 5–10 years, the Soviet Union's living standards would exceed those of even the most advanced capitalist country in Europe, and within 10–15 years, they would exceed those of the United States. With the "right initiative," this could even be achieved 3–4 years ahead of schedule.[9]

Buoyed by these and other such optimistic calculations, Khrushchev concluded that "full communism" was now clearly visible on the horizon, and the Party should focus its efforts in this direction. Hundreds of experts were mobilized to construct an ambitious new Communist Party program that both distanced Khrushchev's regime from that of his predecessor and revitalized the Soviet project, as Alexander Titov has argued.[10] The first Party program had been adopted in 1903, when the Bolsheviks had vowed to overthrow Tsarism in the name of the working class. The second was adopted in 1917, when the Communist Party had declared its ambition to build socialism in Russia. The third aimed to complete the Bolsheviks' project of building communism in the Soviet Union. Khrushchev personally insisted that material provisioning of the population be included as one of its key components.[11] When he unveiled it at the Twenty-Second Party Congress in October 1961, he proudly declared that, not only would communism be achieved by 1980, but already within the first 10 years of embarking upon the new plan, "every stratum [*sloi*] of the Soviet population will be able to make use of their wealth, and will be materially provided for. In this way, communism will demonstrate its decisive superiority over capitalism, regarding the question of which system directly benefits everyone. For the first time in history, we will fully and finally eliminate poverty."[12]

The full-value ruble would play a critical role in building communism, facilitating the steady economic growth the population's growing prosperity depended upon in the meantime. "The correct combination of material and moral incentives is our course, our line, during the entire process of building communism," Khrushchev explained in the same speech.[13] While society was in the socialist stage, it was impossible to dispense with distribution according to labor, commodity-money relationships, and capitalist economic concepts such as price, profit, finance, and credit; however, these economic instruments, he went on, contained "socialist content" and served communist goals. When communism was established, they would become obsolete, and would be replaced by more advanced moneyless economic concepts such as "direct accounting" and the "distribution of social labor." In the interim, "our task during communist construction consists in making ever more use of and improving financial-credit levers, and control by means of the ruble, prices, and profit."[14]

Not one year later, by the spring of 1962, the Soviet Union's economic prospects looked much less rosy. Planners' calculations and Khrushchev's triumphant claims about the country's growing prosperity were unrealistic, to say the least. Already by the late 1950s, the economy had begun to exhaust its postwar sources of growth, and, by the early 1960s, it was suffering diminishing returns on its long-standing focus on building up heavy industry—a crisis of overinvestment that it had presumed was possible only in a capitalist, not socialist, economy.[15] According to Philip Hanson, industrial growth slowed from 8.9% per annum in the period 1953–1960 to 6.6% per annum in 1960–1964.[16] That decrease was partly due to Khrushchev's disruptive "hobbyhorse" reforms, but it also stemmed from the rigidity built into the planning system, which worked against implementing desired structural changes.[17] For example, as discussed in Chapter 2, the wage reforms that were scheduled to conclude in 1962 constituted a glorified pay cut for many low-paid workers, while traditional priority sectors of the economy managed to protect their high earnings and circumvent changes intended to incentivize higher quality and greater productivity. Even more problematically, Khrushchev's initially successful agricultural reforms of the mid-1950s gave way to devastating failures in the early 1960s. Restrictions on private agricultural activities imposed when the state's food supply was increasing, fraud in the campaign to "catch up and overtake" the United States in meat production, and poor harvests had produced serious shortages both in state stores and in the kolkhoz markets. After years of claiming that the Soviet Union was on the verge of overtaking the United States in agricultural output, it was, to its great humiliation, forced to import grain from America in 1963. Hunger was knocking on Soviet citizens' doors once again.

Unspendable money stemming from increased wages, pensions, and other state payments to the population, such as interest on savings, combined with shortages in state stores and rising market prices, threw off the carefully planned balance of the population's money income and expenses, undermining the promises associated with the full-value ruble, as seen in each of this book's chapters. This imbalance between money and goods to spend it on had grown severe and undeniable by the spring of 1962. To correct it, over the remainder of that year, the Soviet government progressively rescinded its assurances about the full-value ruble, replacing them with a new and unpopular austerity program. The increased meat and milk prices announced on June 1 were, to many, a stunning reversal of Khrushchev's promise that price reductions, which were still depicted as essential to increasing real wages and to communist construction, even if Stalinist consecutive price cuts had ceased, would soon resume. No doubt because of this backlash, the promised minimum wage raise that was slated for 1962 was more quietly postponed, as was the abolition of taxes that fall. Extending pensions to collective farmers was also postponed until 1964, and, when it was finally accomplished, the pensions they received were much more modest than those offered to workers. Despite these shifts, during the remainder of Khrushchev's rule, the population continued to acquire more unspendable or, to put it in Soviet terms, "uncovered" rubles. This excess money contributed to market-price inflation, ended up in interest-paying bank accounts and bonds that only increased the state's financial liability to the people and caused the savings glut to grow, and it made workers grumble even louder about the difficulties of making ends meet. In many Soviet citizens' eyes, the new 1961 ruble came to symbolize not imminent communist abundance but the socialist government's failure to deliver upon its promises.

No one was criticized more harshly for this state of affairs than Khrushchev, both within the Soviet government, itself, and in the population at large. Soviet bureaucrats and planners yearned to see the economy recentralized after it became clear that Khrushchev's experiments in decentralization had produced chaos and a loss of control instead of more accurate plans as promised.[18] Khrushchev's lack of respect for collective policy-making, constant reshuffling of personnel, and dictatorial streak also rubbed many of Stalin's cadres the wrong way; his successor, Leonid Brezhnev, would not make the same mistake, coming to power declaring himself the guarantor of "collective leadership."[19] Just as importantly, ordinary citizens and central authorities alike were growing restless about obviously declining living standards, which Khrushchev did not acknowledge in spite of the new culture of openness and public discussion he, in principle, promoted. Among the many accusations leveled against Khrushchev when he was kicked out of office in October 1964, one of the most damning was that his policies had failed to bring about the dramatic improvements that he had personally repeatedly guaranteed. "The data here are very worrying," a transcript of the Central Committee's report on his conduct reads.[20] Growth of the national wealth was down to about a third of 1950–1953 levels by 1963, a fact that was attributed to "unsatisfactory leadership over the economy." Growth of workers' real wages was also disappointing: the Seven-Year Plan was supposed to see growth of 40%, but over the past five years, it had grown by only 20%. In the meantime, prices in the kolkhoz markets had risen by 17%, while prices in state cooperatives had grown 13% since 1963 alone. The state had been forced to postpone its efforts to raise minimum wages and bring taxes to an end. "All these and other facts inspire great dissatisfaction in the population," the report concluded.[21] Meanwhile, Khrushchev continued to trumpet the excellent situation the country found itself in, the fact that "we have a little piece of heaven on earth." "Isn't this demagoguery?" the report asked.[22] If the situation did not improve, "people will start to say: 'To hell with you, if you can't direct and manage the economy. If you're only going to make promises and not fulfill them, put someone else in charge who can lead and can keep his word.' And they would be right."[23]

After Khrushchev was removed from office, the Soviet government swiftly abandoned his more disruptive economic reforms in the name of expediting communism. It recentralized the Soviet economy and rolled back Khrushchev's experiments in devolving control and decision-making to the local level. However, Khrushchev's living standards campaign, with its emphasis on better-stocked shelves and improved consumption, was not, as Natalya Chernyshova notes, something the new leadership could easily abandon even if it had wanted to.[24] The Brezhnev years are often remembered as the Soviet Union's "golden age," when living standards were relatively high and the Soviet system settled into a comfortable stability, despite the economy's continuing slump. The paternalistic wage, price, and pension policies of the relatively more prosperous mid- to late 1950s became key components of the late Soviet social contract until the mid-1980s, when the country's economic difficulties could no longer be glossed over. As Aleksei Makarkin emphasizes, the government became more cautious in its dealings with the public after the furor surrounding price increases in 1962, and its new source of economic prosperity—oil profits—allowed for another two decades of generosity when funding its social policy.[25] It provided full and secure employment, relatively egalitarian wage policies and lax performance pressures in industry, state-controlled and heavily subsidized retail prices for essential goods, and free or discounted education, medical care, and child care, and, as Linda J. Cook argues, in return for their social and economic security, Soviet workers gave the regime their political compliance and quiescence.[26]

Consumer shortages persisted and the trade system continued to anticipate and respond poorly to consumer demand, but there were no more major spikes in retail prices or the cost of living, as in 1962, until the Mikhail Gorbachev years. Although it did not revive the late Stalin era's consecutive price reductions, the Brezhnev government resumed its more paternalistic approach to retail price policy. Under the banner of the Kosygin reforms of 1965 onward, planners attempted to establish a more concrete correspondence between supply and demand, and reward enterprises for greater efficiency and productivity—initiatives that had, in fact, been discussed earlier in connection with Khrushchev's policy of "economically grounded" prices in the early 1960s, but which had stalled after the events of 1962. Beginning in the mid-1960s, mathematically minded economists like Vasily Nemchinov attempted to revamp the government's approach to prices in order to use them more "scientifically" and produce greater efficiency.[27] Retail prices were not publicly depicted in such terms, however. Much as in the Stalin years, the Brezhnev government portrayed retail prices as the primary driver of real wage growth. It also resumed Stalinist public rituals surrounding price adjustments. "Holiday trade," or increased supply ahead of important events complemented by price cuts on those goods, was portrayed as an important demonstration of the Communist Party's concern for the population's material prosperity.[28] At other times, keeping prices stable became a hallmark of the Brezhnev regime's relationship to consumers, and it emphasized that prices could only go down, though the prices of many consumer goods crept up in reality.[29]

Although there were attempts to rework incentives within the Soviet industrial workplace, another major overhaul of the wage system did not occur under Brezhnev. The minimum wage was brought up to 60 rubles (new money) in 1968, 70 rubles in 1971, and 80 rubles in 1980. Collective farmers, for their part, received guaranteed minimum wages from the kolkhoz starting in 1966. Significant changes to industrial wages did not come until Gorbachev's last-ditch efforts to stimulate better work and higher productivity by tying wage levels to enterprises' income levels rather than central funds in the mid-1980s, in several ways, a throwback to Khrushchev's wage reforms of 1956–1962.[30] Workers' and collective farmers' pension minimums were also raised under Brezhnev, but, as with wages, there were few substantive reforms to the pension system until perestroika, when Gorbachev finally revisited the issue of pension financing and raised the possibility of asking workers to pay into their own pensions. He also sought to redress some of the inequities that had persisted after the adoption of the 1956 pension law, proposing to raise peasants' pensions to the levels enjoyed by workers and provide pensions to those who had spent inadequate time in the workplace.[31] The Soviet Union collapsed before these reforms could be implemented.

At the Twenty-Fourth Party Congress, on March 30, 1971, Brezhnev announced in passing that the Soviet government would begin redeeming the frozen mass subscription bonds earlier than anticipated, beginning in 1974–1975 and finishing in 1990, a full six years ahead of schedule.[32] This was good news to millions of bondholders across the country eager to recoup the money the government had effectively confiscated in 1957; however, by that point, inflation had reduced the value of their investments and many bondholders, as some angry letter writers had predicted, had died without seeing their investments returned. The abolition of taxes was never resumed. It was not until 1990 that the elimination of the bachelor tax was set into motion, beginning with married women. With the collapse of the Soviet Union, the bachelor tax died with it, although there have been repeated efforts to revive it since as a solution to post-Soviet states' ongoing demographic crises.[33] As for the income tax, minor changes to the tax scale were made only in the early 1970s, before more substantive changes to income tax connected to the reemergence of private enterprise in the late 1980s during perestroika.

The late Soviet government continued to turn to market bonds, lotteries, and savings deposits to absorb excess cash in circulation. It never managed to solve the problem of the savings glut. As the 1947 3% lottery bond reached the end of its 20-year term, the government issued a new 3% bond in 1966 to partially redeem it. By then, state debt on market bonds totaled over 1.5 billion rubles.[34] By 1978, over 15 billion rubles was held in these bonds, and the average ruble saved now spent 830 days in a bank account.[35] Brezhnev issued yet another 3% market bond to redeem the 1966 issues in 1982. By January 1, 1991, the Soviet state owed around 185.5 billion rubles to the population on these investments.[36] These debts were left unpaid when the Soviet Union collapsed in December 1991. While other post-Soviet republics reneged on repayment, their fate is yet to be decisively settled in post-Soviet Russia.[37]

Communism was not achieved by 1980, and the ruble outlived the Soviet Union.[38] Yet, in the postwar period, as this book has shown, there was real hope within the Soviet leadership that the socialist economy was performing well enough to move in the direction of a moneyless economy. That did not mean reducing the role and significance of the ruble in Soviet life as the country recuperated from the war's damage and moved toward the glorious communist future, but just the opposite: the ruble had to become even more "full-value" within the planned economy and in Soviet citizens' hands, before money could be made obsolete. This argument had been advanced well before the war, most vehemently by Stalin, and Khrushchev maintained the same line into the early 1960s. Despite his desire to get back to "Leninist" norms, Khrushchev did not revisit the issue of money's problematic existence in a postrevolutionary economy; instead, he affirmed the importance of the full-value ruble during the socialist transition and his notion of prosperity, while more inclusive than that of his predecessor, fundamentally rested upon Stalinist foundations.

One important reason why Soviet leaders and experts, from Stalin to Khrushchev, did not revisit the issue of whether or not money should play such an important role in Soviet life was because they still needed it as an incentive for compliance with their plans decades after the revolution. Full communism, as Marx had instructed and as the Bolsheviks understood him, required a state of abundance; producing abundance required tangible incentives for the hard work that needed to be done to overcome Russia's historic economic deficits and the Second World War's enormous damage employing a population that had not yet fully developed communist "consciousness." Soviet authorities accordingly invested great effort in trying to maintain the full-value ruble by striking the proper balances between currency in circulation and goods available for purchase and between paternalism and personal responsibility in their social welfare policies in order to boost its incentive value. As this book has shown, in the roughly 20 years after the war, if not for the remainder of the Soviet period, these balances eluded them.

The Bolsheviks' turn to the full-value ruble to deliver upon the promise of prosperity had important consequences for citizens' experience of Soviet power. As a nexus mediating the relationship between citizens and the state, it communicated the former's assigned importance to the economy and, more broadly, to the communist project. Even after Khrushchev's attempts to reduce income inequality and move beyond the harshest consequences of the Stalinist "struggle against leveling," the full-value ruble articulated who was entitled to experience Soviet prosperity first. Although their economic prospects improved over the course of the 1950s and they were increasingly integrated into the Soviet money economy, peasants remained at the back of the line. Party and cultural elites continued to be in the "vanguard," a position that not only entitled them to higher salaries and more spending power, but which entitled them to one of the most useful privileges of all in the Soviet Union: the ability to treat money as irrelevant. Lacking access and personal connections, and amid persistent deficits of consumer goods to spend it on, ordinary people accumulated massive savings that could not be easily spent and did not have social currency to cash in instead. Despite the government's sustained efforts to improve the purchasing power of the Soviet ruble, the reality was that it was not "full-value." It was much more frequently useless. This undercut ordinary citizens' confidence in the ruble, which, in turn, diminished its value as a labor incentive and hindered economic growth and productivity toward the abundance that was believed to be needed before resources could be distributed more equitably. It undercut the population's faith in a government that continually promised, but failed, to eliminate their money troubles once and for all.

Appendixes

APPENDIX A

Unified State Retail Prices as of December 16, 1947

Prices of Bread and Other Manufactured Goods (in rubles, per kilogram)

	Zone I	Zone II	Zone III
Rye bread	2.80	3.00	3.20
Wheat bread, second-class	4.00	4.40	4.80
Wheat bread, first-class	6.20	7.00	7.80
Whole-grain rye bread	4.40	4.80	5.20
Second-class wheat flour	5.70	6.20	7.00
First-class wheat flour	7.00	8.00	9.00
First-class ground flour	5.50	6.00	6.50
Buckwheat grains	11.00	12.00	13.00
First-class macaroni	9.00	10.00	11.00
Refined sugar	13.50	15.00	16.50
First-class beef	28.00	30.00	32.00
High-quality salted butter	62.00	64.00	66.00
Refined and unrefined sunflower oil	28.00	30.00	32.00
Fresh pike-perch fish	10.50	12.00	10.50
Vatted salted herring	17.00	20.00	17.00
Ground salt, second kind	1.60	1.60	1.80
Ground salt, third kind	1.40	1.40	1.60
Oats	2.20	2.50	2.80

Prices of Fruits, Milk, and Eggs (in rubles, by season)

	Zone I		Zone II		Zone III	
	from	to	from	to	from	to
First-group "Kandil'" apples, per kg.	8.00	12.00	12.00	18.00	16.00	25.00
Whole milk, per liter	2.50	3.50	3.00	4.00	4.00	5.00
Eggs, first-category, for 10	10.00	14.00	12.00	16.00	14.00	18.00

Unified Prices of Certain Goods for All Zones (in rubles)

Georgian loose-leaf tea	100 gr.	16.00
Roasted coffee grains	1 kg.	75.00
Bottled "Zhigulevskoe" beer	0.5 liter	7.00
Ice cream	1 kg.	20.00
Caviar	1 kg.	400.00
"Moskovskaia" vodka	0.5	60.00

Prices of Industrially Produced Goods (in rubles)

	Article no.	Unit	In the cities	In the countryside
Calico	6	meter	10.10	11.20
Satin	144	meter	25.20	28.00
Wool-blend fabrics	384	meter	108.00	120.00
Pure wool "Boston" fabric	125	meter	450.00	510.00
Crêpe de Chine	5	meter	137.00	151.75
Women's cotton dresses	157–208	piece	77.00	86.00
Women's wool dresses	141–23	piece	510.00	560.00
Men's double-breasted wool-blend suits	12–16	piece	430.00	450.00
Men's suits made from "Boston" fabric	12–46	piece	1,400.00	1,500.00
Men's leather boots	R4004chsh	pair	260.00	288.00
Women's shoes	R4144chsh	pair	260.00	288.00
Men's rubber boots	110	pair	45.00	45.00
Men's felt boots	0129n	pair	195.00	216.00
Women's wool-blend jackets	534	piece	190.00	210.00
Women's cotton stockings	8	pair	7.00	7.50
Men's patterned and viscose socks	86	pair	17.00	19.00
Cotton thread in black and white colors	–	spool	1.75	1.75
Matches	–	box	0.20	0.20
Perfumed soap	–	100 g.	4.00	4.00
Household soap	–	100 g.	5.20	5.20
Kerosene	–	liter	2.00	2.50
"Kazbek" rolling papers, 25 pieces	–	box	6.30	6.30
Women's celluloid comb	462–130	piece	4.00	4.00
"Zvezda" and "ZIF" metal watches	T18	piece	900.00	900.00
Gramophone, model PT-3	–	piece	900.00	900.00
"Rekord" radio set	–	piece	600.00	600.00
"Fed-1" camera	–	piece	1,100.00	1,100.00

Data sources: GARF, f. 5446, op. 1, d. 316, l. 282–284 (Order No. 550 from the Ministry of Trade on the new unified prices). See also "Prikaz No. 550 ministerstva torgovli SSSR 14 dekabria 1947 g. gor. Moskvy: Novye edinye gosudarstvennye roznichnye tseny na prodovol'stvennye i promyshlennye tovary," *Pravda,* December 16, 1947, 3.

APPENDIX B

Pension Norms

New Pension Norms in the Draft Law, May 8, 1956

			Types of Workers and Employees								
			Standard workers and employees			Workers and employees who worked underground, in dangerous jobs, or in hot conditions			Workers and employees in other difficult jobs		
Pension Categories and Subcategories			% of wage	Wage cap	Above cap	% of wage	Wage cap	Above cap	% of wage	Wage cap	Above cap
Old-age	Monthly Wage	Up to 350 (incl.)	100	–	–	100	–	–	–	–	–
		350–500	85	–	–	90	–	–	–	–	–
		500–600	75	–	–	80	–	–	–	–	–
		600–800	65	–	–	70	—	—	—	—	—
		800–1,000	55	–	–	60	–	–	–	–	–
		1,000 and above	50	–	–	55	–	–	–	–	–
Workers and employees who became disabled as a result of a work-related injury or illness	Disability Group	I	100	500	+ 10%	100	600	+ 20%	100	500	+ 15%
		II	90	450	+ 10%	90	600	+ 20%	90	500	+ 15%
		III	65	400	+ 10%	65	600	+ 20%	65	500	+ 15%
Workers and employees who became disabled not as a result of a work-related illness	Disability Group	I	100	500	+ 10%	100	600	+ 20%	100	500	+ 15%
		II	90	450	+ 10%	90	600	+ 20%	90	500	+ 15%
		III	65	400	+ 10%	65	600	+ 20%	65	500	+ 15%
Dependent family members of workers and employees who died on the job	Number of Dependents	3 or more	100	500	+ 10%	100	600	+ 20%	100	500	+ 15%
		2	90	450	+ 10%	90	600	+ 20%	90	500	+ 15%
		1	65	400	+ 10%	65	600	+ 20%	65	500	+ 15%

Data source: "Zakon o gosudarstvennykh pensiiakh," *Pravda*, May 9, 1956, 1–2.

Draft Pension Norms, May 8, 1956, in Rubles (continued)

Pension Categories and Subcategories			Types of Workers and Employees								
			Standard workers and employees			Workers and employees who worked underground, in dangerous jobs, or in hot conditions			Workers and employees in other difficult jobs		
			% of wage	Wage cap	Above cap	% of wage	Wage cap	Above cap	% of wage	Wage cap	Above cap
Dependent family members of workers and employees who died as a result of an illness and who had the necessary labor period to obtain a disability pension	Number of Dependents	3 or more	85	500	+ 10%	85	600	+ 20%	85	500	+ 15%
		2	65	450	+ 10%	65	600	+ 20%	65	500	+ 15%
		1	45	400	+ 10%	45	600	+ 20%	45	500	+ 15%
Soldiers who were workers or employees prior to being conscripted who were injured or became ill as a result of frontline or other military responsibilities	Disability Category	I	100	500	+ 10%	100	600	+ 20%	100	500	+ 15%
		II	90	450	+ 10%	90	600	+ 20%	90	500	+ 15%
		III	65	400	+ 10%	65	600	+ 20%	65	500	+ 15%
Soldiers who were workers or employees prior to being conscripted who were injured or became ill not as a result of frontline or other military responsibilities	Disability Category	I	85	500	+ 10%	85	600	+ 20%	85	500	+ 15%
		II	65	450	+ 10%	65	600	+ 20%	65	500	+ 15%
		III	45	400	+ 10%	45	600	+ 20%	45	500	+ 15%

Data source: "Zakon o gosudarstvennykh pensiiakh," *Pravda*, May 9, 1956, 1–2.

Draft Minimum and Maximum Pension Amounts, May 8, 1956, in Rubles

Type of Pensioner	Subcategory	Minimum	Maximum
Old-age	–	360	1,200
Workers who became disabled as a result of an injury or illness resulting from their professional responsibilities	I-group	360	1,200
	II-group	285	900
	III-group	210	450
Workers who became disabled as a result of an illness not resulting from their professional responsibilities	I-group	300	900
	II-group	230	600
	III-group	160	450
Dependent family members of workers and employees who died on the job	3 or more	300	1,200
	2	230	900
	1	160	450
Dependent family members of workers and employees who died as a result of an illness and who had the necessary labor period to obtain a disability pension	3 or more	300	900
	2	230	600
	1	160	400
Soldiers who were workers or employees prior to being conscripted who were injured or became ill as a result of frontline or other military responsibilities	I-group	385	1,200
	II-group	285	900
	III-group	210	450
Soldiers who were workers or employees prior to being conscripted who were injured or became ill not as a result of frontline or other military responsibilities	I-group	330	900
	II-group	230	600
	III-group	160	400

Data source: "Zakon o gosudarstvennykh pensiiakh," *Pravda,* May 9, 1956, 1–2.

Draft Pension Bonuses, May 8, 1956

Category	Requirement	Bonus percentage added to pension
For a Continuous Labor Period		
Old-age pensioners	More than 15 years	10%
I- and II-group invalids due to a nonwork-related illness	10–15 years	10%
	15 years or more	15%
Dependents of workers and employees who died on the job	10–15 years	10%
	15 years or more	15%
Dependents of workers and employees who died as a result of a nonwork-related illness	10–15 years	10%
	15 years or more	15%
For Care of Nonworking Dependents*		
Nonworking old-age pensioners	1 dependent	10%
	2 dependents or more	15%

(*Continued*)

Draft Pension Bonuses, May 8, 1956 (continued)

Category	Requirement	Bonus percentage added to pension
Nonworking I- and II-group invalids (regardless of the cause of disability)	1 dependent	10%
	2 dependents or more	15%
I-group invalids (regardless of the cause of disability)	To care for dependents	15% (not to exceed 30% of the total amount of the pension)
Dependents of workers who died on the job	3 or more dependents	15%

* "Dependents" included children, brothers, sisters, and grandchildren under the age of 16 or, if they were in school, 18 years of age; disabled individuals exceeding these ages, including brothers, sisters, and grandchildren, providing they did not have labor-capable parents; fathers, mothers, wives, and husbands who were older than 60 years for men and 55 years for women or who were disabled; a parent or spouse, regardless of age or labor capacity who did not work and who was engaged in caring for a deceased breadwinner's children, brothers, sisters, or grandchildren who were not older than 8 years of age; grandfathers and grandmothers in the absence of other individuals who, by law, were required to provide care to them.

Data source: "Zakon o gosudarstvennykh pensiiakh," *Pravda,* May 9, 1956, 1–2.

Amended Required Labor Periods for Workers Who Became Disabled as a Result of Nonwork-Related Illness

	Labor period required		
Age	Men	Women	Workers and employees who worked underground, in dangerous jobs, or in hot conditions
20–23 years	2	1	1
23–26 years	3	2	2
26–31 years	5	3	3
31–36 years	7	5	5
36–41 years	10	7	6
41–46 years	12	9	7
46–51 years	14	11	8
51–56 years	16	13	10
56–61 years	18	14	12
61 years and older	20	15	14

Data source: "Zakon o gosudarstvennykh pensiiakh," *Pravda,* July 15, 1956, 1.

Amended Pension Bonuses

Category	Requirement	Bonus percentage added to pension
For a Continuous Labor Period		
Male old-age pensioners	15 years, with a 35-year labor period	15%
Female old-age pensioners	15 years, with a 30-year labor period	10%
I- and II-group invalids due to a nonwork-related illness	10–15 years 15 years or more	10% 15%
Dependents of workers and employees who died on the job	10–15 years 15 years or more	10% 15%
Dependents of workers and employees who died as a result of a nonwork-related illness	10–15 years 15 years or more	10% 15%
For Care of Nonworking Dependents		
Nonworking old-age pensioners	1 dependent 2 dependents or more	10% 15%
Nonworking I- and II-group invalids (regardless of the cause of disability)	1 dependent 2 dependents or more	10% 15%
I-group invalids (regardless of the cause of disability)	To care for dependents	15% (not to exceed 30% of the total amount of the pension)
Dependents of workers who died on the job	3 or more dependents	15%
Dependents of deceased soldiers who were not workers prior to conscription	1 dependent 2 dependents or more	10% 15%
Nonworking I- and II-group war invalids (regardless of the cause of disability)	1 dependent 2 dependents or more	10% 15%
For Military Rank		
War invalids who were workers prior to conscription	Attained the rank of sergeant or higher	10%
Families of deceased soldiers who were workers prior to conscription	Attained the rank of sergeant or higher	10%
Families of deceased soldiers who were workers in a producers' cooperative prior to conscription	Attained the rank of sergeant or higher	10%

Data source: "Zakon o gosudarstvennykh pensiiakh," *Pravda,* July 15, 1956, 1–2.

Pension Norms for War Veterans Who Were Not Workers prior to Conscription

Soldiers who were not workers prior to being conscripted who were injured defending the USSR or as a result of other military responsibilities, or as a consequence of an illness related to frontline service	Disability Category	I-group	385 rubles per month
		II-group	285 rubles per month
		III-group	210 rubles per month
Soldiers who were not workers prior to being conscripted who were injured or who became ill due to circumstances not related to the fulfillment of their official military or frontline duties	Disability Category	I-group	330 rubles per month
		II-group	230 rubles per month
		III-group	160 rubles per month

Data source: "Zakon o gosudarstvennykh pensiiakh," *Pravda,* July 15, 1956, 1.

Pension Norms for the Families of Deceased Soldiers Who Were Not Workers prior to Conscription

Labor-incapable family members of a deceased soldier who was not a worker prior to conscription, regardless of the cause of his death	Number of Dependents	3 or more	385 rubles per month
		2	285 rubles per month
		1	210 rubles per month

Data source: "Zakon o gosudarstvennykh pensiiakh," *Pravda,* July 15, 1956, 2.

Notes

Introduction

1. "Postanovlenie soveta ministrov SSSR i TsKP(b) o provedenii denezhnoi reformy i otmene kartochek na prodovol'stvennye i promyshlennye tovary," *Pravda,* December 15, 1947, 1.

2. Ibid.

3. From the mid-1930s on, Stalinist authorities drew an explicit link between prosperity and "culturedness," understood as a clean, "civilized," and materially comfortable life, which Soviet citizens were promised in exchange for more efficient work. See Vadim Volkov, "The Concept of Kul'turnost'," in *Stalinism: New Directions,* ed. Sheila Fitzpatrick (London: Routledge, 2000), 216.

4. This belief was not merely aspirational, according to the Russian economist G. I. Khanin. On the basis of his recalculations of Soviet figures, Khanin argues that the 1950s were a period of unprecedented financial stabilization, and this was one of the immense economic and social achievements that, in his opinion, helped make the 1950s the decade of the "Soviet economic miracle." See G. I. Khanin, "The 1950s—the Triumph of the Soviet Economy," *Europe-Asia Studies,* Vol. 55, No. 8 (2003): 1198–1199.

5. Marx suggested that, after the socialist revolution, workers might initially receive paper vouchers entitling them to a certain number of goods from the common store in correlation with the amount of labor time they had contributed, but these vouchers would not be money because they would not circulate. Communism would be a state of abundance, and when it had been achieved, these vouchers would become unnecessary. See Karl Marx, *Capital: A Critique of Political Economy,* vol. 2, *The Process of Circulation of Capital,* ed. Friedrich Engels, trans. Ernest Untermann (Chicago: Charles H. Kerr, 1933), 412.

6. "Doklad tovarishcha N. S. Khrushcheva; IV. Ob izmenenii masshtaba tsen i zamene nyne obrashchaiushchikhsia deneg novymi den'gami," *Izvestiia,* May 6, 1960, 3.

7. On the emergence of the "balance of the population's money income and expenses" as a planning tool, see N. S. Margolin, *Balans denezhnykh dokhodov i raskhodov naseleniia* (Moskva: Gosplanizdat, 1940), 3–5. These calculations were classified beginning in the early 1930s but have been recently declassified and collated as a data set. See Iu. I. Kashin and V. V. Mikov, eds., *Po stranitsam arkhivnykh fondov tsentral'nogo banka rossiiskoi federatsii,* vypusk 1, *Denezhnye dokhody i raskhody naseleniia, 1924–1990 gg.* (Moskva: Tsentral'nyi bank Rossiiskoi federatsii, 2006).

8. On the Khrushchev-era Thaw as a rupture with the Stalinist past, see Denis Kozlov and Eleonory Gilburd, "The Thaw as an Event in Russian History," in *The Thaw: Soviet Society and Culture during the 1950s and 1960s*, ed. Denis Kozlov and Eleonory Gilburd (Toronto: University of Toronto Press, 2013), 27–28.

9. Notable entries include Susan E. Reid, "Cold War in the Kitchen: Gender and the De-Stalinization of Consumer Taste in the Soviet Union under Khrushchev," *Slavic Review*, Vol. 61, No. 2 (2002): 211–252; Mark B. Smith, *Property of Communists: The Urban Housing Program from Stalin to Khrushchev* (DeKalb: Northern Illinois University Press, 2010); Steven E. Harris, *Communism on Tomorrow Street: Mass Housing and Everyday Life after Stalin* (Baltimore: Johns Hopkins University Press, 2013); Christine Varga-Harris, *Stories of House and Home: Soviet Apartment Life during the Khrushchev Years* (Ithaca, N.Y.: Cornell University Press, 2015).

10. Alec Nove, "Toward a 'Communist Welfare State'?," *Problems of Communism*, Vol. 1, No. 9 (1960): 8.

11. Ibid., 9.

12. For example, Tony Judt's sweeping study of postwar Europe is perhaps the most well-known overview of these developments, but the Soviet Union is mentioned only fleetingly in this connection: Judt points out that, in the Soviet Union, infant mortality rates declined in the 1950s due to improved nutrition, housing, and medical care. See Tony Judt, *Postwar: A History of Europe since 1945* (New York: Penguin Books, 2005), 331.

13. A relative consensus exists among economic historians that the Soviet Union achieved high growth rates after the Second World War. Philip Hanson notes that, in spite of the government's "notoriously exaggerated" figures heralding astronomic growth and rapid recovery during the Fourth Five-Year Plan, even Western recalculations for the period 1946–1950 show that, by 1948, gross national product had returned to 1940 levels, the 1950 level was one-fifth above that of 1940, and by the time of Stalin's death, it was 50% higher. See Philip Hanson, *The Rise and Fall of the Soviet Economy: An Economic History of the USSR from 1945* (London: Longman, 2003), 25–26. Mark Harrison suggests that the post-1945 Soviet economy was not particularly depressed compared to other European economies; Soviet growth was knocked back by about 10 years, while other countries were set back by decades. Harrison suggests that the Soviet Union was still rebounding from earlier economic shocks, such as the Civil War, collectivization, and the Great Terror, helping to explain high growth rates after the Second World War. He writes: "Because this backlog existed and was so large, the economy could spend thirty years making it up and, while it did so, put on the appearance of dynamism." He locates another cause of growth in more efficient use of repression; if before the war, terror was indiscriminate, affecting the loyal and disloyal alike, postwar repression was "selective, focused, and efficient" by comparison. See Mark Harrison, "The Soviet Union after 1945: Economic Recovery and Political Repression," *Past and Present*, Vol. 210, No. 6 (2011): 111–120.

14. Donald A. Filtzer, *The Hazards of Urban Life in Late Stalinist Russia: Health, Hygiene, and Living Standards, 1943–1953* (New York: Cambridge University Press, 2010), 4–6.

15. Although by the 1930s, money was important as a "unitary measuring stick," as David Granick called it, "natural criteria," such as output produced and materials consumed, were still considered important economic indicators and profitability was rejected as the basic criterion for evaluating managers' decisions and firms' work. See David Granick, *Management of the Industrial Firm in the USSR: A Study in Soviet Economic Planning* (New York: Columbia University Press, 1954), 157–161.

16. As Oscar Sanchez-Sibony has shown, the Soviet government used the possibility of trade without hard currency as a selling point in its economic dealings with the decolonizing world, which also suffered from a deficit of hard currency. See Oscar Sanchez-Sibony, *Red Globalization: The Political Economy of the Soviet Cold War from Stalin to Khrushchev* (Cambridge: Cambridge University Press, 2014), 149.

17. János Kornai, *The Socialist System: The Political Economy of Communism* (Princeton, N.J.: Princeton University Press, 1992), 131.

18. Ibid., 140–143.

19. Ibid., 148, 273.

20. Ibid., 239.

21. Elena Osokina, *Our Daily Bread: Socialist Distribution and the Art of Survival in Stalin's Russia, 1927–1941,* ed. Kate Transchel, trans. Kate Transchel and Greta Bucher (Armonk, N.Y.: M. E. Sharpe, 2001), 104.

22. Sheila Fitzpatrick, *Everyday Stalinism: Ordinary Life in Extraordinary Times: Soviet Russia in the 1930s* (New York: Oxford University Press, 1999), 62. James Heinzen has recently pushed back on the idea that *blat* was consistently more useful than money. He points out that most people did not have *blat* and personal connections were not always enough to solve their problems. In the postwar period, everyday life provided prolific opportunities for the illicit exchange of cash, which was often the only payment accepted for certain goods and favors procured illegally and semi-legally. Heinzen concludes that, given the extent of these transactions, at least in the postwar period, the "stereotype that money had little value in the Soviet system is clearly incorrect." See James Heinzen, *The Art of the Bribe: Corruption under Stalin, 1943–1953* (New Haven, Conn.: Yale University Press, 2016), 283, 107.

23. Fitzpatrick, *Everyday Stalinism,* 63.

24. Ibid., 96–99.

25. Yegor Gaidar, "Russian Reform" (November 27, 1996), 10, Social Science Research Network, http://papers.ssrn.com/sol3/papers.cfm?abstract_id=2144676.

26. See Evgenii Preobrazhenskii, *Bumazhnye den'gi v epokhu proletarskoi diktatury* (Tiflis: Gos. izd-vo, 1921), 4. As Steven G. Marks notes, this "rhetorical flourish" on Preobrazhenskii's part was little more than "fantasizing," for, in reality, the Bolsheviks had no other source of revenue than printing money and they did so to prevent the government from collapsing. Steven G. Marks, "The Russian Experience of Money, 1914–1924," in *Russian Culture in War and Revolution, 1914–22,* bk. 2, ed. Murray Frame et al. (Bloomington, Ind.: Slavica Publishers, 2014), 131.

27. Julie Hessler, *A Social History of Soviet Trade: Trade Policy, Retail Practices, and Consumption, 1917–1953* (Princeton, N.J.: Princeton University Press, 2004), 61–62.

28. Marks, "The Russian Experience of Money," 136–137.

29. Ibid., 138.

30. The chervonets, named after an old Tsarist currency, was introduced in 1922. It was primarily intended to be used for foreign trade, and, despite its nonconvertibility, it was ostensibly on the gold standard. The *sovznak* was removed from circulation in the first half of 1924. The ruble was drastically devalued three times during the currency reform, in 1922 and 1923 and in 1924, when a new ruble was issued that was worth 1/50,000 of a 1923 ruble, 1/5,000,000 of a 1922 ruble, and 1/10 of a chervonets. The chervonets was eventually discontinued with 1947 currency reform.

31. On Stalin's anticapitalism, see Oleg V. Khlevniuk, *Stalin: New Biography of a Dictator,* trans. Nora Seligman (New Haven, Conn.: Yale University Press, 2015), 7.

32. In their famous Civil War–era textbook, *The ABC of Communism,* Nikolai Bukharin and Evgenii Preobrazhenskii claimed that "communist society will know nothing of money." It was needed in the meantime, they acknowledged, because commodities would still be produced during the socialist transition, private trade could not yet be supplanted by socialist distribution, and trade with the countryside was conducted in money. Nevertheless, since socialism was "incomplete communism," money had already begun to lose its significance. See Nikolai Bukharin and E. A. Preobrazhenskii, *The ABC of Communism: A Popular Explanation of the Program of the Communist Party of Russia,* trans. Eden and Cedar Paul (London: Communist Party of Great Britain, 1922), 333–334. Bukharin suggested elsewhere that money was in the process of "self-destruction": it was becoming an "empty shell" as workers' wages materialized into a "social-labor share." Nikolai Bukharin, *Ekonomika perekhodnogo perioda,* chast' 1, *Obshchaia teoriia transformatsionnogo protsessa* (Moskva: Gosudarstvennoe izdatel'stvo, 1920), 135.

33. Iosif Vissarionovich Stalin, "XIV s"ezd VKP(b) 18–31 dekabria 1925 g.," in *Sochineniia* (Moskva: Gosudarstvennoe izdatel'stvo politicheskoi literatury, 1951), tom 7, 369. The extent to which Sokol'nikov was, in fact, the opponent of money that Stalin depicted him as is debatable. In the early 1920s, he criticized more radical communists like Preobrazhenskii who, in his opinion, failed to realize that the depreciation of money's value did not reduce its significance within the economy. Samuel A. Oppenheim suggests that Sokol'nikov supported a "rational" financial policy and strengthening the Soviet currency. See Samuel A. Oppenheim, "Between Right and Left: G. Ia. Sokolnikov and the Development of the Soviet State, 1921–1929," *Slavic Review,* Vol. 48, No. 4 (1989): 596–597. Marks goes even further, suggesting that Sokol'nikov represented an "alternative vision of the future," for he believed that the "monetary equivalent of the laws of gravity imposed limits on the state's ability to act. . . . A normal economic life governed by the normal rules of markets and money was tantamount to the victory of capitalism over the socialist state. And that was anathema to party radicals, including Stalinists, who yearned for the destruction of the old society and the creation of a new one." See Marks, "The Russian Experience of Money," 147.

34. For criticism of the prevailing idea within the Stalinist leadership that inflation could not affect a planned economy, see Leon Trotsky, *The Revolution Betrayed: What Is the Soviet Union and Where Is It Going?* (Garden City, N.Y.: Doubleday, Doran, 1937), 54.

35. Paul R. Gregory and Aleksei Tikhonov, "Central Planning and Unintended Consequences: Creating the Soviet Financial System, 1930–1939," *Journal of Economic History,* Vol. 60, No. 4 (December 2000): 1017. See also Franklyn D. Holzman, "Soviet Inflationary Pressures, 1928–1957: Causes and Cures," *Quarterly Journal of Economics,* Vol. 74, No. 2 (1960): 173.

36. Gregory and Tikhonov, "Central Planning and Unintended Consequences," 1018.

37. Ibid., 1024–1025.

38. Writing in exile around the same time, Trotsky evinced a much less radical attitude regarding the problem of money than Stalin accused him and his colleagues on the left of possessing. He argued that "money cannot be arbitrarily 'abolished'" because it first had to "exhaust [its] historic mission, evaporate, and fall away." He suggested that, during the socialist transition, the "personal interests of the producer and consumer, their egoism," needed to be taken into consideration in a planned system, and thus a "reliable and flexible instrument" like money was needed, ideally a currency backed by gold and one that was convertible rather than shut in an autarkic system, as the Soviet ruble was. Indeed, the 1924 ruble was assigned a gold value, but in practice, it was not convertible into gold in any meaningful sense. Even worse, under Stalin, "Soviet money has ceased to be money; it serves no longer as a measure of value." Though Stalinist leaders declared inflation incompatible with the Soviet Union's planned economy, the ruble was far from a stable, reliable currency with real value, but extremely was inflated, Trotsky emphasized, and "currency inflation, inevitably producing credit inflation, entails a substitution of fictitious for real magnitudes, and corrodes the planned economy from within." This meant that the gains associated with the First Five-Year Plan were merely "statistical," and, in reality, workers received only dubious gains from "socialism achieved with the help of inflation." Once the pitfalls of this approach were realized, Stalin and his "obedient professors" then came up with a 'socialist theory of money' only "after the twilight of inflationist illusions." See Trotsky, *The Revolution Betrayed,* 50, 52, 54–55, 57.

39. I. V. Stalin, "Otchetnyi doklad XVII s"ezdu partii o rabote TsK VKP(b) 26 ianvaria 1934 g.," in *Sochinenie* (Moskva: Gosudarstvennoe izdatel'stvo politicheskoi literatury, 1951), tom 13, 343.

40. Ibid.

41. Ibid., 360.

42. Ibid.

43. Oleg V. Khlevniuk and R. W. Davies emphasize that the First Five-Year Plan did not envision rationing or the switch to a moneyless economy, but envisioned the switch to a high-productivity industrial system and increased consumer goods. However, this was unrealistic due to the inflationary pressures it produced. See Oleg V. Khlevniuk and R. W. Davies, "The End of Rationing in the Soviet Union, 1934–1935," *Europe-Asia Studies,* Vol. 51, No. 4 (1999): 559–560.

44. On the hierarchy of ration recipients and those excluded from the ration system, see Osokina, *Our Daily Bread,* 134.

45. Kristy Ironside, "Stalin's Doctrine of Price Reductions during the Second World War and Postwar Reconstruction," *Slavic Review,* Vol. 75, No. 3 (2016): 659.

46. Rossiiskii gosudarstvennyi arkhiv sotsial'no-politicheskoi istorii (RGASPI), f. 558, op. 11, d. 1118, l. 42 (Stalin's response to Molotov's speech on the end of rationing, November 1934).

47. RGASPI, f. 558, op. 11, d. 1118, l. 44.

48. RGASPI, f. 558, op. 11, d. 1118, l. 46.

49. RGASPI, f. 558, op. 11, d. 1118, l. 55.

50. "Bez kartochek," *Pravda,* September 26, 1935, 1.

51. Ibid.

52. On shortages at this time, and the state's response to them, see Hessler, *A Social History of Soviet Trade,* 241–243.

53. RGASPI, f. 82, op. 2, d. 780, l. 77 (report on the state of the currency supply from Gosbank to Molotov, December 12, 1945).

54. On abuses of the ration system, in particular the use of ration cards to purchase goods for resale, see Elena Dmitrievna Tverdiukova, "Bor'ba so zloupotrebleniiami v sfere kartochnogo snabzheniia naseleniia v SSSR, 1941–1947 gg.," *Vestnik Sankt-Peterburgskogo Universiteta,* seriia 2, *Istoriia,* June 2010, 37–38; Hessler, *A Social History of Soviet Trade,* 271–272.

55. RGASPI, f. 82, op. 2, d. 780, l. 84.

56. On the expansion of barter during the war, see William Moskoff, *The Bread of Affliction: The Food Supply in the USSR during World War II* (Cambridge: Cambridge University Press, 1990), 161–162, 170.

57. On wartime commercial price adjustments, see Ironside, "Stalin's Doctrine of Price Reductions," 664–667. On wartime fundraising campaigns' role in draining excess cash from circulation, especially that held by the peasantry, see Kristy Ironside, "Rubles for Victory: The Social Dynamics of State Fundraising on the Soviet Home Front," *Kritika: Explorations in Russian and Eurasian History,* Vol. 15, No. 4 (2014): 815.

58. As Hessler observes, in the first half of the war, private trade was a "survivalist" response to dire shortages; however, by the second half of the war, private economic ventures became "untethered from survival" and were thriving until the government, worried by this, clamped down on them in 1947–1948. See Hessler, *A Social History of Soviet Trade,* 279–281. Heinzen similarly observes that, by the midpoint of the war in 1943, illegal underground economic activity, the theft of state property, and bribery were significant sources of concern for Communist Party leaders, because these pursuits seemed to have become deeply embedded in Soviet life. See Heinzen, *The Art of the Bribe,* 1.

59. "Obzor pisem po voprosu denezhnogo obrasheniia Narodnomu komissaru finansov SSSR tov. Zverevu A. G.," in *Denezhnaia reforma v SSSR 1947 goda: Dokumenty i materialy,* ed. L. N. Dobrokhotov (Moskva: ROSSPEN, 2010), 667–668.

60. Julie Hessler, "Postwar Normalisation and Its Limits in the USSR: The Case of Trade," *Europe-Asia Studies,* Vol. 53, No. 3 (2001): 446.

61. Ibid.

62. "Stenogramma vystupleniia A. G. Zverev na soveshchanii po voprosam denezhnogo obrashcheniia, 28 ianvaria 1943 g.," in Dobrokhotov, *Denezhnaia reforma v SSSR 1947 goda,* 31. Note that, prior to March 1946, the Ministry of Finance was known as the Commissariat of Finance.

63. "Neobkhodimost' denezhnoi reform i ee predposylki," in *Po stranitsam arkhivnykh fondov tsentral'nogo banka rossiiskoi federatsii,* vypusk 3, *Denezhnaia reforma 1947 goda v dokumentax: Podgotovka, provedenie i otsenka rezul'tatov,* ed. Iu. I. Kashin (Moskva: Tsentral'nyi bank Rossiiskoi federatsii, 2007), 12.

64. "Postanovlenie soveta ministrov SSSR i TsKP(b) o provedenii denezhnoi reformy i otmene kartochek na prodovol'stvennye i promyshlennye tovary," 1.

65. P. Charles Hachten, "Property Relations and the Economic Organization of Soviet Russia, 1941–1948" (PhD diss., University of Chicago, 2005), 409.

66. Ibid., 412. As Holzman pointed out, the Soviet government often boasted that the average Soviet worker enjoyed a low income-tax burden and thus nominally high wages, for example, but this concealed how much workers paid in indirect taxes and the fact that the real value of their wages was desperately low—an example of the "money illusion." See Franklyn D. Holzman, *Soviet Taxation: The Fiscal and Monetary Problems of a Planned Economy* (Cambridge, Mass.: Harvard University Press, 1955), 62–65.

67. Holzman, *Soviet Taxation,* 65.

68. Elena Zubkova, *Russia after the War: Hopes, Illusions, and Disappointments, 1945–1957,* trans. Hugh Ragsdale (Armonk, N.Y.: M. E. Sharpe, 1998), 54–55.

69. Ibid.

70. Donald A. Filtzer, *Soviet Workers and Late Stalinism: Labour and the Restoration of the Stalinist System after World War II* (Cambridge: Cambridge University Press, 2002), 79.

71. Ibid., 80–87.

72. Filtzer explains his choice of the word "attenuated" to describe the process of recovery in the period 1948–1953 as follows: "The main determinants of the quality of life improved slowly but palpably, but in the end still could not cover more than the most essential needs of urban citizens." Ibid., 115.

73. I find Charles S. Maier's approach to the study of historical political economy most instructive here. As Maier argues, "Political economy . . . regards economic ideas and behavior not as frameworks for analysis, but as beliefs and actions that must themselves be explained. They are contingent and problematic; that is, they might have been different and they must be explained within particular political and social contexts." By examining "revealed preferences," the historian can explore "social choice," or the intended outcome and the risks accepted to achieve it. See Charles S. Maier, *In Search of Stability: Explorations in Historical Political Economy* (Cambridge: Cambridge University Press, 1987), 6.

74. See I. V. Stalin, *Ekonomicheskie problemy sotsializma v SSSR* (Moskva: Gosudarstvennoe izdatel'stvo politicheskoi literatury, 1952). On the dispute over the textbook on socialist political economy and Stalin's role in it, see Ethan Pollock, *Stalin and the Soviet Science Wars* (Princeton, N.J.: Princeton University Press, 2006), 168–211. The resulting textbook was published in 1954. See K. V. Ostrovitianov et al., *Politicheskaia ekonomika; Uchebnik* (Moskva: Gosudarstvennoe izdatel'stvo politicheskoi literatury, 1954).

75. Stalin, *Ekonomicheskie problemy sotsializma v SSSR*, 17–18.

76. Ibid., 69.

77. Yoram Gorlizki and Oleg V. Khlevniuk, *Cold Peace: Stalin and the Ruling Circle, 1945–1953* (Oxford: Oxford University Press, 2004), 123–124.

78. The social sciences, including economics, were presumed to be bourgeois and obsolete before the war, but enjoyed something of a renaissance after it. See Maya Haber, "Socialist Realist Science: Constructing Knowledge about Rural Life in the Soviet Union, 1943–1958" (PhD diss., University of California Los Angeles, 2013). On the rise of economics as a social science in the postwar period, see Yakov Feygin, "Building a Ruin: Cold War Economics and the Politics of Reform in the Post-Stalin USSR" (unpublished book manuscript, 2019), 16. On the rise of economic forecasting in the wake of Stalin's death, see Eglė Rindzevičiūtė, "A Struggle for the Soviet Future: The Birth of Scientific Forecasting in the Soviet Union," *Slavic Review*, Vol. 75, No. 1 (2016): 52–76. On the increasing use of the social sciences, particularly economics, to raise living standards beginning in the Khrushchev era, see Artemy Kalinovsky, *Laboratory of Socialist Development: Cold War Politics and Decolonization in Soviet Tajikistan* (Ithaca, N.Y.: Cornell University Press, 2018), 78–84.

79. Kalinovsky, *Laboratory of Socialist Development*, 68.

80. Chris Miller, "Economic Ideas Crossing Borders: The Transnational Turn in Soviet Economic History," *Soviet and Post-Soviet Review*, Vol. 46, No. 1 (2019): 57.

81. Feygin, "Building a Ruin," 2–3.

82. For example, Grigorii Mar'iakhin, an expert on Soviet taxes who pushed the idea of legalizing and taxing private trade as a source of postwar revenue in the late 1940s, a suggestion that was deemed impermissible and which put him in the crosshairs of the secret police, potentially risked not only losing his job but losing his liberty and his life, as Hessler emphasizes. See Julie Hessler, "A Postwar Perestroika? Toward a History of Private Enterprise in the USSR," *Slavic Review*, Vol. 57, No. 3 (1998): 531. As it turns out, he simply lost his job as head of the Department on Taxes and Collections of the Ministry of Finance but remained a respected expert on taxation and state revenue into the 1960s. He is a key player in Chapters 4 and 5 in this book. A better-known example of this phenomenon is Nikolai Voznesenskii, a key economic authority during the Second World War and the Chairman of Gosplan after it, who was executed in 1950 during one of the last major purges of the Stalin era. Giovanni Cadioli suggests Voznesenskii was targeted, in part, for his "rational" reformist economic initiatives, in particular his attempts to reconceptualize the Marxist concept of the "law of value" under Soviet socialism. Voznesenskii argued for the increased use of "economic levers" including prices, money, credit, profit, and bonuses. He was politically disgraced not only due to accusa-

tions that he had embezzled resources to unfairly benefit Leningrad (the so-called Leningrad Affair), but because of a concurrent downturn in economic growth presumed to be due to his "manipulations" of figures and of reality (the "Gosplan Affair"). See Giovanni Cadioli, "Soviet Economic Thought and Economic Policy in the 1940s: Influence on 1950s–1960s Reforms" (PhD thesis, Oxford University, 2018), 122, 124, 169–180.

1. Our Low-Price Guarantee

1. As the price expert A. N. Malafeev explained, during the socialist transition, there existed two "antagonistic tendencies" in pricing, socialist and market-capitalist, and a dual law of value. The government set its prices based on the goals of socialist construction and satisfying the material and cultural needs of workers; private traders, such as black marketers and kolkhoz market vendors, sought to maximize their own profits and, as a result, attempted to "derail" these goals. A vicious battle thus unfolded between the state and the private sector; however, with the decisive victory of socialist relations of production, such "variegation in commodity-money relations" would be "liquidated" and a single, socialist law of value would regulate the Soviet economy. See A. N. Malafeev, *Istoriia tsenoobrazovaniia v SSSR, 1917–1963 gg.* (Moskva: Mysl', 1964), 6–7. On the concept of the "persistent private sector," or the remnants of the market that stubbornly survived in spite of Stalinist repression, see Hessler, *A Social History of Soviet Trade,* 251.

2. Fitzpatrick, *Everyday Stalinism,* 97.

3. In reality, not everyone who paid higher prices at commercial shops could easily afford to do so. As Golfo Alexopoulos notes, those who were disenfranchised by the Soviet system because they were considered "class enemies," such as priests and their children, were shut out of the ration system on the argument that, in a country of limited resources, bread should go to workers first and foremost. See Golfo Alexopoulos, *Stalin's Outcasts: Aliens, Citizens, and the Soviet State, 1926–1936* (Ithaca, N.Y.: Cornell University Press, 2003), 28–29. Elena Osokina observes that many customers at Torgsin outlets, which were supposed to service foreign specialists and where goods were traded for hard currency and in exchange for valuables like antiques, jewelry, and precious metals, were people who were shut out of the state distribution system, often trading in their last valuable possessions for bread. Osokina called Torgsin "the biggest speculator in the country." See Osokina, *Our Daily Bread,* 122–123.

4. RGASPI, f. 558, op. 11, d. 1118, l. 49–50.

5. RGASPI, f. 558, op. 11, d. 1118, l. 51.

6. RGASPI, f. 558, op. 11, d. 1118, l. 51.

7. RGASPI, f. 558, op. 11, d. 1118, l. 53.

8. "Bez kartochek," *Pravda,* September 26, 1935, 1.

9. In fact, during this period, as Vyacheslav Molotov later acknowledged, the government even put the prices of many goods up. See Feliks Ivanovich Chuev and Vyacheslav Mikhailovich Molotov, *Sto sorok besed s Molotovym: Iz dnevnika F. Chueva* (Moskva: Terra, 1991), 367.

10. Wendy Z. Goldman, "Not by Bread Alone: Food, Workers, and the State," in *Hunger and War: Food Provisioning in the Soviet Union during World War II*, ed. Wendy Z. Goldman and Donald A. Filtzer (Bloomington: Indiana University Press, 2015), 65.

11. On commercial prices during the war, see Hessler, *A Social History of Soviet Trade*, 302. On commercial price cuts beginning in 1944, see Ironside, "Stalin's Doctrine of Price Reductions," 664–667.

12. RGASPI, f. 82, op. 2, d. 780, l. 83.

13. Ironside, "Stalin's Doctrine of Price Reductions," 664–665.

14. I. V. Stalin, "Rech' na predvybornom sobranii izbiratelei Stalinskogo izbiratel'nogo okruga goroda Moskvy, 9 fevralia 1946 goda," in *Sochineniia* (Moskva: Mysl', 1997), tom 16, 14.

15. *Zakon o piatiletnem plane vosstanovleniia i razvitiia narodnogo khoziaistva SSSR na 1946–1950 gg.* (Leningrad: Ogiz, Gosudarstvennoe izdatel'stvo politicheskoi literatury, 1946), 51, 56.

16. Scholarly opinions vary on the extent to which the famine was man-made. V. F. Zima and Michael Ellman both emphasize the Soviet government's responsibility for the food crisis. Zima originated the thesis that the Soviet government demanded impossible grain requisitions from the peasantry and chose to not release its grain stocks for Soviet citizens' consumption in order to sell them abroad. See V. F. Zima, *Golod v SSSR 1946–1947 godov: Proiskhozhdeniie i posledstviia* (Moskva: Rossiiskaia akademiia nauk, In-t rossiiskoi istorii, 1996), 10–11, 149–153. Ellman concurs, deeming the famine a "preventable food availability decline" that might not have resulted in 1–1.5 million deaths if the Soviet government had opted for different policies and had not allowed those who did not have an "entitlement" to food to perish. See Michael Ellman, "The 1947 Soviet Famine and the Entitlement Approach to Famines," *Cambridge Journal of Economics*, Vol. 24, No. 5 (2000): 620–621. Nicholas Ganson assigns more blame to the bad harvest and the resulting scarcity of grain than to human factors. See Nicholas Ganson, *The Soviet Famine of 1946–47 in Global and Historical Perspective* (New York: Palgrave Macmillan, 2009), 5. Donald A. Filtzer emphasizes public health considerations: the Soviet population had not yet recovered from the malnutrition they suffered during the war when another nutrition crisis hit, and environmental factors such as poor sanitation and inadequate housing magnified the famine's impact. See Donald A. Filtzer, "The 1947 Food Crisis and Its Aftermath: Worker and Peasant Consumption in Non-famine Regions of the RSFSR," in *A Dream Deferred: New Studies in Russian and Soviet Labour History*, ed. Donald A. Filtzer et al. (Bern: Peter Lang, 2008), 345. Stephen G. Wheatcroft suggests that the timing and nature of the food problems between 1941 and 1947 conform to a general pattern of Soviet famines, rather than any attempt to punish the peasantry through harsh procurements, and that massive grain stocks, as Zima suggested, were not available, nor could they have been imported amid the world food crisis of 1946–1947. See Stephen G. Wheatcroft, "The Soviet Famine of 1946–1947, the Weather and Human Agency in Historical Perspective," *Europe-Asia Studies*, Vol. 64, No. 6 (2012): 987–1005.

17. On the increased ration prices, see "V sovete ministrov," *Izvestiia*, September 17, 1946, 1. For the declining number of ration recipients, see "Dannye TsSU o normirovannom

snabzhenii naseleniia 1942–1947 gg.," in *Sovetskaia povsednevnost' i massovoe soznanie, 1939–1945*, ed. A. Ia. Livshin and I. B. Orlov (Moskva: ROSSPEN, 2003), 205. The Soviet government portrayed these moves as important steps in the direction of "unifying" prices toward the abolition of rationing. Filtzer portrays this as an effort to depress consumption of grain in response to the severe shortages associated with the famine. See Filtzer, *Soviet Workers and Late Stalinism,* 47–48. Hessler, on the other hand, sees it as consistent with the policy of narrowing the gap between ration and commercial prices that had governed distribution since the later stages of the war, a policy that was predicated on the idea that postwar distribution would advance through the stages laid out during the mid-1930s transition to nonrationed trade. See Hessler, *A Social History of Soviet Trade,* 305. See also Ironside, "Stalin's Doctrine of Price Reductions," 666–667.

18. On the bread allowance as a wage tack-on, see Chapter 2.

19. I expand on this notion of price reductions as a Stalinist "economic doctrine," or a set of normative assumptions and beliefs about the working of the economy, in Ironside, "Stalin's Doctrine of Price Reductions."

20. Khrushchev unambiguously praised the economic strategy of consecutive retail price reductions before Stalin's death. At a meeting of trade workers in Moscow in January 1953, he maintained: "In no country other than ours, with our socialist government, could there be such a situation, in which, even with shortages of many kinds of goods, we managed to lower prices all the same. Capitalists consider this an unbelievable phenomenon. For them, it's just the opposite: shortages of goods create the possibility to earn more money, and for us it leads to lower prices." See "Vystuplenie N. S. Khrushcheva na sobranii aktiva rabotnikov torgovli i obshchestvennogo pitaniia gor. Moskvy," in *Nikita Sergeevich Khrushchev: Dva tsveta vremeni; Dokumenty lichnogo fonda N. S. Khrushcheva,* ed. N. G. Tomilina et al. (Moskva: Mezhdunarodnyi fond "Demokratiia," 2009), tom 1, 427.

21. Malafeev, *Istoriia tsenoobrazovaniia v SSSR,* 269.

22. "Postanovlenie soveta ministrov SSSR i TsKP(b) o provedenii denezhnoi reformy i otmene kartochek na prodovol'stvennye i promyshlennye tovary," 1.

23. The prices of food products in the first zone were lowest and prices in the third zone, which mostly comprised sparsely populated areas in the Far East and North, were the highest. Note that a city, region, or republic might be in one zone for bread prices, but in another for milk products, and in yet another for fruits and vegetables. For example, Moscow and Leningrad oblasts were in the second zone for bread, milk, and eggs, but in the third and most expensive zone for fruit, which was also subject to seasonal variations in price. See Appendix A for a complete price list.

24. The prices of bread and flour dropped on average by 12%, while cereals and macaroni dropped by 10% and the new prices for meat, fish, oil, sugar, candy, salt, potatoes, and vegetables, as well as tobacco and matches, stayed at ration levels. Prices for milk, eggs, tea, and fruit remained "close to" ration levels, while textiles, shoes, and clothing were repriced 3.2 times lower than commercial levels. See "Otmena kartochek na prodovol'stvennye i promyshlennye tovary," *Pravda,* December 15, 1947, 2.

25. Ibid.

26. Gosudarstvennyi arkhiv Rossiiskoi Federatsii (GARF), f. 5446, op. 49, d. 4606, l. 135 (report to Kosygin on trade on December 16 and December 17, undated, but likely December 18, 1947).

27. GARF, f. 5446, op. 49, d. 4606, l. 150 (report on trade in Moscow, December 18, 1947).

28. GARF, f. 5446, op. 49, d. 4606, l. 142.

29. GARF, f. 5446, op. 49, d. 4606, l. 142.

30. GARF, f. 5446, op. 49, d. 4606, l. 30 (report on trade in Sverdlovsk, December 16, 1947).

31. "Otmena kartochek na prodovol'stvennye i promyshlennye tovary," 2.

32. GARF, f. 5446, op. 49, d. 4607, l. 27 (report on market trade in Kiev, December 16, 1947).

33. GARF, f. 259a, op. 6, d. 4663, l. 3 (report on trade in the RSFSR after the currency reform, from Rodionov to Stalin, December 18, 1947).

34. GARF, f. 5446, op. 49, d. 4609, l. 79 (report on market prices by A. Starovskii, January 3, 1948).

35. On grain shortages that persisted throughout the year, see Zima, *Golod v SSSR,* 151–153.

36. RGASPI, f. 17, op. 135, d. 10, l. 53 (report on trade in Kaluga from Panov to Malenkov, early 1948).

37. See, for example, RGASPI, f. 17, op. 135, d. 10, l. 77–79 (report from K. Mokichev to A. A. Kuznetsov, early 1948).

38. GARF, f. 374a, op. 3, d. 2209, l. 16; op. 2566, l. 2 (statistical calculation of the balance of workers' income and expenses in 1947).

39. GARF, f. 5446, op. 50, d. 2409, l. 66 (letter from a group of workers, January 13, 1948).

40. "O povyshenii pokupatel'noi sposobnosti rublia i real'noi zarabotnoi platy," in Dobrokhotov, *Denezhnaia reforma v SSSR 1947 goda,* 437.

41. Ibid., 438.

42. Ibid., 437.

43. Ibid., 439.

44. GARF, f. 5446, op. 50, d. 2435, l. 23 (draft changes to alcohol prices, March 25, 1948).

45. GARF, f. 5446, op. 50, d. 2435, l. 32 (report on alcohol prices, March 20, 1948).

46. See, for example, GARF, f. 5446, op. 50, d. 2435, l. 39 (request to lower caviar prices from the Minister of Fish Production to Molotov, March 25, 1948).

47. "Vtoroi etap snizheniia tsen," *Izvestiia,* April 10, 1948, 1.

48. On the car as the ultimate "deficit commodity," see Lewis H. Siegelbaum, *Cars for Comrades: The Life of the Soviet Automobile* (Ithaca, N.Y.: Cornell University Press, 2008) 188–189.

49. GARF, f. 5446, op. 120, d. 936, l. 113 (report on the implementation of the 1948 trade plan by I. Zhavoronkov, undated).

50. GARF, f. 5446, op. 51, d. 2610, l. 34 (report on trade in 1948 from Zhavoronkov, circa late 1948 or early 1949).

51. GARF, f. 5446, op. 51, d. 2610, l. 34.

52. On the importance of the turnover tax to the Soviet state budget, see Holzman, *Soviet Taxation.*

53. "Po voprosu o denezhnom obrashchenii," in *Po stranitsam arkhivnykh fondov v tsentral'nogo banka rossiiskoi federatsii,* vypusk 6, *Obmen deneg v SSSR 1961 goda v dokumentakh: Podgotovka, provedenie i otsenka rezul'tatov,* ed. Iu. I. Kashin (Moskva: Tsentral'nyi bank Rossiiskoi federatsii, 2008), 8.

54. Ibid.

55. Ibid.

56. "Postanovlenie Soveta Ministrov SSSR i TsK VKP(b) o novom snizhenii s 1 marta 1949 goda gosudarstvennykh roznichnykh tsen na tovary massovogo potrebleniia," *Pravda,* March 1, 1949, 1.

57. Ibid.

58. *Pravda,* March 1, 1949, 1.

59. "Eto vozmozhno tol'ko v nashei strane!," *Pravda,* March 1, 1949, 2.

60. RGASPI, f. 17, op. 135, d. 22, l. 60 (report on trade on March 1, 1949, from Sazonov to Ponomarenko, March 3, 1949).

61. RGASPI, f. 17, op. 135, d. 22, l. 75 (report on the sale of main products after the March price reduction to Stalin from V. Pavliukov, April 4, 1949).

62. GARF, f. 5446, op. 51, d. 2517, l. 105 (anonymous letter to the Council of Ministers, March 15, 1949).

63. GARF, f. 5446, op. 51, d. 2518, l. 160 (anonymous letter to the Council of Ministers, July 6, 1949).

64. GARF, f. 5446, op. 51, d. 2518, l. 160.

65. Dmitrii Shepilov, *The Kremlin's Scholar: A Memoir of Soviet Politics under Stalin and Khrushchev,* ed. Stephen V. Bittner, trans. Anthony Austin (New Haven, Conn.: Yale University Press, 2007), 245.

66. GARF, f. 5446, op. 120, d. 939, l. 202 (report on goods reserves in trade organizations in the first quarter of 1949, undated).

67. "Po voprosu o denezhnom obrashchenii," 9.

68. "O novom snizhenii gosudarstvennykh tsen na prodovol'stvennye i promyshlennye tovary," *Pravda,* March 1, 1950, 1–2.

69. "Stalinskaia zabota o blagosostoianii naroda," *Pravda,* March 1, 1950, 1.

70. "O perevode kursa rubl'ia na zolotuiu bazu i o povyshenii kursa rubl'ia v otnoshenii inostranykh valiut," *Pravda,* March 1, 1950, 2. Note that the British pound was devalued

by 30% in 1949 in an effort to solve its postwar balance of payments problem, a development that was probably beneficial to the Soviet Union, as Oscar Sanchez-Sibony points out, given that the latter owed wartime debts to the United Kingdom and it was moving some of its foreign currency reserves out of the United States dollar and into European banks due to its anxiety about American plans for postwar Europe and their consequences for its foreign currency reserves. See Oscar Sanchez-Sibony, "Capitalism's Fellow Traveler: The Soviet Union, Bretton Woods, and the Cold War, 1944–1958," *Comparative Studies in Society and History,* Vol. 56, No. 2 (2014): 304.

71. The gold content of the ruble was pegged at 0.222168 grams. The ruble's exchange rate vis-à-vis the American dollar was adjusted to 4 rubles, instead of the previous 5.30 rubles, and its exchange rate vis-à-vis the British pound was adjusted to 11.20 rubles from 14.80 rubles.

72. As Holzman argues, the primary rationale, given that consumer prices had decreased since December 1947, "contains elements of truth but is not entirely relevant as a rationalization of the revaluation." Prices for consumer goods did decline sharply, but these were only a small fraction of Soviet trade and they contained a huge amount of turnover tax, he emphasizes. Instead, Holzman argues that the relationship between domestic prices for nonconsumption goods and world prices was more important. Between 1937 and 1950, domestic prices of producers' goods and raw materials, excluding petroleum products, increased substantially. By 1950, the ruble was overvalued, in Holzman's opinion, and there was no economic justification for overvaluing it further. That said, by then, the Soviet government was expanding its trade relations with its satellite states in Central and Eastern Europe through the Council for Mutual Economic Assistance and Stalin identified the ruble as the trading currency of this emerging bloc. The upward reevaluation of the ruble may have been designed to give the impression of its increased usefulness. See Franklyn D. Holzman, "The Ruble Exchange Rate and Soviet Foreign Trade Pricing Policies, 1929–1961," *American Economic Review,* Vol. 58, No. 4 (1968): 815–816.

73. "O novom snizhenii gosudarstvennykh tsen na prodovol'stvennye i promyshlennye tovary," *Pravda,* March 1, 1951, 1; "O novom snizhenii gosudarstvennykh roznichnykh tsen na prodovol'stvennye tovary," *Pravda,* April 1, 1952, 1.

74. "Deviatnatsatyi s"ezd KPSS, Moskva, 5–15 oktiabria 1952 g.," in *Kommunisticheskaia Partiia Sovetskogo soiuza v rezoliutsiakh i resheniiakh, s"ezdov, konferentsii i plenumov* (Moskva: Izdatel'stvo politicheskoi literatury, 1985), 280.

75. Stalin, *Ekonomicheskie problemy sotsializma v SSSR,* 69.

76. Malafeev, *Istoriia tsenoobrazovaniia v SSSR,* 261.

77. "Na osnovne postoiannogo rosta narodnogo khoziaistva . . . ," *Pravda,* March 1, 1950, 1.

78. "Snizhenie roznichnykh tsen i sovetskaia torgovlia," *Pravda,* March 2, 1951, 2.

79. "Inostrannye otkliki na postanovlenie Soveta Ministrov SSSR i TsIK VKP(b) 'O novom snizhenii gosudarstvennykh roznichnykh tsen na prodovol'stvennye tovary,'" *Pravda,* April 3, 1952, 3.

80. See Jeffrey Brooks, *Thank You, Comrade Stalin! Soviet Public Culture from Revolution to Cold War* (Princeton, N.J.: Princeton University Press, 2000), xv.

81. GARF, f. 5451, op. 25, d. 4238, l. 1 (report on the first day of trade after the new lower prices in Leningrad, March 1, 1949).

82. GARF, f. 5446, op. 86, d. 2221, l. 181 (report to Mikoyan on workers' responses to the new lower prices for consumer goods, April 2, 1951).

83. Jukka Gronow, *Caviar with Champagne: Common Luxury and the Ideals of the Good Life in Stalin's Russia* (Oxford, U.K.: Berg, 2003), 42.

84. Rossiiskii gosudarstvennyi arkhiv noveishei istorii (RGANI), f. 5, op. 30, d. 68, l. 49 (report on trade after the April 1, 1954, price reduction to Khrushchev and Malenkov from I. Kapitonov, April 21, 1954).

85. See, for example, "Novosti dnia/khroniki nashikh dnei 1954 No. 20" (Tsentral'noi studii dokumental'nykh fil'mov, 1954). Available online: https://www.net-film.ru/film-10113/.

86. RGASPI, f. 17, op. 135, d. 22, l. 77.

87. GARF, f. 5446, op. 51, d. 2518, l. 124 (anonymous letter from a Soviet worker to the Council of Ministers, circa July 1949).

88. For more on the labor day as a standard of measurement emanating from distrust of peasant psychology, see Haber, "Socialist Realist Science," 153, 162.

89. Alec Nove, "The Income of Soviet Peasants," *Slavonic and East European Review,* Vol. 38, No. 91 (1960): 314.

90. G. L. Mar'iakhin, *Ocherki istorii nalogov s naseleniia v SSSR* (Moskva: Izdatel'stvo "Finansy," 1964), 209.

91. Rossiiskii gosudarstvennyi arkhiv ekonomiki (RGAE), f. 679, op. 2, d. 939, l. 2 (report on the agricultural tax to Zverev from K. Plotnikov, June 24, 1953).

92. GARF, f. 5446, op. 87, d. 1202, l. 64 (report on the draft law on the agricultural tax from Zverev to Malenkov, July 22, 1953).

93. GARF, f. 5446, op. 87, d. 1202, l. 64.

94. GARF, f. 5446, op. 87, d. 1202, l. 64.

95. RGANI, f. 5, op. 30, d. 68, l. 14 (preliminary report on trade in 1953 to Malenkov and Khrushchev from Mikoyan, January 20, 1954).

96. RGANI, f. 5, op. 30, d. 68, l. 13.

97. Gorlizki and Khlevniuk, *Cold Peace,* 141.

98. "O novom snizhenii gosudarstvennykh tsen na prodovol'stvennye i promyshlennye tovary," *Pravda,* April 1, 1953, 1.

99. GARF, f. 5446, op. 120, d. 1057, l. 65 (transcript of Mikoyan's comments at a meeting of the Council of Ministers on March 3, 1953).

100. GARF, f. 5446, op. 120, d. 1057, l. 64.

101. On reforms to the agricultural tax, see "Zakon o sel'skokhoziaistvennom naloge," *Pravda,* August 10, 1953, 2–3.

102. "Zasedanie verkhovnogo soveta SSSR; Rech' predsedatelia Soveta ministrov soiuza SSR tovarishcha G. M. Malenkova," *Pravda,* August 9, 1953, 2.

103. "O merakh dal'neishego razvitiia sel'skogo khoziaistva SSSR; Doklad Sekretaria TsK KPSS tov. Khrushcheva N. S. na Plenume TsK KPSS 3 sentiabria 1953 goda," *Izvestiia,* September 15, 1953, 1.

104. "O merakh dal'neishego razvitiia sel'skogo khoziaistva SSSR," 2.

105. Anatolii Strelianyi, "Khrushchev and the Countryside," in *Nikita Khrushchev,* ed. William Taubman, Sergei Khrushchev, and Abbott Gleason, trans. David Gehrenbeck, Eileen Kane, and Alla Bashenko (New Haven, Conn.: Yale University Press, 2000), 113–114.

106. Ibid.

107. RGAE, f. 679, op. 2, d. 1025, l. 2 (report on the rise in collective farms' money incomes by M. Nesmii, 1955).

108. RGAE, f. 679, op. 2, d. 1025, l. 31.

109. RGAE, f. 679, op. 2, d. 1025, l. 8.

110. "V Sovete Ministrov SSSR i Tsentral'nom Komitete KPSS: O merakh dal'neishego razvitiia sovetskoi torgovli," *Pravda,* October 23, 1953, 1.

111. Ibid., 2.

112. "O novom snizhenii gosudarstvennykh roznichnykh tsen na prodovol'stvennye i promyshlennye tovary," *Pravda,* March 1, 1954, 1.

113. RGANI, f. 5, op. 20, d. 96 (anonymous letter to *Pravda,* August 2, 1954).

114. RGANI, f. 5, op. 30, d. 68, l. 70 (report on bread trade and worker's complaints about bread sales, November 25, 1954).

115. RGANI, f. 5, op. 30, d. 68, l. 207 (reports on letters sent to the newspaper *Sel'skoe khoziaistvo* on bread trade in rural areas, compiled by K. Shaposhnikov, November 19, 1954).

116. RGANI, f. 5, op. 30, d. 135, l. 7 (report on letters to the Central Committee of the Communist Party about food shortages, April 25, 1955).

117. "Zapiska N. S. Khrushcheva v presidium TsK KPSS po voprosam uporiadocheniia zarabotnoi platy i pensionnogo dela," in *Nikita Sergeevich Khrushchev: Dva tsveta vremeni; Dokumenty lichnogo fonda N. S. Khrushcheva,* ed. N. G. Tomilina et al. (Moskva: Mezhdunarodnyi fond "Demokratiia," 2009), tom 2, 279.

118. Ibid.

119. "XX s"ezd Kommunisticheskoi partii Sovetskogo soiuza; Prodolzhenie doklada tovarishcha N. S. Khrushcheva," *Pravda,* February 15, 1956, 7.

120. Ibid.

121. Ibid.

122. RGANI, f. 5, op. 30, d. 266, l. 17 (report on the outcome of family budget studies in 1957 to the Council of Ministers from A. Starovskii, March 5, 1958).

123. Tsentral'noe statisticheskoe upravlenie pri Sovete ministrov RSFSR, in *Biudzhety rabochikh, sluzhashchikh i kolkhoznikov RSFSR za 1940, 1953, 1956, 1957, 1958 gody: Statisticheskii sbornik* (Moskva: TsSU, 1959), 28–29.

124. RGANI, f. 5, op. 20, d. 193, l. 93 (report by A. Kudriatsev to the Central Committee of the Communist Party on measures to bring down prices in the kolkhoz markets ahead of the currency reform, September 2, 1960).

125. RGANI, f. 5, op. 20, d. 193, l. 93.

126. This demand, in part, explains Khrushchev's aggressive push for the expansion of the textile industry and for the introduction of cheaper synthetic fabrics. See Nataliia Lebina, "Plus the Chemicalization of the Entire Wardrobe," *Russian Studies in History,* Vol. 48, No. 1 (2009): 40.

127. RGANI, f. 5, op. 30, d. 149, l. 71 (statistical report on the growth of the national income of the USSR to Suslov from A. Starovskii, October 10, 1956).

128. GARF, f. 374a, op. 31, d. 2069, l. 65 (report on the material conditions of workers', ITRs' white-collar workers' and peasants' material conditions in 1958 from B. Kolpakov to I. E. Skvorsov, March 24, 1959).

129. GARF, f. 374a, op. 31, d. 2069, l. 65.

130. On Khrushchev's post-1957 efforts to transform collective farmers into wage earners and thus maximize their labor incentives, see Aaron Hale-Dorrell, *Corn Crusade: Khrushchev's Farming Revolution in the Post-Stalin Soviet Union* (Oxford: Oxford University Press, 2018), 137–166.

131. RGAE, f. 679, op. 2, d. 1130, l. 6 (report on budgetary questions regarding the financing of agriculture in 1957 by S. I. Nedelin).

132. RGANI, f. 5, op. 30, d. 149, l. 71.

133. GARF, f. 374a, op. 31, d. 2069, l. 64.

134. GARF, f. 374a, op. 31, d. 2069, l. 65.

135. Alexandra Oberländer, "Eggs versus Rubles: Hatching Money in the Soviet Countryside" (unpublished paper presented at the Association for Slavic, East European, and Eurasian Studies annual convention, 2018).

136. RGANI, f. 5, op. 20, d. 170, l. 52.

137. RGANI, f. 5, op. 20, d. 170, l. 50.

138. GARF, f. 5446, op. 93, d. 679, l. 166.

139. RGANI, f. 5, op. 20, d. 192, l. 15.

140. "V blizhaishie gody dognat' soedinennye shtaty ameriki po proizvodstvu miasa, masla i moloka na dushu naseleniia," *Pravda,* May 24, 1957, 1.

141. "Postanovlenie Soveta Ministrov SSSR 'O snizhenii gosudarstvennykh roznichnikh i zakupochnykh tsen na svininu, miaso gusei, i utok,'" in *Prezidium TsK KPSS 1954–1964,* tom 2, *Postanovleniia 1954–1958,* ed. A. A. Fursenko (Moskva: ROSSPEN, 2003), 708.

142. "Rastet narodnoe potreblenie," *Pravda,* November 21, 1957, 4.

143. "V ministerstve torgovli SSSR," *Izvestiia,* January 3, 1958, 1.

144. RGANI, f. 5, op. 20, d. 170, l. 65–70.

145. RGANI, f. 5, op. 20, d. 170, l. 3.

146. GARF, f. 5446, op. 93, d. 1240, l. 70 (draft proposal to reduce selected prices to Kosygin from Garbuzov and Perov, April 17, 1959).

147. GARF, f. 5446, op. 93, d. 1240, l. 70.

148. GARF, f. 5446, op. 93, d. 1240, l. 68.

149. GARF, f. 5446, op. 93, d. 1240, l. 66.

150. GARF, f. 5446, op. 93, d. 1240, l. 65.

151. "O snizhenii gosudarstvennykh roznichnykh tsen na nekotorye tovary narodnogo potrebleniia," *Pravda,* July 1, 1959, 2.

152. "Ob otmene nalogov s rabochikh i sluzhashchikh i drugikh meropriatiiakh, napravlennykh na povyshenie blagosostoianiia sovetskoi naroda; Doklad tovarishcha N. S. Khrushcheva na sessii Verkhovnogo soveta SSSR," *Izvestiia,* May 6, 1960, 2.

153. Ibid.

154. "Vvedenie," in Kashin, *Po stranitsam arkhivnykh fondov v tsentral'nogo banka rossiiskoi federatsii,* vypusk 6, 4.

155. See "Postanovlenie Prezidiuma TsK KPSS ot 30 oktiabria 1958 goda," in Kashin, *Po stranitsam arkhivnykh fondov v tsentral'nogo banka rossiiskoi federatsii,* vypusk 6, 44.

156. The circumstances surrounding Zverev's departure remain unclear. In his memoirs, he does not mention this episode, or anything to do with his involvement in the 1961 currency reform. See Arseny Grigorevich Zverev, *Zapiski ministra* (Moskva: Politizdat, 1973). In a recently reissued version of the same book, in the foreword, the author repeats the Stalinist author Iurii Mukhin's assertion that Zverev disagreed with Khrushchev over the currency reform and was forced into retirement, and that rumors circulated at the time that he had threatened to shoot Khrushchev. See Arseny Grigorevich Zverev, *Stalin i den'gi* (Moskva: Algoritm, 2012), 1–2.

157. Sergei Khrushchev, *Khrushchev in Power: Unfinished Reforms, 1961–1964,* trans. George Shriver (Boulder, Colo.: Lynne Rienner Publishers, 2014), 4.

158. Ibid.

159. A. Korovyshkin, "Novyi masshtab tsen i obmen deneg," *Pravda,* December 31, 1960, 2.

160. Holzman suggests that, unlike in 1950, the adjustment of the ruble's exchange rate vis-à-vis foreign currencies represented a depreciation of the ruble, though it was not publicly presented as such; though internal prices were decreased by a factor of 10, the ruble's value in relation to other currencies was adjusted only by a factor of 4.4, or a 55.6% depreciation. See Holzman, "The Ruble Exchange Rate," 817. This would be consistent with efforts to create more "economically grounded" prices in the early 1960s, as discussed later in this chapter.

161. Ibid., 818.

162. See "Ob osveshchenii v pechati nekotorykh voprosov, sviazannykh s izmeneniem masshtaba tsen v SSSR i zamene nyne obrashchaiushchikhsia deneg novymi den'gami," in Kashin, *Po stranitsam arkhivnykh fondov v tsentral'nogo banka rossiiskoi federatsii,* vypusk 6, 47–49.

163. Vasilii Garbuzov, "Otvechaem na voprosy chitatelei; Novye den'gi i tseny na tovary," *Pravda,* October 12, 1960, 3.

164. GARF, f. 5446, op. 94, d. 688, l. 15 (letter from P. N. Maslov to Khrushchev, November 11, 1960).

165. RGANI, f. 5, op. 20, d. 193, l. 94.

166. RGANI, f. 5, op. 20, d. 193, l. 94.

167. RGANI, f. 2, op. 30, d. 364, l. 3, 15 (report on the progress of the introduction of new currency and prices in Moscow to the Central Committee of the Communist Party from V. Stepakov, January 2, 1961).

168. GARF, f. 259a, op. 42, d. 6345, l. 39, 41 (report on the exchange of currency in the RSFSR from Zotov to Sokolov, January 6, 1961).

169. GARF, f. 259a, op. 42, d. 6345, l. 11 (report on the progress of the introduction of new currency and prices in the RSFSR in the first 10 days of January, from Sokolov to Iasnov, January 11, 1961).

170. RGANI, f. 2, op. 30, d. 364, l. 5, 11.

171. RGANI, f. 2, op. 30, d. 364, l. 20.

172. RGANI, f. 2, op. 30, d. 364, l. 20.

173. The process of converting wages and pensions began in late 1960 and was completed ahead of the introduction of the new ruble, prices, and payments on January 1, 1961. However, in many parts of the Soviet Union, mistakes were made when rounding workers' tariff rates and pensions, which their recipients quickly discovered when they were next paid, and many areas were not sent enough new money or sufficient coins, leading to wage and pension arrears. See, for example, GARF, f. 259a, op. 42, d. 6345, l. 11–12.

174. Nikita Sergeevich Khrushchev, *Memoirs of Nikita Khrushchev, Reformer,* ed. Sergei Khrushchev (University Park: Pennsylvania State University Press, 2006), 409.

175. Ibid., 410.

176. G. A. E. Smith, "Agriculture," in *Khrushchev and Khrushchevism,* ed. Martin Mc Cauley (Bloomington: Indiana University Press, 1987), 110. On the Sovnarkhoz reform, see Nataliya Kibita, *Soviet Economic Management under Khrushchev: The Sovnarkhoz Reform* (London: Routledge, 2013).

177. RGANI, f. 5, op. 20, d. 163, l. 105 (report on food and goods shortages in the state trade sector from D. Pavlov to the Central Committee of the Communist Party, June 4, 1957).

178. Haber, "Socialist Realist Science," 170–171.

179. Aaron Hale-Dorrell points out that Khrushchev was frequently mocked for his corn campaign, which he pursued with almost religious devotion, and its failure figured heavily in critiques of his leadership. Hale-Dorrell argues that this interpretation is mistaken, however: the corn campaign was "more sensible" than its critics portrayed it, if one considers it as one part of a larger model of industrial agriculture Khrushchev hoped to adopt from the United States. See Hale-Dorrell, *Corn Crusade,* 1–3.

180. The most egregious case of fraud emerged out of Riazan, which claimed to have tripled meat production in 1959 and was held up as an example to be emulated by other regions, but was soon revealed to have cheated to the tune of 50,000 tons of meat. On the Riazan scandal, see Oleg V. Khlevniuk, "The Economy of Illusions: The Phenomenon of Data-Inflation in the Khrushchev Era," in *Khrushchev in the Kremlin: Policy and Government in the Soviet Union, 1953–1964,* ed. Jeremy Smith and Melanie Ilič (Milton Park, Abingdon, Oxon: Routledge, 2011), 171–189.

181. Karl-Eugen Wädekin, *The Private Sector in Soviet Agriculture,* ed. George F. Karcz, trans. Keith Bush (Berkeley: University of California Press, 1973), 265–267.

182. Nikita Sergeevich Khrushchev, "Ob otmene obiazatel'nykh postavok i naturoplaty za raboty MTS, o novom poriadke, tsenakh i usloviakh zagotovok sel'skokhozaistvennykh produktov; Doklad na Plenume TsK KPSS, 17 iulia 1958 goda," in *Stroitel'stvo kommunizma,* tom 3, *Ianvar' 1958 goda–mai 1959 goda* (Moskva: Gosudarstvennoe izdatel'stvo politicheskoi literatury, 1962), 391.

183. Ibid.

184. GARF, f. 5446, op. 94, d. 688, l. 30 (letter of complaint to Mikoyan from O. M. Piletskaia, September 28, 1960).

185. RGANI, f. 5, op. 30, d. 325, l. 84 (letter of complaint to Suslov from I. I. Zhukov, December 26, 1960).

186. RGANI, f. 5, op. 30, d. 325, l. 84.

187. Among their ranks were not just ordinary citizens, but also former members of the Stalinist political elite. Dmitrii Shepilov, who, by then, had been ousted from the government after the Anti-Party scandal and who hated Khrushchev, praised Stalin's policy of consecutive retail price cuts and argued that its abandonment during the "Khrushchevshchina" "caused serious harm to the entire economic and political situation in the country." See Shepilov, *The Kremlin's Scholar,* 245.

188. GARF, f. 5446, op. 96, d. 1040, l. 13 (letter of complaint to the Council of Ministers from G. V. Miroliubov, April 10, 1962).

189. GARF, f. 5446, op. 96, d. 1040, l. 22 (letter of complaint to Khrushchev from N. M. Siniutin, circa spring 1962).

190. Feygin, "Building a Ruin," 73–74.

191. As Oscar Sanchez-Sibony has noted, around this time, Gosekonomsovet experts began enthusiastically advocating for the expansion of foreign trade; though it remained nonconvertible, changes to the ruble's purchasing power at this time may have been connected to the government's desire to boost the ruble's use in world trade by bringing its value into a greater state of equilibrium with foreign currencies. On the push for more foreign trade, see Sanchez-Sibony, *Red Globalization,* 119. On the connection between the 1961 currency reform, price reforms, and global trade, see Holzman, "The Ruble Exchange Rate," 818. Gosekonomsovet was liquidated in November 1962, however, and the price-setting reform initiated in the early 1960s was not resumed until after Khrushchev was kicked out of office. See Gertrude E. Schroeder,

"The 1966–67 Soviet Industrial Price Reform: A Study in Complications," *Soviet Studies*, Vol. 20, No. 4 (1969): 462–477.

192. Viktor Danilovich Belkin, *Tseny edinogo urovnia i ekonomicheskie izmereniia na ikh osnove* (Moskva: Izdatel'stvo ekonomicheskoi literatury, 1963), 28.

193. "Programma kommunisticheskoi partii Sovetskogo soiuza," *Pravda*, July 30, 1961, 6.

194. Belkin acknowledges the new approach to price setting was, in part, behind the government's thinking when it raised prices on meat and milk. See Belkin, *Tseny edinogo urovnia*, 59.

195. "Obrashchenie TsK KPSS i soveta ministrov SSSR ko vsem rabochim i rabotnitsam, kolkhoznikam i kolkhoznitsam, rabochim i rabotnitsam sovkhozov, sovetskoi intelligentsii, ko vsemu sovetskomu narodu," *Pravda*, June 1, 1962, 1.

196. "O snizhenii gosudarstvennykh roznichnykh tsen na sakhar, tkani iz viskoznoi shtapel'noi priazhi i izdeliia iz etikh tkanei," *Pravda*, June 1, 1962, 1.

197. RGANI, f. 2, op. 30, d. 394, l. 70.

198. Ibid.

199. RGANI, f. 89, op. 6, d. 11, l. 1 (report on the population's reaction to the new prices to the Central Committee from P. Ivashutin, June 1, 1962).

200. RGANI, f. 89, op. 6, d. 11, l. 2.

201. RGANI, f. 89, op. 6, d. 11, l. 2.

202. RGANI, f. 89, op. 6, d. 13, l. 1 (report on the population's reaction to the new prices to the Central Committee from V. Semichastnyi, June 2, 1962).

203. RGANI, f. 89, op. 6, d. 13, l. 1.

204. GARF, f. 5446, op. 96, d. 1325, l. 22 (letter to Khrushchev from M. S. Glazunova, June 1, 1962).

205. GARF, f. 5446, op. 96, d. 1325, l. 29 (letter to Khrushchev from Agapovich, June 1, 1962).

206. GARF, f. 5446, op. 96, d. 1326, l. 9 (anonymous letter to Khrushchev, June 1, 1962).

207. GARF, f. 5446, op. 96, d. 1327, l. 41 (letter to Khrushchev from T. A. Laletina, June 1, 1962).

208. GARF, f. 5446, op. 96, d. 1327, l. 41.

209. Alec Nove, "Industry," in McCauley, *Khrushchev and Khrushchevism*, 63.

210. GARF, f. 5446, op. 96, d. 1327, l. 96 (letter to Khrushchev from A. O. Vershinin, June 1, 1962).

211. GARF, f. 5446, op. 96, d. 1327, l. 96.

212. GARF, f. 5446, op. 96, d. 1327, l. 59 (letter to the Council of Ministers from Savel'ev, June 1, 1962).

213. Vladimir A. Kozlov, *Mass Uprisings in the USSR: Protest and Rebellion in the Post-Stalin Years*, trans. and ed. Elaine McClarnand MacKinnon (Armonk, N.Y. M. E. Sharpe,

2002), 228. See also Samuel H. Baron, *Bloody Saturday in the Soviet Union: Novocherkassk, 1962* (Stanford, Calif.: Stanford University Press, 2001).

214. "Rech' tovarishcha N. S. Khrushcheva," *Pravda*, June 20, 1962, 2.

215. Nikita Sergeevich Khrushchev, "Vsemerno ukrepliat' proizvodstvennye kolkhozno-sovkhoznye upravleniia; Rech' na soveshchanii rabotnikov proizvodstvennykh upravlenii raionov tsentra rossiiskoi federatsii v Moskve, 27 iunia 1962 goda," in *Stroitel'stvo kommunizma v SSSR i razvitie sel'skokhoziaistva*, tom 7, *Mart 1962–mart 1963 goda* (Moskva: Gospolizdat, 1963), 50–51.

216. Ibid., 51.

217. RGANI, f. 3, op. 20, d. 310, l. 124–125 (report to the Central Committee of the Communist Party on the outcome of a study of the population's budgets in the first nine months of 1962 after the increase in the retail prices of meat, meat products, and butter, from I. Matiukha, circa late 1962).

218. RGANI, f. 3, op. 20, d. 310, l. 124, 128.

219. RGANI, f. 3, op. 20, d. 310, l. 132.

220. RGANI, f. 2, op. 30, d. 394, l. 213 (report to the Central Committee of the Communist Party on letters of complaint to the newspapers *Pravda* and *Izvestiia* on unsatisfactory trade in bread, from V. Ievlev and V. Chistiakov, October 30, 1962).

221. RGANI, f. 2, op. 30, d. 394, l. 215.

222. Hanson, *The Rise and Fall of the Soviet Economy*, 74.

223. Zima, *Golod v SSSR*, 62.

224. RGANI, f. 5, op. 20, d. 128, l. 56 (letter of complaint to *Pravda* from S. I. Shukin, April 27, 1955).

225. Chuev and Molotov, *Sto sorok besed s Molotovym*, 442.

226. Elena Iurievna Zubkova, *Poslevoennoe sovetskoe obshchestvo: Politika i povsednevnost', 1945–1953* (Moskva: ROSSPEN, 2000), 87–88.

227. Ironside, "Stalin's Doctrine of Price Reductions," 659.

2. Income Redistribution without "Leveling"

1. "Zapiska N. S. Khrushcheva v presidium TsK KPSS po voprosam uporiadocheniia zarabotnoi platy i pensionnogo dela," 277.

2. Ibid. "Auxiliary workers" were those who performed low-skilled jobs and non-production-oriented tasks, such as repairing and cleaning equipment, maintaining quality control, or loading and unloading trucks.

3. Ibid., 278.

4. Ibid.

5. "XX s"ezd Kommunisticheskoi partii Sovetskogo soiuza," 7.

6. Ibid.

7. "Direktivy XX s"ezda KPSS po shestomu piatiletnemu planu razvitiia narodnogo khoziaistva SSSR na 1956–1960 gody," *Pravda*, February 26, 1956, 6.

8. The term *uravnilovka* is sometimes translated as "equalitarianism." It retains a distinctly negative connotation.

9. As Moshe Lewin points out, workplace hierarchies were strengthened and orderly careerism was promoted in the 1930s in an attempt to stabilize the body social and develop cadres of skilled workers. Moshe Lewin, *The Making of the Soviet System: Essays in the Social History of Interwar Russia* (New York: Pantheon Books, 1985), 222. On the making of loyal Stalinist cadres, see Sheila Fitzpatrick, "Stalin and the Making of a New Elite, 1928–1939," *Slavic Review*, Vol. 38, No. 3 (1979): 377–402.

10. Aleksandr Antonovich Iliukhov, *Kak platili bol'sheviki: Politika sovetskoi vlasti v sfere oplaty truda v 1917–1941 gg.* (Moskva: ROSSPEN; Fond pervogo prezidenta Rossii B. N. El'tsina, 2010), 370.

11. On Kremlin rations in the 1930s, see Fitzpatrick, *Everyday Stalinism*, 96–97. On the evolution of Kremlin rations into the later Soviet period, see Mervyn Matthews, *Privilege in the Soviet Union: A Study of Elite Life-Styles under Communism* (London: G. Allen & Unwin, 1978), 38.

12. Quote by Yuri Bodarev, cited in Bernice Q. Madison, *Social Welfare in the Soviet Union* (Stanford, Calif.: Stanford University Press, 1968), 59.

13. Fitzpatrick, *Everyday Stalinism*, 96.

14. Ibid.

15. This criticism of gilded, Westernized youth who avoided socially useful labor continued well into the Khrushchev years. See Sheila Fitzpatrick, "Social Parasites: How Tramps, Idle Youth, and Busy Entrepreneurs Impeded the Soviet March to Communism," *Cahiers du monde russe*, Vol. 47, No. 1–2 (2006): 387–388, 401–403.

16. B. Protopopov and I. Shatunovskii, "Plesen'," *Komsomol'skaia pravda*, November 19, 1953, 3. Historians are divided on if the *stiliagi* were wealthy and if this was a defining characteristic of this group. Mark Edele argues that the *stiliagi* were the "golden youth" of the middle class, and their style can be linked to the postwar embourgeoisement of the Stalinist elite. See Mark Edele, "Strange Young Men in Stalin's Moscow: The Birth and Life of the Stiliagi, 1945–1953," *Jahrbücher für Geschichte Osteuropas*, Vol. 50, No. 1 (2002): 38. Juliane Fürst disagrees that the *stiliagi* were all wealthy and privileged, attaching more importance to other markers of belonging, such as their fashion, hairstyles, and musical tastes. See Juliane Fürst, "The Importance of Being Stylish: Youth, Culture and Identity in Late Stalinism," in *Late Stalinist Russia: Society Between Reconstruction and Reinvention*, ed. Juliane Fürst (London: Routledge, 2006), 217. For more on the "moral panic" concerning *stiliagi* and other youths during the postwar years, see Juliane Fürst, *Stalin's Last Generation: Soviet Post-war Youth and the Emergence of Mature Socialism* (Oxford: Oxford University Press, 2010) 190–197.

17. On ideologically correct approaches to child-rearing in the 1950s, see Edward D. Cohn, *The High Title of a Communist: Postwar Party Discipline and the Values of the Soviet*

Regime (DeKalb: Northern Illinois University Press, 2015), 151; and Deborah A. Field, *Private Life and Communist Morality in Khrushchev's Russia* (New York: Peter Lang, 2007), 82–97.

18. A. Sukontsev and I. Shatunovskii, "Za golubym zaborom," *Komsomol'skaia pravda,* March 17, 1954, 3.

19. "V prezidiume SSP SSSR," *Pravda,* May 6, 1954, 2.

20. The decree raising ration prices had initially included a provision prohibiting raising wages; however, the Soviet government decided to excise this, likely to avoid a negative public response. It was issued as a separate decree. See "Telefonogramma I. V. Stalina L. P. Berii o proekte postanovleniia o zapreshchenii povysheniia zarplaty," in *Politbiuro TsK KPSS(b) i Sovet Ministrov SSSR 1945–1953,* ed. O. V. Khlevniuk, I. Gorlitskii, and L. P. Kosheleva (Moskva: ROSSPEN, 2002), 210.

21. RGANI, f. 5, op. 30, d. 101, l. 20 (compilation of letters of complaint to the Central Committee of the Communist Party from Kabashkin, April 22, 1955). The feuilleton in question was "Na verkhnem 'do,'" *Pravda,* January 9, 1955, 2.

22. RGANI, f. 5, op. 30, d. 101, l. 23.

23. RGANI, f. 5, op. 30, d. 101, l. 23.

24. RGANI, f. 5, op. 30, d. 101, l. 19.

25. RGANI, f. 5, op. 30, d. 101, l. 19.

26. RGANI, f. 5, op. 30, d. 101, l. 19.

27. RGANI, f. 5, op. 30, d. 101, l. 23.

28. On the Stalin Prize's connection to privilege, see Oliver Johnson, "The Stalin Prize and the Soviet Artist: Status Symbol or Stigma?," *Slavic Review,* Vol. 70, No. 4 (2011): 819–843.

29. GARF, f. 5446, op. 89, d. 1790, l. 103 (undated anonymous letter, circa 1955).

30. GARF, f. 5446, op. 89, d. 1790, l. 103.

31. For more details related to these accusations and the political fallout from the scandal, see Evgenii Zhirnov, "Razvrat, p'ianka, sovrashchenie devushek," *Kommersant,* November 28, 2005, http://www.kommersant.ru/doc/630490.

32. Ibid.

33. Cohn, *The High Title of a Communist,* 5.

34. Zhirnov, "Razvrat."

35. RGANI, f. 5, op. 30, d. 135, l. 13.

36. RGANI, f. 5, op. 30, d. 135, l. 13.

37. RGANI, f. 5, op. 30, d. 135, l. 14.

38. Eugenia Belova and Valery Lazarev, *Funding Loyalty: The Economics of the Communist Party* (New Haven, Conn.: Yale University Press, 2012), 34.

39. A. B. Konovalov, "Modernizatsiia sistemy nomenklaturnykh l'got i privilegii: Opyt khrushchevkikh reform (1953–1964 gody)," *Istoricheskii ezhegodnik sibirskogo otdeleniia rossiiskoi akademii nauk,* 2007, 8.

40. Ibid.

41. Ibid., 11.

42. Iu. N. Zhukov, *Tainy Kremlia: Stalin, Molotov, Beria, Malenkov* (Moskva: Terra, 2000), 625. See also Galina Mikhailovna Ivanova, *Na poroge "gosudarstva vseobshchego blago-sostoianiia": Sotsial'naia politika v SSSR (seredina 1950-kh–nachalo 1970 godov)* (Moskva: Institut rossiiskoi istorii RAN, 2011), 60.

43. RGANI, f. 5, op. 30, d. 101, l. 28.

44. RGANI, f. 5, op. 30, d. 135, 1. 13. Paying in "envelopes" was a euphemism for paying someone illicitly or "under the table." The envelopes were also sometimes known as "packets" (*pakety*).

45. RGANI, f. 5, op. 30, d. 135, 1. 13.

46. Arseny Grigorevich Zverev, *O gosudarstvennom biudzhete SSSR na 1948 god i ob ispolnenii gosudarstvennogo biudzheta SSSR za 1946: Doklad i zakliuchitel'nye slova ministra finansov SSSR na chetvertoi sessii Verkhovnogo Soveta SSSR 2-go sozyva 31 ianvaria–4 fevralia 1948 g.* (Moskva: Gosudarstvennyi izdatel'stvo politicheskoi literatury, 1948), 32.

47. Arseny Grigorevich Zverev, "Finansovaia distsiplina i kontrol' rublem v narodnom khoziaistve SSSR," *Bolshevik*, No. 12 (1952): 35.

48. RGANI, f. 5, op. 30, d. 135, l. 16–17.

49. RGANI, f. 5, op. 30, d. 135, l. 18–19.

50. RGANI, f. 5, op. 30, d. 135, l. 19.

51. Konovalov, "Modernizatsiia sistemy nomenklaturnykh l'got i privilegii," 11.

52. Ibid., 11–14.

53. See, for example, Ivan Timofeevich Nuzhim, "Berezhlivost'—ne skupost,'" *Izvestiia*, May 31, 1959, 3. On the Komsomol's role in implementing thrifty procedures and preventing costly waste on the shop floor, see, for example, "Berech' narodnye rubli," *Komsomol'skaia pravda*, April 9, 1957, 1.

54. Reid, "Cold War in the Kitchen," 219.

55. Ibid., 218.

56. On images of consumer abundance under Stalin, see Fitzpatrick, *Everyday Stalinism*, 90.

57. Iliukhov, *Kak platili bol'sheviki*, 59.

58. Vladimir Ilich Lenin, "Novaia ekonomicheskaia politika i zadachi politprosvetov," in *Polnoe sobranie sochinenii* (Moskva: Izdatel'stvo politicheskoi literatury, 1964), tom 44, 165.

59. Iliukhov, *Kak platili bol'sheviki*, 46.

60. Previously, the tariff system had only been used in the metal and printing industries.

61. See Iliukhov, *Kak platili bol'sheviki*, 39–41.

62. Rafik Abdulaevich Batkaev and Vladimir Ivanovich Markov, *Differentsiatsiia zarabotnoi platy v promyshlennosti SSSR* (Moskva: Ekonomika, 1964), 42.

63. Donald A. Filtzer, *Soviet Workers and Stalinist Industrialization: The Formation of Modern Soviet Production Relations, 1928–1941* (Armonk, N.Y.: M. E. Sharpe, 1986), 51–55.

64. Lewin, *The Making of the Soviet System,* 221.

65. Filtzer, *Soviet Workers and Stalinist Industrialization,* 59.

66. Iosif Vissarionovich Stalin, "Novaia obstanovka—novye zadachi khoziaistvennogo stroitel'stva," in *Sochineniia* (Moskva: Gosudarstvennoe izdatel'stvo politicheskoi literatury, 1951), tom 13, 56.

67. Ibid., 57.

68. Ibid.

69. Murray Yanowitch, *Social and Economic Inequality in the Soviet Union: Six Studies* (White Plains, N.Y.: M. E. Sharpe, 1977), 24.

70. See, for example, G. Arkad'ev, *Marksizm-leninizm v bor'be s melkoburzhuaznoi uravnilovkoi* (Moskva: Partinoe izdatel'stvo, 1932), 17.

71. Iliukhov, *Kak platili bol'sheviki,* 214.

72. Ibid., 215. In reality, as Iliukhov emphasizes, many of those accused of harboring "opportunist views" were merely carrying out orders from the Central Committee and, in some cases, from Stalin, himself.

73. Ostrovitianov et al., *Politicheskaia ekonomika,* 455.

74. Ibid.

75. Filtzer, *Soviet Workers and Stalinist Industrialization,* 179, 186.

76. On the wartime labor regime, see Martin Kragh, "Stalinist Labour Coercion during World War II: An Economic Approach," *Europe-Asia Studies,* Vol. 63, No. 7 (2011): 1253–1273. Note that the laws were put in place in 1940 before, but in anticipation of, the war.

77. RGASPI, f. 82, op. 2, d. 797, l. 64 (report on the growth of labor productivity and wages in industry during the war to Molotov, circa late 1944).

78. RGASPI, f. 82, op. 2, d. 797, l. 66. The wage fund was centrally determined based on the previous year's performance and changes in the size and qualifications of the labor force, as well as expected productivity. On the wage fund, see Alec Nove, *The Soviet Economy: An Introduction* (New York: Praeger, 1969), 132–134.

79. RGASPI, f. 82, op. 2, d. 789, l. 108 (report on the effects of the currency reform to Molotov from Zverev, circa early 1948).

80. Donald A. Filtzer, *Soviet Workers and De-Stalinization: The Consolidation of the Modern System of Soviet Production Relations, 1953–1964* (Cambridge: Cambridge University Press, 1992), 93.

81. Ibid.

82. Ibid., 93–94.

83. Nove, *The Soviet Economy,* 131–132. Initially, wage setting was the Commissariat of Labor's responsibility, and when that organ was abolished in 1934, some of its functions

were absorbed by the Central Trade Union; however, the latter was not part of the government per se and decisions about wage grades did not fall under its purview. See also Alastair McAuley, *Economic Welfare in the Soviet Union: Poverty, Living Standards, and Inequality* (Madison: University of Wisconsin Press, 1979), 199, 202.

84. McAuley, *Economic Welfare in the Soviet Union,* 198.

85. A. N. Maslin, *Printsip material'noi zainteresovannosti pri sotsializme* (Moskva: Moskovskii rabochii, 1955), 22–23.

86. Ibid., 39.

87. "XX s"ezd Kommunisticheskoi partii Sovetskogo soiuza," 7.

88. A. A. Arakelian, *Pochemu my protiv uravnilovki* (Moskva: Moskovskii rabochii, 1959), 13.

89. Ibid.

90. Ibid., 14–16.

91. Ibid., 17.

92. Ibid., 18.

93. "O povyshenii zarabotnoi platy nizkooplachivaemym rabochikh i sluzhashchikh," *Pravda,* September 9, 1956, 1.

94. "Dlia blaga sovetskykh liudei; Zabota o liudiakh truda," *Pravda,* September 10, 1956, 1.

95. Abel Gezevich Aganbegian and V. F. Maier, *Zarabotnaia plata v SSSR; Nekotorye voprosy teorii i praktiki* (Moskva: Gosplanizdat, 1959), 222.

96. Nove, *The Soviet Economy,* 133.

97. GARF, f. 9595, op. 1, d. 108, l. 6. (undated report to the Central Committee of the Communist Party from the Committee on Questions of Work and Wages, circa 1955).

98. GARF, f. 9595, op. 1, d. 33, l. 31 (undated report on women's wages from N. Tatarinova, March 6, 1957).

99. GARF, f. 9595, op. 1, d. 33, l. 36.

100. GARF, f. 9595, op. 1, d. 33, l. 31.

101. GARF, f. 9595, op. 1, d. 33, l. 31; GARF, f. 374a, op. 30, d. 10132, l. 13 (report on the outcome of the study of workers' and collective farmers' budgets in the RSFSR in 1956, March 9, 1957).

102. GARF, f. 374a, op. 30, d. 10132, l. 13.

103. GARF, f. 374a, op. 31, d. 2069, l. 78 (report on the material situation of workers, ITRs, white-collar employees, and collective farmers in 1958 to A. B. Aristov from B. Kolpakov, March 24, 1959).

104. See Leonard Joel Kirsch, *Soviet Wages: Changes in Structure and Administration since 1956* (Cambridge, Mass., MIT Press, 1972), 2.

105. Batkaev and Markov, *Differentsiatsiia zarabotnoi platy,* 45.

106. Ibid.

107. Filtzer, *Soviet Workers and De-Stalinization*, 97.

108. "V tsentral'nom komitete KPSS Sovete Ministrov i VTsSPS: O perevode v 1958 godu na semi- i shestichasovoi rabochi den' i uporiadochenii zarabotnoi platy rabochikh i sluzhashchikh riada otraslei tiazheloi promyshlennosti," *Pravda*, April 22, 1958, 1.

109. Note that some workers in these industries in the Donbass region had already been shifted to six- and seven-hour workdays in 1956–1957.

110. "V tsentral'nom komitete KPSS Sovete Ministrov i VTsSPS: O perevode na sokrashchenii rabochii den' i uporiadochenii zarabotnoi platy rabochikh i sluzhashchikh mashinostroitel'noi, neftianoi i gazovoi promyshlennosti," *Izvestiia*, November 4, 1958, 1.

111. Matthews, *Privilege in the Soviet Union*, 93.

112. Filtzer, *Soviet Workers and De-Stalinization*, 113.

113. RGANI, f. 5, op. 30, d. 216, l. 33.

114. RGANI, f. 5, op. 30, d. 216, l. 30–31.

115. RGANI, f. 5, op. 30, d. 217, l. 9.

116. See "O povyshenii zarabotnoi platy i stroitel'stve zhilishch dlia rabochikh i inzhenerno-tekhnicheskikh rabotnikov predpriiatii i stroek, raspolozhennykh na Urale, v Sibiri i na Dal'nem Vostoke," *Sobranie postanovlenii i rasporiazhenii Soveta ministrov*, No. 12 (October 14, 1946): 226.

117. Alan Barenberg, *Gulag Town, Company Town: Forced Labor and Its Legacy in Vorkuta* (New Haven, Conn.: Yale University Press, 2014), 181.

118. RGANI, f. 5, op. 30, d. 217, l. 9–10 (proposal to reform wages and transition to a shorter workday for workers and white-collar employees in the USSR's Northern regions, late April 1958).

119. RGANI, f. 5, op. 30, d. 217, l. 9–10.

120. See Barenberg, *Gulag Town, Company Town*, 174.

121. Nikita Sergeevich Khrushchev, *O kontrol'nykh tsifrakh razvitiia narodnogo khoziaistva SSSR na 1959–1965 gody: Doklad na vneocherednom XXI s"ezde Kommunisticheskoi partii Sovetskogo Soiuza 27 ianvaria i 5 fevralia 1959 g.* (Moskva: Gos. izd-vo polit. lit-ry, 1959), 51.

122. Ibid.

123. "V tsentral'nom komitete KPSS, Sovete Ministrov SSSR i VTsSPS; O srokakh zaversheniia perevoda na sokrashchenyi rabochii den' i uporiadocheniia zarabotnoi platy rabochikh i sluzhashchikh," *Izvestiia*, September 20, 1959, 1.

124. Ibid.

125. Ibid.

126. Batkaev and Markov, *Differentsiatsiia zarabotnoi platy*, 46.

127. Filtzer, *Soviet Workers and De-Stalinization*, 101.

128. Ibid.

129. Ibid.

130. Ibid., 102.

131. Ibid., 92.

132. RGANI, f. 5, op. 30, d. 266, l. 135–140 (proposal for increasing republics' responsibility for provisioning goods to the population, signed by I. Ignatev, I. Kuzmin, A. Zverev, et al., circa September 1958).

133. RGANI, f. 5, op. 20, d. 169, l. 9 (transcript of excerpts from Khrushchev's speech to the May 1958 Plenum of the Communist Party).

134. RGANI, f. 5, op. 20, d. 169, l. 9.

135. See "Doklad o sostoianii denezhnogo obrashcheniia SSSR," in Kashin, *Po stranitsam arkhivnykh fondov v tsentral'nogo banka rossiiskoi federatsii,* vypusk 6, 97–98.

136. I. Aralichev, "Otkrovennyi razgovor," *Trud,* November 7, 1956, 2.

137. Ibid.

138. GARF, f. 5446, op. 96, d. 1040, l. 164 (letter of complaint to Khrushchev from Krikunov et al., April 26, 1962).

139. GARF, f. 5446, op. 96, d. 1040, l. 164.

140. GARF, f. 5446, op. 96, d. 1040, l. 167 (letter to Khrushchev from Zametin, April 29, 1962).

141. Matthews, *Privilege in the Soviet Union,* 37.

142. Ibid., 36.

143. Ibid.

144. Konovalov, "Modernizatsiia sistemy nomenklaturnykh l'got i privilegii," 17–18.

145. Ibid., 18.

146. "Ob otmene nalogov s rabochikh i sluzhashchikh i drugikh meropriatiiakh," 3.

147. Ibid.

148. See, for example, "Otvety na voprosy: Tol'ko li ot snizheniia tsen zavisit rost blagosostoianiia naseleniia?," *Politicheskoe samoobrazovanie,* No. 8 (1960): 82–86.

149. Petr Ilich Ermolenko, "Biudzhet rabochei sem'i," *Sovetskie profsoiuzy,* No. 8 (1957): 68.

150. Ibid.

151. Ibid., 70.

152. "Chto prines 1956 god sem'e rabochego Andrianova?," *Komsomol'skaia pravda,* February 22, 1957, 2–3. See also Natal'ia Nikitichna Tatarskaia and Aleksandr Vladimirovich Gurianov, *Biudzhet rabochei sem'i* (Moskva: Gospolitizdat, 1957). The book goes into more depth about the family's life and economic practices.

153. "Chto prines 1956 god sem'e rabochego Andrianova?," 2.

154. Tatarskaia and Gurianov, *Biudzhet rabochei sem'i,* 16.

155. Ibid.

156. Khrushchev, *O kontrol'nykh tsifrakh razvitiia narodnogo khoziaistva SSSR na 1959–1965 gody*, 53.

157. Ibid.

158. RGANI, f. 2, op. 3, d. 364, l. 28–29 (report on expenses from the wage fund in 1961 to the Central Committee of the Communist Party from A. Korovushkin, March 23, 1961).

159. RGANI, f. 2, op. 3, d. 364, l. 29–30.

160. RGANI, f. 2, op. 3, d. 364, l. 30.

161. RGANI, f. 2, op. 3, d. 364, l. 75–77 (report on anticipated expenditures from the wage fund to Khrushchev from V. Grishin and A. Volkov, September 17, 1961).

162. RGANI, f. 2, op. 3, d. 364, l. 75–77.

163. RGANI, f. 2, op. 3, d. 364, l. 78.

164. RGANI, f. 2, op. 3, d. 364, l. 79.

165. RGANI, f. 2, op. 3, d. 364, l. 79.

166. RGANI, f. 2, op. 3, d. 364, l. 79.

167. RGANI, f. 2, op. 3, d. 364, l. 79.

168. "Stenograficheskaia zapis' zasedaniia Prezidiuma TsK KPSS po voprosu 'O korrektivakh zadanii kontrol'nykh tsifr razvitiia narodnogo khoziaistva SSSR na ostavshiisia period semiletki (1963–1965),'" in *Prezidium TsK KPSS 1954–1964,* tom 1, *Chernovye protokoly zapisi zasedanii; Stenogrammy,* ed. A. A. Fursenko (Moskva: ROSSPEN, 2003), 565. A wage increase targeted not at low-income workers as a group, but only at workers in education, health care, and other "service-oriented" professions was later announced alongside pensions for collective farmers at the July 1964 Plenum of the Communist Party. See "Vse vo imia cheloveka, dlia blaga cheloveka," *Pravda,* July 15, 1964, 1.

169. "Stenograficheskaia zapis' zasedaniia Prezidiuma TsK KPSS po voprosu 'O korrektivakh zadanii kontrol'nykh tsifr razvitiia narodnogo khoziaistva SSSR na ostavshiisia period semiletki (1963–1965),'" 566.

170. Ibid.

171. In some industries, piece-workers could earn up to twice as much as time-workers in their same skill grade. See Filtzer, *Soviet Workers and De-Stalinization,* 105.

172. GARF, f. 5446, op. 96, d. 1328, l. 4 (letter of complaint to Khrushchev from E. Zlobin, June 1, 1962).

173. See Mariia Dynina, *Kak organizovana zarabotnaia plata rabochikh* (Moskva: Gos. izd-vo polit. lit-ry, 1961), 3–4.

174. Sergei Khrushchev, *Nikita Khrushchev: Reformator; Trilogiia ob ottse* (Moskva: Vremia, 2010), 355.

175. Ibid.

176. Ibid., 680–681.

177. GARF, f. 5446, op. 96, d. 1327, l. 1 (anonymous letter to Khrushchev, June 1, 1962).

178. Vladimir A. Kozlov, Sheila Fitzpatrick, and Sergei V. Mironenko, eds., *Sedition: Everyday Resistance in the Soviet Union under Khrushchev and Brezhnev,* trans. Olga Livshin (New Haven, Conn.: Yale University Press, 2011), 288.

179. Ibid., 271.

3. Socialist Security

1. RGANI, f. 5, op. 30, d. 128, l. 2 (pension reform proposal to Khrushchev from N. Shvernik and N. Murav'eva, March 19, 1955). On the 300-ruble wage cap, see "O poriadke primeneniia pravil pensionirovaniia utverzhdennykh SSSS 29 fevralia 1932 goda," in *Pensii po sotsial'nomu strakhovaniiu; Sbornik zakonodatel'nykh i direktivnykh materialov,* by R. Kats and N. A. Sorokin (Moskva: Profizdat, 1935), 32.

2. Ibid.

3. "Zapiska N. S. Khrushcheva v presidium TsK KPSS po voprosam uporiadocheniia zarabotnoi platy i pensionnogo dela," 278.

4. For a concise current definition of "pay-as-you-go" versus "funded" pension schemes, see Nicholas Barr, *The Economics of the Welfare State,* 5th ed. (Oxford: Oxford University Press, 2012), 154–155. Many countries have a hybrid version in which a certain amount of the contributions go toward a pension fund.

5. Bernice Q. Madison, a sociologist whose 1968 tome remains one of the few comprehensive English-language treatments of the prerevolutionary and Soviet social welfare systems, states that between the Second World War and 1956, no substantive changes in social insurance were made and 1956 marked the dawn of a new era in income maintenance policy. See Madison, *Social Welfare in the Soviet Union,* 75. In her work on post-Soviet pension reforms, Andrea Chandler writes that, after Stalin's death, the Soviet leadership quietly prepared a comprehensive pension reform, inspired in part by the recognition that Western capitalist countries were establishing their own old-age security systems. See Andrea Chandler, *Shocking Mother Russia: Democratization, Social Rights, and Pension Reform in Russia, 1990–2001* (Toronto: University of Toronto Press, 2004), 25. Mark B. Smith similarly depicts 1953 as a watershed and argues that the 1956 pension law was a move in the direction of the principle of universality: while higher pensions were granted to certain categories of workers, the new pensions "nevertheless amounted to transparent and regularized rights . . . they were not arbitrarily conceived, like Stalin-era apportionments of privilege." See Mark B. Smith, "Social Rights in the Soviet Dictatorship: The Constitutional Right to Welfare from Stalin to Brezhnev," *Humanity: An International Journal of Human Rights, Humanitarianism, and Development,* Vol. 3, No. 3 (2012): 396. Smith expands on this argument in another article, suggesting that the pension reform of 1956 was characteristic of a wider transformation that took place after 1953, and to a more limited extent after 1945, that he calls "the withering away of the danger society": the creation of a universal welfare system in which many social risks were eliminated. He claims that the "traceable origins" of the 1956 and 1964 pension reforms lay in the period immediately after Stalin's death in March 1953. See Mark B. Smith, "The Withering Away of the Danger Society: The Pensions Reforms of 1956 and 1964 in the Soviet Union," *Social Science History,*

Vol. 39, No. 1 (2015): 130–131, 133–135. Galina Mikhailovna Ivanova portrays pension reform as an arena in the competition between Khrushchev and Malenkov over the Soviet leadership after Stalin's death. See Ivanova, *Na poroge "gosudarstva vseobshchego blagosostoianiia,"* 61–70. One outlier in the existing scholarship is Maria Cristina Galmarini-Kabala, whose work on welfare assistance to socially marginal citizens via the Ministry of Social Insurance shows that pension reform for the uninsured, that is, those who were not eligible for a pension on the basis of labor, began in 1949–1950. She links these reforms to the growing competition with the West during the Cold War. These efforts, in her opinion, foreshadowed the more systematic changes that took place in 1956. See Maria Cristina Galmarini-Kabala, *The Right to Be Helped: Deviance, Entitlement, and the Soviet Moral Order* (DeKalb: Northern Illinois University Press, 2016), 218.

6. This fits the pattern of Stalin's postwar governing behavior identified by Gorlizki and Khlevniuk: he increasingly delegated authority in the postwar period but rejected out of hand any talk of "reforms." See Gorlizki and Khlevniuk, *Cold Peace,* 123–124.

7. On the ideological impulses behind early Soviet social welfare initiatives, see David L. Hoffmann, *Cultivating the Masses: Modern State Practices and Soviet Socialism, 1914–1939* (Ithaca, N.Y.: Cornell University Press, 2011), 52–54; Galmarini-Kabala, *The Right to Be Helped,* 37–38.

8. Galmarini-Kabala, *The Right to Be Helped,* 41.

9. Kats and Sorokin, *Pensii po sotsial'nomu strakhovaniiu,* 3.

10. "Postanovlenie TsIK SSSR, SNK SSSR ot 13.02.1930: Polozhenie o pensiiakh i posobiakh po sotsial'nomu strakhovaniiu," *Sobranie zakonov i rasporiazhenii,* No. 11 (March 6, 1930): 220–231.

11. Chandler, *Shocking Mother Russia,* 31.

12. Matthews, *Privilege in the Soviet Union,* 103–104.

13. The Soviet government was still arguing about the merit of personal pensions and trying unsuccessfully to limit them by 1990, as Chandler observes. See Chandler, *Shocking Mother Russia,* 55.

14. Ibid., 37. At the same time, as Galmarini-Kabala has shown, that 'right' to be helped remained internalized by many Soviet citizens and activists, who continued to press the Soviet govermment to meet its ethical commitments to them as members of a socialist society. See Galmarini-Kabala, *The Right to Be Helped,* 146–147.

15. Galmarini-Kabala, *The Right to Be Helped,* 147.

16. See "Postanovlenie tsentral'nogo ispolnitel'nogo komiteta i soveta narodnykh komissarov: O sotsial'nom strakhovanii," *Sobranie zakonov i rasporiazhenii,* No. 41 (July 2, 1931): 501–508.

17. "Ob otnesenii mashinistov pod'emnykh mashin na shakhtakh k vrednym professiiam pri naznachenii pensii; Postanovlenie sekretariata VTsSPS 17 noiabria 1934 g.," in Kats and Sorokin, *Pensii po sotsial'nomu strakhovaniiu,* 30.

18. “O meropriatiiakh po uporiadocheniiu trudovoi distsipliny, ulushcheniiu praktiki gosudarstvennogo sotsial’nogo strakhovaniia i bor’be s zloiupotrebleniami v etom dele; Postanovlenie Soveta narodnykh komissarov soiuza SSR, tsentral’nogo komiteta vsesoiuznoi kommunisticheskoi partii (bol’shevikov) i vsesoiuznogo tsentra’nogo soveta professional’nykh soiuzov,” *Pravda,* December 29, 1938, 1.

19. Ibid., 2.

20. S. Glezin and A. Raikhman, *Gosudarstvennaia finansovaia pomoshch’ voennosluzhashchim i ikh sem’iam* (Moskva: Gosfinizdat, 1942), 3–4.

21. RGASPI, f. 82, op. 2, d. 780, l. 83.

22. Glezin and Raikhman, *Gosudarstvennaia finansovaia pomoshch’ voennosluzhashchim i ikh sem’iam,* 13–14.

23. Ibid., 14.

24. GARF, f. 5446, op. 47, d. 3345, l. 6 (letter on pensions for the families of those who died or went missing in action in 1941–1942 to Voznesenskii from Kosygin, May 8, 1945).

25. GARF, f. 5446, op. 48, d. 3236, l. 222 (letter of complaint to the Council of Ministers from Z. F. Novikova, October 19, 1946).

26. GARF, f. 5446, op. 48, d. 3236, l. 222.

27. “Ob uluschenii pensionnogo obespecheniia po invalidnosti, po sluchaiu poteri kormil’tsa i po starosti; Postanovlenie SSSS pri NKT SSSR 29 fevralia 1932 g. No. 47,” in Kats and Sorokin, *Pensii po sotsial’nomu strakhovaniiu,* 13.

28. Mark Edele, *Soviet Veterans of the Second World War: A Popular Movement in an Authoritarian Society, 1941–1991* (Oxford: Oxford University Press, 2008), 185.

29. Ibid., 191. The Decembrists were a group of soldier-revolutionaries who pushed Tsar Nicholas I to institute liberal reforms in 1825.

30. Ibid., 193.

31. Beate Fieseler, “The Bitter Legacy of the ‘Great Patriotic War’: Red Army Disabled Soldiers under Late Stalinism,” in Fürst, *Late Stalinist Russia,* 48–51. See also Beate Fieseler, “Soviet-Style Welfare: The Disabled Soldiers of the ‘Great Patriotic War,’” in *Disability in Eastern Europe and the Former Soviet Union: History, Policy and Everyday Life,* ed. Michael Rasell and Elena Iarskaia-Smirnova (London: Routledge, 2014), 28–31.

32. Elena Zubkova, “S protianutoi rukoi: Nishchie i nishchenstvo v poslevoennom SSSR,” *Cahiers du monde russe,* Vol. 49, No. 2 (2008): 450.

33. Ibid.

34. Fieseler, “Soviet-Style Welfare,” 27.

35. On veterans’ complaints and petitions at the local level, see Edele, *Soviet Veterans,* 40–41. On their in-person petitions for pension raises and related requests for assistance at the highest level of government, the Presidium of the Supreme Soviet, see Kristy Ironside, “‘I Beg You Not to Reject My Plea’: The Late Stalinist Welfare State and the Politics of One-Time Monetary Aid, 1946–1953,” *Journal of Social History,* Vol. 51, No. 4 (2018): 1052–1057.

36. RGASPI, f. 558, op. 11, d. 893, l. 62 (letter to Stalin from Sofiia Briukhova, May 22, 1946).

37. GARF, f. 5446, op. 47, d. 3334, l. 2 (letter to Kosygin from M. L. Sosunov, June 21, 1945).

38. GARF, f. 5446, op. 47, d. 3334, l. 3 (letter of support for Sosunov's petition from Mitrichev to Kosygin, July 2, 1945).

39. See "O preimushchestvakh i l'gotakh dlia podzemnykh rabochikh, rukovodiashchikh inzhenerno-tekhnicheskikh rabotnikov ugol'noi promyshlennosti i stroitel'stva ugol'nykh shakht," *Sobranie zakonov i rasporiazhenii,* No. 8 (1947): 145–148; "O preimushchestvakh i l'gotakh dlia gornykh i burovykh rabochikh gornykh i burovykh masterov, rukovodiashchikh i inzhenerno-tekhnicheskikh rabotnikov Ministerstva geologii," *Sobranie zakonov i rasporiazhenii,* No. 9 (1947): 172–174.

40. "Instruksiia o poriadke naznacheniia i vyplaty personal'nye pensii republikanskogo i mestnogo znacheniia," *Sobranie postanovleniia i rasporiazheniia soveta ministrov soiuznykh respublik,* No. 4 (1949): 72.

41. Ibid., 74.

42. GARF, f. 5446, op. 87, d. 2124, l. 65 (letter on the necessity of pension reform to Stalin from Chernousov, October 22, 1949).

43. GARF, f. 5446, op. 87, d. 2124, l. 64.

44. GARF, f. 5446, op. 87, d. 2124, l. 64.

45. GARF, f. 5446, op. 87, d. 2124, l. 149 (summary of activities by the pension commission and proposed reforms to the Council of Ministers from Zverev et al., circa July 1950).

46. GARF, f. 5446, op. 87, d. 2124, l. 149.

47. GARF, f. 5446, op. 87, d. 2124, l. 148.

48. GARF, f. 5446, op. 87, d. 2124, l. 147.

49. GARF, f. 5446, op. 87, d. 2124, l. 143.

50. GARF, f. 5446, op. 87, d. 2124, l. 146.

51. GARF, f. 5446, op. 87, d. 2124, l. 145.

52. GARF, f. 5446, op. 87, d. 2124, l. 141.

53. GARF, f. 5446, op. 87, d. 2124, l. 141.

54. GARF, f. 5446, op. 87, d. 2124, l. 45 (letter to the Council of Ministers from Zverev, June 2, 1950).

55. GARF, f. 5446, op. 87, d. 2124, l. 249 (report on proposed reforms to the Council of Ministers from Zverev et al., June 3, 1952).

56. GARF, f. 5446, op. 87, d. 2124, l. 248.

57. GARF, f. 5446, op. 87, d. 2124, l. 325 (letter to the Council of Ministers from Kuznetsov, circa July 1952).

58. GARF, f. 5446, op. 87, d. 2124, l. 315 (draft decree on pension reform, circa July 1952).

59. GARF, f. 5446, op. 87, d. 2124, l. 1 (letter of complaint to the Council of Ministers signed by "labor invalid," undated but circa late 1940s or early 1950s).

60. GARF, f. 5446, op. 87, d. 2124, l. 11 (letter of complaint to the Council of Ministers and the Presidium of the Central Committee of the Communist Party from I. N. Egorov, November 19, 1952).

61. GARF, f. 5446, op. 87, d. 2124, l. 10.

62. GARF, f. 5446, op. 89, d. 1790, l. 29 (summary of letters and complaints regarding pensions to the newspaper *Trud,* April 29, 1955).

63. GARF, f. 5446, op. 89, d. 1790, l. 29. Two hundred ten rubles constituted the minimum pension of 150 rubles plus the bread allowance of 60 rubles.

64. GARF, f. 5446, op. 89, d. 1790, l. 22.

65. GARF, f. 5446, op. 89, d. 1790, l. 22.

66. For an overview of those drafts' provisions, see Ivanova, *Na poroge "gosudarstva vseobshchego blagosostoianiia,"* 65–66.

67. RGANI, f. 5, op. 30, d. 128, l. 2.

68. The document is signed by Nikolai Shvernik, then head of the trade unions, and N. A. Murav'eva, then head of the Ministry of Social Security of the RSFSR. Malenkov was Chairman of the Council of Ministers until February 1955, whereupon he became Deputy Chairman.

69. RGANI, f. 5, op. 30, d. 128, l. 6.

70. RGANI, f. 5, op. 30, d. 128, l. 4.

71. RGANI, f. 5, op. 30, d. 128, l. 13.

72. Ivanova, *Na poroge "gosudarstva vseobshchego blagosostoianiia,"* 60–61.

73. Ibid., 70.

74. See Chandler, *Shocking Mother Russia,* 62.

75. "Zapiska N. S. Khrushcheva v prezidium TsK KPSS po voprosam uporiadocheniia zarabotnoi platy i pensionnogo dela," 278.

76. Ibid.

77. "XX s"ezd Kommunisticheskoi partii Sovetskogo soiuza," 7.

78. This group entailed representatives of ministries that had been involved in pension reform efforts since the late 1940s, namely, the Minister of Finance, Arseny Zverev, who had led earlier efforts. It also entailed the Chairman of the Council of Ministers, Nikolai Bulganin, and Deputies Mikhail Pervukhin and Lazar Kaganovich, and several economic officials who had not played a leading role in earlier efforts, including Maksim Saburov, Nikolai Baibakov, and Aleksei Kosygin of Gosplan—the same Kosygin who would play a role in the 1961 currency reform and price-setting reforms of the early 1960s. The trade union was also represented by L. Solov'ev. See "Zapiska komissii po podgotovke proekta zakona o gosudarstvennykh pensiiakh v okonchatel'noi redaktsii zakona," in Fursenko, *Prezidium TsK KPSS 1954–1964, tom 2, postanovleniia 1954–1958,* 273–274.

79. Ibid., 274.

80. Ibid., 278.

81. Ibid., 277–278.

82. Ibid., 278.

83. Ibid, 274.

84. "Zakon o gosudarstvennykh pensiiakh," *Pravda,* May 9, 1956, 1–2.

85. Ibid., Article 6 and 6a.

86. Ibid., Article 7.

87. Ibid., Article 8a and 8b.

88. Ibid., Article 20.

89. Ibid., Article 30.

90. GARF, f. 5446, op. 90, d. 1020, l. 227 (report on citizens' suggestions for how to improve the pension law to the Central Committee from Bulganin, July 3, 1956).

91. "Bogateet strana," *Izvestiia,* May 10, 1956, 1.

92. "Starost' moia budet spokoinoi," *Trud,* May 10, 1956, 1.

93. Ibid.

94. "Trudovoe stazh—osnovnoe v naznachenii pensii," *Pravda,* June 10, 1956, 2.

95. "O pensiiakh dlia invalidov truda," *Pravda,* June 10, 1956, 2.

96. GARF, f. 5446, op. 90, d. 1021, 227 (letter to the Council of Ministers from A. M. Barashkin, May 23, 1956).

97. GARF, f. 5446, op. 90, d. 1022, l. 90 (letter to the newspaper *Pravda Vostoka* from M. U. Gorlanov, June 15, 1956).

98. GARF, f. 5446, op. 90, d. 1022, l. 119 (undated letter to *Pravda* from A. Tural'skii and B. Novikov, circa May–June 1956).

99. GARF, f. 5446, op. 90, d. 1021, l. 253–254 (letter to the Council of Ministers from N. A. Mikhailov, May 26, 1956).

100. GARF, f. 5446, op. 90, d. 1021, l. 249–250 (undated letter to the Council of Ministers from Ababkov, circa May–June 1956).

101. This suggestion was rejected; however, a law later introduced in 1967 allowed workers in the Far North to retire 5 years early if they had worked there for at least 15 years.

102. GARF, f. 5446, op. 90, d. 1020, l. 224–225.

103. GARF, f. 5446, op. 90, d. 1020, 1. 224.

104. GARF, f. 5446, op. 90, d. 1020, l. 222–223.

105. "Zakliuchitel'noe slovo predsedatel'ia soveta ministrov SSSR N. A. Bul'ganina na zasedaniia soveta natsional'nostei verkhovnogo soveta SSSR 13 iiulia 1956 goda," *Pravda,* July 15, 1956, 3.

106. Ibid.

107. Ibid.

108. Ibid.

109. Ibid.

110. "Zakon o gosudarstvennykh pensiiakh," *Pravda*, July 15, 1956, 1–2.

111. Ibid., Article 9.

112. Ibid., Articles 10 and 11.

113. Ibid., Article 41.

114. Ibid., Article 46.

115. Ibid., Article 58. Science workers' pensions were reformed in separate decrees issued by the end of that year. On March 2, 1957, the terms of pensions for 'length of service' offered to teachers and medical personnel, as existed before October 1, 1956, were officially preserved with no changes. See "O pensiiakh za vyslugu let," *Sobranie postanovlenii pravitel'stva Soiuza sovetskikh sotsialisticheskikh respublik*, No. 4 (1957): 146. Khrushchev preserved and expanded the privileges offered to personal pensioners in a separate decree on November 14, 1956, going into effect in December. Generals' and other career soldiers' pensions were later reformed and reduced according to a decree of July 27, 1959, a move that proved unpopular because he reduced the size of the Red Army shortly thereafter and forced many generals into retirement.

116. These were low-level organs of municipal government that handled pension and other welfare matters. For more on these encounters, see Mark B. Smith, "Faded Red Paradise: Welfare and the Soviet City after 1953," *Contemporary European History*, Vol. 24, No. 4 (2015): 608–612.

117. GARF, f. 5446, op. 90, d. 1312, l. 125 (summary of letters about pensions received by the newspaper *Pravda* between October and November 1956).

118. GARF, f. 5446, op. 90, d. 1312, l. 137.

119. Individuals without a complete labor period were not categorically barred from receiving a pension. They could potentially receive a pension if they met rigid criteria regarding the breaks in their employment: if they had reached the necessary age of retirement; if they had worked no less than a total of five years before becoming a pensioner; if they had worked for a continuous period of three years before applying to receive a pension; if breaks in their employment did not exceed six months in length; and if they applied for a pension no more than a month after ending work. Workers who became first- and second-group invalids and, as a result, did not have a full labor period, were eligible for pensions, but not third-group invalids. See Nina Aleksandrovna Abrosimova, *Pensii pri nepolnom stazhe* (Moskva: Gosudarstvennoe izdatel'stvo iuridicheskoi literatury, 1962), 10–11.

120. This problem is discussed at length in A. Naguevskii and Iu. Khramov, "Pomen'she formalizma," *Sotsial'noe obespechenie*, No. 1 (1957): 11.

121. GARF, f. 5446, op. 90, d. 1312, l. 136.

122. GARF, f. 5446, op. 90, d. 1312, l. 134.

123. GARF, f. 5446, op. 90, d. 1312, l. 134.

124. Some had even anticipated this problem. For example, one legal consultant in Voronezh, which was occupied during the war and whose residents had been evacuated, raised this issue when the Soviet government solicited suggestions on how to change the law. She wrote that many people had come to her asking how evacuation would affect their eligibility for a pension; she asked for clarification on this issue in the finalized law. See GARF, f. 5446, op. 90, d. 1021, l. 226.

125. See, for example, B. Babkin and M. Shishalovskii, "O pravakh i obiazannostiakh komissii po naznacheniiu pensii," *Sotsial'noe obespechenie,* No. 12 (1956): 7.

126. V. Karavaev, "Nepreryvnyi stazh," *Sotsial'noe obespechenie,* No. 3 (1957): 58–63.

127. Ibid., 58.

128. Ibid., 61.

129. Ibid., 63.

130. GARF, f. 5446, op. 91, d. 577, l. 148.

131. GARF, f. 5446, op. 92, d. 622, l. 86.

132. GARF, f. 5446, op. 92, d. 622, l. 84.

133. GARF, f. 5446, op. 92, d. 622, l. 81.

134. "Dokladnaia zapiska Gosbanka SSSR 'O denezhnom obrashchenii v 1957 godu,' 15 marta 1957 goda," in *Po stranitsam arkhivnykh fondov tsentral'nogo banka rossiiskoi federatsii,* vypusk 16, *Iz neopublikovannogo (vedomstvennye materialy),* ed. Iu. I. Kashin and T. V. Kozlova (Moskva: Tsentral'nyi bank Rossiiskoi federatsii, 2014), 131.

135. Ibid.

136. Ibid., 132.

137. Ibid.

138. GARF, f. 5446, op. 92, d. 622, l. 80 (report to the Council of Ministers on the number of pensioners in the Soviet Union, circa 1958).

139. GARF, f. 5446, op. 92, d. 622, l. 80.

140. GARF, f. 5446, op. 92, d. 622, l. 80.

141. GARF, f. 5446, op. 95, d. 1005, l. 97–98 (proposal to the Council of Ministers from the Council of Ministers of the RSFSR to allow pensioners to work, circa June 1961).

142. GARF, f. 5446, op. 95, d. 1005, l. 120 (circular from the Council of Ministers, June 17, 1961).

143. A. G. Novitskii and G. B. Mil', *Zaniatost' pensionerov: Sotsial'no-demograficheskii aspekt* (Moskva: Finansy i statistika, 1981), 37.

144. "O povyshenii material'noi zainteresovannosti pensionerov v rabote na proizvodstve," *Sobranie postanovlenii pravitel'stva Soiuza sovetskikh sotsialisticheskikh respublik,* No. 3 (1964): 16–17.

145. "Ministr otvechaet nashim chitatel'iam," *Izvestiia,* April 3, 1964, 5.

146. Novitskii and Mil', *Zaniatost' pensionerov,* 37.

147. Chandler, *Shocking Mother Russia,* 41.

148. Liubov Denisova, *Rural Women in the Soviet Union and Post-Soviet Russia,* ed. and trans. Irina Mukhina (Milton Park, Abingdon, Oxon: Routledge, 2010), 79–80.

149. Iurii Aksiutin, *Khrushchevskaia "ottepel'" i obshchestvennye nastroeniia v SSSR v 1953–1964 gg.* (Moskva: ROSSPEN, 2004), 158–159.

150. GARF, f. 5446, op. 94, d. 883, l. 24 (undated letter to Khrushchev from Likev, after October 1959).

151. GARF, f. 5446, op. 94, d. 883, l. 24.

152. Ivanova, *Na poroge "gosudarstva vseobshchego blagosostoianiia,"* 96.

153. Nikita Sergeevich Khrushchev, "Intensifikatsiia proizvodstva—glavnoe napravlenie v razvitii sel'skogo khoziaistva; Rech' na Plenume TsK KPSS 14 fevraliia 1964 goda," in *Stroitel'stvo kommunizma v SSSR i razvitie sel'skogo khoziaistva* (Moskva: Politizdat, 1964), tom 8, 438.

154. Ibid., 440.

155. Ibid., 441.

156. Ibid., 441–442.

157. "Vse vo imia cheloveka, dlia blaga cheloveka," 1.

158. Ibid.

159. "Zakon soiuza sovetskikh sotsialisticheskikh respublik o pensiiakh i posobiiakh chenlov kolkhozov," *Pravda,* July 16, 1964, 1–2.

160. Ol'ga Vladimirovna Kapustina, "Deiatel'nost' sovetskogo gosudarstva po sovershenstvovaniiu pensionnogo obespecheniia grazhdan (vtoraia polovina 1950-kh–1980-e gody)" (dissertation, Pushkin Leningrad State University, 2010), 115–116.

161. Khrushchev, *Memoirs of Nikita Khrushchev, Reformer,* 338.

162. Ibid.

163. Ibid., 338–339.

164. "Postanovlenie prezidiuma TsK KPSS 'O material'nom obespechenii t. Khrushcheva N. S.,'" in *Nikita Khrushchev 1964: Stenogrammy plenuma TsK KPSS i drugie dokumenty,* ed. A. N. Artizov et al. (Moskva: Mezhdunarodnyi fond "Demokratiia", 2007), 437.

165. Khrushchev, *Memoirs of Nikita Khrushchev, Reformer,* 422.

166. Madison, *Social Welfare in the Soviet Union,* 76.

167. Sarah D. Phillips, "'There Are No Invalids in the USSR!': A Missing Soviet Chapter in the New Disability History," *Disability Studies Quarterly,* Vol. 29, No. 3 (2009), http://dsq-sds.org/article/view/936/1111.

4. All Your Wages in Hand

1. On Soviet taxes' purported "social-return character," see G. L. Mar'iakhin and D. V. Burmistrov, *Nalogi s naseleniia v SSSR; Dopushcheno v kachestve ucheb. posobiia dlia fin. i finansovo-kreditnykh tekhnikumov* (Moskva: Gosudarstvennoe finansovoe izdatel'stvo, 1957), 5.

2. Ibid., 1.

3. D. V. Burmistrov, Z. Kosareva, and F. A. Uriupin, *Vtoroi etap otmeny nalogov s rabochikh i sluzhashchikh v SSSR* (Moskva: Gosudarstvennoe finansovoe izdatel'stvo, 1961), 23.

4. See A. V. Bachurin, *Pribyl' i naloga s oborota v SSSR* (Moskva: Gosudarstvennoe finansovoe izdatel'stvo, 1955), 3.

5. Ibid.

6. Franklyn D. Holzman, "The Burden of Soviet Taxation," *American Economic Review,* Vol. 43, No. 4 (1953): 548.

7. Ibid., 560.

8. Ibid., 562.

9. Holzman, *Soviet Taxation,* 64–65.

10. Holzman argued that, at the very least, they were a form of forced savings, though he acknowledged that it was possible some workers did purchase them out of revolutionary fervor, especially initially. See Franklyn D. Holzman, "An Estimate of the Tax Element in Soviet Bonds," *American Economic Review,* Vol. 47, No. 3 (1957): 390–393. See also Holzman, *Soviet Taxation,* 200–208.

11. Holzman, "An Estimate of the Tax Element," 395.

12. Mar'iakhin, *Ocherki istorii nalogov s naseleniia,* 204.

13. Fursenko, *Prezidium TsK KPSS 1954–1964,* tom 1, 234.

14. "Iz stenogrammy vystupleniia N. S. Khrushcheva na soveshchanii rabotnikov sel'skogo khoziaistva v gor. Gor'kom," in Tomilina et al., *Nikita Sergeevich Khrushchev,* tom 2, 342.

15. Karl Marx, "Moralizing Criticism and Critical Morality: A Contribution to German Cultural History contra Karl Heinzen," in *The Collected Works of Karl Marx and Frederick Engels,* vol. 6, *General Works, 1844–1895* (New York: International Publishers, 1976), 328.

16. Ibid.

17. Ibid., 329.

18. Karl Marx and Friedrich Engels, "Manifesto of the Communist Party," in *The Marx-Engels Reader,* ed. Robert C. Tucker (New York: Norton, 1978), 490.

19. Mar'iakhin, *Ocherki istorii nalogov v naseleniia,* 25.

20. It should be noted that personal income taxes were a relatively new phenomenon in Russia by the time the Bolsheviks seized power. One of the nobility's long-standing and formally recognized privileges was exemption from taxation. Peasants, who bore the brunt of taxation, both in money form and in conscripts toward the military, paid it collectively through the commune. The Tsar had introduced personal income taxes in the Russian Empire only in 1916 and amid the fiscal crisis of the First World War, a policy that was continued by the Provisional Government. On the introduction of the 1916 income tax in Tsarist Russia, see Yanni Kotsonis, *States of Obligation: Taxes and Citizenship in the Russian Empire and Early Soviet Republic* (Toronto: University of Toronto Press, 2014), 174.

21. Mar'iakhin and Burmistrov, *Nalogi s naseleniia v SSSR,* 18, 20.

22. Holzman, *Soviet Taxation,* 181–183.

23. Ibid., 183.

24. Although they offered to partially repay some Tsarist-era debts and aggressively sought out foreign loans in the interwar period, the first credit the Bolshevik government received from a foreign government was matériel delivered under the auspices of the Lend-Lease agreement with the United States during the Second World War.

25. Peter Tufano, "Saving whilst Gambling: An Empirical Analysis of UK Premium Bonds," *American Economic Review,* Vol. 98, No. 2 (2008): 321.

26. Pavel Iakovlevich Dmitrichev, *Gosudarstvennye zaimy v SSSR; Dopushcheno v kachestve uchebnogo posobiia dlia finansovykh i finansovo-kreditnykh tekhnikumov* (Moskva: Gosudarstvennoe finansovoe izdatel'stvo, 1956), 27. See also Alexei Rykov's speech on this subject before Communist Party leaders: "Konferentsiia VKP(b). Khoziaistvennoe polozhenie strany i zadachi partii. Doklad tov. A. I. Rykova; Nakopleniia, ego istochniki i temp khoziaistvennogo razvitiia," *Izvestiia,* October 30, 1926, 1.

27. M. Panovko, *Zaimy SSSR: V voprosakh i otvetakh* (Moskva: Gosudarstvennoe finansovoe izdatel'stvo, 1934), 7.

28. Ibid., 7–8.

29. U. G. Cherniavskii, *Voina i prodovol'stvie: Snabzhenie gorodskogo naseleniia v Velikuiu Otechestvennuiu voinu, 1941–1945 gg.* (Moskva: Izdatel'stvo "Nauka," 1964), 160.

30. In the mid-1930s, *komsody* members received bonuses of 0.15% in the cities and 0.25% in the countryside. See M. V. Rosliakov, ed., *Kartoteka finansovogo rabotnika* (Leningrad: Vsesoiuznaia spravochnaia kartoteka, Leningradskoe otdelenie, 1934), 100.

31. Harvard Project on the Soviet Social System Online, Vol. 35, Case 97/(NY) 1528 (interviewer M.T., type A4), 11, http://pds.lib.harvard.edu/pds/view/5607127?n=11.

32. Harvard Project on the Soviet Social System Online, Schedule A, Vol. 23, Case 456 (interviewer J.R., type A4), 11, http://pds.lib.harvard.edu/pds/view/5357432?n=12.

33. On collective responsibility, see Alena V. Ledeneva, *Russia's Economy of Favours: Blat, Networking and Informal Exchange* (Cambridge: Cambridge University Press, 1998), 81–83; Alena V. Ledeneva, "The Genealogy of Krugovaia Poruka: Forced Trust as a Feature of Russian Political Culture," in *Trust and Democratic Transition in Post-Communist Europe,* ed. Ivana Marková (Oxford: Oxford University Press for the British Academy, 2004), 85–86; Alena V. Ledeneva, *How Russia Really Works: The Informal Practices That Shaped Post-Soviet Politics and Business* (Ithaca, N.Y.: Cornell University Press, 2006), 99–114. As Oleg Kharkhordin notes, during the Soviet period, the term "collective" came to connote mutual surveillance and conformity. See Oleg Kharkhordin, *The Collective and the Individual in Russia: A Study of Practices* (Berkeley: University of California Press, 1999), 76–87, 110. I expand on how collective responsibility animated state fundraising campaigns during the Second World War in Ironside, "Rubles for Victory."

34. Belova and Lazarev, *Funding Loyalty,* 76–77.

35. See "Ukaz prezidiuma verkhovnogo soveta SSSR: Ob ustanovlenii na voennoe vremia vremennoi nadbavki k sel'skokhoziaistvennomu nalogu i k podokhodnomu nalogu s naseleniia," *Izvestiia,* July 4, 1941, 1.

36. "Ukaz prezidiuma verkhovnogo soveta SSSR o naloge na kholostiakhov, odinokikh i bezdetnykh grazhdan SSSR," *Izvestiia,* November 25, 1941, 1. On the government's wartime and postwar pronatalism, see Mie Nakachi, "Replacing the Dead: The Politics of Reproduction in the Postwar Soviet Union, 1944–1955" (PhD diss., University of Chicago, 2008), 159–160. See also Mie Nakachi, "N. S. Khrushchev and the 1944 Soviet Family Law: Politics, Reproduction, and Language," *East European Politics and Societies,* Vol. 20, No. 1 (2006): 45.

37. The war tax now ranged from 120 rubles owed on a yearly salary of up to 1,800 rubles per year to 2,700 owed on a salary of 24,000 rubles and higher. Collective farmers owed 130–600 rubles per member of the farm.

38. On tax privileges as a form of state financial support for the needy, see G. L. Mar'iakhin, D. V. Burmistrov, and Z. Maeva, *Posobiia, pensii i nalogovye l'goty voennosluzhashchim, chlenam ikh semei i invalidam otechestvennoi voiny* (Moskva: Gosudarstvennoe finansovoe izdatel'stvo, 1944), 3.

39. "Ukazy prezidiuma verkhovnogo soveta SSSR o podokhodnom naloge s naseleniia," *Vedomosti verkhovnogo soveta SSSR,* No. 17 (May 1, 1943): 4.

40. "Ukaz prezidiuma verkhovnogo soveta SSSR ob uvelichenii gosudarstvennoi pomoshchi beremennym zhenshchinam, mnogodetnym i odinokym materiam, usilenii okhrany materinstva i detstva, ob ustanovlenii pochetnogo zvaniia 'mat'-geroin' i uchrezhdenii ordena 'materinskaia slava' i medali 'medal' materinstva,'" *Pravda,* July 9, 1944, 1.

41. To get a sense of how quickly subscription quotas were overfulfilled, see reports to the Council of Ministers in the days after each bond was announced: GARF, f. 5446, op. 43a, d. 3757, l. 84; f. 5446, op. 44, d. 757, l. 5; f. 5446, op. 46, d. 2171, l. 6; f. 5446, op. 47, d. 1943, l. 7 (Reports on subscriptions across the USSR, 1942–1945).

42. GARF, f. 7523, op. 17, d. 29, l. 41 (transcript of a meeting of the subcommittee on taxes from the people, state bonds, and other sources of budgetary revenue, August 28, 1946).

43. GARF, f. 7523, op. 17, d. 29, l. 41.

44. RGASPI, f. 82, op. 2, d. 789, l. 111.

45. Immediately after the war, industries began petitioning to have their workers exempted from the war tax on the grounds that, with the return to normal production, workers' wages had declined and the tax inflicted a substantial financial hardship upon them. For example, see GARF, f. 5446, op. 47, d. 1893, l. 80 (letter to Kosygin from Alekhin, August 7, 1945).

46. GARF, f. 5446, op. 47, d. 1893, l. 138 (letter to Voznesenskii from Zverev, December 22, 1945).

47. "O povyshenii razmera neoblagaemogo podokhodnym nalogom minimum zarabotnoi platy rabochikh i sluzhashchikh," *Vedomosti,* No. 36 (October 8, 1946): 3.

48. RGAE, f. 679, op. 2, d. 685, l. 18 (analysis of the system and practice of the bachelor tax by G. L. Mar'iakhin, 1949).

49. RGAE, f. 679, op. 2, d. 685, l. 20.

50. RGAE, f. 679, op. 2, d. 685, l. 21.

51. The post-Stalinist agricultural tax reform of August 8, 1953, contained the stipulation that, from January 1, 1954, the only rural citizens now required to pay the bachelor tax were those who were not officially registered as part of a given farm but who were subject to the agricultural tax, rural citizens who earned wages outside the farm, non-cooperated artisans, and handicraft workers. This effectively exempted most peasants from paying the tax. See RGAE, f. 679, op. 2, d. 1224, l. 58 (report on the bachelor tax and other local taxes by Burmistrov, September 1, 1965).

52. Kristy Ironside, "Between Fiscal, Ideological, and Social Dilemmas: The Soviet 'Bachelor Tax' and Post-war Tax Reform, 1941–1962," *Europe-Asia Studies,* Vol. 69, No. 6 (2017): 855–856.

53. Ibid., 865–866.

54. GARF, f. 5446, op. 81, d. 2368, l. 75 (circular from the Council of Ministers, January 30, 1951).

55. GARF, f. 7523, op. 17, d. 29, l. 39.

56. GARF, f. 5446, op. 48a, d. 2078, l. 1–2 (petition to Voznesenskii from Rodionov to lower the RSFSR's subscription quota, April 10, 1946).

57. GARF, f. 5446, op. 48, d. 1958, l. 3 (report on the collection of subscriptions to the State Bond for the Reconstruction and Development of the National Economy, May 10, 1946).

58. GARF, f. 7523, op. 39, d. 968, l. 24 (Protokol No. 3 of the subcomission on taxes from the people, state bonds and other sources of budgetary revenue, January 31, 1947).

59. GARF, f. 7523, op. 40, d. 845, l. 21 (transcript of a meeting of the subcomission on taxes from the people, state bonds, and other sources of budgetary revenue, January 23, 1948).

60. GARF, f. 7523, op. 50, d. 2520, l. 205 (report on the conversion of the bonds to Stalin from Kosygin, circa 1948).

61. Ironside, "Rubles for Victory," 812–814.

62. "Pis'mo B. Ivanovoi v Sovet Ministrov SSSR," in *Sovetskaia zhizn' 1945–1953,* ed. E. Iu. Zubkova (Moskva: ROSSPEN, 2003), 544.

63. *Pryguny* refers to members of an evangelical religious cult who jump up and down during their worship practices.

64. GARF, f. 5446, op. 49a, d. 3007, l. 42–50 (report to Voznesenskii from Mekhlis, August 16, 1947). See also GARF, f. 5446, op. 49a, d. 3110 (reports on unauthorized collection of subscriptions in 1947).

65. GARF, f. 5446, op. 49a, d. 3007, l. 38 (decree on distortions in the collection of subscriptions to the second State Bond for the Reconstruction and Development of the National Economy of the USSR, July 1, 1947).

66. See, for example, GARF, f. 5446, op. 50a, d. 3629, l. 29 (report on advance subscriptions in Kalinin raion to the Council of Ministers from Shevliakov, April 26, 1948).

67. For these criteria, see GARF, f. 5685, op. 1, d. 83, l. 13 (instructions regarding decisions to allow bondholders to sell back or mortgage the bonds, May 5, 1934).

68. Dmitrichev, *Gosudarstvennye zaimy v SSSR*, 31.

69. RGAE, f. 7733, op. 33, d. 107, l. 3–4 (report to Molotov from Zverev on the bond conversion process, February 18, 1948).

70. GARF, f. 7523, op. 65, d. 583, l. 31 (yearly report on the Reception's activities, circa early 1947).

71. GARF, f. 7523, op. 33, d. 7, l. 188 (personal statement from N. M. Maralin, April 4, 1947).

72. GARF, f. 5446, op. 51, d. 2653, l. 128 (letter to Stalin from V. N. Samoshkin, May 31, 1949).

73. GARF, f. 5446, op. 51, d. 2653, l. 129, 132 (letter to Samoshkin from P. Ia. Dmitrichev, July 17, 1949).

74. GARF, f. 5446, op. 51, d. 2653, l. 132 (letter to Zverev from the administrative department of the Council of Ministers, September 21, 1949).

75. "Dokladnaia zapiska ministra finansov SSSR A. G. Zverev, 1951 god," in *Po stranitsam arkhivnykh fondov v tsentral'nogo banka rossiiskoi federatsii,* vypusk 13, *Gosbank SSSR i MinFin SSSR v protsesse mobilizatsii i ispol'zovaniia sberezhenii naseleniia (vedomstvennye materialy),* ed. Iu. I. Kashin and T. V. Kozlova (Moskva: Tsentral'nyi bank Rossiiskoi federatsii, 2012), 85.

76. Ibid.

77. RGANI, f. 5, op. 20, d. 136, l. 6 (instructions from Zverev to financial workers, February 12, 1955).

78. RGANI, f. 5, op. 20, d. 136, l. 3.

79. RGANI, f. 5, op. 30, d. 149, l. 6 (report on the plan for developing the national economy in 1956–1960 to Khrushchev from Zverev, January 31, 1956).

80. RGANI, f. 5, op. 30, d. 149, l. 6.

81. RGANI, f. 5, op. 30, d. 149, l. 7.

82. RGANI, f. 5, op. 20, d. 152, l. 2 (instructions from the Central Committee to financial workers, February 3, 1956).

83. RGANI, f. 5, op. 30, d. 179, l. 61 (report to the Central Committee on the progress of the subscription campaign for the State Bond for the Development of the National Economy in workplaces and enterprises in Moscow, May 15, 1956).

84. RGANI, f. 5, op 30, d. 179, l. 62.

85. GARF, f. 5446, op. 90, d. 902, l. 86 (letter to Kosygin from Suslova, May 6, 1956).

86. GARF, f. 5446, op. 90, d. 902, l. 86–87.

87. "Protokol No. 83 zasedaniia 19 marta 1957," in Fursenko, *Prezidium TsK KPSS 1954–1964,* tom 1, 234–235.

88. "Protokol No. 86 zasedaniia 4 aprelia 1957 g.," in Fursenko, *Prezidium TsK KPSS 1954–1964,* tom 1, 246.

89. Ibid., 247.

90. "Iz stenogrammy vystupleniia N. S. Khrushcheva," 340. Khrushchev's speech was cleaned up and published in *Pravda* two days later as "Rech' tov. N. S. Khrushcheva na soveshchanii rabotnikov sel'skogo khoziaistva Gor'kovskoi, Arzamasskoi, Kirovskoi oblastei, Mariiskoi, Mordovskoi i Chuvashskoi ASSR 8 aprelia 1957 goda v gorode Gor'kom," *Pravda,* April 10, 1957, 1–3.

91. "Rech' tov. N. S. Khrushcheva na soveshchanii rabotnikov sel'skogo khoziaistva," 2.

92. "Iz stenogrammy vystupleniia N. S. Khrushcheva," 341.

93. Georgii Zhukov, the Minister of Defense and an ally of Khrushchev's during the 1957 Anti-Party scandal, recalled that the Central Committee accused Khrushchev of promising this without consulting them, and upon Khrushchev's return from Gorki, they had to have "yet another unpleasant conversation with him." It was only after this that the government decided not to default on the bonds and came up with the plan to freeze them for 25 years. See "Posle smerti Stalina; Zapis' vospominanii G. K. Zhukova," 1999, Fond Aleksandra N. Yakovleva, http://www.alexanderyakovlev.org/fond/issues-doc/1004992.

94. "Iz stenogrammy vystupleniia N. S. Khrushcheva," 342.

95. Ibid.

96. RGAE, f. 7599, op. 21, d. 107, l. 67–68 (data prepared by the Ministry of Finance for use in propaganda, undated but circa April–May 1957).

97. See N. Sukhanov, "Materialy dlia besedy: V interesakh sovetskogo gosudarstva i vsego naroda," *Bloknot agitatora,* No. 12 (April 1957): 1–2.

98. Ironside, "Rubles for Victory," 822.

99. GARF, f. 5446, op. 91, d. 508, l. 70–71 (telegram to Bulganin from a collective of workers at the Surovskii auto garage, April 10, 1957)

100. GARF, f. 5446, op. 91, d. 790, l. 1–3.

101. GARF, f. 5446, op. 91, d. 790, l. 1–3.

102. GARF, f. 5446, op. 91, d. 817, l. 14 (summary of workers' letters regarding the bonds, addressed to Bulganin, April 18, 1957).

103. GARF, f. 5446, op. 91, d. 817, l. 13.

104. GARF, f. 5446, op. 91, d. 817, l. 13.

105. GARF, f. 5446, op. 91, d. 817, l. 13.

106. GARF, f. 5446, op. 91, d. 817, l. 13.

107. GARF, f. 5446, op. 91, d. 817, l. 7.

108. GARF, f. 5446, op. 1, d. 663, l. 144 (joint decree of the Central Committee and Council of Ministers No. 435, "On state bonds collected by subscription among workers of the Soviet Union," April 19, 1957).

109. GARF, f. 5446, op. 1, d. 663, l. 145.

110. "V interesakh gosudarstva, v interesakh naroda," *Pravda,* May 15, 1957, 1.

111. GARF, f. 7523, op. 75, d. 1663, l. 59 (report to the Supreme Soviet's subcommittee on revenue for the state budget regarding plans for the state savings bank system for 1958 from Dmitrichev, December 6, 1957).

112. GARF, f. 7523, op. 75, d. 1663, l. 59.

113. RGAE, f. 7733, op. 46, d. 477, l. 215 (letter to Khrushchev from I. M. Tokarev, April 19, 1957).

114. RGAE, f. 7733, op. 46, d. 477, l. 50 (letter to *Pravda,* forwarded to the Ministry of Finance, from G. N. Chukaev, circa April 1957).

115. RGAE, f. 7733, op. 46, d. 477, l. 31 (letter to Khrushchev and Zverev from F. V. Popov, circa April 1957).

116. GARF, f. 5446, op. 84, d. 37, l. 8 (report comparing Soviet family tax benefits to those in the People's Democracies and in the capitalist West, undated but circa late 1956).

117. RGAE, f. 7733, op. 46, d. 478, l. 288 (summary of letters of complaint regarding taxes sent to Bulganin, December 30, 1956).

118. RGAE, f. 7733, op. 46, d. 476, l. 89 (letter to Khrushchev from A. P. Belyi, March 31, 1957).

119. RGAE, f. 679, op. 2, d. 685. See also Ironside, "Between Fiscal, Ideological, and Social Dilemmas," 864–865.

120. "Rech' tovarishcha N. S. Khrushcheva na sobranii komsomol'tsev i molodezhi g. Moskvy, iz'iavivshikh zhelanie poekhat' rabotat' na tselinnye zemli, 7 ianvaria 1955 goda," *Izvestiia,* January 9, 1955, 2.

121. RGAE, f. 7733, op. 46, d. 478, l. 7–14 (report to Khrushchev from Zverev, undated but between August and December 1957).

122. RGAE, f. 7733, op. 46, d. 478, l. 38 (draft decree "On improving the material provisioning of workers with large families and freeing workers with one or two children . . . ," undated but circa early 1958).

123. *Izvestiia,* December 21, 1957, 1.

124. RGANI, f. 5, op. 30, d. 222, l. 214.

125. RGANI, f. 5, op. 30, d. 222, l. 215.

126. See, for example, the objections voiced in GARF, f. 7523, op. 75, d. 786, l. 4 (report on citizens' responses to the December 19, 1957, decree, April 4, 1958).

127. RGAE, f. 679, op. 2, d. 1097, l. 1 (report "On the Paths to Modernizing the Soviet System of Taxes from the People" to Zverev from Mar'iakhin, circa late 1958).

128. RGAE, f. 679, op. 2, d. 1097, l. 1.

129. RGAE, f. 679, op. 2, d. 1097, l. 1.

130. RGAE, f. 679, op. 2, d. 1097, l. 9.

131. RGAE, f. 679, op. 2, d. 1097, l. 10.

132. RGAE, f. 679, op. 2, d. 1097, l. 11.

133. These are far from the only problems Mar'iakhin identified in this lengthy report, all of which resulted in underpayment of taxes and lost revenue for the government. He took aim at the common practice, especially among academics, of having more than one job, but paying taxes only on the primary salary, as well as the tax privileges enjoyed by the literary intelligentsia, whose royalties and other payments were not always included in their taxable income. Even the manner in which workers paid taxes was problematic: at present, it was being taken off the previous months' earnings because of the premium piece-rate system; however, if workers' pay went up for one reason or another, that meant that they did not pay the full amount of tax they owed on it. The opposite situation was also common: workers' pay frequently went down, and they were overtaxed. Another major issue was the fact that, among those who did not earn standard wages and who paid their taxes directly to local financial organs, the tax rates for these groups had not been revised in years and had been set when the Soviet government sought to put non-cooperated artisans, nonunionized doctors, and other individuals who earned money outside state employment channels out of business. At present, nobody earned enough to pay the current highest tax rate of 69%, Mar'iakhin emphasized. See RGAE, f. 679, op. 2, d. 1097, l. 5–62.

134. RGAE, f. 679, op. 2, d. 1097, l. 43.

135. RGAE, f. 679, op. 2, d. 1097, l. 65–66.

136. RGAE, f. 679, op. 2, d. 1097, 66.

137. RGANI, f. 5, op. 20, d. 188, l. 1 (secret report to the Central Committee from Zverev on abolishing taxes, circa late 1958).

138. RGANI, f. 5, op. 20, d. 188, l. 2.

139. RGANI, f. 5, op. 20, d. 188, l. 3.

140. RGANI, f. 5, op. 20, d. 188, l. 7.

141. Khrushchev, *O kontrol'nykh tsifrakh razvitiia narodnogo khoziaistva SSSR na 1959–1965 gody*, 50–51.

142. Ibid., 52.

143. "N. S. Khrushchev's Broadcast over U.S. Television, September 27, 1959," in *Khrushchev in America; Full Texts of the Speeches Made by N. S. Khrushchev, Chairman of the Council of Ministers of the USSR on His Tour of the United States, September 15–27, 1959* (New York: Crosscurrents Press, 1960), 205.

144. Franklyn D. Holzman, "Soviet Taxes Defined: Abolition of Levy on Income Held Little Relief for Population," *New York Times*, October 6, 1959, 68.

145. "Zapiska komissii TsK KPSS i soveta ministrov SSSR po voprosu ob otmene nalogov s naseleniia," in *Prezidium TsK KPSS 1954–1964*, tom 3, *Postanovleniia 1959–1964*, ed. A. A. Fursenko (Moskva: ROSSPEN, 2008), 107.

146. Ibid.

147. Ibid., 108.

148. Ibid., 110.

149. Ibid., 111.

150. Ibid., 112.

151. Ibid., 106.

152. "Ob otmene nalogov s rabochikh i sluzhashchikh i drugikh meropriatiiakh," 2.

153. Ibid., 2.

154. Ibid., 6.

155. Ibid.

156. "Zakon soiuza sovetskikh sotsialisticheskikh respublik ob otmene nalogov s zarabotnoi platy rabochikh i sluzhashchikh," *Pravda,* May 7, 1960, 1.

157. Those who earned between 1,001 and 2,000 rubles per month were promised "higher take-home pay based on their base pay rates and salaries" through tax reductions: a 79% reduction in taxes paid on an income of 1,001–1,200; 46% on pay of 1,201–1,400; 29% on pay of 1,401–1,600; 15% on pay of 1,601 to 1,800; and 10% on pay of 1,801–2,000 rubles per month. However, their base pay rates and salaries would simultaneously be reduced by the remaining portion of the tax. In other words, workers who earned 1,001 rubles per month would receive a pay reduction totaling 21% of what they had previously paid in income taxes, while those earning 2,000 rubles would see a reduction in base pay totaling 90% of the amount they had previously paid in taxes, and those who earned over 2,000 rubles would see a reduction in base pay totaling 100% of what they had previously paid in income taxes. All those earning over 1,000 rubles per month paid 82 rubles plus 13% of the amount of their monthly wages that exceeded 1,000 rubles under the 1943 income tax law. Workers earning 1,001 rubles per month would, then, receive a base wage reduction of 64.88 rubles (79% of 82.13 rubles), but a net gain of 17.25 rubles—the difference between the reduction and the amount they had previously paid in tax. Workers earning 2,001 rubles, however, would simply lose 212.13 rubles in monthly salary, the amount they had previously paid in tax.

158. "Razgovor shel o nas," *Magnitogorskii metall,* May 8, 1960, 2.

159. "Moscow 'Abolishes' Taxes," *New York Times,* May 7, 1960.

160. D. V. Burmistrov and Z. Kosareva, *Obiazatel'nye postavki sel'khozproduktov gosudarstvu khoziaistvami kolkhoznikov i drugikh grazhdan: Prakticheskoe posobie dlia finansovykh rabotnikov* (Moskva: Gosudarstvennoe finansovoe izdatel'stvo, 1956), 22.

161. Ibid., 23.

162. Ibid.

163. "Amerikanets i nalogi," *Izvestiia,* May 5, 1960, 10.

164. "Siamskie bliznetsy," *Izvestiia,* May 5, 1960, 10.

165. Valentin Sergeevich Zorin, *Amerikanets, monopolii, nalogi* (Moskva: Gosudarstvennoe izdatel'stvo iuridicheskoi literatury, 1960), 21.

166. Ibid., 32, 39.

167. Stepan Zlobin, *Bez nalogov, bez voiny!* (Moskva: Gosudarstvennoe izdatel'stvo iuridicheskoi literatury, 1960), 32.

168. Akiva L'vovich Akimov, *Obshchestvo bez nalogov* (Leningrad: Lenizdat, 1961), 41.

169. RGANI, f. 5, op. 30, d. 364, l. 80.

170. RGANI, f. 5, op. 30, d. 364, l. 80.

171. RGANI, f. 5, op. 30, d. 364, l. 81.

172. "Vtoroi etap otmeny nalogov v SSSR," *Pravda,* October 3, 1961, 6.

173. GARF, f. 7523, op. 78, d. 2061, l. 84 (materials regarding the plan for state revenue in 1961, undated but late 1961).

174. "Stenograficheskaia zapis' zasedaniia Prezidiuma TsK KPSS po voprosu 'O korrektivakh zadanii kontrol'nykh tsifr razvitiia narodnogo khoziaistva SSSR na ostavshiisia period semiletki (1963–1965),'" 566.

175. "Ukaz prezidiuma verkhovnogo soveta SSSR o perenesenii srokov osvobozhdeniia sluzhashchikh ot nalogov zarabotnoi platy," *Izvestiia,* September 24, 1962, 1.

176. "V interesakh razvitiia ekonomiki i ukrepleniia oboronosposobnosti strany," *Izvestiia,* September 24, 1962, 3. Note that this announcement was published just weeks before the Cuban Missile Crisis.

177. Ibid.

178. Franklyn D. Holzman, "The Soviet Bond Hoax," *Problems of Communism,* Vol. 6, No. 5 (1957): 48–49.

179. Ibid., 49. Note that Holzman's interpretation was challenged by James R. Millar, who gave more weight to the default's redistributive functions, since the bonds' purchase had been, in effect, progressive—higher-earning citizens gave proportionally more money to the bonds. Millar argued that the default was an attempt to decrease the tax burden of the bonds and transfer purchasing power to the population. The decision to cease paying lottery premiums and to freeze outstanding bonds, in his opinion, simply substituted a new tax to compensate for the lost revenue. See James R. Millar, "History and Analysis of Soviet Domestic Bond Policy," *Soviet Studies,* Vol. 27, No. 4 (1975): 613.

180. Holzman, "The Soviet Bond Hoax," 47.

181. "A Tale about Tsar Nikita," in Kozlov, Fitzpatrick, and Mironenko, *Sedition,* 144–145.

5. Real Returns

1. "Ukrupnennye stat'i balansa denezhnykh dokhodov i raskhodov naseleniia SSSR (1924–1990)," in Kashin and Mikov, *Po stranitsam arkhivnykh fondov tsentral'nogo banka rossisskoi federatsii,* vypusk 1, 10–12.

2. Kornai, *The Socialist System,* 239.

3. RGAE, f. 7599, op. 21, d. 107, l. 31 (report on sums held in savings banks, undated but after January 1, 1957).

4. "Analiticheskii doklad 'O razvitii denezhnogo obrashcheniia, kreditovaniia, finansovaniia, raschetov i drugikh voprosakh deiatel'nosti Gosudarstvennogo banka SSSR, 21 dekabria 1965 goda,'" in Kashin, *Po stranitsam arkhivnykh fondov v tsentral'nogo banka rossiiskoi federatsii,* vypusk 13, 115.

5. "Razdel 'sberegatel'noe delo' godogo otcheta Gosbanka SSSR za 1964 god," in Kashin, *Po stranitsam arkhivnykh fondov v tsentral'nogo banka rossiiskoi federatsii,* vypusk 13, 114.

6. L. V. Valler and P. Ia. Dmitrichev, *Sberegatel'nye kassy v SSSR* (Moskva: Gosudarstennoe finansovoe izdatel'stvo, 1946), 3.

7. Ibid., 4.

8. Ibid.

9. I expand on this shift in the case of the state lottery in Kristy Ironside, "Khrushchev's Cash-and-Goods Lotteries and the Turn Toward Positive Incentives," *Soviet and Post-Soviet Review,* Vol. 41, No. 3 (2014): 296–323.

10. "Ustav gosudarstvennykh trudovykh sberegatel'nykh kass SSSR," *Sobranie postanovlenii i rasporiazhenii soveta ministrov soiuza sovetskykh sotsialisticheskhikh respublik,* No. 7 (December 17, 1948): 89.

11. See "Pis'mo Gosbanka SSSR po dokladnoi zapiske N. Glushakova, 18 dekabria 1958 goda," in Kashin, *Po stranitsam arkhivnykh fondov v tsentral'nogo banka rossiiskoi federatsii,* vypusk 13, 95–98.

12. Feygin, "Building a Ruin," 58–59.

13. Serguei Alex Oushakine, "'Against the Cult of Things': On Soviet Productivism, Storage Economy, and Commodities with No Destination." *Russian Review,* Vol. 73, No. 2 (2014): 209.

14. At the Twenty-Second Party Congress, the "code of the builders of communism" was issued, a set of twelve tenets regarding the moral qualities expected of Soviet citizens during communist construction. See Field, *Private Life and Communist Morality,* 9–12.

15. Valler and Dmitrichev, *Sberegatel'nye kassy v SSSR,* 28.

16. GARF, f. 5446, op. 43a, d. 3757, l. 88 (report to Voznesenskii, Kosygin, and Zverev from Nozyrev on the work of savings banks during the war, late 1941).

17. See GARF, f. 5446, op. 44a, d. 4758, l. 6–14 (proposals to remove restrictions on savings accounts, March–June 1943). On proposals to remove restrictions on market bonds as an incentive for investing in a proposed market bond that never materialized, see, for example, "Analiticheskii doklad Gosplana SSSR 'Puti sokrashcheniia defitsita gosbiudzheta,' 7 aprelia 1942 goda," in Kashin, *Po stranitsam arkhivnykh fondov v tsentral'nogo banka rossiiskoi federatsii,* vypusk 13, 71.

18. Ironside, "Rubles for Victory," 821.

19. L. V. Valler, *Denezhnye sberezheniia—na delo razgroma vraga; Posobie dlia obshchestvennogo aktiva po sberegatel'nomu delu* (Moskva: Gosudarstvennoe finansovoe izdatel'stvo, 1942), 29.

20. GARF, f. 7523, op. 17, d. 29, l. 43.

21. "Analiticheskii doklad 'Denezhnoe obrashchenie SSSR v period Velikoi Otechestvennoi voiny i likvidatsiia posledstvii voiny v denezhnom obrashchenii,' 1951 god," in Kashin, *Po stranitsam arkhivnykh fondov v tsentral'nogo banka rossiiskoi federatsii,* vypusk 13, 83.

22. Ibid.

23. "Rost vkladov naseleniia v sberegatel'nye kassy i gosbank SSSR posle 1 dekabria 1947 g.; Zapiska A. Zvereva na imia I. Stalina," in Dobrokhotov, *Denezhnaia reforma v SSSR 1947 goda,* 324.

24. "Rasprostraniaiutsia slukhi o reforme," in Dobrokhotov, *Denezhnaia reforma v SSSR 1947 goda,* 367–370.

25. "Rost vkladov naseleniia v sberegatel'nye kassy i gosbank SSSR posle 1 dekabria 1947 g.," 325.

26. Ibid.

27. RGAE, f. 7733, op. 32, d. 328, l. 2 (letter from N. M. Fadeev to the Ministry of Finance, December 17, 1947).

28. See Article 8a and 8b, in "Postanovlenie soveta ministrov SSSR i TsKP(b) o provedenii denezhnoi reformy i otmene kartochek na prodovol'stvennye i promyshlennye tovary," 1.

29. See Article 8v, in ibid.

30. It chose to deal with Party members' trangressions extrafinancially. As Edward D. Cohn shows, the high number of Party members who were caught trying to protect their savings through illegal means accounts for the sharp increase in expulsions from the Party in 1948. See Cohn, *The High Title of a Communist,* 128.

31. "Analiticheskii doklad 'Denezhnoe obrashchenie SSSR v period Velikoi Otechestvennoi voiny i likvidatsiia posledstvii voiny v denezhnom obrashchenii,' 1951 god," 84.

32. "Pochemu ia dolzhen teriat' tak tiazhelo nazhitye sberezheniia? Pis'mo na imia pomoshchnika I. V. Stalina A. N. Poskrebysheva," in Dobrokhotov, *Denezhnaia reforma v SSSR 1947 goda,* 678.

33. RGAE, f. 7733, op. 32, d. 328, l. 29 (letter to the Ministry of Finance from V. Molchanov, December 16, 1947).

34. "Protokol 344: Sekretariata TsK VKP(b) ot 12. III–8. IV. 1948 g. reshenie sekretariata ot 12. III–48 g.," in Dobrokhotov, *Denezhnaia reforma v SSSR 1947 goda,* 414–415.

35. Ibid., 415–416.

36. GARF, f. 7523, op. 40, d. 845, l. 49–50 (protocol of the morning meeting of the Supreme Soviet's subcommission on taxes from the people, bonds, and other sources of state revenue, January 24, 1948).

37. GARF, f. 7523, op. 41, d. 888, l. 13 (transcript of a meeting of the Supreme Soviet's subcommission on taxes from the people, bonds, and other sources of state revenue, February 25, 1949).

38. See GARF, f. 5446, op. 49a, d. 3007, l. 59 (report to Voznesenskii from Zverev, circa mid-1946).

39. GARF, f. 5446, op. 50, d. 2520, l. 210.

40. GARF, f. 5446, op. 50, d. 2520, l. 210.

41. GARF, f. 7523, op. 41, d. 888, l. 6.

42. GARF, f. 7523, op. 40, d. 845, l. 26.

43. On "cultured trade" as "the watchword for the retail sector," see Hessler, *A Social History of Soviet Trade,* 198.

44. "Uluchshit' rabotu sberegatel'nykh kass; Obzor pisem v redaktsiu," *Pravda,* July 25, 1946, 3.

45. GARF, f. 7523, op. 40, d. 845, l. 26.

46. GARF, f. 7523, op. 40, d. 859, l. 76 (transcript of a meeting of the Supreme Soviet's subcommission on taxes from the people, bonds, and other sources of state revenue, January 23, 1948).

47. P. Martynov, "Sberkassa No. 171," *Literaturnaia gazeta,* November 27, 1952, 1.

48. Ibid.

49. GARF, f. 7523, op 42, d. 677, l. 24 (transcript of a meeting of the Supreme Soviet's subcommission on taxes from the people, bonds, and other sources of state revenue, May 29, 1950).

50. GARF, f. 7523, op 42, d. 677, l. 24.

51. GARF, f. 7523, op. 75, d. 1641, l. 19 (report to the Council of Ministers from Zhavoronkov, circa 1957).

52. GARF, f. 7523, op. 75, d. 1641, l. 19.

53. Soviet market bonds were bearer bonds, which is why many Soviet citizens chose to leave their bonds in the bank for safekeeping.

54. GARF, f. 7523, op. 75, d. 1641, l. 18.

55. GARF, f. 7523, op. 42, d. 677, l. 24.

56. GARF, f. 7523, op. 75, d. 1663, l. 63 (report to the Supreme Soviet's subcommission on taxes from the people, bonds, and other sources of state revenue from Dmitrichev, December 6, 1957).

57. For examples of theft by savings bank employees, see RGAE, f. 7599, op. 21, d. 94, l. 40–41.

58. "Za vysokuiu kul'turu obsluzhivaniia naseleniia," *Izvestiia,* November 23, 1956, 1.

59. Vladimir Ilich Lenin, "K derevenskoi bednote," in *Polnoe sobranie sochinenii* (Moskva: Gosudarstvennoe izdatel'stvo politicheskoe literatury, 1959), tom 7, 163.

60. Ironside, "Khrushchev's Cash-and-Goods Lotteries," 302.

61. As Evgenii Kovtun emphasizes, this did not, in fact, prevent them from being organized, and even more lotteries were organized after the ban than before it. Evgenii Kovtun, *Azart v strane sovetov,* tom 2, *Loterei* (Moskva: ZAO "Olimp-Biznes," 2012), 40.

62. For more on the failed state lottery of 1922, see Vladimir Nikandrovich Terebov, "Sud'ba loterei," *Kollektsioner,* No. 31–32 (1996): 194–195, http://www.bonistikaweb.ru/terebov.htm; and Kovtun, *Azart v strane sovetov,* tom 2, 61–66.

63. Millar, "History and Analysis of Soviet Domestic Bond Policy," 600.

64. Ironside, "Rubles for Victory," 820.

65. Ibid., 818–819.

66. GARF, f. 5446, op. 47, d. 2005, l. 4 (report to Voznesenskii from Zverev, October 16, 1945).

67. Note that a 100-ruble denomination of the 1947 3% bond could be purchased, but that entitled the bearer to only half of a prize should it win. In the case of the Reconstruction and/or Development of the National Economy Bonds, 25-ruble and 50-ruble issues could be purchased, but these entitled one to only one-quarter and one-half of a prize, respectively. The 200- and 500-ruble issues of mass subscription bonds consisted of two and five bonds of the same series but different numbers, and entitled the bearer to two or five chances to win a prize on those numbers, respectively.

68. A. S. Vashchuk and E. Iu. Selezneva, "Fiskal'naia politika na dal'nem vostoke Rossii (seredina 1940-kh–1950-e gody)," *Vestnik DVO RAN,* No. 1 (2007): 94.

69. GARF, f. 5446, op. 87, d. 1181, l. 3.

70. The bond draw as public spectacle was depicted in the 1925 silent comedy film *The Tailor from Torzhok,* about a wayward winning lottery bond. See *Zakroishchik iz Torzhka* (Mezhrabpom-Rus', 1925).

71. RGAE, f. 7599, op. 21, d. 206, l. 7.

72. GARF, f. 7523, op. 75, d. 1680, l. 88. See also Ironside, "Khrushchev's Cash-and-Goods Lotteries," 317.

73. "Sberegatel'nye kassy prinimaiut vyigryshnye vklady," *Izvestiia,* March 30, 1951, 4.

74. L. Kats, "Za korennoe uluchshchenie deiatel'nost sberegatel'nykh kass," *Finansy SSSR,* No. 11 (1956): 36.

75. Fursenko, *Prezidium TsK KPSS 1954–1964,* tom 1, 235.

76. GARF, f. 5446, op. 91, d. 817, l. 2.

77. GARF, f. 5446, op. 1, d. 670, l. 88.

78. GARF, f. 259a, op. 7, d. 9127, l. 38; op. 42, d. 823, l. 24–26. The lottery was overseen by the Ministry of Finance but was implemented in a decentralized way by each of the republics, which bore the costs of their respective lottery but kept its revenue.

79. GARF, f. 5446, op. 1, d. 670, l. 89.

80. RGAE, f. 7733, op. 47, d. 19, l. 3. See also the public announcements regarding these violations in the major newspapers, for example, "V TsK KPSS i Sovete Ministrov SSSR; O faktakh narusheniia printsipa dobrovol'nosti v razmeshchenii biletov denezhno-veshchevoi loterei sredi naseleniia," *Pravda,* February 2, 1958, 2.

81. "V TsK KPSS i Sovete Ministrov SSSR," 2.

82. RGAE, f. 7733, op. 47, d. 21, l. 47.

83. RGAE, f. 7733, op. 47, d. 21, l. 47.

84. RGAE, f. 7733, op. 47, d. 21, l. 58.

85. RGAE, f. 7733, op. 47, d. 21, l. 58.

86. RGAE, f. 7733, op. 47, d. 15, l. 13–14.

87. RGAE, f. 7599, op. 21, d. 206, l. 1 (report on Gostrudsberkass activities in Moscow to mobilize the population's spare money, circa early 1958).

88. RGAE, f. 7599, op. 21, d. 206, l. 1.

89. RGAE, f. 7599, op. 21, d. 206, l. 3.

90. RGAE, f. 7599, op. 21, d. 206, l. 2.

91. "Kakim emu khotelos' by videt nomer bileta . . . ," *Krokodil,* April 30, 1958, 14.

92. See, for example, "Vyigrana Vol'gu," *Sovetskaia Rossiia,* May 28, 1958, 6.

93. "Vyigraly!," *Ogonek,* No. 4 (January 1959): 26.

94. See RGAE, f. 7733, op. 47, d. 37, l. 86 (report to Zverev from A. Belyi, November 25, 1958).

95. GARF, f. 259a, op. 42, d. 4466, l. 16 (summary of letters of complaint regarding undelivered prizes sent to the newspaper *Sovetskaia Rossiia* to D. S. Polianskii from I. Pustovalov, March 31, 1959).

96. RGAE, f. 7733, op. 47, d. 37, l. 86.

97. RGAE, f. 7733, op. 47, d. 32, l. 11 (report to Zverev from Dmitrichev, August 12, 1958).

98. RGAE, f. 7733, op. 47, d. 32, l. 11.

99. RGAE, f. 7733, op. 47, d. 32, l. 14.

100. RGAE, f. 7733, op. 47, d. 32, l. 11.

101. "Denezhno-veshchevaia lotereiia 1963 goda; Shest' tirazhei v god, deciatki tysiach tsennykh vyigryshei," *Pravda,* October 25, 1962, 4.

102. Ironside, "Khrushchev's Cash-and-Goods Lotteries," 321.

103. RGAE, f. 7599, op. 21, d. 94, l. 6–8.

104. RGAE, f. 7599, op. 21, d. 94, l. 8.

105. RGAE, f. 7599, op. 21, d. 94, l. 9.

106. RGAE, f. 7599, op. 21, d. 94, l. 10.

107. RGAE, f. 7599, op. 21, d. 94, l. 17.

108. RGAE, f. 7599, op. 21, d. 94, l. 18.

109. RGAE, f. 7599, op. 21, d. 94, l. 18.

110. RGAE, f. 7599, op. 21, d. 94, l. 374 (transcript of Zverev's speech to financial workers, February 23, 1957).

111. RGAE, f. 7599, op. 21, d. 94, l. 375.

112. RGAE, f. 7599, op. 21, d. 94, l. 377.

113. RGAE, f. 7599, op. 21, d. 94, l. 377.

114. *Komissiia sodeistva goskreditu i sberegatel'nomu delu* (Moskva: Gosudarstvennoe finansovoe izdatel'stvo, 1959), 12.

115. On embedding agents of the savings banks in workplaces, see A. Bilenko, "Za uluchshchenie deiatel'nosti sberegatel'nykh kass," *Finansy SSSR,* No. 4 (1956): 76–78. On automatic transfers from wages to savings accounts, see GARF, f. 7523, op. 75, d. 1680, l. 78–79.

116. *Komissiia sodeistviia,* 68–69.

117. Ibid., 32.

118. Pavel Iakovlevich Dmitrichev, "Razvivat' sberezhennoe delo," *Izvestiia,* October 9, 1958, 2.

119. *Komissiia sodeistviia,* 26.

120. For a common complaint regarding this phenomenon, see P. Smirnov, "Biudzhet molodogo rabochego," *Komsomol'skaia pravda,* September 15, 1956, 2.

121. *Molodoi kommunist,* No. 2 (February 1958), back cover.

122. GARF, f. 7523, op. 78, d. 2026, l. 26.

123. *Tverdyi kharakter* (Tsentrnauchfil'm, 1959), https://www.net-film.ru/film-39254/.

124. GARF, f. 7523, op. 74, d. 1663, l. 62–63.

125. GARF, f. 7523, op. 74, d. 1663, l. 62–63.

126. GARF, f. 7523, op. 75, d. 1680, l. 77.

127. GARF, f. 7523, op. 75, d. 1680, l. 77.

128. GARF, f. 7523, op. 78, d. 2026, l. 14.

129. GARF, f. 7523, op. 75, d. 1680, l. 86.

130. GARF, f. 7523, op. 75, d. 1680, l. 86.

131. GARF, f. 7523, op. 78, d. 2026, l. 19.

132. GARF, f. 7523, op. 78, d. 2026, l. 19.

133. "Proekt zapiski 'O problemakh denezhnogo obrashcheniia v general'nom perspective razvitiia narodnogo khoziaistva SSSR,' 1 marta 1960 goda," in Kashin, *Po stranitsam arkhivnykh fondov v tsentral'nogo banka rossiiskoi federatsii,* vypusk 13, 99.

134. Ibid.

135. Ibid., 108.

136. "Nauchnyi doklad G. L. Mar'iakhina 'Narodnye sberezheniia i ikh akkumuliatsiia cherez finansovuiu sistemu v protsesse stroitel'stva kommunizma, 1962 goda," in Kashin, *Po stranitsam arkhivnykh fondov v tsentral'nogo banka rossiisskoi federatsii,* vypusk 13, 104.

137. Ibid., 105.

138. Ibid., 106.

139. "Rost vkladov v sberkassy," *Pravda,* July 11, 1961, 4.

140. "Zasedaniia verkhonogo soveta SSSR; O gosudarstvennom biudzhete SSSR na 1962 god i ob ispolnenii gosudarstvennogo biudzheta SSSR za 1960 god; Doklad ministra finansov SSSR deputata V. F. Garbuzova," *Pravda,* December 7, 1961, 4.

141. "Proekt sovmestnogo doklada Minfina SSSR, Gosbanka SSSR i TsSU SSSR 'O sostoianii denezhnogo obrashcheniia v SSSR,' 20 sentiabria 1963 goda," in Kashin, *Po stranitsam arkhivnykh fondov v tsentral'nogo banka rossiisskoi federatsii,* vypusk 13, 110.

142. Ibid.

143. "Za dal'neishee razvitie sberegatel'nogo dela," in Kashin, *Po stranitsam arkhivnykh fondov v tsentral'nogo banka rossiisskoi federatsii,* vypusk 13, 112.

144. L. Vysokoostrovskii, "Zakhazivaite," *Sovetskaia Rossiia,* June 7, 1962, 2.

Conclusion

1. G. Maksimov, G. Ovodov, and L. El'iashev, *Novyi masshtab tsen* (Moskva: Gosudarstvennoe finansovoe izdatel'stvo, 1960), 3.

2. RGANI, f. 5, op. 17, d. 325, l. 23 (Volkov's report to Khrushchev on the perspective plan for the development of the national economy in 1961–1980, February 22, 1960).

3. RGANI, f. 5, op. 17, d. 325, l. 24.

4. RGANI, f. 5, op. 17, d. 325, l. 25.

5. RGANI, f. 5, op. 17, d. 325, l. 25.

6. RGANI, f. 5, op. 17, d. 325, l. 26–28.

7. RGANI, f. 5, op. 17, d. 325, l. 30–31.

8. RGANI, f. 5, op. 17, d. 325, l. 33.

9. RGANI, f. 5, op. 17, d. 325, l. 35–36.

10. Alexander Titov, "The 1961 Party Programme and the Fate of Khrushchev's Reforms," in *Soviet State and Society under Nikita Khrushchev,* ed. Melanie Ilič and Jeremy Smith (London: Routledge, 2009), 10.

11. Ibid.

12. "O programme kommunisticheskoi partii sovetskogo soiuza; Doklad tovarishcha N. S. Khrushcheva na XXII s"ezde Kommunisticheskoi partii Sovetskogo Soiuza 18 oktiabria 1961 goda," *Pravda,* October 19, 1961, 5.

13. Ibid., 6.

14. Ibid.

15. On the Soviet Union's sources of postwar economic growth, see Harrison, "The Soviet Union after 1945," 111–115. On diminishing returns on its investments, see Feygin, "Building a Ruin," 78.

16. Hanson, *The Rise and Fall of the Soviet Economy,* 73.

17. Ibid.

18. Feygin, "Building a Ruin," 101. As Giovanni Cadioli points out, the various institutions that Khrushchev had created to obtain and feed more accurate local information back to the center were progressively brought back under central organs as the failures of Khrushchev's policy of regionalization became apparent: from 1962 on, the number

of sovnarkhozy was reduced before they were abolished altogether, while Gosekonomsovet was remerged into Gosplan and new central economic planning institutions, including the Supreme Council of the National Economy, were introduced. See Cadioli, "Soviet Economic Thought and Economic Policy," 248–249.

19. Susanne Schattenberg, "Trust, Care, and Familiarity in the Politburo: Brezhnev's Scenario of Power," *Kritika: Explorations in Russian and Eurasian History,* Vol. 16, No. 4 (2015): 839–843.

20. "Doklad prezidiuma TsK KPSS na oktiabr'skom plenume TsK KPSS (variant)," in Artizov et al, *Nikita Khrushchev 1964,* 191.

21. Ibid, 192.

22. Ibid, 193.

23. Ibid, 193.

24. Natalya Chernyshova, *Soviet Consumer Culture in the Brezhnev Era* (New York: Routledge, 2013), 17.

25. See Aleksei Makarkin, "The Russian Social Contract and Regime Legitimacy," *International Affairs,* Vol. 87, No. 6 (2011): 1465–1466.

26. See Linda J. Cook, "Brezhnev's 'Social Contract' and Gorbachev's Reforms," *Soviet Studies,* Vol. 44, No. 1 (1992): 37.

27. Feygin, "Building a Ruin," 73.

28. Chernyshova, *Soviet Consumer Culture,* 38–39.

29. Ibid., 39. See also James R. Millar, "The Little Deal: Brezhnev's Contribution to Acquisitive Socialism," *Slavic Review* 44, No. 4 (1985): 696.

30. Donald A. Filtzer, *Soviet Workers and the Collapse of Perestroika: The Soviet Labour Process and Gorbachev's Reforms, 1985–1991* (Cambridge: Cambridge University Press, 2008), 59.

31. Chandler, *Shocking Mother Russia,* 44–49.

32. "Prodolzheniia doklada tovarishcha L. I. Brezhneva," *Izvestiia,* March 31, 1971, 5.

33. Ironside, "Between Fiscal, Ideological, and Social Dilemmas," 876.

34. "Razdely 'sberegatel'noe delo': Godovykh otchetov Gosbanka SSSR za 1966–1969 gody," in Kashin and Kozlova, *Po stranitsam arkhivnykh fondov v tsentral'nogo banka Rossiiskoi federatsii,* vypusk 13, 120.

35. Ibid., 162.

36. GARF, f. 5446, op. 163, d. 33, l. 77.

37. Étienne Forestier-Peyrat and Kristy Ironside, "A Communist World of Public Debt? The Failure of a Counter-model," in *A World of Public Debts: A Political History,* ed. Nicolas Barreyre and Nicolas Delalande (London: Palgrave Macmillan, 2020), 336.

38. The 1961 ruble was converted in 1993, when post-Soviet Russia finally severed its financial system from those of the other former Soviet republics; that 1993 ruble was, in turn, converted again during the financial crisis of 1997–1998.

Bibliography

Archives

Gosudarstvennyi arkhiv Rossiiskoi Federatsii (GARF)

f. 259a: Sovet ministrov RSFSR

f. 374a: Gosudarstvennyi komitet RSFSR po statistike

f. 472a: Upravlenie gosudarstvennykh trudovykh sberegatel'nykh kass i gosudarstvennogo kredita RSFSR gosudarstvennogo banka SSSR

f. 5446: Sovet ministrov SSSR

f. 5451: Vsesoiuznyi tsentral'nyi sovet professional'nykh soiuzov

f. 5685: Tsentral'naia komissiia sodeistviia gosudarstvennomu kreditu i sberegatel'nomu delu pri prezidiume tsentral'nogo ispolnitel'nogo komiteta SSSR

f. 7523: Verkhovnyi sovet SSSR

f. 9595: Nauchno-issledovatel'skii institut truda i gosudarstvennogo komiteta SSSR po trudu i sotsial'nym voprosam

Rossiiskii gosudarstvennyi arkhiv ekonomiki (RGAE)

f. 679: Nauchno-issledovatel'skii finansovyi institut Ministerstva finansov SSSR

f. 1562: Tsentral'noe statisticheskoe upravlenie

f. 7599: Glavnoe upravlenie gostrudsberkass i goskredita SSSR

f. 7733: Ministerstvo finansov SSSR

Rossiiskii gosudarstvennyi arkhiv noveishei istorii (RGANI)

f. 5: Apparat TsK KPSS

f. 89: Kollektsiia kopii dokumentov, rassekrechennykh pri vypolnenii tematicheskikh zaprosov v protsesse nauchno-issledovatel'skoi raboty

Rossiiskii gosudarstvennyi arkhiv sotsial'no-politicheskoi istorii (RGASPI)

f. 17: Tsentral'nyi komitet KPSS

f. 82: Molotov, Viacheslav Mikhailovich

f. 558: Stalin, Iosif Vissarionovich

Films

"Novosti dnia / khroniki nashikh dnei 1954 No. 20." Tsentral'noi studii dokumental'nykh fil'mov, 1954. https://www.net-film.ru/film-10113/.

Tverdyi kharakter. Tsentrnauchfil'm, 1959. https://www.net-film.ru/film-39254/.
Zakroishchik iz Torzhka. Mezhrabpom-Rus', 1925.

Image Collections

Ne Boltai: A Collection of 20th-Century Century Propaganda. http://www.neboltai.org/.

Newspapers, Journals, and Magazines

Izvestiia
Komsomol'skaia pravda
Krokodil
Literaturnaia gazeta
Magnitogorskii metall
Ogonek
Pravda
Sobranie postanovleniia i rasporiazheniia soveta ministrov soiuznykh respublik
Sobranie postanovlenii pravitel'stva Soiuza sovetskikh sotsialisticheskikh respublik
Sobranie zakonov i rasporiazhenii
Sotsial'noe obespechenie
Sovetskaia Rossiia
Trud
Vecherniaia Moskva
Vedomosti verkhovnogo soveta SSSR

Memoirs

Chuev, Feliks Ivanovich, and Vyacheslav Mikhailovich Molotov. *Sto sorok besed s Molotovym: Iz dnevnika F. Chueva.* Moskva: Terra, 1991.

Khrushchev, Nikita Sergeevich. *Memoirs of Nikita Khrushchev, Reformer.* Edited by Sergei Khrushchev. University Park: Pennsylvania State University Press, 2006.

———. *Memoirs of Nikita Khrushchev, Statesman.* Edited by Sergei Khrushchev. University Park: Pennsylvania State University Press, 2013.

Khrushchev, Sergei. *Khrushchev in Power: Unfinished Reforms, 1961–1964.* Translated by George Shriver. Boulder, Colo.: Lynne Rienner Publishers, 2014.

———. *Nikita Khrushchev: Reformator; Trilogiia ob ottse.* Moskva: Vremiia, 2010.

Mikoyan, Anastas. *Tak bylo: Razmyshleniia o minuvshem.* Moskva: Vagrius, 1999.

Shepilov, Dmitrii. *The Kremlin's Scholar: A Memoir of Soviet Politics under Stalin and Khrushchev.* Edited by Stephen V. Bittner. Translated by Anthony Austin. New Haven, Conn.: Yale University Press, 2007.

Zverev, Arsenii Grigorevich. *Stalin i den'gi.* Moskva: Algoritm, 2012.

———. *Zapiski ministra.* Moskva: Politizdat, 1973.

BIBLIOGRAPHY

Published Collections of Archival Documents

Arkhiv kinokroniki i dokumental'nykh filmov. Online: https://www.net-film.ru/.

Artizov, A. N., ed. *Nikita Khrushchev 1964: Stenogrammy plenuma TsK KPSS i drugie dokumenty*. Moskva: Mezhdunarodnyi fond "Demokratiia," 2007.

Dobrokhotov, L. N., ed. *Denezhnaia reforma v SSSR 1947 goda: Dokumenty i materialy*. Moskva: ROSSPEN, 2010.

Dobrokhotov, L. N., V. N. Kolodezhnyi, and V. S. Pushkarev, eds. *Denezhnaia reforma 1921–1924 gg.: Sozdanie tverdoi valiuty; Dokumenty i materialy*. Moskva: ROSSPEN, 2008.

Fond Aleksandra N. Yakovleva. Available online: http://www.alexanderyakovlev.org/db-docs.

Fursenko, A. A., ed. *Prezidium TsK KPSS 1954–1964*. Tom 1, *Chernovye protokoly zapisi zasedanii; Stenogrammy*. Moskva: ROSSPEN, 2003.

———. *Prezidium TsK KPSS 1954–1964*. Tom 2, *Postanovleniia 1954–1958*. Moskva: ROSSPEN, 2003.

———. *Prezidium TsK KPSS 1954–1964*. Tom 3, *Postanovleniia 1959–1964*. Moskva: ROSSPEN, 2003.

Harvard Project on the Soviet Social System Online. http://hcl.harvard.edu/collections/hpsss/index.html.

Kashin, Iu. I., ed. *Po stranitsam arkhivnykh fondov tsentral'nogo banka rossiiskoi federatsii*. Vypusk 3, *Denezhnaia reforma 1947 goda v dokumentax: Podgotovka, provedenie i otsenka rezul'tatov*. Moskva: Tsentral'nyi bank Rossiiskoi federatsii, 2007.

———. *Po stranitsam arkhivnykh fondov v tsentral'nogo banka rossiiskoi federatsii*. Vypusk 6, *Obmen deneg v SSSR 1961 goda v dokumentakh: Podgotovka, provedenie i otsenka rezul'tatov*. Moskva: Tsentral'nyi bank Rossiiskoi federatsii, 2008.

———. *Po stranitsam arkhivnykh fondov v tsentral'nogo banka rossiiskoi federatsii*. Vypusk 13, *Gosbank SSSR i MinFin SSSR v protsesse mobilizatsii i ispol'zovaniia sberezhenii naseleniiu (vedomstvennye materialy)*. Moskva: Tsentral'nyi bank Rossiiskoi federatsii, 2012.

———. *Po stranitsam arkhivnykh fondov tsentral'nogo banka rossiiskoi federatsii*. Vypusk 16, *Iz neopublikovannogo (vedomstvennye materialy)*. Moskva: Tsentral'nyi bank Rossiiskoi federatsii, 2014.

Kashin Iu. I., and V. V. Mikov, eds. *Po stranitsam arkhivnykh fondov tsentral'nogo banka rossiiskoi federatsii*. Vypusk 1, *Denezhnye dokhody naseleniia 1924–1990 gg*. Moskva: Tsentral'nyi bank Rossiiskoi federatsii, 2006.

Khlevniuk, O. V., I. Gorlitskii, and L. P. Kosheleva, eds. *Politbiuro TsK KPSS(b) i Sovet ministrov SSSR 1945–1953*. Moskva: ROSSPEN, 2002.

Kozlov, Vladimir A., Sheila Fitzpatrick, and Sergei V. Mironenko, eds. *Sedition: Everyday Resistance in the Soviet Union under Khrushchev and Brezhnev*. Translated by Olga Livshin. New Haven, Conn.: Yale University Press, 2011.

Livshin, A. Ia., and I. B. Orlov, eds. *Sovetskaia povsednevnost' i massovoe soznanie, 1939–1945*. Moskva: ROSSPEN, 2003.

Tomilina, N. G., et al., eds. *Nikita Sergeevich Khrushchev: Dva tsveta vremeni; Dokumenty lichnogo fonda N. S. Khrushcheva (v dvukh tomakh).* Moskva: Mezhdunarodnyi fond "Demokratiia," 2009.

Zubkova, E. Iu., ed. *Sovetskaia zhizn' 1945–1953.* Moskva: ROSSPEN, 2003.

Published Primary Sources in Russian

Abrosimova, Nina Aleksandrovna. *Pensii pri nepolnom stazhe.* Moskva: Gosudarstvennoe izdatel'stvo iuridicheskoi literatury, 1962.

Aganbegian, Abel Gezevich, and V. F. Maier. *Zarabotnaia plata v SSSR; Nekotorye voprosy teorii i praktiki.* Moskva: Gosplanizdat, 1959.

Aizenberg, I. "K voprosu o soderzhanii deneg pri sotsializme." *Den'gi i kredit,* No. 2 (1963): 12–22.

Akimov, Akiva L'vovich. *Obshchestvo bez nalogov.* Leningrad: Lenizdat, 1961.

Arakelian, A. A. *Pochemu my protiv uravnilovki.* Moskva: Moskovskii rabochii, 1959.

Arkad'ev, G. *Marksizm-leninizm v bor'be s melkoburzhuaznoi uravnilovkoi.* Moskva: Partiinoe izdatel'stvo, 1932.

Astrakhan, E. I. *Printsipy pensionnogo obespecheniia rabochikh i sluzhashchikh v SSSR.* Moskva: Gosudarstvennoe izdatel'stvo iuridicheskoi literatury, 1961.

Atlas, Zakharii Veniaminovich. "Denezhnaia politika sovetskoi vlasti." *Den'gi i kredit,* No. 10 (1957): 33–43.

———. *Denezhnoe obrashchenie i kredit SSSR.* Moskva: Gosudarstvennoe finansovoe izdatel'stvo, 1957.

———. *Sotsialisticheskaia denezhnaia sistema: Problemy sotsialisticheskogo preobrazovaniia i razvitiia denezhnoi sistemy SSSR.* Moskva: Finansy, 1969.

Babkin, B., and M. Shishalovskii. "O pravakh i obiazannostiakh komissii po naznacheniiu pensii." *Sotsial'noe obespechenie,* No. 12 (1956).

Bachurin, A. V. *Pribyl' i naloga s oborota v SSSR.* Moskva: Gosudarstvennoe finansovoe izdatel'stvo, 1955.

Batkaev, R. A., and V. I. Markov. *Differentsiatsiia zarabotnoi platy v promyshlennosti SSSR.* Moskva: Ekonomika, 1964.

Batyrev, V. "Ob odnoi nepravil'noi teorii stoimosti, deneg i tseny pri sotsializme." *Den'gi i kredit,* No. 1 (1961): 7–17.

Belkin, V. D. *Tseny edinogo urovnia i ekonomicheskie izmereniia na ikh osnove.* Moskva: Izdatel'stvo ekonomicheskoi literatury, 1963.

Bilenko, A. "Za uluchshchenie deiatel'nosti sberegatel'nykh kass." *Finansy SSSR,* No. 4 (1956): 76–78.

Borisov, G. Ia., and V. I. Merkulova. *Pensionnoe obespechenie v SSSR: Sbornik ofitsial'nykh materialov.* Moskva: Gosudarstvennoe izdatel'stvo iuridicheskoi literatury, 1958.

Bubentsov, V. F, and Aleksandr Ivanovich Volkov. *O pensiiakh i posobiiakh kolkhoznikam: Sotsial'noe obespechenie kolkhoznikov v SSSR.* Moskva: Znanie, 1965.

Bukharin, Nikolai. *Ekonomika perekhodnogo perioda.* Chast' 1, *Obshchaia teoriia transformatsionnogo protsessa.* Moskva: Gosudarstvennoe izdatel'stvo, 1920.

Burmistrov, D. V., and Z. Kosareva. *Obiazatel'nye postavki sel'khozproduktov gosudarstvu khoziaistvami kolkhoznikov i drugikh grazhdan: Prakticheskoe posobie dlia finansovykh rabotnikov.* Moskva: Gosudarstvennoe finansovoe izdatel'stvo, 1956.

Burmistrov, D. V., Z. Kosareva, and F. A. Uriupin. *Otmena nalogov s rabochikh i sluzhashchikh v SSSR: Prakticheskoe posobie dlia finansovykh rabotnikov i bukhgalterov predpriiatii i organizatsii.* Moskva: Gosudarstvennoe finansovoe izdatel'stvo, 1960.

———. *Vtoroi etap otmeny nalogov s rabochikh i sluzhashchikh v SSSR.* Moskva: Gosudarstvennoe finansovoe izdatel'stvo, 1961.

Cherniavskii, U. G. *Voina i prodovol'stvie: Snabzhenie gorodskogo naseleniia v Velikuiu Otechestvennuiu voinu, 1941–1945 gg.* Moskva: Izdatel'stvo "Nauka," 1964.

"Dal'neishee ukreplenie sovetskogo rublia." *Den'gi i kredit,* No. 6 (1960): 1–8.

Dikhtiar, G. A. *Sovetskaia torgovlia v period sotsializma i razvernutogo stroitel'stva kommunizma.* Moskva: Izdatel'stvo "Nauka," 1965.

Dmitrichev, Pavel Iakovlevich. *Gosudarstvennye zaimy v SSSR; Dopushcheno v kachestve uchebnogo posobiia dlia finansovykh i finansovo-kreditnykh tekhnikumov.* Moskva: Gosudarstvennoe finansovoe izdatel'stvo, 1956.

Domashneva T. V., and V. A. Aralov. *Trudovoe ustroistvo invalidov v SSSR: Sbornik normativnykh aktov i metodicheskikh materialov.* Moskva: Gosudarstvennoe izdatel'stvo iuridicheskoi literatury, 1963.

Dymshits, I. "K voprosu o sushchnosti i roli deneg v sotsialisticheskom obshchestve." *Den'gi i kredit,* No. 5 (1957): 19–28.

Dynina, Mariia. *Kak organizovana zarabotnaia plata rabochikh.* Moskva: Gosudarstvennoe izdatel'stvo politicheskoi literatury, 1961.

Ermolenko, Petr Ilich. "Biudzhet rabochei sem'i." *Sovetskie profsoiuzy,* No. 8 (1957): 68–70.

Fefilov, Afanasii Ivanovich. *Roznichnaia torgovlia v SSSR.* Moskva: Gosudarstvennoe izdatel'stvo torgovoi literatury, 1957.

Glezin, S., and A. Raikhman. *Gosudarstvennaia finansovaia pomoshch' voennosluzhashchim i ikh sem'iam.* Moskva: Gosudarstvennoe finansovoe izdatel'stvo, 1942.

Gorodskaia planovaia komissiia i upravlenie narodnokhoziaistvennogo ucheta g. Moskvy. *Materialy o khoziaistve Moskvy v itogo pervoi piatiletki.* Moskva: Izdanie Mosgorplana, 1934.

Ikonnikov, V. V. *Naznachenie i funktsii deneg v sovetskoi sotsialisticheskoi sisteme khoziaistva; Stenogramma publichnoi lektsii prochitannoi v tsentral'noi lektorii obshchestva v Moskve.* Moskva: Izdatel'stvo "Pravda," 1951.

———. "Rol' i funktsii sovetskikh deneg." *Bol'shevik,* No. 8 (1949): 37–50.

Kapustin, E. "Chto takoe uravnilovka v oplate truda i pochemu ona nedopustima v sotsialisticheskom obshchestve?" *Politicheskoe samoobrazovanie,* No. 6 (1958): 94–98.

Karavaev, V. "Nepreryvnyi stazh." *Sotsial'noe obespechenie,* No. 3 (1957): 58–63.

Kats, L. "Za korennoe uluchshchenie deiatel'nost sberegatel'nykh kass." *Finansy SSSR,* No. 11 (1956): 36–47.

Kats, R., and N. A. Sorokin. *Pensii po sotsial'nomu strakhovaniiu; Sbornik zakonodatel'nykh i direktivnykh materialov.* Moskva: Profizdat, 1935.

Khrushchev, Nikita Sergeevich. *O kontrol'nykh tsifrakh razvitiia narodnogo khoziaistva SSSR na 1959–1965 gody: Doklad na vneocherednom XXI s"ezde Kommunisticheskoi partii Sovetskogo Soiuza 27 ianvaria i 5 fevralia 1959 g.* Moskva: Gos. izd-vo polit. lit-ry, 1959.

———. *Stroitel'stvo kommunizma.* Tom 3, *Ianvar' 1958 goda–mai 1959 goda.* Moskva: Gosudarstvennoe izdatel'stvo politicheskoi literatury, 1962.

———. *Stroitel'stvo kommunizma v SSSR i razvitie sel'skogo khoziaistva.* Tom 8. Moskva: Politizdat, 1964.

———. *Stroitel'stvo kommunizma v SSSR i razvitie sel'skokhoziaistva.* Tom 7, *Mart 1962–mart 1963 goda.* Moskva: Gospolizdat, 1963.*Komissiia sodeistva goskreditu i sberegatel'nomu delu.* Moskva: Gosudarstvennoe finansovoe izdatel'stvo, 1959.

Kommunisticheskaia Partiia Sovetskogo soiuza v rezoliutsiakh i resheniiakh, s"ezdov, konferentsii i plenumov. Moskva: Izdatel'stvo politicheskoi literatury, 1985.

Konnik, I. I. *Den'gi v period kommunisticheskogo obshchestva.* Moskva: Finansy, 1966.

Korobushkin, Aleksandr Konstantinovich. *Novyi sovetskii rubl'.* Moskva: Gosudarstvennoe izdatel'stvo politicheskoi literatury, 1960.

Kozlov, Genrikh Abramovich. "Den'gi pri sotsializme." *Bol'shevik,* No. 8 (1952): 58–68.

———. *Sovetskie den'gi.* Moskva: Gosudarstvennoe finansovoe izdatel'stvo, 1939.

Kronrod, Ia. A. *Den'gi v sotsialisticheskom obshchestve; Ocherki teorii.* Moskva: Gosudarstvennoe finansovoe izdatel'stvo, 1954.

———. *Ukreplenie denezhnogo obrashcheniia v SSSR, inflatsiia v stranakh kapitalizma.* Moskva: Gos. izd-vo polit. lit-ry, 1950.

Lebedev, B., and V. Bliakher. *Nuzhny li den'gi v Sovetskom soiuze?* Moskva: Gosudarstvennoe finansovoe izdatel'stvo, 1931.

Lenin, Vladimir Ilich. *Polnoe sobranie sochinenii.* Tom 7. Moskva: Gosudarstvennoe izdatel'stvo politicheskoe literatury, 1959.

———. *Polnoe sobranie sochinenii.* Tom 44. Moskva: Izdatel'stvo politicheskoi literatury, 1964.

Lopatkin, V. G. *Raspredelenie po trudu i formy ego osushchestvleniia; Lektsiia.* Moskva: VPSh, 1960.

Maksimov, G., G. Ovodov, and L. El'iashev. *Novyi masshtab tsen.* Moskva: Gosudarstvennoe finansovoe izdatel'stvo, 1960.

Malafeev, A. N. *Istoriia tsenoobrazovaniia v SSSR, 1917–1963 gg.* Moskva: Mysl', 1964.

Margolin, N. S. *Balans denezhnykh dokhodov i raskhodov naseleniia.* Moskva: Gosplanizdat, 1940.

Mar'iakhin, G. L. *Ocherki istorii nalogov s naseleniia v SSSR.* Moskva: Izdatel'stvo "Finansy," 1964.

Mar'iakhin, G. L., and D. V. Burmistrov. *Nalogi s naseleniia v SSSR; Dopushcheno v kachestve ucheb. posobiia dlia fin. i finansovo-kreditnykh tekhnikumov.* Moskva: Gosudarstvennoe finansovoe izdatel'stvo, 1957.

Mar'iakhin, G. L., D. V. Burmistrov, and Z. Maeva. *Posobiia, pensii i nalogovye l'goty voennosluzhashchim, chlenam ikh semei i invalidam otechestvennoi voiny.* Moskva: Gosudarstvennoe finansovoe izdatel'stvo, 1944.

Maslin, A. N. *Printsip material'noi zainteresovannosti pri sotsializme.* Moskva: Moskovskii rabochii, 1955.

Molotov, V. M. *Ob otmene kartochnoi sistema po khlebu.* Moskva: Partizdat, 1934.

Naguevskii A., and Iu. Khramov. "Pomen'she formalizma." *Sotsial'noe obespechenie,* No. 1 (1957): 10–11.

Novitskii, A. G., and G. V. Mil'. *Zaniatost' pensionerov: Sotsial'no-demograficheskii aspekt.* Moskva: Finansy i statistika, 1981.

O snizheniia tsen na khleb i otmene kartochnoi sistemy na miaso, rybu, sakhar, zhiry i kartofel'; Postanovlenie soveta narodnykh komissarov soiuza SSR i tsentral'nogo komiteta VKP(b). Moskva: Partizdat TsK VKP(b), 1935.

Ob uporiadochenii kartochnoi sistemy na khleb, nekotorye prodovol'stvennye i promyshlennye tovary: Prikaz narodnogo komissariata torgovli SSSR 380 ot 13 noiabria 1942 g. i instruktsii o poriadke vydachi, ucheta i khraneniia kartochek na normirovanye tovary i o poriadke otpuska normirovannykh tovarov v torgovoi seti. Kirov: Izdanie Oblastnogo biuro prod. i promtovarnykh kartochek, 1943.

Ostrovitianov, K. V., D. T. Shepilov, L. A. Leont'ev, I. D. Laptev, I. I. Kuz'minov, and L. M. Gatovskii. *Politicheskaia ekonomika; Uchebnik.* Moskva: Gosudarstvennoe izdatel'stvo politicheskoi literatury, 1954.

"Otvety na voprosy: Tol'ko li ot snizheniia tsen zavisit rost blagosostoianiia naseleniia?" *Politicheskoe samoobrazovanie,* No. 8 (1960): 82–86.

Panovko, M. *Zaimy SSSR: V voprosakh i otvetakh.* Moskva: Gosudarstvennoe finansovoe izdatel'stvo, 1934.

Preobrazhenskii, E. A. *Bumazhnye den'gi v epokhu proletarskoi diktatury.* Tiflis: Gos. izd-vo, 1921.

Rosliakov, M. V., ed. *Kartoteka finansovogo rabotnika.* Leningrad: Vsesoiuznaia spravochnaia kartoteka, Leningradskoe otdelenie, 1934.

RSFSR and Tsentral'noe statisticheskoe upravlenie. *Sovetskaia torgovlia v RSFSR: Statisticheskii sbornik.* Moskva: Gos. stat. izd-vo, 1958.

Shkurko, Sergei Ivanovich. *Raspredelenie po trudu i uporiadochenie zarabotnoi platy v SSSR.* Moskva: Izd-vo "Znanie," 1960.

"Sovetskie obligatsii bol'she ne vyigraiut." *Kommersant,* May 22, 2013. http://www.kommersant.ru/doc/2194452.

"Spornye voprosy teorii sovetskikh deneg." *Den'gi i kredit,* No. 2 (1954): 53–57.

Stalin, I. V. *Ekonomicheskie problemy sotsializma v SSSR.* Moskva: Gospolizdat, 1952.

———. *Sochineniia.* Tom 7. Moskva: Gosudarstvennoe izdatel'stvo politicheskoi literatury, 1951.

———. *Sochineniia.* Tom 13. Moskva: Gosudarstvennoe izdatel'stvo politicheskoi literatury, 1951.

———. *Sochineniia.* Tom 16. Moskva: Mysl', 1997.

Sukhanov, N. "Materialy dlia besedy: V interesakh Sovetskogo gosudarstva i vsego naroda." *Bloknot agitatora,* No. 12 (April 1957): 1–11.

Tatarskaia, Natal'ia Nikitichna, and Aleksandr Vladimirovich Gurianov. *Biudzhet rabochei sem'i.* Moskva: Gospolitizdat, 1957.

Tsentral'noe statisticheskoe upravlenie pri Sovete Ministrov RSFSR. *Biudzhety rabochikh, sluzhashchikh i kolkhoznikov RSFSR za 1940, 1953, 1956, 1957, 1958 gody: Statisticheskii sbornik.* Moskva: TsSU, 1959.

Tsentral'noe statisticheskoe upravlenie pri Sovete Ministrov SSSR. *Sovetskaia torgovlia: Statisticheskii sbornik.* Moskva: Gostatizdat, 1956.

Uriupin, F. *Posobiia, pensii i nalogovye l'goty voennosluzhashchim, chlenam ikh semei i invalidam otechestvennoi voiny.* Moskva: Gosudarstvennoe finansovoe izdatel'stvo, 1944.

Valler, L. V. *Denezhnye sberezheniia—na delo razgroma vraga; Posobie dlia obshchestvennogo aktiva po sberegatel'nomu delu.* Moskva: Gosudarstvennoe finansovoe izdatel'stvo, 1942.

Valler, L. V., and P. Ia. Dmitrichev. *Sberegatel'nye kassy v SSSR.* Moskva: Gosudarstvennoe finansovoe izdatel'stvo, 1946.

Vorov'ev, V., and N. Gorichev. "K voprosu o roli deneg v perspektive razvitiia narodnogo khoziaistva SSSR." *Den'gi i kredit,* No. 8 (1960): 1–13.

Zabozlaev, A. A., A. V. Levshin, and V. A. Aralov. *Sotsial'noe obespechenie v SSSR: Sbornik ofitsialnykh materialov.* Moskva: Profizdat, 1962.

Zakon o piatiletnem plane vosstanovleniia i razvitiia narodnogo khoziaistva SSSR na 1946–1950 gg. Leningrad: Ogiz, Gosudarstvennoe izdatel'stvo politicheskoi literatury, 1946.

Zaslavskaia, Tatiana Ivanovna. *Raspredelenie po trudu v kolkhozakh.* Moskva: Izd. Ekonomika, 1966.

Zlobin, I. D. *Den'gi pri kapitalizme.* Moskva: Gosudarstvennoe finansovoe izdatel'stvo, 1945.

———. *Sovetskii rubl'.* Moskva: Izdatel'stvo "Znanie," 1961.

———. *Sushchnost' i funktsii deneg v SSSR.* Moskva: Gosudarstvennoe finansovoe izdatel'stvo, 1956.

Zlobin, Stepan. *Bez nalogov, bez voiny!* Moskva: Gosudarstvennoe izdatel'stvo politicheskoi literatury, 1960.

Zorin, Valentin Sergeevich. *Amerikanets, monopolii, nalogi.* Moskva: Gos. izd-vo polit. lit-ry, 1960.

Zverev, Arsenii Grigorevich. "Finansovaia ditsiplina i kontrol' rublem v narodnom khoziaistve SSSR." *Bol'shevik,* No. 12 (1952): 24–35.

———. *Finansovaia sistema v novykh usloviiakh upravleniia khoziaistvom; Lektsiia, prochitannaia v vysshei partiinoi shkole pri TsK KPSS.* Moskva: Izdatel'stvo VPSh i LON pri TsK KPSS, 1958.

———. *Gosudarstvennye biudzhety Soiuza SSR, 1938–1945 gg.* Moskva: Gosudarstvennoe finansovoe izdatel'stvo, 1946.

———. *Gosudarstvennye zaimy v SSSR i vklady v sberegatel'nye kassy.* Moskva: Gosudarstvennoe finansovoe izdatel'stvo, 1957.

———. *Khoziaistvennoe razvitie i finansy v semiletke, 1959–1965.* Moskva: Gosudarstvennoe finansovoe izdatel'stvo, 1959.

———. *O gosudarstvennom biudzhete SSSR na 1945 god i ispolnenii gosudarstvennogo biudzheta SSSR za 1943 god: Doklad i zakliuchitel'nye slova Narodnogo komissara finansov SSSR na odinnadtsatoi sessii Verkhovnogo Soveta SSSR 1-go sozyva 24–27 aprelia 1945 g.* Moskva: Gos. izd-vo polit. lit-ry, 1945.

———. *O gosudarstvennom biudzhete SSSR na 1946 god i ispolnenii biudzheta za 1944 i 1945 gody: Doklad i zakliuchitel'nye slova Ministra finansov SSSR na vtoroi sessii Verkhovnogo Soveta SSSR 2-go sozyva 15–18 oktiabria 1946 g.* Moskva: Gos izd-vo polit. lit-ry, 1946.

———. *O gosudarstvennom biudzhete SSSR na 1947 god: Doklad i zakliuchitel'nye slova Ministra Finansov SSSR na tret'ei sessii Verkhovnogo Soveta SSSR 2-go sozyva 20–25 fevralia 1947 g.* Moskva: Gosudarstvennoe izdatel'stvo politicheskoi literatury, 1947.

———. *O gosudarstvennom biudzhete SSSR na 1948 god i ob ispolnenii gosudarstvennogo biudzheta SSSR za 1946 god: Doklad i zakliuchitel'nye slova ministra finansov SSSR na chetvertoi sessii Verkhovnogo Soveta SSSR 2-go sozyva 31 ianvaria–4 fevralia 1948 g.* Moskva: Gosudarstvennoe izdatel'stvo politicheskoi literatury, 1948.

———. *O gosudarstvennom biudzhete SSSR na 1949 god i ob ispolnenii gosudarstvennogo biudzheta SSSR za 1947 god: Doklad i zakliuchitel'nye slova Ministra finansov SSSR A. G. Zvereva na vtoroi sessii Verkhovnogo Soveta SSSR 2-go sozyva 10–14 marta 1949 g.* Moskva: Gosudarstvennoe izdatel'stvo politicheskoi literatury, 1949.

———. *O Gosudarstvennom biudzhete SSSR na 1949 god i ob ispolnenii gosudarstvennogo biudzheta SSSR za 1947 god: Doklad i zakliuchitel'nye slova Ministra Finansov SSSR na piatoi sessii Verkhovnogo Soveta Soiuza SSR 2-go sozyva 10–14 marta 1949 g.* Moskva: Gosudarstvennoe izdatel'stvo politicheskoi literatury, 1949.

———. *O gosudarstvennom biudzhete SSSR na 1950 god i ob ispolnenii gosudarstvennogo biudzheta SSSR za 1948 i 1949 gody: Doklad i zakliuchitel'nye slova ministra finansov SSSR na pervoi sessii Verkhovnogo Soveta SSSR 3-go sozyva 13–17 iiunia 1950 g.* Moskva: Gosudarstvennoe izdatel'stvo politicheskoi literatury, 1950.

———. *O gosudarstvennom biudzhete SSSR na 1952 god i ob ispolnenii gosudarstvennogo biudzheta SSSR za 1950 god.* Moskva, 1952.

———. *O gosudarstvennom biudzhete SSSR na 1953 god i ob ispolnenii gosudarstvennogo biudzheta SSSR za 1951 i 1952 gody: Doklad i zakliuchitel'noe slovo Ministra finansov SSSR A. G. Zvereva na piatoi sessii Verkhovnogo Soveta SSSR 5 i 8 avgusta 1953 g.; Zakon o gosudarstvennom biudzhete SSSR na 1953 god; Zakon o sel'skokhoziaistvennom naloge.* Moskva: Gospolitizdat, 1953.

———. *O gosudarstvennom biudzhete SSSR za 1951 god: Doklad i zakliuchitel'nye slova.* Moskva: Gosudarstvennoe izdatel'stvo politicheskoi literatury, 1951.

———. *Problemy tsenoobrazovaniia i finansy.* Moskva: Izd-vo "Nauka," 1966.

Translated Published Primary Sources

Bukharin, Nikolai, and E. A. Preobrazhenskii. *The ABC of Communism: A Popular Explanation of the Program of the Communist Party of Russia.* Translated by Eden and Cedar Paul. London: Communist Party of Great Britain, 1922.

Khrushchev in America; Full Texts of the Speeches Made by N. S. Khrushchev, Chairman of the Council of Ministers of the USSR on His Tour of the United States, September 15–27, 1959. New York: Crosscurrents Press, 1960.

Marx, Karl. *Capital: A Critique of Political Economy.* Vol. 2, *The Process of Circulation of Capital,* edited by Friedrich Engels, translated by Ernest Untermann. Chicago: Charles H. Kerr, 1933.

———. "Moralizing Criticism and Critical Morality: A Contribution to German Cultural History Contra Karl Heinzen." In *The Collected Works of Karl Marx and Frederick Engels*, vol. 6, *General Works, 1844–1895*, 312–340. New York: International Publishers, 1976.

Marx, Karl, and Friedrich Engels. "Manifesto of the Communist Party." In *The Marx-Engels Reader*, edited by Robert C. Tucker, 469–500. New York: Norton, 1978.

Trotsky, Leon. *The Revolution Betrayed: What Is the Soviet Union and Where Is It Going?* Garden City, N.Y.: Doubleday, Doran, 1937.

Zverev, A. G. *What Soviet Citizens Get besides Wages.* London: Soviet Booklets, 1959.

English-Language Primary Sources

Rose, Scott. "Brezhnev Bonds Haunt Putin as Investors Hunt $785 Billion." *Bloomberg*, August 31, 2012. http://www.bloomberg.com/news/2012-08-27/brezhnev-bonds-haunt-putin-as-investors-hunt-for-785-billion.html.

Secondary Sources

Aksiutin, Iurii. *Khrushchevskaia "ottepel'" i obshchestvennye nastroeniia v SSSR v 1953–1964 gg.* Moskva: ROSSPEN, 2004.

Alexopoulos, Golfo. *Stalin's Outcasts: Aliens, Citizens, and the Soviet State, 1926–1936.* Ithaca, N.Y.: Cornell University Press, 2003.

Attwood, Lynne. "Housing in the Khrushchev Era." In *Women in the Khrushchev Era*, edited by Melanie Ilicč, Susan E. Reid, and Lynne Attwood, 177–202. Houndmills, Basingstoke, Hampshire: Palgrave Macmillan, 2004.

Barber, John, and Mark Harrison. *The Soviet Home Front, 1941–1945: A Social and Economic History of the USSR in World War II.* London: Longman, 1991.

Barenberg, Alan. "'For a Single, Clear Pension Law': Legislating and Debating Soviet Pensions, 1956–1965." Master's thesis, University of Chicago, 2000.

———. *Gulag Town, Company Town: Forced Labor and Its Legacy in Vorkuta.* New Haven, Conn.: Yale University Press, 2014.

Baron, Samuel H. *Bloody Saturday in the Soviet Union: Novocherkassk, 1962.* Stanford, Calif.: Stanford University Press, 2001.

Barr, Nicholas. *The Economics of the Welfare State.* 5th ed. Oxford: Oxford University Press, 2012.

Belova, Eugenia, and Valery Lazarev. *Funding Loyalty: The Economics of the Communist Party.* New Haven, Conn.: Yale University Press, 2012.

Bornstein, Morris. "The Reform and Revaluation of the Ruble." *American Economic Review*, Vol. 51, No. 1 (1961): 117–123.

Brooks, Jeffrey. *Thank You, Comrade Stalin! Soviet Public Culture from Revolution to Cold War.* Princeton, N.J.: Princeton University Press, 2000.

Cadioli, Giovanni. "Soviet Economic Thought and Economic Policy in the 1940s: Influence on 1950s–1960s Reforms." PhD thesis, Oxford University, 2018.

Campbell, Colin D., and Rosemary G Campbell. "Soviet Price Reductions for Consumer Goods, 1948–1954." *American Economic Review*, Vol. 45, No. 4 (1955): 609–625.

Chandler, Andrea. *Shocking Mother Russia: Democratization, Social Rights, and Pension Reform in Russia, 1990–2001.* Toronto: University of Toronto Press, 2004.

Chernyshova, Natalya. *Soviet Consumer Culture in the Brezhnev Era.* New York: Routledge, 2013.

Cohn, Edward D. *The High Title of a Communist: Postwar Party Discipline and the Values of the Soviet Regime.* DeKalb: Northern Illinois University Press, 2015.

Cook, Linda J. "Brezhnev's 'Social Contract' and Gorbachev's Reforms." *Soviet Studies,* Vol. 44, No. 1 (1992): 37–56.

———. *The Soviet Social Contract and Why It Failed: Welfare Policy and Workers' Politics from Brezhnev to Yeltsin.* Cambridge, Mass.: Harvard University Press, 1993.

Davies, R. W. *The Development of the Soviet Budgetary System.* Cambridge: Cambridge University Press, 1958.

Denisova, Liubov. *Rural Women in the Soviet Union and Post-Soviet Russia.* Edited and translated by Irina Mukhina. Milton Park, Abingdon, Oxon: Routledge, 2010.

Dunham, Vera Sandomirsky. *In Stalin's Time: Middleclass Values in Soviet Fiction.* Cambridge: Cambridge University Press, 1976.

Edele, Mark. *Soviet Veterans of the Second World War: A Popular Movement in an Authoritarian Society, 1941–1991.* Oxford: Oxford University Press, 2008.

———. "Strange Young Men in Stalin's Moscow: The Birth and Life of the Stiliagi, 1945–1953." *Jahrbücher für Geschichte Osteuropas,* Vol. 50, No. 1 (2002): 37–61.

Ellman, Michael. "The 1947 Soviet Famine and the Entitlement Approach to Famines." *Cambridge Journal of Economics,* Vol. 24, No. 5 (2000): 603–630.

Feygin Yakov. "Building a Ruin: Cold War Economics and the Politics of Reform in the Post-Stalin USSR." Unpublished book manuscript, 2019.

Field, Deborah A. *Private Life and Communist Morality in Khrushchev's Russia.* New York: Peter Lang, 2007.

Fieseler, Beate. "The Bitter Legacy of the 'Great Patriotic War': Red Army Disabled Soldiers under Late Stalinism." In *Late Stalinist Russia: Society between Reconstruction and Reinvention,* edited by Juliane Fürst, 46–61. London: Routledge, 2006.

———. "Soviet-Style Welfare: The Disabled Soldiers of the 'Great Patriotic War.'" In *Disability in Eastern Europe and the Former Soviet Union: History, Policy and Everyday Life,* edited by Michael Rasell and Elena Iarskaia-Smirnova, 18–41. London: Routledge, 2014.

Filtzer, Donald A. *The Hazards of Urban Life in Late Stalinist Russia: Health, Hygiene, and Living Standards, 1943–1953.* New York: Cambridge University Press, 2010.

———. "The 1947 Food Crisis and Its Aftermath: Worker and Peasant Consumption in Non-famine Regions of the RSFSR." In *A Dream Deferred: New Studies in Russian and Soviet Labour History,* edited by Donald A. Filtzer, Wendy Z. Goldman, Gijs Kessler, and Simon Pirani, 345–383. Bern: Peter Lang, 2008.

———. *Soviet Workers and De-Stalinization: The Consolidation of the Modern System of Soviet Production Relations, 1953–1964.* Cambridge: Cambridge University Press, 1992.

———. *Soviet Workers and Late Stalinism: Labour and the Restoration of the Stalinist System after World War II.* Cambridge: Cambridge University Press, 2002.

———. *Soviet Workers and Stalinist Industrialization: The Formation of Modern Soviet Production Relations, 1928–1941.* Armonk, N.Y.: M. E. Sharpe, 1986.

———. *Soviet Workers and the Collapse of Perestroika: The Soviet Labour Process and Gorbachev's Reforms, 1985–1991.* Cambridge: Cambridge University Press, 2008.

———. "Standard of Living versus Quality of Life: Struggling with the Urban Environment in Russia during the Early Years of Post-war Reconstruction." In *Late Stalinist Russia: Society between Reconstruction and Reinvention,* edited by Juliane Fürst, 81–102. London: Routledge, 2006.

Fitzpatrick, Sheila. "Blat in Stalin's Time." In *Bribery and Blat in Russia: Negotiating Reciprocity from the Middle Ages to the 1990s,* edited by Stephen Lovell, Alena V. Ledeneva, and A. B. Rogachevskii, 166–182. New York: St. Martin's Press, 2000.

———. *Everyday Stalinism: Ordinary Life in Extraordinary Times: Soviet Russia in the 1930s.* New York: Oxford University Press, 1999.

———. "Social Parasites: How Tramps, Idle Youth, and Busy Entrepreneurs Impeded the Soviet March to Communism." *Cahiers du monde russe,* Vol. 47, No. 1–2 (2006): 377–408.

———. "Stalin and the Making of a New Elite, 1928–1939." *Slavic Review,* Vol. 38, No. 3 (1979): 377–402.

———. *Stalin's Peasants: Resistance and Survival in the Russian Village after Collectivization.* New York: Oxford University Press, 1994.

Forestier-Peyrat, Étienne, and Kristy Ironside. "A Communist World of Public Debt? The Failure of a Counter-model." In *A World of Public Debts: A Political History,* edited by Nicolas Barreyre and Nicolas Delalande, 317–345. London: Palgrave Macmillan, 2020.

Fürst, Juliane. "The Importance of Being Stylish: Youth, Culture and Identity in Late Stalinism." In *Late Stalinist Russia: Society between Reconstruction and Reinvention,* edited by Juliane Fürst, 210–230. London: Routledge, 2006.

———. *Stalin's Last Generation: Soviet Post-war Youth and the Emergence of Mature Socialism.* Oxford: Oxford University Press, 2010.

Galmarini-Kabala, Maria Cristina. *The Right to Be Helped: Deviance, Entitlement, and the Soviet Moral Order.* DeKalb: Northern Illinois University Press, 2016.

Ganson, Nicholas. *The Soviet Famine of 1946–47 in Global and Historical Perspective.* New York: Palgrave Macmillan, 2009.

Gatrell, Peter. *Russia's First World War: A Social and Economic History.* London: Pearson-Longman, 2005.

Goland, Yurii. "Currency Regulation in the NEP Period." *Europe-Asia Studies,* Vol. 46, No. 8 (1994): 1251–1296.

Goldman, Wendy Z. "Not by Bread Alone: Food, Workers, and the State." In *Hunger and War: Food Provisioning in the Soviet Union during World War II,* edited by Wendy Z. Goldman and Donald A. Filtzer, 44–97. Bloomington: Indiana University Press, 2015.

Gorlizki, Yoram, and Oleg V. Khlevniuk. *Cold Peace: Stalin and the Ruling Circle, 1945–1953.* Oxford: Oxford University Press, 2004.

Granick, David. *Management of the Industrial Firm in the USSR: A Study in Soviet Economic Planning.* New York: Columbia University Press, 1954.

Gregory, Paul R., and Aleksei Tikhonov. "Central Planning and Unintended Consequences: Creating the Soviet Financial System, 1930–1939." *Journal of Economic History,* Vol. 60, No. 4 (December 2000): 1017–1040.

Gronow, Jukka. *Caviar with Champagne: Common Luxury and the Ideals of the Good Life in Stalin's Russia.* Oxford, U.K.: Berg, 2003.

Haber, Maya. "Socialist Realist Science: Constructing Knowledge about Rural Life in the Soviet Union, 1943–1958." PhD diss., University of California, Los Angeles, 2013.

Hachten, P. Charles. "Property Relations and the Economic Organization of Soviet Russia, 1941–1948." PhD diss., University of Chicago, 2005.

Hale-Dorrell, Aaron. *Corn Crusade: Khrushchev's Farming Revolution in the Post-Stalin Soviet Union.* Oxford: Oxford University Press, 2018.

Hanson, Philip. *The Rise and Fall of the Soviet Economy: An Economic History of the USSR from 1945.* London: Longman, 2003.

Harris, Steven E. *Communism on Tomorrow Street: Mass Housing and Everyday Life after Stalin.* Baltimore: Johns Hopkins University Press, 2013.

Harrison, Mark. "The Soviet Union after 1945: Economic Recovery and Political Repression." *Past and Present,* Vol. 210, No. 6 (2011): 103–120.

Heinzen, James. *The Art of the Bribe: Corruption under Stalin, 1943–1953.* New Haven, Conn.: Yale University Press, 2016.

Hessler, Julie. "Cultured Trade: The Stalinist Turn toward Consumerism." In *Stalinism: New Directions,* edited by Sheila Fitzpatrick, 182–209. London: Routledge, 2000.

———. "Postwar Normalisation and Its Limits in the USSR: The Case of Trade." *Europe-Asia Studies,* Vol. 53, No. 3 (2001): 445–471.

———. "A Postwar Perestroika? Toward a History of Private Enterprise in the USSR." *Slavic Review,* Vol. 57, No. 3 (1998): 516–542.

———. *A Social History of Soviet Trade: Trade Policy, Retail Practices, and Consumption, 1917–1953.* Princeton, N.J.: Princeton University Press, 2004.

Hoffmann, David L. *Cultivating the Masses: Modern State Practices and Soviet Socialism, 1914–1939.* Ithaca, N.Y.: Cornell University Press, 2011.

Holzman, Franklyn D. "The Burden of Soviet Taxation." *American Economic Review,* Vol. 43, No. 4 (1953): 548–571.

———. "Commodity and Income Taxation in the Soviet Union." *Journal of Political Economy,* Vol. 58, No. 5 (1950): 425–433.

———. "An Estimate of the Tax Element in Soviet Bonds." *American Economic Review,* Vol. 47, No. 3 (1957): 390–396.

———. "The Ruble Exchange Rate and Soviet Foreign Trade Pricing Policies, 1929–1961." *American Economic Review,* Vol. 58, No. 4 (1968): 803–825.

———. "The Soviet Bond Hoax." *Problems of Communism,* Vol. 6, No. 5 (1957): 47–49.

———. "Soviet Inflationary Pressures, 1928–1957: Causes and Cures." *Quarterly Journal of Economics,* Vol. 74, No. 2 (1960): 167–188.

———. *Soviet Taxation: The Fiscal and Monetary Problems of a Planned Economy.* Cambridge, Mass.: Harvard University Press, 1955.

———. "Soviet Taxes Defined: Abolition of Levy on Income Held Little Relief for Population." *New York Times,* October 6, 1959.

Ilič, Melanie, and Jeremy Smith, eds. *Soviet State and Society under Nikita Khrushchev.* London: Routledge, 2009.

Iliukhov, Aleksandr Antonovich. *Kak platili bol'sheviki: Politika sovetskoi vlasti v sfere oplaty truda v 1917–1941 gg.* Moskva: ROSSPEN; Fond pervogo prezidenta Rossii B. N. El'tsina, 2010.

Ironside, Kristy. "Between Fiscal, Ideological, and Social Dilemmas: The Soviet 'Bachelor Tax' and Post-war Tax Reform, 1941–1962." *Europe-Asia Studies,* Vol. 69, No. 6 (2017): 855–878.

———. "'I Beg You Not to Reject My Plea': The Late Stalinist Welfare State and the Politics of One-Time Monetary Aid, 1946–1953." *Journal of Social History,* Vol. 51, No. 4 (2018): 1045–1068.

———. "Khrushchev's Cash-and-Goods Lotteries and the Turn toward Positive Incentives." *Soviet and Post-Soviet Review,* Vol. 41, No. 3 (2014): 296–323.

———. "Rubles for Victory: The Social Dynamics of State Fundraising on the Soviet Home Front." *Kritika: Explorations in Russian and Eurasian History,* Vol. 15, No. 4 (2014): 799–828.

———. "Stalin's Doctrine of Price Reductions during the Second World War and Postwar Reconstruction." *Slavic Review,* Vol. 75, No. 3 (2016): 655–677.

Ivanova, Galina Mikhailovich. *Na poroge "gosudarstva vseobshchego blagosostoianiia": Sotsial'naia politika v SSSR (seredina 1950-kh–nachalo 1970 godov).* Moskva: Institut rossiiskoi istorii RAN, 2011.

Jasny, Naum. "The Soviet Price System." *American Economic Review,* Vol. 40, No. 5 (1950): 845–863.

———. *The Soviet Price System.* Stanford, Calif.: Stanford University Press, 1951.

Johnson, Oliver. "The Stalin Prize and the Soviet Artist: Status Symbol or Stigma?" *Slavic Review,* Vol. 70, No. 4 (2011): 819–843.

Judt, Tony. *Postwar: A History of Europe since 1945.* New York: Penguin Books, 2005.

Kalinovsky, Artemy. *Laboratory of Socialist Development: Cold War Politics and Decolonization in Soviet Tajikistan.* Ithaca, N.Y.: Cornell University Press, 2018.

Kapustina, Ol'ga Vladimirovna. "Deiatel'nost' sovetskogo gosudarstva po sovershenstvovaniiu pensionnogo obespecheniia grazhdan (vtoraia polovina 1950-kh–1980-e gody)." Dissertation, Pushkin Leningrad State University, 2010.

Kerblay, Basile. *Les marchés paysans en URSS.* Paris: Mouton, 1968.

Khanin, G. I. "The 1950s—the Triumph of the Soviet Economy." *Europe-Asia Studies,* Vol. 55, No. 8 (2003): 1187–1212.

Kharkhordin, Oleg. *The Collective and the Individual in Russia: A Study of Practices.* Berkeley: University of California Press, 1999.

Khlevniuk, Oleg V. "The Economy of Illusions: The Phenomenon of Data-Inflation in the Khrushchev Era." In *Khrushchev in the Kremlin: Policy and Government in the*

Soviet Union, 1953–1964, edited by Jeremy Smith and Melanie Ilicč, 171–189. Milton Park, Abingdon, Oxon: Routledge, 2011.

———. *Stalin: New Biography of a Dictator.* Translated by Nora Seligman. New Haven, Conn.: Yale University Press, 2015.

Khlevniuk, Oleg V., and R. W. Davies. "The End of Rationing in the Soviet Union, 1934–1935." *Europe-Asia Studies,* Vol. 51, No. 4 (1999): 557–609.

Kibita, Nataliya. *Soviet Economic Management under Khrushchev: The Sovnarkhoz Reform.* London: Routledge, 2013.

Kirsch, Leonard Joel. *Soviet Wages: Changes in Structure and Administration since 1956.* Cambridge, Mass.: MIT Press, 1972.

Konovalov, A. B. "Modernizatsiia sistemy nomenklaturnykh l'got i privilegii: Opyt khrushchevskikh reform (1953–1964 gody)." *Istoricheskii ezhegodnik Sibirskogo otdeleniia rossiiskoi akademii nauk,* 2007, 6–20.

Kornai, János. *The Socialist System: The Political Economy of Communism.* Princeton, N.J.: Princeton University Press, 1992.

Kotsonis, Yanni. "'Face-to-Face': The State, the Individual, and the Citizen in Russian Taxation, 1863–1917." *Slavic Review,* Vol. 63, No. 2 (2004): 221–246.

———. "'No Place to Go': Taxation and State Transformation in Late Imperial and Early Soviet Russia." *Journal of Modern History,* Vol. 76, No. 3 (2004): 531–577.

———. *States of Obligation: Taxes and Citizenship in the Russian Empire and Early Soviet Republic.* Toronto: University of Toronto Press, 2014.

Kovtun, Evgenii. *Azart v strane sovetov.* Tom 2, *Loterei.* Moskva: ZAO "Olimp-Biznes," 2012.

Kozlov, Denis, and Eleonory Gilburd. "The Thaw as an Event in Russian History." In *The Thaw: Soviet Society and Culture during the 1950s and 1960s,* edited by Denis Kozlov and Eleonory Gilburd, 18–81. Toronto: University of Toronto Press, 2013.

Kozlov, Vladimir A. *Mass Uprisings in the USSR: Protest and Rebellion in the Post-Stalin Years.* Translated and edited by Elaine McClarnand MacKinnon. Armonk, N.Y.: M. E. Sharpe, 2002.

Kragh, Martin. "Stalinist Labour Coercion during World War II: An Economic Approach." *Europe-Asia Studies,* Vol. 63, No. 7 (2011): 1253–1273.

Lebina, Nataliia. "Plus the Chemicalization of the Entire Wardrobe." *Russian Studies in History,* Vol. 48, No. 1 (2009): 33–45.

Ledeneva, Alena V. "The Genealogy of Krugovaia Poruka: Forced Trust as a Feature of Russian Political Culture." In *Trust and Democratic Transition in Post-communist Europe,* edited by Ivana Marková, 85–108. Oxford: Oxford University Press for the British Academy, 2004.

———. *How Russia Really Works: The Informal Practices That Shaped Post-Soviet Politics and Business.* Ithaca, N.Y.: Cornell University Press, 2006.

———. *Russia's Economy of Favours: Blat, Networking and Informal Exchange.* Cambridge: Cambridge University Press, 1998.

Lévy-Ullmann, Henri. "Lottery Bonds in France and in the Principal Countries of Europe." *Harvard Law Review,* Vol. 9, No. 6 (1896): 386–405.

Lewin, Moshe. *The Making of the Soviet System: Essays in the Social History of Interwar Russia.* New York: Pantheon Books, 1985.

Madison, Bernice Q. *Social Welfare in the Soviet Union.* Stanford, Calif.: Stanford University Press, 1968.

Maier, Charles S. *In Search of Stability: Explorations in Historical Political Economy.* Cambridge: Cambridge University Press, 1987.

Makarkin, Aleksei. "The Russian Social Contract and Regime Legitimacy." *International Affairs,* Vol. 87, No. 6 (2011): 1459–1474.

Marks, Steven G. "The Russian Experience of Money, 1914–1924." In *Russian Culture in War and Revolution, 1914–22,* bk. 2, edited by Murray Frame et al., 121–148. Bloomington, Ind.: Slavica Publishers, 2014.

Matthews, Mervyn. *Privilege in the Soviet Union: A Study of Elite Life-Styles under Communism.* London: G. Allen & Unwin, 1978.

McAuley, Alastair. *Economic Welfare in the Soviet Union: Poverty, Living Standards, and Inequality.* Madison: University of Wisconsin Press, 1979.

———. "Social Policy." In *Khrushchev and Khrushchevism,* edited by Martin McCauley, 138–155. Bloomington: Indiana University Press, 1987.

Millar, James R. "History and Analysis of Soviet Domestic Bond Policy." *Soviet Studies,* Vol. 27, No. 4 (1975): 598–614.

———. "The Little Deal: Brezhnev's Contribution to Acquisitive Socialism." *Slavic Review,* Vol. 44, No. 4 (1985): 694–706.

Millar, James R., and James A. Gentry. "The Soviet Experiment with Domestic Lottery Bonds." *Financial Management,* Vol. 9, No. 4 (1980): 21–29.

Miller, Chris. "Economic Ideas Crossing Borders: The Transnational Turn in Soviet Economic History." *Soviet and Post-Soviet Review,* Vol. 46, No. 1 (2019): 55–66.

Moskoff, William. *The Bread of Affliction: The Food Supply in the USSR during World War II.* Cambridge: Cambridge University Press, 1990.

Nakachi, Mie. "N. S. Khrushchev and the 1944 Soviet Family Law: Politics, Reproduction, and Language." *East European Politics and Societies,* Vol. 20, No. 1 (2006): 40–68.

———. "Replacing the Dead: The Politics of Reproduction in the Postwar Soviet Union, 1944–1955." PhD diss., University of Chicago, 2008.

Nove, Alec. *An Economic History of the U.S.S.R.* Reprinted with revisions. Harmondsworth, Middlesex, England: Penguin Books, 1982.

———. *An Economic History of the U.S.S.R., 1917–1991.* 3rd ed. London: Penguin Books, 1992.

———. "The Income of Soviet Peasants." *Slavonic and East European Review,* Vol. 38, No. 91 (1960): 314–333.

———. "Industry." In *Khrushchev and Khrushchevism,* edited by Martin McCauley, 61–70. Bloomington: Indiana University Press, 1987.

———. *The Soviet Economy: An Introduction.* New York: Praeger, 1969.

———. "Toward a 'Communist Welfare State'?" *Problems of Communism,* Vol. 1, No. 9 (1960): 1–10.

Oberländer, Alexandra. "Eggs versus Rubles: Hatching Money in the Soviet Countryside." Unpublished paper presented at the Association for Slavic, East European, and Eurasian Studies annual convention, 2018.

Oppenheim, Samuel A. "Between Right and Left: G. Ia. Sokolnikov and the Development of the Soviet State, 1921–1929." *Slavic Review,* Vol. 48, No. 4 (1989): 592–613.

Osokina, Elena. *Our Daily Bread: Socialist Distribution and the Art of Survival in Stalin's Russia, 1927–1941.* Edited by Kate Transchel. Translated by Kate Transchel and Greta Bucher. Armonk, N.Y.: M. E. Sharpe, 2001.

Oushakine, Serguei Alex. "'Against the Cult of Things': On Soviet Productivism, Storage Economy, and Commodities with No Destination." *Russian Review,* Vol. 73, No. 2 (2014): 198–236.

Phillips, Sarah D. "'There Are No Invalids in the USSR!': A Missing Soviet Chapter in the New Disability History." *Disability Studies Quarterly,* Vol. 29, No. 3 (2009). http://dsq-sds.org/article/view/936/1111.

Pollock, Ethan. *Stalin and the Soviet Science Wars.* Princeton, N.J.: Princeton University Press, 2006.

Reid, Susan E. "Cold War in the Kitchen: Gender and the De-Stalinization of Consumer Taste in the Soviet Union under Khrushchev." *Slavic Review,* Vol. 61, No. 2 (2002): 211–252.

Rindzevičiūtė, Eglė. "A Struggle for the Soviet Future: The Birth of Scientific Forecasting in the Soviet Union." *Slavic Review,* Vol. 75, No. 1 (2016): 52–76.

Sanchez-Sibony, Oscar. "Capitalism's Fellow Traveler: The Soviet Union, Bretton Woods, and the Cold War, 1944–1958." *Comparative Studies in Society and History,* Vol. 56, No. 2 (2014): 290–319.

———. *Red Globalization: The Political Economy of the Soviet Cold War from Stalin to Khrushchev.* Cambridge: Cambridge University Press, 2014.

Schattenberg, Susanne. "Trust, Care, and Familiarity in the Politburo: Brezhnev's Scenario of Power." *Kritika: Explorations in Russian and Eurasian History,* Vol. 16, No. 4 (2015): 835–858.

Schroeder, Gertrude E. "The 1966–67 Soviet Industrial Price Reform: A Study in Complications." *Soviet Studies,* Vol. 20, No. 4 (1969): 462–477.

Siegelbaum, Lewis H. *Cars for Comrades: The Life of the Soviet Automobile.* Ithaca, N.Y.: Cornell University Press, 2008.

———. *Stakhanovism and the Politics of Productivity in the USSR, 1935–1941.* Cambridge: Cambridge University Press, 1988.

Smith, G. A. E. "Agriculture." In *Khrushchev and Khrushchevism,* edited by Martin McCauley, 95–117. Bloomington: Indiana University Press, 1987.

Smith, Jeremy, and Melanie Ilič, eds. *Khrushchev in the Kremlin: Policy and Government in the Soviet Union, 1953–1964.* Milton Park, Abingdon, Oxon: Routledge, 2011.

Smith, Mark B. "Faded Red Paradise: Welfare and the Soviet City after 1953." *Contemporary European History,* Vol. 24, No. 4 (2015): 597–617.

———. *Property of Communists: The Urban Housing Program from Stalin to Khrushchev.* DeKalb: Northern Illinois University Press, 2010.

———. "Social Rights in the Soviet Dictatorship: The Constitutional Right to Welfare from Stalin to Brezhnev." *Humanity: An International Journal of Human Rights, Humanitarianism, and Development,* Vol. 3, No. 3 (2012): 385–406.

———. "The Withering Away of the Danger Society: The Pensions Reforms of 1956 and 1964 in the Soviet Union." *Social Science History,* Vol. 39, No. 1 (2015): 129–148.

Strelianyi, Anatolii. "Khrushchev and the Countryside." In *Nikita Khrushchev,* edited by William Taubman, Sergei Khrushchev, and Abbott Gleason, translated by David Gehrenbeck, Eileen Kane, and Alla Bashenko, 113–137. New Haven, Conn.: Yale University Press, 2000.

Terebov, Vladimir Nikandrovich. *Katalog lotereinykh biletov RSFSR i SSSR tsentral'nykh vypuskov (1922–1992).* Saransk: Tip. "Kras. Okt.," 2005.

———. "Sud'ba lotereii." *Kollektsioner,* No. 31–32 (1996): 194–195. http://www.bonistikaweb.ru/terebov.htm.

Titov, Alexander. "The 1961 Party Programme and the Fate of Khrushchev's Reforms." In *Soviet State and Society under Nikita Khrushchev,* edited by Melanie Ilicč and Jeremy Smith, 8–25. London: Routledge, 2009.

Tufano, Peter. "Saving whilst Gambling: An Empirical Analysis of UK Premium Bonds." *American Economic Review,* Vol. 98, No. 2 (2008): 321–326.

Tverdiukova, Elena Dmitrievna. "Bor'ba so zloupotrebleniiami v sfere kartochnogo snabzheniia naseleniia v SSSR, 1941–1947 gg." *Vestnik Sankt-Peterburgskogo Universiteta,* seriia 2, *Istoriia,* June 2010, 32–40.

Varga-Harris, Christine. *Stories of House and Home: Soviet Apartment Life during the Khrushchev Years.* Ithaca, N.Y.: Cornell University Press, 2015.

Vashchuk, A. S., and E. Iu. Selezneva. "Fiskal'naia politika na dal'nem vostoke Rossii (seredina 1940-kh–1950-e gody)." *Vestnik DVO RAN,* No. 1 (2007): 90–97.

Volkov, Vadim. "The Concept of Kul'turnost'." In *Stalinism: New Directions,* edited by Sheila Fitzpatrick, 210–230. London: Routledge, 2000.

Wädekin, Karl-Eugen. *The Private Sector in Soviet Agriculture.* Edited by George F. Karcz. Translated by Keith Bush. Berkeley: University of California Press, 1973.

Wheatcroft, Stephen G. "The Soviet Famine of 1946–1947, the Weather and Human Agency in Historical Perspective." *Europe-Asia Studies,* Vol. 64, No. 6 (2012): 987–1005.

Yanowitch, Murray. "Changes in the Soviet Money Wage Level since 1940." *American Slavic and East European Review,* Vol. 14, No. 2 (April 1955): 195–223.

———. *Social and Economic Inequality in the Soviet Union: Six Studies.* White Plains, N.Y.: M. E. Sharpe, 1977.

———. "The Soviet Income Revolution." *Slavic Review,* Vol. 22, No. 4 (1963): 683–697.

Zhirnov, Evgenii. "Razvrat, p'ianka, sovrashchenie devushek." *Kommersant,* November 28, 2005. http://www.kommersant.ru/doc/630490.

Zhukov, Iu. N. *Tainy Kremlia: Stalin, Molotov, Beria, Malenkov.* Moskva: Terra, 2000.

Zima, V. F. *Golod v SSSR 1946–1947 godov: Proiskhozhdeniie i posledstviia.* Moskva: Rossiiskaia akademiia nauk, In-t rossiiskoi istorii, 1996.

Zubkova, Elena Iurievna. *Poslevoennoe sovetskoe obshchestvo: Politika i povsednevnost', 1945–1953.* Moskva: ROSSPEN, 2000.

———. "The Rivalry with Malenkov." In *Nikita Khrushchev,* edited by William Taubman, Sergei Khrushchev, and Abbott Gleason, translated by David Gehrenbeck, Eileen Kane, and Alla Bashenko, 67–84. New Haven, Conn.: Yale University Press, 2000.

———. *Russia after the War: Hopes, Illusions, and Disappointments, 1945–1957.* Translated by Hugh Ragsdale. Armonk, N.Y.: M. E. Sharpe, 1998.

———. "S protianutoi rukoi: Nishchie i nishchenstvo v poslevoennom SSSR." *Cahiers du monde russe,* Vol. 49, No. 2–3 (2008): 441–474.

Acknowledgments

This book is the product of over a decade of research and writing that would not have been possible without the support and encouragement of many people and institutions. The idea to write on money in the postwar Soviet Union grew out of a seminar on the history of everyday life co-taught at the University of Chicago by Sheila Fitzpatrick and her colleague Leora Auslander. Having recently reread *The Master and Margarita,* whose protagonist is able to quit his job and fund his literary pursuits after winning the lottery (more precisely, after one of the semi-compulsory mass subscription bonds I discuss in Chapter 4 wins), I decided to write on exactly that. I was left with more questions than answers—what could one do with a grand prize of 100,000 rubles in a "shortage economy" in which money was typically thought of as useless? Sheila Fitzpatrick encouraged me to consider money in Soviet life as a topic and that sent me down the rabbit hole that ended up becoming this book.

Throughout the process of writing, Dr. Fitzpatrick provided an excellent model of how to do social history, and I am grateful for her guidance. The finished book is certainly more "economic" than earlier drafts, and it takes a more top-down perspective, but it is enriched by the superior training in listening to the "voices from below" that I received from her. Tara Zahra and Leora Auslander were also extremely supportive throughout the research and writing process. I especially want to thank Dr. Zahra for her generosity and advice when I was cutting my teeth on the academic job market and in publishing.

One of the best things about studying at the University of Chicago is its intellectual atmosphere. The many discussions I had with my peers during my time there, often over pints of beer in Hyde Park's dive bars or in each other's apartments, were formative during the earliest stages of this project. In particular, I want to thank Natalie Belsky, Flora Roberts, Rachel Applebaum, Leah Goldman, Esther Peters, and Cheryl Stephenson for their company, conversation, and commiseration. I also want to thank Faith Hillis, Eleonory Gilburd, Michael Geyer, and the broader community of Russianists and Europeanists in Chicago and the American Midwest, who provided feedback on chapter drafts at the Modern European History Workshop, the Midwest Russian History workshop, and the Chicago-area *kruzhok* (circle).

This book was the product of extended research trips to Moscow over the course of several years. These were facilitated by generous support from the History Department at the University of Chicago, Sheila Fitzpatrick, and the Social Science Research Council. Financial support for writing, as well as a final trip to Moscow, was provided by a fellowship from the American Council of Learned Societies. I want to extend my warmest thanks to the staff at the State Archive of the Russian Federation, the Russian State Archive of the Economy, the Russian State Archive for Socio-Political History, and the Russian State Archive for Contemporary History for their assistance and their patience as I fumbled to articulate what I was looking for. Outside of the archives, I was lucky to find "comrades" among those also on research trips and through the Foreign Historians' Congress. In particular, I want to Philippa Hetherington, Masha Kirasirova, Johanna Conterio, and Alan Roe for their ongoing friendship.

I spent a year as fellow at the International Center for the History and Sociology of World War II and Its Consequences at the Higher School of Economics in Moscow. This opportunity proved crucial for filling in the potholes in my research and beginning the process of transforming my early manuscript into a book. I was surrounded by an incredible community of mentors and scholars there. I want to thank Oleg Budnitskii, Liudmila Novikova, Oleg Khlevniuk, Michael David-Fox, Seth Bernstein, Franziska Exeler, Tomasso Piffer, and Jonathan Brunstedt for making this such a rewarding experience. I also want to thank Natalia Melikova and Julia Reysner for their friendship and for letting me borrow their kitchens while I was living without one and could not indulge my cooking hobby in Moscow.

I was able to sharpen the ideas in this book as a result of years of—arcane and, let's be honest, sometimes alienating—conversations about the peculiarities of the Soviet economy at Association for Slavic, East European, and Eurasian Studies (ASEEES) conventions, over the internet, and in person. I'm grateful to Yakov Feygin for continuing to be a sounding board for my half-baked ideas and for being my academic "little brother." I also want to thank Chris Miller, Artemy Kalinovsky, Alessandro Iandolo, Aaron Hale-Dorrell, Oscar Sanchez-Sibony, and Andrew Sloin, all of whose feedback and whose work have been influential upon my own thinking about the Soviet economy. Thanks must also go to Elena Osokina, who told me where to find some of Stalin's more colorful quotations about money, and to Yanni Kotsonis, for encouraging my interest in Soviet taxes.

I was also fortunate to receive feedback on full and partial drafts of chapters during various invited talks and conferences, including at New York University, University College London's School of Slavonic and East European Studies, New York University–Abu Dhabi, Birkbeck–University of London, the University of Basel, and New York University–Paris. Thank you to Yanni Kotsonis, Philippa Hetherington, Masha Kirasirova, Jessica Reinisch, Vanessa Ogle, Juliette Cadiot, and Anne O'Donnell for inviting me. I workshopped a draft of the introduction at the University of Toronto's Russian reading group; I want to thank Lynne Viola, Alison Smith, and the other members of the group for their extremely useful comments, which helped me tame an otherwise unwieldily long introduction to this book. On that note, I'm grateful to Lynne Viola for encouraging me to pursue the study of Soviet history in the first place while I was a student at the Center for European, Russian, and Eurasian Studies (CERES) at the University of Toronto. I'm also grateful to Robert Austin, Jeffrey Kopstein, and other members of the CERES community who fostered my burgeoning interest in the region while I was trying to figure out what to do with my life.

ACKNOWLEDGMENTS

During the time I was writing and revising this manuscript, I was fortunate to have had fantastic colleagues at the two universities I have worked at. Among my colleagues at the University of Manchester, I especially want to thank Peter Gatrell (who gifted me his entire collection of Russian and Soviet economic history books!); Yoram Gorlizki, who read early drafts of the first two chapters; and Christian Goeschel, Sarah Roddy, Eloise Moss, Alexia Yates, Jo Laycock, and Anna Strowe. At McGill University, I want to thank my colleagues for their moral support during the final stages of shaping up the manuscript, in particular Lorenz Lüthi, Darian Totten, and Alex Tipei. I also want to thank my research assistant Yaroslav Gouzenko for his heroic last-minute assistance with fact-checking and citations.

Thank you to my editor Andrew Kinney for believing in this book project, and for helping to make it more accessible to non-Soviet specialists. Thanks also go to the three anonymous reviewers whose detailed feedback undoubtedly made for a more coherent and polished final product. Thank you to Anna Loginova for her assistance in securing the rights to images from the Ne Boltai collection. For remaining images, I've made every effort to identify copyright holders and obtain their permission for the use of copyrighted material. Notification of any additions or corrections that should be incorporated in future reprints or editions of this book would be greatly appreciated.

Chapter 1 builds on ideas first discussed in "Stalin's Doctrine of Price Reductions during the Second World War and Postwar Reconstruction," *Slavic Review,* Vol. 75, No. 3 (2016): 655–677. "Between Fiscal, Ideological, and Social Dilemmas," *Europe-Asia Studies,* Vol. 69, No. 6 (2017): 855–878, informs Chapter 4. Chapters 4 and 5 expand on research presented in "Khrushchev's Cash-and-Goods Lotteries and the Turn toward Positive Incentives," *Soviet and Post-Soviet Review,* Vol. 41, No. 3 (2014): 296–323.

Finally, I would never have ended up in academe, let alone writing this book, without the support of my family. I want to thank my parents for their unflagging love, for putting up with me when I'm insufferable, and for taking care of my dog, Reggie, when I gallivanted off to a conference or to an archive on the other side of the world. I also want to thank my in-laws, Jack and Dottie Pratt, for their support, our ongoing conversations about history and academe over the breakfast table, and for Jack's help with indexing. I am eternally grateful to my husband and partner-in-crime, Daniel Webster Pratt, to whom this book is dedicated. Much of it was written when we were separated by an ocean, several time zones, and international borders, and while we missed each other terribly. I am grateful that is no longer the case because I am a better scholar as a result of our conversations, and I am an all-around better person for having him in my life.

Index